The Gattegno Effect

The Gattegno Effect

100 VOICES ON ONE OF HISTORY'S GREATEST EDUCATORS

Copyright © 2011 Educational Solutions Worldwide Inc.
All rights reserved
ISBN 978-0-87825-365-4
Educational Solutions Worldwide Inc.
Suite 1581 - 244 Fifth Avenue, New York, NY 10001
www.EducationalSolutions.com

Acknowledgments

This memoir has been produced by a dedicated team:

EDITING: Amy Logan
LAYOUT: Laura Boyle
PHOTOGRAPHY: Agata Waliczek
COVER ART: Christopherr Mendoza
COMMUNICATIONS: Laura Boyle and Sima Gandhi
PUBLICITY: Martin Power

Contents

Preface
Bill Bernhardt

Introduction
Eaton Donald

Gattegno's Aphorisms
Bill Bernhardt..............3

In Pursuit of a Science of Education
Alf Coles.............5

Standing on the Shoulders of Dr. G
John Pint.............8

How Caleb Gattegno Influenced My Life
Dr. Roslyn Young..............12

Silence: The Most Powerful Tool of All
沈黙：最も強力な教具
Fusako Allard..............14

'A Cat that Walked by Himself'
Dr. Caroline Brandt..............20

Transcending Barriers to Become a Better Learner
Lindsay Pearson..............23

"I Didn't Do it, You Did": A Great Lesson Learned
Dr. Leslie Turpin..............25

A Responsibility to Learn
Dr. Cecilia Bartoli..............26

Facing Change the Gattegno Way
Edna Shaw..............30

Une nouvelle vision grâce à la Lecture en couleurs
Véronique Rodoz..............33

Meine Begegnungen mit dem Genie Dr. Gattegno
Klara Miller-Fuehren..............34

Exceeding Expectations
Dr. Marilyn Maye..............36

No Tricks, But There is Magic in the Technique
Luigi Magnano..............39

The Maori Revival
Te Ataarangi..............40

Transferable Skills
Bill Robbins..............44

Revolutionizing My Teaching By Doing the Opposite
Hugh Birdsall..............48

Life is a Grand Experiment
Robert P. Echter..............52

How Could I Prevent Turning Into A Teaching Zombie?
Dr. Patricia Benstein..............55

Living, Learning, Teaching
En vivant, en apprenant, en enseignant
Brendan Marcus..............58

The Audacious Learner and Teacher in Me
Michiko Watabe..............63

From the Congo to the Bronx
Daniel Tamulonis..............66

Leading Ways
Ghislaine Graf..............70

Une enseignante française à Bobo Dioulasso
Geneviève Godard..............72

An Educational Awakening
David B. Davies..............76

The Silent Way: A Pedagogy of Life
Dr. Marti Anderson..............77

Life Through a Silent Way Lens
Manuela Bartoli..............78

Dr. Gattegno and the Riverside
Language Program
P. Berman, L. Serota, N. Elliott, L. Pesce..............82

He Said Nothing,
But I Understood Everything
Dr. Clifton de Cordoba..............86

Caleb Gattegno, une expérience de
maïeutique
Philippe Fagot 88

The Heart of the Matter: Gattegno's
Awareness of the Powers of Children
Laurinda Brown..............90

Transformation:
From Ideology to Science
Dr. Arthur B. Powell..............92

Silent Way au Japon
Malik Berkane..............95

The Foundation of My Teaching:
A Belief in the Genius of Human Beings
Dr. Paula Hajar..............98

How Staying With a Question
Pays Off
Maria Gagliardo..............102

Je n'imagine pas enseigner
le français autrement
Maritée Juge 104

A Mother and Daughter Story
Rachel Adams Goertel and Carole Adams 107

The Summer with Dr. G
Jim Reed..............109

Caleb Gattegno aujourd'hui :
quelques réflexions
Maurice Laurent..............110

An Experiment in Humanizing Education
Ann Crary Evans..............112

Humanism in Language Teaching
Dr. Earl Stevick..............115

Caleb Gattegno and the Well-Crafted
Pedagogical Challenge
Eaton Donald..............120

Fractions Are Not Parts of Wholes
Dr. A. J. (Sandy) Dawson 124

"Why Am I Doing This?"
Dr. Patrick Moran..............127

Gattegno en Haïti
Raymonde Rocourt..............128

The Road to Inspired Teaching
Andrew Weiler..............130

A Man Ahead of His Time
Recuerdos Agradecidos
Laura Guajardo..............133

To the Best of Our Abilities
Carol Rose..............135

Two Simple Drawings
That Changed My Teaching Forever
Dr. Jane Orton..............138

Trois Enseignantes De Genève
A- L Ferro-Luzzi,
A. Fayolle Dietl et R. Wisler 144

Reflections on Gattegno,
Learning Lakota, and More
Dr. Jim Green..............152

Gattegno's Body of Work:
Providing Lessons For Life
Dr. Roann Altman..............154

Ordinary Miracles
Claudie Gattegno..............158

This Work Transformed Me
Ce travaille m'a transformé
Christiane Rozet..............162

Insights from Gattegno
Dr. Piers Messum..............166

It Takes the Time it Takes
何かをするのに かかるだけの時間がかかる
Kazuko Shimizu..............168

Taking the Learner into Account:
An Effective Remedy for Becoming a
Better Teacher
Wojciech Łukaszewicz..............174

A Father's Reading Laboratory
Michel Zobel..............176

I Have Experienced the Gattegno Approach
Mon expérience avec l'approche Gattegno
Nathanaël Zobel..............177

The Talk of the Town
Dr. Ubiratan D'Ambrosio..............180

Caleb Gattegno: As I Remember Him
Dr. Katherine A. Mitchell..............182

Silence, apprentissage et
méta-apprentissage
Dr. Michel Sagaz..............187

Voices from AURAMA
A. Bregani, D. Cerretti, M-C Challandes, C.
Delétra, B. Mesot, C. de Sybourg,
M. Weinmann 192

My Personal Journey Towards
Letting Go of "No"
Christian Duquesne..............196

A Fascination with Pronunciation
発音の魅力
Junko Shinada..............198

Sharing the Gift of Math, Learning and A
Better Way to Teach
Dr. Joyce F. Baynes..............202

Small Vocabulary as a Big Idea!
Dr. Bob Coe..............204

A Less-Damaging Career
Donald Cherry..............208

Une rencontre avec Gattegno
ou plus précisément avec sa pédagogie
Daniel Roder..............210

Education From My Father
Alma Arnould, née Gattegno..............212

The Silent Way Down Under
De Silent Way Downunder
Dr. Marietta Elliott-Kleerkoper..............215

Three Lessons Learned From
An Uncompromising Man
Dr. Theodore Swartz..............219

Seeing 'I' to 'I'
Steve Hirschhorn..............221

A "Maverick" Among Thinkers
Dr. Alvino Fantini..............223

Un plaisir pour la vie
Alain L'Hôte..............225

The Real Learning:
Educating My Self
Noriko Ogino..............229

Approaching the Approach
L'évolution d'une approche
Isabelle Luter Doussain 230

"Have You Ever Thought
You Might Be Boring?"
Donald Freeman..............235

Le rôle que Caleb Gattegno peut jouer au
Burkina Faso
Soré Hadara..............237

My Time with Dr. G and His Overwhelming
Flow of Creativity
Michael J. Hollyfield..............238

I Went Looking for a Match
And Found a Volcano
Yoko Yasuda..............242

Ignoring the Threat of Violence for the Hope
of Becoming a Better Teacher
Esaie Pierre..............244

Witnessing the Truth
En témoin de la vérité
Jean-Jacques Dutrait 246

Caleb Gattegno, Scientist:
A Learner Remembers
Stephen DeGiulio..............252

Working on the Edge of Discomfort:
Threads of a Complex Journey into Awareness
Chris Breen..............254

Where do Good Results Come From?
Dr. Bruce Ballard..............256

In the Midst of a Whirlwind
Dr. Masayuki Onishi..............260

Some Facts of Awareness
Allen Rozelle..............264

Etre disponible:
Un art de vivre façon Caleb Gattegno
Martine Widmer..............266

An Original Thinker
Dr. Diane Larsen-Freeman..............269

Silence Amplifies: The Loud Silent Way
Adrian Underhill..............270

So this is the Silent Way!
原点へ近づく喜び
Etsuko Nagasawa..............272

Working for Caleb Gattegno
Jeremy Steele..............276

Dancing a Dialogue: Interaction with the
Learner and Interaction in Learning
Janice Mattina..............280

Une fortune sur un plateau
Suzanne Lachaise..............283

Gattegno and the McCarthy-Towne
Elementary School
J. Parker Damon..............284

Changing Expectations
Le trajet d'un métier
Sylvain Dufros..............288

A Letter to Dr. G
Dr. Barbara Villez..............291

The "Only" Statements
Dr. John Mason..............292

Ein Tor zu einer neuen Welt
Rosaria Dell'Eva..............294

Respect for the Child's Ability
to do First Class Thinking
John Holt..............296

Une approche pour l'Afrique
Zouré Moumouni..............300

Why I Love Joining Silent Way Workshops
Kyoko Nishio..............302

The Faster Way
Steven Quinn..............304

Caleb Gattegno: A Profound and
Continuing Personal Influence
Henry Liebling..............308

A Teacher's Perspective on
the Power of Observation
Dr. Kathleen Graves..............310

The Influence of Gattegno –
Direct and Indirect
Rosie McAndrew 312

Appendix

About the Authors..............317
Chronology of Dr. Caleb Gattegno..............341
Bibliography of Dr. Caleb Gattegno..........343

Preface

The Association for the Science of Education is honored to co-publish this Memoir with Educational Solutions Inc., the company originally founded by Dr. Caleb Gattegno to make his compelling vision of human learning available to teachers and students. The Association's purpose is to help realize that vision of human and humane learning.

It was in the early 1970s at the Educational Solutions offices in New York City that many of the members of our Association first encountered Dr. Gattegno's work and, indeed, the man himself. The contributions to this Memoir by our members and non-members alike recall "Dr. G" in the context of East 12th Street, Fifth Avenue, or University Place, each one a memorable space in its own right. Participants hail from Europe, Africa, Asia, Australia, North America and South America, attesting to the world-wide reach and appeal of Dr. Gattegno's work.

We are hoping that the publication of this Memoir will increase the cadre of educators all over the world who share the certainty that the future of education is bright with promise. They will move forward into the twenty-first century with the confidence and creativity that find surety in the profound learning powers that are our birthright.

Bill Bernhardt
President, The Association for the Science of Education

Introduction

No one who ever consciously set out to make a difference in the world will tell you it was an easy choice to make, or that it was smooth sailing once that choice was made. The path less traveled can be extremely bumpy, especially in the field of contemporary education since its structures and policies do not readily lend themselves to change.

In this collective memoir, many of the contributors took the road less traveled by adopting a radically different approach to teaching, one that has made a difference in transforming both their lives and the lives of their students.

The path they chose was blazed by scientist and educator Dr. Caleb Gattegno. Gattegno did not advocate changing the window dressing in the 'house of education'. Rather, he suggested a new foundation was in order – one built not on imitation and memorization but on the powers and strengths that all of us use every day effortlessly, easily and effectively. Among other things, Gattegno offered a vision for a new and enhanced role for the teacher and suggested elevating the position to one in which educators themselves become associates in the elaboration of a new Science of Education.

Gattegno, who would have turned 100 this year, ranged far and wide in his thinking. He incorporated mathematics, litcracy, psychology, epistemology, language, learning, evolution, physics, health and what it means to be human into his consideration set.

We felt certain that many voices were better than one to provide a window into Gattegno's pedagogy, and it was during a conversation with Piers Messum and Roslyn Young that the construct of a collective memoir emerged at their suggestion. This collective memoir is about the work of Gattegno as seen through the eyes and told in the voices of those who put his vision into practice and volunteered to forget what they knew about traditional teaching in order to truly become better teachers.

Gattegno worked in more than 40 countries and in multiple languages, with academics, teachers, parents and students across a spectrum of ages, ethnicities and capabilities. We felt it appropriate to include contributions from a similar spectrum of individuals – geographically diverse, multi-lingual, and across a range of professional interests. Readers will notice a variety of experiences, each written in the author's unique style.

This is a book of stories. It is not a textbook, or a how-to manual, nor is it designed to be summary of Gattegno's thinking. For those interested in pursuing a more in-depth understanding of Gattegno's works and writings, this book contains a complete bibliography of his existing and newly republished library.

There is good reason to be optimistic about the future of formal education. Gattegno's vision is an effective, proven alternative and remedy to the deep-rooted problems weighing down current educational systems. The stories of those working within Gattegno's pedagogy provide inspiration and evidence that positive change, personal growth, and true learning are available and accessible to all who are interested.

Eaton Donald
President, Educational Solutions Worldwide Inc.

> The use of words for expression does not necessarily imply their use for communication... Because of this we can safely say that in verbal relationships 'communication is almost a miracle.'
>
> — Dr. Caleb Gattegno

The Common Sense of Teaching Foreign Languages, Second Edition (2010), pages 60-61.

Gattegno's Aphorisms

Bill Bernhardt

Anyone who ever had the opportunity to listen to Caleb Gattegno speak noticed his slow, deliberate, manner of talking. In common with many others who spent time with him, I adopted some of his characteristic inflections and mannerisms of speech with the result that I sounded slightly ridiculous talking in the measured cadencies of the master.

His own voice, however, always carried conviction and sounded perfectly in accord with his presence. Listening to him speak was an act of discovery, even though it could be difficult to follow the exact thread of his discourse. As he often remarked, "language is for expression rather than for communication. Communication, when it occurs, is a miracle."

It was always striking to me that I could never anticipate what the next word in a phrase was going to be. It was as if he were inventing the language (whatever language he happened to be speaking at any particular moment) as he went along. He often told stories — personal reminiscences, historical synopses or summaries were characteristic — but never the same story twice. I can't recall a single story that he told more than once in my hearing over a 20-year period. Nor can I remember ever encountering in print any story that I had heard him utter previously.

His stories were usually quite short, often humorous. One that springs to mind at the moment is about a young man who wrote job application letters for two different positions in colonial, Anglophone Africa. Each position had a different age requirement, so when the young man came for an interview, he was asked, "How old are you?" His answer was, "Which position am I being considered for?"

In contrast with his singular use of stories, Gattegno had many aphorisms that he often repeated, in a variety of different contexts. When I say "aphorisms," I am thinking, above all, of phrases that provide short, concise statements of principle, such as "the Silent Way," "working on oneself," "surrendering to the problem," "taking the time it takes," "the subordination of teaching to learning," and so on.

> "I don't prepare a lesson — I prepare myself."

In many cases, a Gattegno aphorism of this type gains some of its richness of meaning from what is not said — that is, words or concepts to which the aphorism provides an implicit contrast or challenge. To take an example, the Silent Way implies a comparison and contrast to the noisy, talkative manner of most teachers. And the second term in the expression (way) suggests a relative orientation or approach rather than an absolute prescription. The teacher is trying to move herself/himself in the direction of quietness, of letting the learners do as much of the talking as possible, but there is no prohibition against speaking. "Silence" is an approach rather than a method.

Another type of aphorism favored by Gattegno consists of short, pointed sentences expressing wise or clever observations or general truths. Examples that come to mind include, "The students are

(Bernhardt Cont'd.)

working on the material, and the teacher is working on the students;" "The problem of reading is solved;" "I don't prepare a lesson — I prepare myself;" "When you write a note, the paper remembers — you forget."

Originally coined in workshops and seminars, many of Gattegno's aphorisms later appeared in print on the pages of his many publications. Some of them struck me forcibly at the moment when I heard them for the first time, but it was only when I encountered them again, in one of his books, or the *Educational Solutions Newsletter*, that they truly became memorable and a permanent part of my own repertoire.

The aphoristic dimension of Gattegno's speech seemed to some hearers to contrast with his description of himself as a "scientist" and put him more in the company of philosophers and sages. I find that understandable, but also misleading. There really is no necessary contradiction between the pursuit of scientific truth on the one hand, and a gift for aphoristic utterance on the other. §

Dr. Caleb Gattegno and a colleague selecting colors for Word Charts at the Educational Solutions office in New York City, circa 1980. (Educational Solutions file photo.)

In Pursuit of a Science of Education

Alf Coles

Gattegno calls on teachers to become scientists of education in their classrooms by using the tool of watchfulness. A problem, as Gattegno was aware, is that watching and seeing is more complex than it may appear. There is a problem with perception – which arises because seeing (or hearing, or any other sense) is an act of categorizing.

A STORY

A parish magazine is delivered to my house every month. One month I noticed, as part of an article, our parish council had a logo, which is an arrangement of three standing stones. I reflected at the time that for this to be the parish council logo, these standing stones must be near where I live, yet I had never seen nor heard of them. The next day I was driving down a road outside our village that I must have gone down and back on several hundred times. Whilst traveling close to 60 mph, without conscious deliberation, I turned my head fully 90 degrees to the right and glimpsed for a fraction of a second, at a break in the wall by the road, the configuration of standing stones.

I do not believe this story is one of chance. I needed to see the stones in the magazine to recognize them in the many fleeting glimpses I must have unknowingly had along the road. Because I see in categories, I only see what I am familiar with – the problem then arises – how am I ever able to see anything 'new'? If, to see something, I need to connect it to something I already know, how can I learn? What can I do to see the strange in the familiar? Foundation art-degree courses run lectures on 'learning to see' in a way that is perhaps not so widespread in initial teacher training.

Yet arguably it is as necessary; to become a teacher, and certainly to become a scientist of education, I need to use myself in a way that allows me to expand my categories of perception. Laurinda Brown puts it simply as, "seeing more, seeing differently," or in Gattegno's language making myself "vulnerable" to the new.

One technique for opening ourselves to the new is to stay with the detail of our observations – and this is what, in part, I read into Gattegno's call for 'watchfulness.' John Mason distinguishes 'accounts of' from 'accounts for' phenomena – the former containing the detail, the latter the interpretation. Of course all description no matter how detailed is interpretation, since all categories impose a splitting up of the world that could have been done differently. Yet there is a difference between saying (of the same imagined event): "I asked a question and no one put up their hand to answer," and "The class seemed

> Gattegno calls on teachers to become scientists of education in their classrooms by using the tool of watchfulness.

(Coles Cont'd.)

disengaged today." If we begin with 'accounts of,' without judgment, we have the chance of noticing something we had not observed before – particularly if we are able to keep records over time and look back at similarities and differences. Someone else might see 'thoughtful' where I see 'disengaged' – holding off interpretation and judgment means alternative descriptions become possible.

And what of the students – how can we work with them to 'see more' and 'see differently' in relation to mathematics? The same distinction between accounts 'of' and 'for' is equally valid. Offer students something visible or tangible, and everyone can say what they see (an 'account of'). If the context is rich enough, then mathematics (moving to an agreed 'account for') can follow from what students notice.

To start with, then, I need a context in which students have something to say.

ANOTHER STORY

My two-year-old daughter was given a balance bicycle for Christmas – this is basically a bicycle with no pedals that you push and then freewheel. In a matter of weeks she was confidently freewheeling downhill and leaning in to go around corners. As I know from seeing her elder brother it will be a short while before she can use these awarenesses to ride a pedal bicycle. In contrast, children given pedal bicycles with stabilizers learn to lean out as they go around corners. This must be unlearnt, and the transition to riding without stabilizers can be hard.

I wonder how much of what we offer students is the equivalent of a stabilizer – fractions as pieces of cake; 'a' stands for 'apple'; the separate treatment of addition and subtraction, or of any two inverse processes. And, more importantly, what are the balance-bike equivalents we can give students? Dick Tahta, who collaborated over many years with Gattegno, would perennially offer the challenge for someone to come up with the minimal set of images needed to cover the whole mathematics curriculum (up to, say, aged 16) – in Dick's words, what are the canonical images of mathematics?

Gattegno was certain there could be no images for algebra, since algebra is an awareness of dynamics; which I find easier to think about as an awareness of process, or an awareness of similarity and difference.

1 -> 2

3 -> 4

10 -> 11

20 -> ??

This function game puzzle will be straightforward to most school students. It requires a stepping back from the simple giving of the answer, however, to recognize structure, and the operation being performed, to become aware of the dynamic or process – i.e., the shift from 'it's one more' to 'I am adding one to the number' – and hence to providing the algebraic notation: n -> n+1.

As a teacher, a favorite activity was working with students on creating graphs of this and other more complex rules. A student might choose to draw graphs of these rules: n-> n+1; n-> 2*n+1; n-> 3*n+1, and notice they cross the y-axis at the same point. Awareness of this similarity can lead a student to conjecture about graphs of the form: n -> m*n+1, and further practice to test this idea. If algebra is awareness of dynamics, it must be around whenever we are doing mathematics – if we can hear it.

By starting with images (I would include a function game as an image – indeed a canonical one), and letting the algebra arise from the dynamics of such work, worries about 'understanding' can disappear. Consider learning about percentages using the Gattegno 'tens' chart below (surely another canonical image).

1000	2000	3000	4000	5000	6000	7000	8000	9000
100	200	300	400	500	600	700	800	900
10	20	30	40	50	60	70	80	90
1	2	3	4	5	6	7	8	9

I begin: "Ten percent of 1,000 is 100. What is 10% of 3,000?" [touching it with a stick]. You call out "300." Ten percent of 600? 60. Ten percent of 320? 32, etc. Finding 10% of a number may initially become associated with 'moving down one row.' (And since inverse functions can always be treated together, moving from 10% to 100%, associated with moving up one row.) The action can be repeated, to give the relations between 1% and 100% as a move up or down two rows. I recognize the 'me' that began teaching in 1994 might have been worried that, in this approach, students do not really 'understand' what they are doing. Yet what else, really, is there to get? It is true there is no linking 'metaphor' (e.g., that 'percent' means 'out of a hundred,' or that percentages can be connected to shading squares on a 10 by 10 grid). The treatment is 'metonymic' - i.e., not about an alternative meaning, but a substitution within the same context. Instead of a metaphoric shift to some (usually unconnected) other domain, the substitution involved here means that finding 10% gets linked to an action students perform (moving down a row) and can see.

In a reverse of my thinking when I began teaching, I now see the kind of 'teaching metaphors' that I used to offer students as 'stabilizers.' I would explain negative numbers as cold bricks, positives as hot bricks, altering the temperature of my pot, so taking out a cold brick, or subtracting a negative – abracadabra – makes it warmer. Such translations may support learners over an initial hurdle, but quickly become barriers – how do you multiply by a cold brick! Gattegno's metonymic approach focuses attention on how to perform key operations (e.g., finding a third of a number by finding three identical Cuisenaire Rods that fit along it; finding the Sine of an angle by finding the perpendicular distance from the x-axis to a point on the circumference of a unit circle). Such operations are actions, real or virtual, that need to be practiced. However, by avoiding metaphor, the focus easily shifts to the transformations themselves, and hence to the inherent algebra, like finding a third of a third, or finding angles with the same Sine length. Gattegno provides the context, the operations (as actions), the notation, and often a challenge – he leaves to students the task of making sense of it all. §

Vintage photograph of elementary-school students working on primary mathematics using Cuisenaire rods. (Educational Solutions file photo.)

Standing on the Shoulders of Dr. G

John Pint

Caleb Gattegno wrote a book called *The Mind Teaches the Brain*. The title is provocative, challenging established concepts. It also relates to a theme developed in Gattegno's *The Universe of Babies* – that our mind is at work from the moment of our conception; that even before leaving the womb, we are equipped with astounding mental powers.

For much of his life, Gattegno studied the workings of the mind and managed to get many people to join him in this fascinating inner exploration.

He might have left things right there, in the realm of ideas, but he didn't. Instead, he took the ideas and painstakingly applied them to mundane school subjects like the teaching of reading, mathematics and foreign languages. Once again, instead of expostulating theories at conventions, he walked into classrooms and showed us how it's done.

Amazing things happened: primary school children were able to speak Italian with great fluency and precision after only one year of study; first graders were doing algebra with full understanding of the equations they were proving; so-called dyslexic children suddenly learned to read within days, sometimes within hours.

It was these verifiable results that grabbed the attention of teachers and brought them to Gattegno's workshops. Thanks to these practical demonstrations, Cuisenaire Rods found their way into every classroom in the world and entire school systems adopted Words in Color and Gattegno Math.

So what went wrong? Why isn't half the world using Gattegno's approaches in their classrooms?

Those of us who worked with Gattegno as teachers of teachers know the answer: these approaches require teachers to change their behavior, to become more sensitive to what's happening inside the students, and to look at the learning process in terms of awareness. This means that instead of filling students' memories with data, a teacher must help students discover things by themselves, to move from awareness to awareness. This in turn requires what Gattegno called The Subordination of Teaching to Learning – the

> Instead of expostulating theories at conventions, he walked into classrooms and showed us how it's done.

teacher constantly monitoring the students' learning and changing tactics accordingly.

So here's the rub. Good schools can't program what is going to happen in the classroom hour by hour or day by day, as is now the custom. Instead, the teacher must learn to be sensitive to what is happening inside the students and to devise exercises and activities that make sense in the here and now. Teachers would no longer be able to walk into the classroom and teach out of a book.

speak from their own experiences and observations rather than quote an authority.

This restriction often produced the most wonderful results, leading the group into areas never before explored. Many observations would be thrown into the pool and eventually, as Gattegno said, the truth would rise to the top.

When I was conducting sessions of this kind with teachers unfamiliar with Gattegno's approaches, I

"This Gattegno approach to group study seemed to me the ultimate refinement of the Socratic Method."

Teaching teachers turned out to be a real challenge. How could you help them work on their own awareness and in particular to discover the awareness of awareness? Gattegno developed a unique way of conducting workshops, designed exactly to open teachers' eyes. These workshops were conducted basically the same way, whether the members of the group were teachers gathering together after watching a demonstration class, or long-time practitioners of Gattegno's approaches, investigating obscure questions like: What is time? What is love? Why do we sleep?

The members of the group would be seated in a big circle. If they had just seen a language-teaching demonstration, the group might be asked a question like: What did you see? Or, what is the most difficult language for a person to learn? Or, why do babies babble?

People could reply if and when they wanted to. If anyone in the group offered something like, "Chomsky says…" the moderator would cut him or her off and request that the members of the group

would eventually hear people in the group whispering to one another, "He's doing with us exactly what he did with the students — instead of giving us answers, he's making us find the answers for ourselves."

Inevitably, at the end of such a study session, the question "What did you learn?" would be asked, and this time every individual in the group would be required to speak. Here it was often very evident that "the truth had risen to the top," and the summaries presented were always enlightening in one way or another. This Gattegno approach to group study seemed to me the ultimate refinement of the Socratic Method.

It might seem amazing that Gattegno could again and again come up with such original and unique solutions to almost every problem that came his way, but he made no secret of how he did it: he examined each problem in terms of awareness. These words will mean nothing to people who are not aware of awareness and may not mean a whole lot more to people who are.

I can only speak for myself. Once I met Gattegno, I found myself often thinking about awareness, but

(Pint Cont'd)

I didn't understand how he used awareness to find solutions to problems until the day he gave a task to a group of us who were studying to get a sort of "certificate of competency" as Silent-Way teachers.

"I want you to use awareness as a tool to study something about your own behavior," he told us, "and then I want you to write about it."

Well, this I found to be a real challenge. It forced me to look awareness square in the eye, so to speak. After much pondering, I decided to look at what I do when a complicated device comes into my hands, for example, upon taking a newly purchased camera out of the box.

To my surprise, I discovered there's a whole routine I follow, inevitably starting with reading the instruction booklet from end to end before even touching the gadget. This study of my own habits was truly revealing; I had been following that routine for most of my life, but only now was I aware of it.

Perhaps, someday on this planet, using awareness as a tool will become commonplace. I could see the history of mankind being totally rewritten in terms of the different awarenesses that jumped up and bit people over the centuries.

Obviously, this way of studying behavior is not in vogue today, even though you'd think awareness would be the number-one topic of interest to academics in all fields, especially education. To me, this just means that Gattegno was a man ahead of his time — but the rest of the world will certainly catch up with him one day and there's no telling what might spark the change.

Tomorrow, Gattegno's writings may prove a godsend to those who will work to transform schools into places of real learning. Meanwhile, today, we who knew him and worked with him need to reassess his and our successes and failures in applying the Science of Education to the real world.

Extremely versatile tools have been developed and we have found myriad ways of using them. We have proven they can actually work in real classroom situations. One of our problems, it seems to me, is to find more efficient ways of teaching teachers to use these tools. We have been successful in transforming tiny percentages of them into truly impressive teachers, but how can this be done on a large scale?

Perhaps trying to fit Gattegno's approaches into standard school systems is the wrong route. Perhaps our real challenge today — 100 years after Gattegno's birth — is to examine the entire question with new eyes. Since the death of Dr. Gattegno, computers have made their way into every home and they will soon be in every pocket. The internet now links the world. One really good teacher can now reach thousands, perhaps millions. Gattegno worked out the technique for teaching unseen audiences via taped lessons. Instead of putting the camera on the teacher, he focused it on a group of students making and resolving mistakes, struggling and succeeding — and found that people watching these tapes could identify with the students on the screen and learn along with them.

Gattegno worked on this under great constraints and only scratched the surface of how to teach through video. Had he lived, he would surely have refined and improved the techniques he pioneered. He would probably have looked at today's sophisticated video games and shouted, "Eureka!"

Caleb Gattegno told us teachers who worked with him that one day we would have to stand on his shoulders. It is time for us to look at the challenge of worldwide education through awareness with new eyes. It's up to us to usher Gattegno's legacy into the new millennium.

§

Student practicing her writing skills using Words in Color. (Educational Solutions file photo.)

How Caleb Gattegno Influenced My Life

Dr. Roslyn Young

I started teaching English as a foreign language in 1968. I soon knew with certainty that I was at best a mediocre teacher of EFL and began wondering how I could do a better job. In 1970, I finally gave myself a year to find a better way of working, and was lucky enough to hear about a weekend workshop to be given by one Caleb Gattegno in Geneva in April 1971. I went along and was deeply moved by the experience.

During this workshop, organized in French, which I didn't yet speak very well, Dr. G, as we always called him, gave a one-hour lesson of Chinese and this hour changed my life. Dr. G said absolutely nothing from the beginning to the end. He worked by pointing and gesturing. I had never been part of a class which was so concentrated, so eager to learn, so implicated in what was happening. I could actually feel myself learning. I left the workshop with the firm intention of using his teaching approach as soon as I could buy the charts and rods.

I knew of no one else who was using the approach at the time, and found it very difficult to put into practice. However, in 1976, I participated in an Italian course with Cecilia Bartoli, and was clearly reminded of what the approach was like when used by an expert. By 1978 or so, my classes were starting to resemble what I could remember of what Dr. G did during that Chinese lesson.

I was teaching intensive courses. By now I could take real pleasure in working with beginners, knowing I was armed to do excellent work with them. No one else wanted to work with the lower level students, since it was considered hard to get beginners to talk. However, my beginners were soon outperforming students in the other classes, particularly in their willingness to express themselves, to try things out. Finally my colleagues wanted to find out what I was doing, and my little secret was out. One by one, they started using the Silent Way, and getting better and better results. In the end, we made up a cohesive team of eight teachers all using the Silent Way approach.

We had pedagogical meetings regularly every week for several years in order to find solutions to the various challenges we had to meet. When we could work well in ordinary intensive classes, we began to take on more varied courses. For example, we did courses in scientific English with the university staff so that they could present their research in congresses and, equally important, understand the questions they were asked at the end of the talk. We worked with both lecturers and students in medicine, pharmacy, computer science, geology, physical education and many other fields. We also invented techniques compatible with the Silent Way for teaching scientists to write articles in English.

We realized quite early that Gattegno's basic tenet, the Subordination of Teaching to Learning, provided us with the ideal way of coordinating as many teachers as necessary into a cohesive team when working with students in a one-to-one setting; we constructed the course around the student's mistakes, here and now. Over the years, we taught dozens of one-to-one intensive courses in which we would put up to five or six teachers into a single team with the student, changing the teacher every two hours while the student worked up to eight or even 10 hours a day. We could do this without having organizational problems because we all knew how to subordinate teaching to learning.

We soon needed a way to provide students with a means of continuing to work on their English after the end of an intensive course. We therefore invented a Silent Way based "English by Telephone" course, called "Anglophone," which was quite a success – Silent Way without the rods and charts. In order to be cost effective, the course was constructed so that the students would have three or four hours of homework for every half-hour of work over the phone with the teacher. We were able to use team-teaching for these courses too, changing teachers after every 10 hours, or 20 sessions, of work on the phone. One of our very first students, quite a sophisticated learner of English, told us that we were headed for disaster, that the course would necessarily be unsuitable for any other student, because it suited him so well that it couldn't possibly work for anyone else. That was a tribute to subordination, if ever there was one!

I also loved to teach catch-up courses for French than we had been getting with 200 hours when I started working at the Centre.

From 1971 when I first met Dr. Gattegno until 1988 when he died, I followed all the workshops I possibly could that he gave in Europe. I realized very quickly that the Silent Way was not just an isolated 'bright idea,' but one of a coherent set of applications of Dr. Gattegno's general theory of learning, a theory which could be applied to all aspects of education. As I worked with him on subjects as varied as reading, mathematics, grammar, French, and other foreign languages, I came to a better understanding of what the approach was actually based on – a very fine analysis of human beings and of how they learn and function.

> I had never been part of a class which was so concentrated, so eager to learn, so implicated in what was happening. I could actually feel myself learning.

high-school students who were completely lost in their English at school. These were 30 hour one-week courses which always took place during the last week of August just before school went back after the summer holidays. These were classes of 'hopeless' students, between 15 and 18 years of age, whose initial test scores indicated an almost complete lack of any understanding of the English language. Once they knew that all the students of the class were uniformly of a very low level, they could be brought to a mental attitude in which they could work. By the end of the week, they could sit round a table and haltingly hold an hour's conversation in English. This involved a complete transformation in their attitude to learning and to the language. Both my students and I always got deep satisfaction out of this course.

Over the years our team was able to reduce the number of hours taught during a course without compromising the results we obtained. Finally we could get better results with 50 hours of course time

However, even more striking for me was the work we did on his model of Man, and Man in the universe. The model gradually unfolded for me as the years passed and he gave workshops as well as weekend or 10-day seminars on subjects as varied as Intuition, Time, Energy and Energies, The Psyche, The Generation of Wealth and Awarenesses. I was astounded by the breadth of his vision. This part of Dr. G's work was even more fascinating for me than the application of the procedures he suggested for the classroom.

He had great respect for the people who came to his seminars, but often little respect for the ideas we held and he pushed us into examining them seriously. He never tried to impose his vision on those who attended his seminars and workshops, but made us work to justify the opinions we held. He could be quite scathing when we had adopted other people's ideas too readily and when he could demonstrate that they were quite obviously false. I learned to become a much sharper thinker during these years.

§

Silence: The Most Powerful Tool of All
沈黙：最も強力な教具

Fusako Allard

I often wonder what my life would have been like had I not met Dr. Gattegno and his invaluable work. At the age of nearly 50 my life took a radical turn when I learned from him, among many other points, how evolution works, and how human beings are made with the ability to change ourselves, the present, the future, and even the past.

photo-copied charts but didn't comment much on them. In later years, as I repeatedly used them with my students, and learned more about the Silent Way little by little, I came to see that I had to make a lot of alterations in order to make a set of charts that really served the learners. This work is still going on, and I don't think it will ever end as long as I continue learning.

I hear his voice saying, 'Don't take anything for granted!'

My first exposure to Dr. Gattegno's work took place in the late 1970s when he gave an intensive 40-hour seminar on the Silent Way in Tokyo and Osaka. Although the seminar was far too difficult for me to understand thoroughly, I could tell that it was something completely different from anything I had ever been exposed to, however what little I understood made perfect sense to me.

I was possessed by a desire to open a language center exclusively based on the theory of the Silent Way. At the same time, I felt an urgent need to know more about this approach and to learn how to use the tools of the Silent Way to teach Japanese and English. So in the summer of 1984, I went to New York and took five workshops on languages, theory, and training for language teachers – all led by Dr. Gattegno himself over the course of three weeks.

By that time, I had finished my second trial of a handmade set of Japanese charts and took them to New York to show Dr. Gattegno. He looked at the

Soon after returning from New York, I received a letter from Dr. Gattegno in which he suggested that he come to Japan on his way to Korea the following year and do a seminar for us. This was how our annual three-to-four- week seminars and workshops at my Center for Learning started. It lasted for five years until the spring of 1988.

Dr. Gattegno was a strict vegetarian in those days, but it was almost impossible to find a place in the neighborhood that didn't use any fish or meat stock in their cooking. The only solution seemed to be to ask Dr. Gattegno to stay at my humble apartment so that I could prepare meals for him.

As nervous as I was at that time, in retrospect, it was an extremely lucky occurrence for me. I was given the unthinkable opportunity to spend time with Dr. Gattegno outside of the seminar site!

Fortunately, it didn't take long for me to know that Dr. Gattegno was one of the easiest guests I have ever hosted: extremely polite, gentle, and considerate. He didn't fail to express his appreciation for my new challenge of "vegetarian cooking." Sensing my constant tension, he also took every chance to make me feel easy, often with his rich sense of humor – even when he was already quite ill.

He told me that he had been fighting cancer for almost three years, but he never seemed to let it stop him from working long hours, or traveling all over the world. I knew, nevertheless, that he was quite ill and that I had to be prepared for his worsening condition, especially when I saw him on his last visit to Japan. He had lost quite a bit of weight, and he had warned me previously that I may not recognize him at the airport.

Considering his strong presence, I took it for granted that I would miss him immensely when he was no longer with us. This, however, was not the case for me. (I hear his voice saying, "Don't take anything for granted!") I found out that Dr. Gattegno's presence never fades as long as I keep working on and learning from the abundant legacy he has left for us. He also taught me that sometimes a presence can become clearer and more significant when the person is no longer with us.

Now that I physically cannot use charts and rods when I work with high school and junior high students helping them to catch up with their school work, I'm with a new challenge to find out how to apply Dr. Gattegno's Science of Education to my work. What can I do in order to work effectively with an invisible set of charts, an invisible box of rods, and invisible pointers? On such occasions, I'm often struck by a strong awareness that I still have the most powerful tool of all, and that is silence. I'm feeling the real power of silence more strongly than ever, and this has generated an awareness about the importance of 'waiting.'

Being the slow learner that I have always been, I'm finally learning that only when I'm silently waiting can I truly be with each student. And this is when I can truly tell that while not all my students are intellectuals, they are all intelligent human beings, and I get an endless joy from being with them. It is a precious gift from Dr. Gattegno.

沈黙：最も強力な教具

ガテーニョ先生とガテーニョ・アプローチの画期的な理念に出会っていなければ、どのような人生をたどっていただろうかを想像するたびに、私は自分のこのトない幸運を祝さずにはいられない気持ちになる。50歳近くなって、ガテーニョ先生から「万物がいかなる進化をたどるか」、そして、「人間というものがどのような存在であるか」を学んだとき、私の人生は根底から揺さぶられ、そこからの進路に大きな方向転換が起こった。自分の現在も、未来も、過去さえも変えることが出来るという認識は、他の数え切れないどの教えよりも強力なインパクトで私に迫った。

ガテーニョ・アプローチとの最初の出会いは1970年代で、先生の東京と大阪でのサイレントウェイ40時間の集中講座を受けたときであった。そのセミナーは私には難し過ぎて、とてもついていけるようなものではなかったが、そこに提唱されていることが、今まで私の触れたことのない、全くレベルの違ったものであることを感じ取ることはできた。そして、わずかに理解できた初対面の言葉や理念は、なぜかストンと私の腑に落ちて、抵抗なく、快くそこに収まった。

私は、サイレントウェイの理念だけを基にした言語習得センターのようなものを開きたいという無謀な願望に心を奪われた。100%　サイレントウェイで日本語と英語を教えたい。それにはサイレントウェイの理論をもっと知らなくてはならない。そして、サイレントウェイの教具の使い方を学ばなくてはならない。そうしてこそ、この理念が正しく実践できるのだと切実に感じた。

1984年の夏、私はニューヨークに3週間滞在し、エデュケーショナル・ソリューションズで言語習得、理論、教師養成などに関する5つの講座を受講した。幸いにも、全て、ガテーニョ先生自らが教鞭をとられた。その頃までに出来上がっていた2版目の手作り日本語チャートを携えて行ってガテーニョ先生に見せたのだが、先生は特に何も言われず、苦心を重ねて作り、複写した写真のコピーを見て心を動かされた様子はみられなかった。

その後何年にもわたって生徒とともにそのチャートを使って勉強し、サイレントウェイの理念と技法をゆっくり理解していくうちに、真に学習者の役に立つチャートを作るには、何度も手を加えて改良し続けなければならないことが徐々に分かってきた。この作業は今も続いている。おそらく、私が学ぶことを止めない限り、終わることはないだろう。

ニューヨークから帰って間もなく、ガテーニョ先生から一通のエアレターをいただいた。先生は翌年韓国に仕事で行かれることになり、途中日本に立ち寄って、私達のためにもセミナーすることが出来るのだが、という提案のお手紙であった。3週間から4週間ガテーニョ先生を日本に招いて、理論・言語習得・教師養成などの集中講座を主催するという語学文化協会の最も輝かしい年中行事はこうして始まり、1988年の春までの5年間続けられた。

そのころのガテーニョ先生は、厳格な菜食主義者だった。当時、純粋に菜食だけの飲食店を近辺で見つけるのは今よりまだ困難で、精進料理を食べさせる店などめったになく、普通の飲食店では肉や魚そのものは避けられても、出汁に肉や魚を使わない店を見つけるのは不可能に近かった。唯一私に考えられた解決策は、先生を我が家にお泊めして、何とか野菜だけの料理に挑戦してみることだった。

ガテーニョ先生を私の質素なアパートにお泊めするなど、考えても身のすくむ思いで、私は狼狽のあまり、それがどれほど幸運なことかに気づく余裕など全くなかった。思えば、セミナーの場以外での先生に接することができたことは、私に与えられた稀な特権だったのだ。それに、先生が、この上なく、もてなし易い客人だということは、すぐにわかった。私は、礼節を重んじ優しく思いやりのある理想的な訪問客に恵まれた。私のつたない菜食料理にさえ、ねぎらいと感謝の言葉を惜しまず、折あるごとに、私の緊張をゆるめるために、豊かなユーモアのセンスを駆使された。このようなお気遣いは、先生の病状がかなり進んでからも変わらなかった。

お会いした当初から、私は先生が三年間、癌をコントロールされているということを聞いていた。先生は、それを気にもかけないかのように、連日長時間の仕事をこなされ、文字通り世界中を駆け巡って全身全霊を仕事に打ち込まれた。しかし、私は先生の病状がかなり進んでいることを感知しており、急激な変化を覚悟していなければならないと自らに言い聞かせていた。特に、先生の最後の日本訪問の際、空港で見た先生が、前もって予告してくださっていたにもかかわらず、別人かと思うほど痩せ細っておられたのを目の当たりにしてその念を強くした。

> 「沈黙」という最も強力な教具が残されているという認識である。

先生の強烈な存在感を思うとき、それを失うことはとても淋しい、悲しいことだろうと私は決め込んでいた。しかし、私にとって、現実はそうではなかった。（先生の、「何事も、当然と思うな！」という声が今も響いてくる。）それとは逆に、私の中から先生の存在感が薄れることはない、先生が残された有り余る遺産を究明し、そこから学び続ける限り、、、という実感を日に日に強く感じる。先生はまた、ある存在は、その人が私の近くにいなくなってからいっそう明確に、意義深く感じられるようになるということを、教えてくださった。

現在私は、中高生が学校の英語の授業についていくための手伝いに生き甲斐を感じている。チャートやロッドが使えなくとも、どうにかしてガテーニョ先生の「科学としての教育」を効率よく実践していこうと情熱を燃やしている。この新しい挑戦に際して、常に心強く思うことは、「沈黙」という最も強力な教具が残されているという認識である。私は沈黙の真の力を今ほど強く感じたことはない。そしてこの気づきは、「待つ」ということの大切さを私に認識させてくれた。

どうしようもない slow learner である私は、黙って待つことによってのみ、学習者一人一人とともに居ることができるという真実をようやく学び始めている。黙って待つ姿勢になってこそ、「私の生徒は一人残らず聡明な学び手なのだ」と明言することができ、ともに学ぶことから限りない悦びを得るのである。ガテーニョ先生からの、最高の贈り物である。§

Young Caleb Gattegno. (Educational Solutions file photo.)

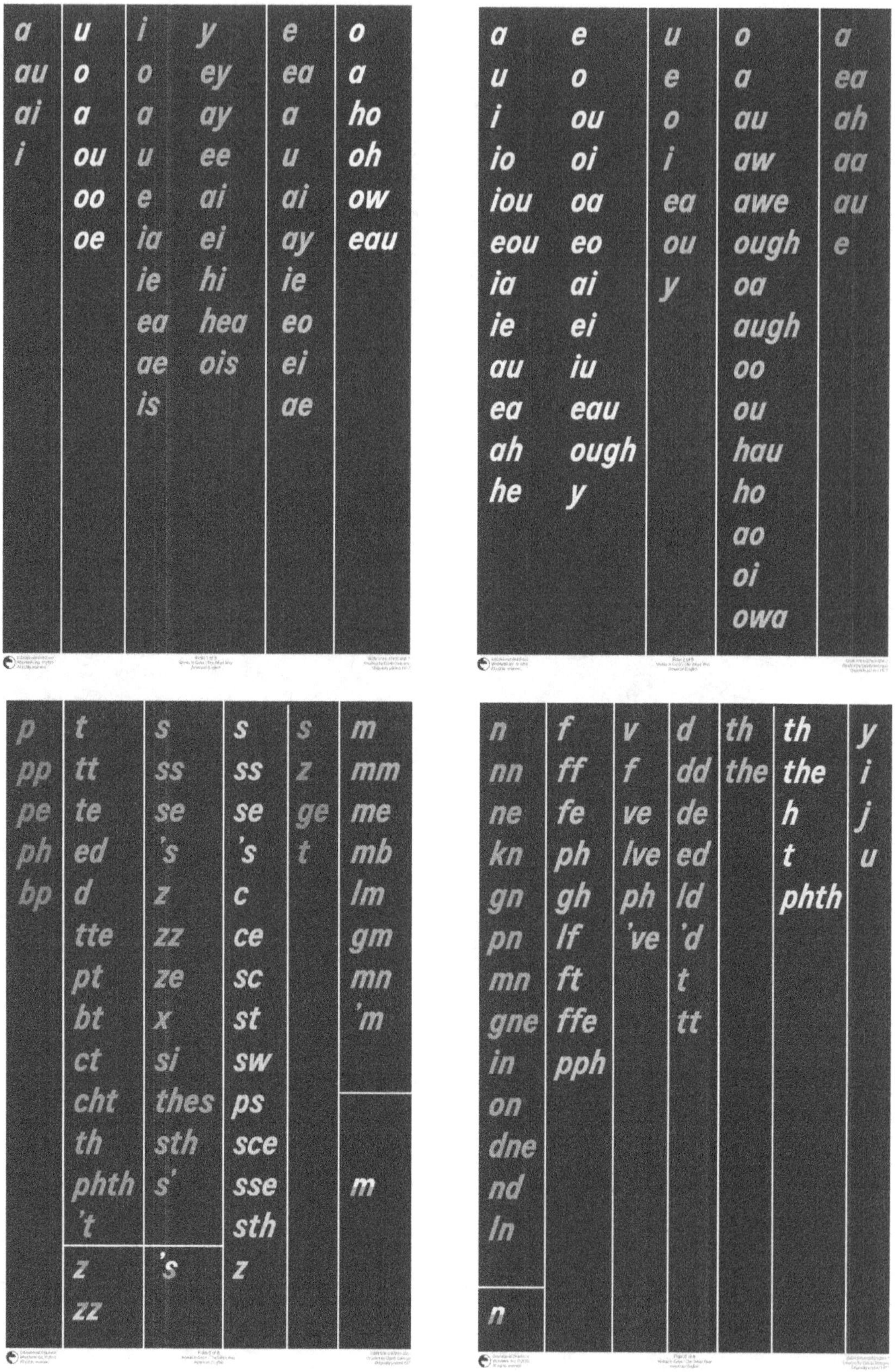

The Fidel Phonic Code was originally conceived in 1957 during Dr. Gattegno's work with UNESCO. Shown here are charts 1-8 of the American English Fidel (2009 reprint) representing a complete panorama of the sounds and spellings of English organized into color-coded columns. ©Educational Solutions Worldwide Inc.

o	e	a	oo	o
oo	ee	ai	ou	a
ew	ea	ea	u	au
ou	y	e	o	oa
ui	ie	ei		oo
u	ei	hei		ou
oe	i	ae	u	ho
ue	eo	aye	eu	ao
eu	ey	ayo	ue	oi
ough	ay	ey		owa
wo	oe			
ieu	ae			
	is			

I	a	o	u	ou
i	ai	oe	ew	hou
y	ay	ow	iew	ow
ie	ey	owe	eau	ough
ye	ei	oa	ue	
igh	eigh	ou	ieu	oi
eye	ea	ew	ewe	oy
eigh	aigh	oh	hu	aw
is	et	ough	eu	
ais	ae	eau	eue	oi
ei	au	oo		
aye	e	au		o
	ee	eo		
		ot		

l	w	k	r	b	h	g
ll	wh	kk	rr	bb	wh	gg
le	u	ke	re	be	j	gu
lle	o	ck	wr	bu		gh
'll		c	rh	pb		gue
		cc	rps			ckgu
		ch	rp			
l	wh	lk	rt			
le		qu	rrh			
'll		que	rre			
		che	lo			
		cqu	're			
		cch	r			
		co	re			
		kh	're			

sh	ch	ng	j	qu	x
ch	tch	n	g	cqu	xe
t	t	ngue	d		cc
s	c	nd	dge		xc
ss	che		ge		
c			gg		
sch			dg		x
sc			dj		
che					x
chs					
					x

'A Cat that Walked by Himself'

Dr. Caroline Brandt

While in my early 20s, in 1982 I moved to Hastings, a small town on the south coast of England, in order to take an initial teacher training course at International House, the precursor to what is now the Cambridge Certificate in English Language Teaching to Adults (CELTA). I took to teaching and was asked to stay after qualifying, and soon found myself immersed in an environment humming with humanistic fervor.

The environment was exceptional, the result of a unique confluence of minds. Seminars, workshops and resources on humanistic themes were made available to all who were interested: there were workshops exploring the concepts and practice of Georgi Lozanov's Suggestopedia; Charles Schmidt's Learning in a New Dimension; Sheila Ostrander and Lynn Schroeder's Superlearning; James Asher's Total Physical Response; Charles Curran's Community Language Learning and Caleb Gattegno's Silent Way. The resource center grew to include books such as Carl Rogers' *Freedom to Learn for the Eighties*, Earl Stevick's *A Way and Ways*, Gertrude Moscowitz' *Caring and Sharing in the Foreign Language Class: A Sourcebook on Humanistic Techniques*, Caleb Gattegno's *The Common Sense of Teaching Foreign Languages* and W. Timothy Gallwey's *The Inner Game of Tennis*. Subscriptions were purchased to the *Brain/Mind Bulletin* and orders placed for Gattegno's newsletters. A group of us met regularly to explore Sufism, particularly as expressed through Idries Shah's *Seeker After Truth*, *Learning How to Learn* and *The Way of the Sufi*.

It was not all plain sailing. People were questioning themselves, others, and the times, and this sometimes provoked resistance, expressed through mockery from those less interested. International House Hastings acquired a singular culture and a different reputation from our sister schools elsewhere: as far as many were concerned we sailed too close to the 'touchy-feely' wind, and, perhaps it seemed to some that we were nothing but dilettantes.

These rough seas threatened to overwhelm at times. It is uniquely seductive, especially when young, to feel that not only do you belong on the inside of a select group, but that enlightenment lies in so belonging. Membership of this group was particularly important to me, as it helped me to define myself; but it also exposed vulnerabilities and created and reinforced dependencies. It was during this period that I formed an influential but extraordinarily difficult relationship which caused not only great emotional distress, but several legal and financial difficulties, and it was many years before I had successfully extricated myself. Such work, at least at that stage of my life, had its risks.

I found, however, that I had the will to work through these traumas. I recall regularly experiencing a potent surge of this will as I walked from my home in Hastings Old Town along the esplanade to the

> " ... his work is all encompassing; his Science of Education is in fact a Science of Life."

classrooms of Palace Chambers. Will, a feature of Gattegno's fourth realm, is "capable of holding down instinctual emotions and of letting the individual explore what is unknown and even threatening." Of all the thinking that I explored during this period, it was Gattegno's work that endured, serving as an anchor in a sea of uncertainty and unsettledness. I know now that this is because his work is all encompassing; his Science of Education is in fact a Science of Life.

It may seem overly grandiose, but I would compare Gattegno's works to classical masterpieces, for three reasons. First, masterpieces are distinguished by their capacity to provide their audience with different perspectives and therefore different experiences when revisited in the course of a lifetime. Second, masterpieces are often intellectually challenging and provocative. Third, any one masterpiece appeals simultaneously to different aspects of the self. These features apply to all of Gattegno's work. While revisits to Gattegno's writings have challenged and provoked me and continue to do so (I use 'provoke' advisedly), certain concepts have remained of central importance over the years. One of those that I draw on most often is the Subordination of Teaching to Learning. This alone has influenced everything that I have done and it suffuses everything I do, from eventually achieving a fulfilling marriage, to raising three happy children, completing a doctorate, living and working in several countries and writing well-received books.

The idea of subordinating teaching to learning is essentially humbling in its spirit, and it helped me greatly to move away from self-absorption (ironically, one of the frequent criticisms of those who search for greater awareness) towards empathy with others, finding great satisfaction in the latter.

In the research for my doctorate, for example, I investigated the experiences of those taking CELTA courses around the world. At the time, the idea of examining such a course primarily from the perspective of those taking it was relatively innovative. Previous research had approached the problem from the perspective of, for example, tutors, assessment, the curriculum or other construct. Perhaps because my approach was unusual, I soon faced difficulties, presented by the closed system, resistant to change. I persevered and managed to establish appropriate access to data; however, once complete, I found that I was not content to let my work gather dust on the British Library shelves, nor did I want to write for those who had developed the course or who taught on it. Instead I was determined to turn the academic, rational, and rather dry analysis (which had after all served its purpose) into a book that could inform and guide those about to take, or in the early stages of taking, a CELTA course: the very course that had once helped to gently nudge me along my own path. No other book serving such a purpose had existed up until that point, not least because more attention is still being paid, it seems to me, to teaching rather than to those taught. There remains much work to do, and it could not be otherwise.

"The idea of subordinating teaching to learning is essentially humbling in its spirit..."

A closing vignette. Unknown to me in those early days in Hastings, Gattegno's work had touched me many years previously, as a child growing up in Edinburgh in the 1960s. I still have the small cotton drawstring bag that was home to the Cuisenaire Rods being used to teach mathematics in my particular primary school at the time, a direct consequence of Gattegno's collaboration with Georges Cuisenaire in the 1950s. I can therefore confidently end this essay with the observation that I have had the great good fortune to be influenced by Gattegno's work nearly all my life, in my quest to become a 'cat that walks by herself' and to create the conditions necessary for those around me to be able to do the same.

(The title of this article is inspired by *Caleb Gattegno's Achievements, as Recounted by Him*, in Newsletter, Volume XVI, Number 5, June 1987.)

§

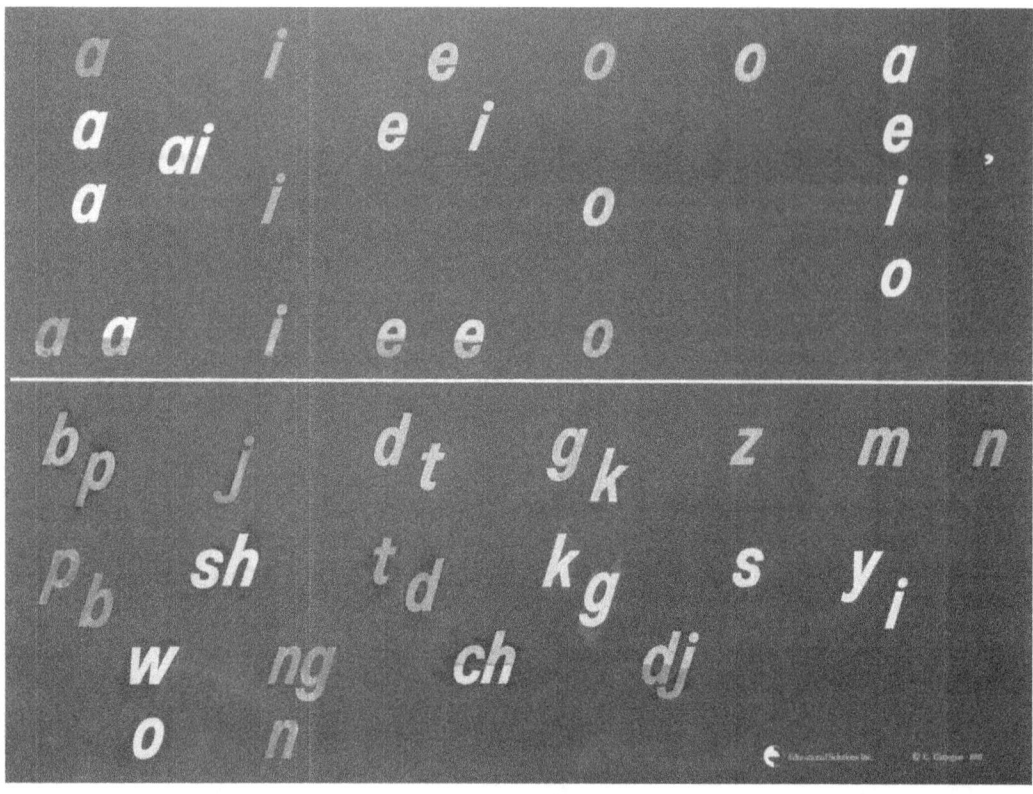

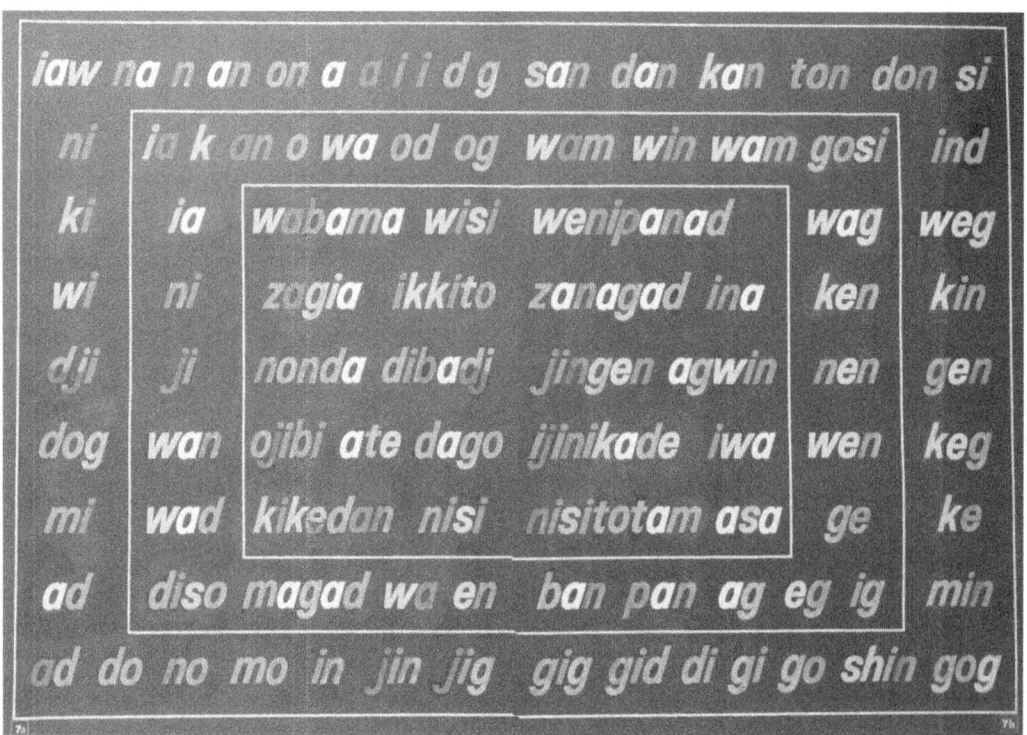

Ojibwe Fidel (top) and Word Charts 7a and b (bottom) in the prototype stage, made 1985.
©Educational Solutions Worldwide Inc.

Transcending Barriers to Become a Better Learner

Lindsay Pearson

Caleb Gattegno's influence on me was pivotal, yet I can't presume to describe him. However, this memoir is more about his effect than him.

The week-long workshop in teaching reading that first drew me to Educational Solutions, Dr. Gattegno's institute, had "feedback" sessions twice a day. At each session, others in the class reported insights that I didn't understand. Then one day, I had an insight that set the course of my life from that day to this. What

As I became more and more "myself," and learned more and more easily, I felt an appreciation for my powers that set me on fire, the way you feel when you are wildly in love. After the class, at home alone, I experienced some kind of psychological or even spiritual breakthrough. It was an understanding of what it takes to overcome one's barriers. That to do so doesn't necessarily involve working through one's problems; that if one does the right thing, one can just transcend those barriers. This from a language class!

> What I saw was hard for me to believe: a way of teaching that had more respect for people's intelligence than anything I had experienced.

I saw was hard for me to believe: a way of teaching that had more respect for people's intelligence than anything I had experienced in teaching, in studying, or in social interactions of any kind. The respect it offered students was not based on their success but on an understanding of the powers we each have.

I thought that I should pursue this calling by studying at Educational Solutions, and so I took as many language classes at Educational Solutions as I could: Chinese, German, Spanish, and Italian. All were absorbing and had lasting linguistic effects. All were taught by Dr. Gattegno's exceptional teachers, but it was in Cecilia Bartoli's Italian class that I had a transcendental experience. Dr. Bartoli is a gifted Silent Way teacher – so much so that at times I thought she was inside my head. But more than sensing her students' needs, Cecilia made us increasingly better learners. She freed me from functioning through my usual persona, and helped me become my most essential learner, which turned out to be brilliant.

I then thought that becoming a Silent Way teacher would give me the same thrill I experienced as a student. Wrong! It took me years before I felt the thrill, and that was when I felt that I was in my student's head. During those years I seemed, from the outside, to do what Silent Way teachers do, i.e. what I had seen other Silent Way teachers do. I copied their lessons. I took practicums. I spent hours and hours planning and reading. But what I didn't do was take in my students, because I didn't know how. I asked myself "What should I do?" and so was nervous, as before a performance. I later realized the question could be "What will I see?" and it's a question that can't be answered before seeing the students. I have noticed some other teachers achieving the correct internal "climate" much sooner than I. I think some people are "naturals," and then there are people, like me, who take a longer time to learn this way of relating to others. The learning has not been tedious; it has been uplifting.

(Pearson Cont'd)

Keen on more training, I attended a series of workshops that Dr. Gattegno conducted for teachers. In the morning, while we watched, he taught a class of foreign-born community college students (brought by one of the attending teachers) who wanted to improve their English. I wrote down every detail of what he did. Then, after the students were dismissed, he would ask us questions about what we saw. These were not easy questions. If we answered blithely, he was likely to scold us, so we were not very forth-coming. And at one point he asked in mock exasperation, "Well, why do you come here? It can't be to see what I do, because you can't see what I do." At the time I just gulped, and wondered what he really meant. After 35 years of teaching, I understand much better. So much of what I understand while teaching is invisible from outside and has nothing to do with planning.

I believe I was already working at Educational Solutions when Dr. Gattegno taught a weekend French class for beginners. I speak French and wanted to observe a master teacher. Dr. Gattegno dealt simultaneously with those beginners and with us observers in a way that made me think, "He's like Pavlova. He is so graceful in his teaching." During the coffee break, I spoke to a few of the students and was disappointed to see that they were just regular folk, not the brilliant people that they appeared to be during the lesson. It was the teacher who could bring all of that out of these students. When the lesson resumed, I felt a wave of admiration for this teacher who could elevate people like that. He was almost completely silent while teaching, and the students seemed to be enjoying themselves. They were relaxed yet deeply engrossed.

Dr. Gattegno was hard to feel comfortable with, and hard to ignore. His social interactions were anything but light, although he had a sense of humor. He did not chitchat about insignificant things, and his presence discouraged the same. What he did say, however, has for years given me food for thought, particularly about teaching. I sometimes wish he would appear in my dreams and give me answers. Unfortunately he, who believed in reincarnation, has not made an appearance and is possibly busy elsewhere.

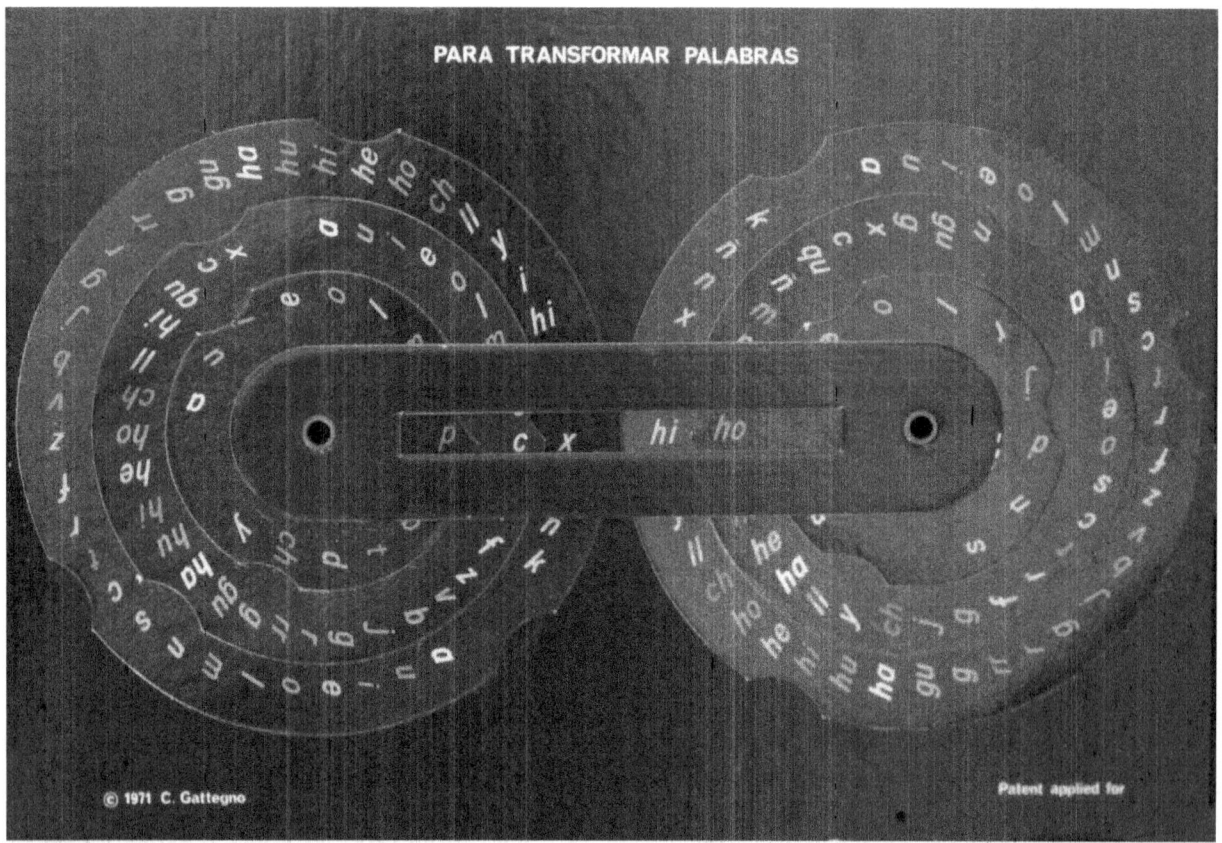

A handheld word transformer tool for Leo Color (the Spanish version of Words in Color), 1971. ©Educational Solutions Worldwide Inc.

"I Didn't Do it, You Did":
A Great Lesson Learned

Dr. Leslie Turpin

My introduction to the Silent Way and Caleb Gattegno began as a student in the MAT program at the School for International Training. In the fall of 1982, I was seated in a large semi-circle of students. Dr. Gattegno had asked my class to share our thoughts on a question he'd posed about learning and teaching. After each insight offered, Gattegno replied simply, "Tell me something I don't know." Many people were miffed by his crustiness, but I was captivated by his request to go deeper and probe beyond the superficial, to dig past the teacher: to do it, whatever it is, better.

Dr. Gattegno's philosophy came from a keen observation of children and of the human experience, so I was not surprised when his philosophy began to permeate my entire life, particularly my raising of two small children.

I began "to get" these deeper applications of Gattegno's teachings one afternoon while riding in the back seat of our Toyota pick-up cab with my five-year-old daughter. I was teaching her to tie her shoes and she was practicing making and passing the bunny ears into a bow. I made the fatal mistake of interfering in her process by doing one of the

> Short-cutting the learning process, offering false praise, or praise at all, is no match for the delight that comes from doing one's own work and making one's own learning discoveries.

Sadly my personal contacts with Dr. Gattegno were few. Instead, I learned his ideas through his wife, Shakti, from his materials and writings and from my teachers (and later colleagues) in the MAT Program. Student autonomy, staying out of the way of the learner and abandoning praise for self-awareness became core teaching values that began to shape my teaching philosophy.

As a shy young woman, I learned that purposeful silence could become the source of my strength as a teacher and not my liability — that silence could be my teaching voice.

crucial passes myself. When she completed the bow, I chirped with praise. She responded by ripping the knot out, tearing off and throwing the shoes and screaming furiously, "I didn't do it, you did!" In that moment I learned Gattegno's greatest lesson — that any learner is capable of knowing what they have and have not done on their own. A teacher can, with her own self-awareness and understanding of the learner's relationship to their challenge, work to support that self-discovery, or she can work to undermine it. Short-cutting the learning process, offering false praise, or praise at all, is no match for the delight that comes from doing one's own work and making one's own learning discoveries. §

A Responsibility to Learn

Dr. Cecilia Bartoli

It was not unusual that at Dr. G's seminars people got upset. For example, when he said that we were all still pre-human there would be protests from some of those who heard the statement for the first time. They immediately interpreted the expression as meaning non-human or sub-human. For them it was inconceivable to consider people pre-human. Yet the prefix "pre" simply means "before" such as "pre-cook" or "pre-Christian." Why would one get upset by such a neutral little word? This is only one example of his provocative techniques to "force awareness," as he would say. Indeed it did force his listeners to pay close attention, with open minds, rather than "pre-judices" to the issue under examination.

As I understand it, for him "pre-humanity" is simply the stage we find ourselves, since the on-going process of evolution has not ended. As a scientist, he always tried to look at phenomena in a neutral way and his hypothesis was that the more individuals cling to current values (given by society, religion, tradition, etc.) and identify with them, the less they are free to tap their inner powers and consequently to evolve. Questioning with a suspended judgment leads to a better understanding and acceptance of the complexity of others as well as oneself, thus facilitating the process of evolution. In essence, his strong suggestion was that in this way we are "responsible" for our own evolution.

> My lessons became far more dynamic and lively and soon everybody realized that working in a group was a great advantage.

"Responsibility," "Being at the center of your universe," "prejudices," "having a place, but not the whole place": these are concepts that Dr. G elaborated extensively and have made a profound impact on my life. Until then I had never realized how simple and useful they could be once they are stripped of any connotation of "good" and "bad." Once I looked at them just for what they are, they have become effective tools both in the classroom and in life.

For example, if responsibility simply means to "respond" in the best way I know to a situation, then I can look even at my inadequate response in a different, more neutral way. It doesn't have to be loaded with feelings of shame or guilt. Analyzing a response from a distance, without identifying with it, makes it easier to learn from it and to accept the consequences, whatever they are. Understanding responsibility – with this new connotation – has made my life a lot easier. If we truly accept that each of us is much more than any given response, then we can give this response (even if it is mistaken, silly, or unwise) its relative place and consider it an opportunity to learn. This is definitely true both in life and in the classroom. Especially in the latter where the context is more restricted, and there are specific tasks to perform, using wrong answers as an opportunity becomes a very useful technique. An inadequate response – wrong answer – may be revised or changed by making different hypotheses and testing them. In short, your classroom becomes a laboratory where the main focus is not in some pre-determined objective, but in your interest in finding the best way to respond to the different challenges your students present.

When I began to use "responsibility" as a technique, the shift in my teaching was a very dramatic one: concentrating on my learning, not only on my students' learning, I realized that the first thing I had to do was to clearly distinguish my tasks from theirs. In other words, I had a place, they had theirs, and attention had to be paid not to trespass on each other's grounds. It had never occurred to me, for instance, that if I helped them with an answer I was in fact taking their place, and taking someone's place is also lack of respect for, and trust in, the intelligence and capacity of that person to untangle a problem.

Working in this way as an experimenter, you become a far keener observer, which in turn empowers your curiosity and imagination. If you become truly engrossed in a process rather than only in results, then you become patient, very patient, because anxiety doesn't take over. What happened to me was that I stopped wanting. Somehow students feel the difference in your attitude: their work often becomes far more imaginative and efficient and results come as a by-product.

Becoming aware of my prejudices and working on them was also very useful. I realized how strong they are, even in the very young, and what a negative effect they may have. How many times have I heard a student say: "I can't learn a foreign language, I'm hopeless"? Or watched younger people teasing each other, at times even in cruelly about different cultural behavior? The challenge in this case is to

> "Somehow students feel the difference in your attitude: their work often becomes far more imaginative and efficient and results come as a by-product."

Another challenge was not to take things for granted when presenting a problem and to make it as unambiguous as possible so the students could "respond" adequately. When the response was not appropriate it was my responsibility to re-present the same problem in a slightly different way so they would have the chance to make different hypotheses, and test them until they found a correct answer. In other words, my task, as a teacher, was also to make my students take "responsibility" for their learning. My lessons became far more dynamic and lively and soon everybody realized that working in a group was a great advantage: some problems were more accessible because of multiple responses, and through them there was also the opportunity to build one's own criteria.

surprise your students by working in ways they are not used to. And there is no better way than tapping the many wonderful mental powers all humans (or pre-humans) have – sight, hearing, imagination, sense of humor, ability to stress and ignore, etc. – and at the same time encouraging them to respect and trust these powers in themselves and in others.

Certainly, the materials Dr. Gattegno developed for teaching foreign languages called the Silent Way are a blessing. They allow a teacher to rely primarily on students' mental powers. Personally I don't think that I could teach without them.

I consider myself very fortunate to have met Dr. G and I'm very grateful to him for helping me to become not only a more responsible teacher, but a person more at peace with herself. §

> "Each of us has been by far the best teacher each of us has had."
>
> — Dr. Caleb Gattegno

The Universe of Babies, Second Edition (2010), page 186.

Dr. Gattegno teaching elementary-school children using Words in Color. (Image from *Women's Day*, Sept. 1971.)

Facing Change the Gattegno Way

Edna Shaw

Back in the 1960s, after a four-year degree in Fine Arts and Philosophy at Melbourne University, followed by a teacher-training course, I commenced work with the Victorian Education Department. My first appointment was at an all-girls secondary school in Brunswick, a strictly working-class suburb to the north of Melbourne. The pupils there were largely native-speakers of English, though an influx of the post-war immigrants to the area had obviously begun.

My central challenge that year was to confront the everyday reality of the classroom, namely of full-time teaching aimed at producing adequate achievement in my pupils, but it was soon obvious that a sense of limitation prevailed both socially and in language at the school. The children, by contrast, were alert and spontaneously responsive to my efforts, appearing as bundles of potential waiting to be tapped.

After a year, I was promoted to Macleod High School at the heart of the burgeoning middle-class suburb in north-eastern Melbourne where I taught English only. I chose to work fully at the first-form level where classes were graded from A to E on the basis of the primary school achievements of the incoming children.

Classes were large and my load heavy, but for me personally, the experience was richly insightful, firing my quest to understand the reasons underlying the discrepancies in my pupils' performance, particularly in English. At the lower end of the spectrum, I had seen truly creative responses come from my somewhat tentative young pupils which heartened me, giving incentive to my quest.

Within the State Education system, the '60s were a period of incipient change, uncertainty too, triggered by numerous issues. The return of married women to the workforce, the push for equal pay and childcare for women, and with a plethora of new methods and terminology surfacing in education, an overall sense of flux prevailed. And with sizeable immigration already underway, the need to teach and the question of how to teach Australian English to children from non-English-speaking backgrounds invited a mix of controversy and disdain.

At the primary school level, the traditional approach to imparting oral and written English to school beginners was being sorely contested by new concepts in method and setting. For example, the look/say method and the open classroom held considerable sway whilst the Gattegno way and the burgeoning concept of dyslexia were sporadically filtering through.

Naturally, official educational seminars were regularly staged and were attended by serious thinkers from the primary through to the tertiary level in education.

It was at one such seminar that I had the privilege of meeting and hearing the great, unpretentious scholar, Caleb Gattegno whose insights confirmed my conviction to move to an inner-Melbourne school where under-privilege, illiteracy and immigrant influx were all in high proportion. My two years at Macleod High School had been productive, but now the excitement of a true challenge beset me.

I felt instinctively that Gattegno's Words in Color offered something both explicit and implicit for the learner – explicit in its structured informed pattern of entry into the language for both illiterate and non-native learners of English, and implicit in that it gave entry into the fullness of life. Its mastery would bring to the learner the inner joy of self-fulfillment, but with it an ability to appreciate wider facets of life through confident communication in speech or writing. For the migrant child it was the key to mastery and happiness in his new life's venture.

I shall never forget a particular moment in the above seminar when an almost palpable silence gripped the group. Caleb had spoken and minds were obviously reflecting, even perhaps questioning the insights given. Then suddenly a voice emerged, "But where do we make the start?" to which a quietly confident Caleb replied, "Being a human being is the right start." How true the response!

Soon entrenched in inner-Melbourne at Fitzroy Girls Secondary School, where local underprivilege was rife and educational goals for girls similarly restricted, I found programming for my pupils at first somewhat unsettling. As well, 45% of my pupils were from migrant families.

I mused often on the planning of an appropriate English syllabus for my pupils, hoping to build into it literary and creative experiences, but then clearly saw that my first priority lay in making the local children literate whilst giving the migrant children a legitimate introduction to English. Combining the two, the Gattegno way would make that possible.

As a start, only the lower forms were addressed though interest in the scheme soon reverberated through to the uppermost level, Form 5. One day after some weeks of instruction, a Form 3 child suddenly asked if I had "a poetry." The outcome of her request saw brief but regular poetry reading by me after each instructional lesson. The children would beam, even if they didn't fully understand. On another occasion from the same class, an excited child politely asked "Please miss, can we have a Shakerpeea (Shakespeare)?" The outcome to that request saw lunchtime readings of Shakespearean plays (in full or part) to a packed reading room.

I was fortunate to have the help of two devoted, able teachers with the Gattegno instruction, and in the art room one teacher brought her radiogram to school playing classical music as the children created. The effect was moving and the outcome poignant.

These children obviously sensed a larger life, whilst at the staff level a mix of excitement and apprehension prevailed. After all, change from entrenched patterns of social disadvantage was not easily met, and the lack of an official program of instruction for English as a Second Language did not help build certainty.

> The children were delighted. Their allotted classroom soon became a hive of anticipation, even joy.

Fortunately strong interest and support came from the two Education Department psychologists visiting the school, their responses soon stemming upwards to the Inspectorial Division itself. The impact of the Gattegno experiment was undeniable, and hence had wider implications for State Education. In fact, I was asked to consider a similar experiment in the Technical Schools Division where the majority of primary school literacy/arithmetic failures were routinely channeled.

The next year saw me back in middle-class suburbia at the Mitcham Technical School, where at the nearby Rooks Road Immigration Hostel the first influx of non-English-speaking migrants had arrived. Here again were the dual categories to be addressed. This time however the 200 Form 1 children, 77% of whom were not functionally literate, formed one experiment and the migrant children of Rooks Road another.

Mitcham staff generally viewed my intrusion with apprehension. Almost a fixed vision of the restricted capabilities of the children prevailed. Even the principal with a mix of compassion and politeness asked, "Don't you really think these children have reached their ceiling?" Silence followed then, in hesitation I finally replied, "No. Actually I don't really think they have looked up yet." Again, silence ensued ending fortunately with a warm assurance from the principal to cooperate fully with my endeavours. And he did.

(Shaw Cont'd)

The Form 1 experiment was buoyant producing not only raised literacy levels but growth to the children in outlook and confidence. A new future confronted them; whereas formerly there was a marked exodus of underachievers at the approved legal age (usually Form 3) to become labourers and low income earners, now they had every chance of reaching Forms 4 or 5 to follow an apprenticeship of their choice. Changes occurred in teacher attitudes too, with the arithmetic teacher giving remedial instruction, and trade teachers actually inserting written questions in their exam processes.

Handling the migrant group was by contrast complex. Certain parents, often in culture shock, viewed their middle-class environment and the school with a measure of distrust and apprehension, and within the group cross-racial tensions existed. Even within the classroom, initially their children gave way to racial sparring. Thus it became imperative for me to establish a welcoming, supportive bond with these families, meeting a need in some cases to visit them on an evening with a welfare officer. For the pupils, the need to give them shared identity with the school was also imperative, and was met in part by gifts of unwanted school uniforms. The children were delighted. Their allotted classroom soon became a hive of anticipation, even joy. Confronting Gattegno's Words in Color both individually and collectively, the pupil responses showed strong application and despite there being six different cultures involved, they unfolded largely with ease.

Within a few months these pupils were grappling rather ably with other areas of the curriculum, especially the more practical subjects; in all a kind of prelude to their upward progress in the school. Concurrent with my work at Mitcham was a growing interest in the Gattegno way at the Education Faculty at Monash University. Students in the Diploma of Special Education program visited my classes, and I in turn addressed them at Monash.

My quest to know consequently took me into post-graduate studies in language acquisition and development, working from a large corpus of material I collected from 5, 7 and 10-year-olds at a local middle class primary school.

Unfortunately space does not permit appraisal of this research nor of my other attempts to test the workability of the Gattegno approach for a successful language remediation or acquisition. Suffice it to say that working with adult migrants at Immigration Department night classes, the response was very positive and productive; that an adult migrant student tutored individually gained Year 12 English in four and a half months and with it entry into tertiary education, and that three hard-core, long-standing illiterate students each taken individually had a complete turnaround and soared upwards.

Throughout this period the term dyslexia was growing in usage, being rather liberally applied to young learners who failed to handle the written word. However, at the first International Symposium on Dyslexia held in Melbourne, I fully supported the contention of the opening speaker, the late renowned eye-specialist Sir Thomas Travers, that dyslexia was rare. In my research paper I showed that our literacy problems were largely "education created."

And so in Caleb Gattegno's centenary year, I remember the path he opened to me and the myriad of learners to whom he brought mastery of language – so enriching and so fundamental to confronting the vicissitudes of life.

§

> "Don't you really think these children have reached their ceiling?" Silence followed then, in hesitation I finally replied, "No. Actually I don't really think they have looked up yet."

Une nouvelle vision grâce à la Lecture en couleurs

Véronique Rodoz

Je suis enseignante spécialisée travaillant en ce moment auprès d'élèves autistes. J'ai rencontré l'approche Gattegno à la fin de ma formation spécialisée, en juin 1999 (j'avais été jusqu'alors enseignante en maternelle pendant 13 ans en petite section): une collègue de cette formation nous a présenté la Lecture en Couleurs dans un temps très court. Sa façon d'être avec chacun (même et surtout avec ceux qui ricanaient un peu ou qui étaient très sûrs d'eux) m'a immédiatement interpellée. Tellement à l'écoute, mais « bousculante » aussi (les « ricaneurs » redevenaient eux-mêmes en prenant le pointeur.)

L'approche attisait aussi ma curiosité: bien que n'ayant jamais enseigné en CP, avec des apprenants lecteurs, je sentais les nombreuses possibilités offertes. Je me suis donc inscrite au stage de lecture proposé par UEPD dès juillet.

Cela n'a pas transformé ma vie d'un seul coup, cela a questionné ma vie de plus en plus consciemment, et de plus en plus fort.

A la rentrée de septembre 1999, j'ai travaillé avec des enfants en difficultés, cela jusqu'en septembre 2006: je n'avais aucune expérience de la lecture (à part la mienne, enfant). J'ai donc commencé à utiliser ce que j'avais appris en stage Lecture en couleurs. Mais, avec réticence, en utilisant le Fidèl seulement, de temps en temps seulement, sans me jeter complètement dedans car j'avais le sentiment que beaucoup de choses m'échappaient sans pouvoir expliquer quoi.

Parallèlement, je continuai à faire des stages avec UEPD, d'orthographe, de grammaire, avec une soif de mieux comprendre ce qu'il y avait derrière cette approche. Puis vinrent les stages de math, plus longtemps après, (parce que je me considérais comme nulle dans ce domaine), qui ont commencé à me faire prendre conscience du travail que j'avais à faire sur moi-même, qui ont beaucoup réparé au niveau de ma pratique, justement parce que je travaillais essentiellement sur moi.

En 2006, j'ai postulé pour un poste en IME (institut médico-éducatif). Il n'y avait pas d'enseignante dans cet établissement assez récent (2003) qui accueillait un public TED (troubles envahissants du développement).

Dans les mêmes temps, je m'engageai dans l'association UEPD, au conseil d'administration, car je me sentais si reconnaissante de tout ce que j'avais reçu de cette association, malgré mes résistances et le temps que je mettais à me laisser transformer.

Cela fait 5 ans que je travaille avec des enfants autistes : il m'aura fallu cette expérience spécifique et difficile pour mettre du sens au concept de la subordination de l'enseignement. Je ne sais pas ce que j'aurais fait sans les outils de la Lecture en couleurs (qu'il a fallu aménager au niveau de la présentation pour mes élèves), sans les outils mathématiques comme les réglettes, sans la poursuite des stages de formation.

Quelques uns de mes élèves sont entrés dans le domaine de la lecture grâce à cette approche très visuelle. D'autres ne lisent pas mais se sont investis (et l'investissement peut sembler compliqué pour des jeunes autistes), sont présents, grâce à ces outils.

Je me suis enseignée aussi pendant ces années, en les utilisant régulièrement, en prenant conscience de façon plus pointue du fonctionnement de mes élèves et du mien, de la richesse de l'outil, de sa vastitude. J'ai encore du travail à faire sur moi, sur ma façon d'appréhender les élèves, sur ma façon d'être avec eux, de l'intérieur. Ma vision du monde a changé grâce à cette approche. Je suis maintenant persuadée du rôle de la conscience dans l'enseignement et les apprentissages.

J'ai du travail à ce niveau jusqu'à la fin de ma vie!

Meine Begegnungen mit dem Genie Dr. Gattegno

Klara Miller-Fuehren

„The Silent Way" kennen zu lernen, war ein bedeutsamer Schritt in meinem Leben.

Es war in den 80er Jahren, als ich in Paris lebte. Als Studentin der Schauspielschule suchte ich Teilzeitarbeit und wurde von „Pour l'Education de Demain" im Büro eingestellt. Allen und Annie Rozelle, die damals die Organisation leiteten, zogen nach Genf, um dort den ‚Silent Way' an der internationalen Schule zu lehren. Deshalb wurde ich schon während der Einarbeitungszeit gefragt von Allen Rozelle und Barbara Villez, ob ich nicht zusätzlich die Ausbildung von ‚Silent Way' machen wolle, um in Paris Deutsch und Englisch zu lehren. In kurzer Zeit war ich so fasziniert von dieser kreativen Annäherung, nicht Methode, dass ich die Ausbildung als ‚Silent Way' Lehrerin mit voller Begeisterung absolvierte. Es ließ sich sehr gut mit meiner Arbeit als junger Schauspielerin vereinbaren.

Faszinierend war für mich, wie schnell die erwachsenen Schüler mit den Color Charts und den Stäbchen lernten, und wie leicht es ihnen fiel, damit die Melodie der Sprache zu erfassen und zu verinnerlichen. Besonders Franzosen haben oft Schwierigkeiten, bestimmte Laute in Englisch zu unterscheiden, wie z.B. das kurze ‚i' für ‚it', denn dieses existiert nicht in der französischen Sprache. Als sie am Color Chart sahen, dass es zwei verschiedene rote Farben für das ‚i' gab, schien das Ohr sich zu neuem Hören zu entwickeln. Es machte ihnen solchen Spaß, völlig anders und kreativer als in anderen Schulen zu lernen. Der Erfolg half dabei:

Nach 10 Stunden schon konnten sie kleine Sätze bilden und trauten sich zu sprechen - und das mit gutem Akzent!

Nach 20 Stunden konnten sie kurze einfache Geschichten in der Fremdsprache erzählen und bekamen ein gutes Gefühl für die Struktur der Sprache - und das auf diese ganz spielerische Art und Weise!

Von Dr. Gattegno lernte ich auch, dass es immer der Fehler des Lehrers ist, wenn die Schüler müde und überfordert sind und nicht mehr aufpassen. Ich gestehe, dass ich die Tendenz hatte, anderen die Schuld zuzuschieben, wenn etwas schief ging.

Dreieinhalb Jahre arbeitete ich für „Pour l'Education de Demain", und es war eine sehr kreative und bereichernde Zeit für mich. Ich verstand immer besser, was Dr. Gattegno zu vermitteln versuchte. Dieses Wissen half mir auch in meinem Privatleben weiter.

Es war eine sehr bereichernde und konstruktive Zeit für mich. Heute noch denke ich gerne daran zurück. Es war die beste Zusammenarbeit, die ich je hatte mit Barbara Villez und Cecilia Bartoli. Auch die Sprachlehrer untereinander waren kollegial und hilfsbereit. Wir vertraten einander, wenn einer krank war, und es gab nie Komplikationen, jeder respektierte den andern. Weder vorher noch nachher erlebte ich eine solch harmonische Zeit.

Dr. Gattegno ließ es den Lehrern frei, wie sie ihren Unterricht gestalteten. Er unterstützte uns mit seinem Know-how, aber nie mit festen Regeln. Er wollte, dass jeder Lehrer sich mit seiner eigenen Art einbringt.

Das großartigste Erlebnis mit Dr. Gattegno war folgendes für mich: Einmal beobachtete ich ihn, wie er mit einem 8-jährigen Jungen arbeitete, der große Probleme mit Mathematik in der Schule hatte. Es war bewundernswert mit welcher Geduld er wartete, bis der Prozess des Verstehens eingetreten war. Er redete nicht dauernd auf ihn ein, er ließ ihn in der Stille nachdenken. Nicht einen Moment übte er Druck auf ihn aus. Es dauerte keine 15 Minuten, da atmete der Junge auf und hatte verstanden! Danach konnte er mit Leichtigkeit Aufgaben lösen, die ihm vorher unmöglich erschienen waren. In meinen Augen ein Geniestreich!

In meiner Ausbildung sollte ich eine Fremdsprache lernen, die ich nicht kannte, und die auch keiner europäischen Sprache ähnelte. So lernte ich chinesisch, japanisch und italienisch. Ich durfte erleben, wie Schüler frustriert sind, wenn sie überfordert werden, und wie wichtig es war, geduldig und klar zu Schülern zu sein, um dies zu meiden.

Das Außergewöhnliche am ‚Silent Way' ist, dass die Sprache einfach im Gedächtnis bleibt, ich kann sie noch heute hervorrufen, wenn nötig.

Vielen Dank an Dr. Gattegno, der die Welt mit seiner Pädagogik so bereichert hat. Er war sicherlich seiner Zeit voraus. Ein Vorreiter hat es oft nicht leicht, seine Sache durchzusetzen, doch sein Werk wird auch heute noch von genügend Lehrern weitergegeben. Und das ist gut so. Dr. Gattegnos' Seminare halfen mir, meine Wahrnehmung für andere Menschen zu öffnen und gleichzeitig meine Sprachkenntnisse enorm zu erweitern. §

In 1954 Dr. Gattegno introduced Cuisenaire Rods to the world starting with a book, *Numbers in Colour*, co-authored with Georges Cuisenaire, which later developed into the Numbers in Colour Math Set. (Educational Solutions file photo.)

Exceeding Expectations

Dr. Marilyn Maye

I began my career in mathematics education in the 1970s, when reform mathematics was in the air. I looked forward to a long career in a field that would continuously evolve, innovate, and include constituencies that had historically been underrepresented.

During my first job after graduate school, I had the good fortune to work in East Harlem in a district where Caleb Gattegno had a contract to work with elementary and intermediate schools. I was assigned the late Marty Hoffman as my Educational Solutions consultant. It was a perfect segue from my pre-service training — ongoing, job-embedded professional development. I would learn to use the language of today's professional development standards and best practices, and I drank in every opportunity to continue to learn more.

Marty came to my eighth grade mathematics classroom at least once per week, and made suggestions about curriculum and instruction. He invited me to afterschool and summer-session workshops led by Dr. Gattegno, both in my school district and at the company. I sat in on parent workshops that Dr. Gattegno conducted at lunch time with parents. And I joined teachers from around the city, on our own incentive with no remuneration, at a Brooklyn cultural center called the East, where mathematics teachers, many of whom had been influenced by Dr. Gattegno, met at least once a week. On our own time, for hours at a stretch, after long work days, we traveled from Harlem and the South Bronx to Brooklyn, to fine tune our understanding of how to "get a lot out of a little," one of Dr. Gattegno's mottos. Our goal was to make it possible for children from Harlem, the South Bronx, Bedford Stuyvesant, and other areas of the city where visible minorities lived, to perform mathematically at advanced levels.

Educators who attended these self-directed professional development gatherings had high expectations. New York City had recently been through a war over "community control" of schools, after a strike by the teachers' union, who opposed it, shut the schools for months. As activists tried to provide instruction during the teachers' absence, communities discovered that they could take some control over the destinies of their educational institutions. Still at university when it happened, young future educators like myself signed on, eager to serve as foot-soldiers. Once employed, both during the school day and afterwards in the evenings, we swapped successful teaching strategies – "How did you get your pre-schoolers to use fractions?" or "How did you get your kids to solve those complicated-looking equations?" We were seeking precocious achievement for our young people. The promise of Gattegno's methods was not just that children would perform at grade level, but that they would perform at levels beyond expectations, and so close or prevent what we now refer to as "the achievement gap."

One of the mathematics educators who convened meetings at the East, the late Professor Everett Barrett, made headlines when fifth-graders he taught at Public School 44, a Brooklyn elementary school, passed the ninth-grade algebra Regents examination (New York State test). Barrett had worked as a "demonstration teacher" at the school teaching students algebra, while their teachers observed, using techniques that tapped into the children's perceptions, introduced algebra before arithmetic, and freed the children from the tedium and limitations of traditional mathematics instruction. I have a godson who was among that group of fifth-graders. He was able to retain those gains despite a lackluster middle school experience, eventually moving on to a magnet high school in mathematics and science, and proceeding to college and a career as a community-based professional working with youth, in another state. He had seen the benefits of community-based education, in a school headed by the dedicated and forward-looking principal, Ms. Doreen Hall. Ms. Hall understood the power of an approach that respects the intelligence of children and that holds them to high expectations. Unfortunately, she was unable to garner support for institutionalizing Barrett's program, even in the wake of the embarrassment to the district when some of her fifth-graders passed the same State algebra exam that their ninth-grade siblings were unable to pass.

Throughout my life, whether I was in education or not, I have always kept bags of Cuisenaire Rods, Geoboards, and a set of miniature Words in Color charts for the occasional child or adult who sought me out in a panic, struggling with traditional learning situations. I've used them with people in my own family, and watched them acquire confidence in understanding proportional reasoning, for example, skills that befuddle the average American. In recent years, I helped found a charter school in my neighborhood, where Dr. Gattegno's approach is the official philosophy and curriculum.

Now, four decades after my introduction to the Subordination of Teaching to Learning, I still go into classroom after classroom in middle and high schools in New York, New Jersey, and other states, and to my horror, observe mathematics instruction that seems uninfluenced in any way by what we learned and tried to accomplish in the 1970s. I find mathematics teachers at the start of their working years, and career changers in midlife, alike, still teaching the way they were taught as schoolchildren and as pre-service educators. The pattern is: procedural presentation of skills and vocabulary at the chalkboard (or "smart"-board), followed by students imitating at their desks what their teachers have modeled, followed by homework from the textbook that repeats the steps seen in class, followed by going over problems the next day, before the next skill in the textbook is tackled. Although it is fashionable to talk about "conceptual" approaches to mathematics instruction, the dominant practice is still to teach disconnected facts and skills, with minimal visualization or student-led discourse to help clarify misconceptions and increase the likelihood of understanding and retention.

The revolution we were a part of did not take hold broadly, for any number of reasons, common to

> The promise of Gattegno's methods was not just that children would perform at grade level, but that they would perform at levels beyond expectations, and so close or prevent what we now refer to as 'the achievement gap.'

many revolutionary movements. The good news, however, is that the pressure for change is as strong, or stronger, than ever. It is fortuitous that the memory of Dr. Gattegno is being invoked, upon the 100th anniversary of his birth, at a time when the push for change in methods and outcomes of mathematics teaching and learning is at a fever pitch. Notwithstanding that much of it is driven by panic over low scores on narrowly-focused tests, and by embarrassingly unfavorable international comparisons, the concerns provide new opportunities to be heard, for those of us who have been affected by and witnessed the power of Dr. Gattegno's approach.

The wide use of technologies – such as YouTube, social media, and smart phones – that make video presentations ubiquitous, instant communication across international borders, and new institutional structures such as charter schools, provide mechanisms for demonstrating and sharing non-traditional

(Maye Cont'd)

instructional strategies, with students and educators alike. We also now have brain-based studies, such as those documented in National Academies Press books, *How People Learn* and *How Students Learn*, that provide additional scientific research affirming the work that Dr. Gattegno did with children. We are positioned to spread the word and the practices, with credibility, as never before.

As those of us who studied with him move into our senior years, and some of us have already transitioned, there is a sense of urgency that we communicate effectively what was not sufficiently captured in writing or other media during Dr. Gattegno's life. Our goal has to be to create a critical mass of young learners who, like those fifth-graders who passed the algebra Regents exam in the 1980s, will become a generation of teachers, whose students will then demonstrate what education can look like when it taps into the powers of the learners' innate intelligence. Every generation that we miss reaching pushes the realization of this vision out another few decades.

§

Box of Algebricks, or Cuisenaire Rods, around which Dr. Gattegno developed his mathematical pedagogy. The rods are a model for the rational number system.

No Tricks, But There is Magic in the Technique

Luigi Magnano

About 40 years ago, while in university, I was given the opportunity to research a new pedagogical language-teaching technique known as the Silent Way, which was being introduced by a certain Dr. Caleb Gattegno. I visited the Educational Solutions office on Fifth Avenue in New York. I didn't know what to expect; perhaps just another one of the many language schools claiming to teach a foreign language quickly.

My contact with Dr. Gattegno was brief but captivating. I enrolled in the workshops to better understand the didactics of Leo Color (Spanish), Words in Color, and the Silent Way. The seminars were conducted by Dr. Gattegno and two other assistants, Steve Schuller and Dr. Dee Hinman, for eight hours per day.

What Dr. Gattegno said, how he presented the technique, and to actively participate and see firsthand the ease with which a foreign language could be taught and learned – without the vocal participation of the teacher, the dreaded grammar rules, the nonsensical homework exercises – was exciting, fascinating, one could say almost magical.

Dr. Gattegno spoke of "ogdens" as the price one pays for learning, and that one should spend as few ogdens as possible to purchase as much language as one can. Simple economics would say that it is baffling this is not applied in most schools.

He discussed for hours the common sense approach to teaching foreign languages, how children learn, breathing techniques and liberating the mind before initiating a course, and his ideas on sleep. "Sleep on it. It will all come back to you in the morning," he said.

I wanted to be able to use the pedagogical "tricks" of his teaching approach, but there were no playbooks, no syllabus, and no formalized program; how can one teach without such aids?

> "Simple economics would say that it is baffling this is not applied in most schools."

By the end of the course I became aware that there were no tricks; it was all in the technique of the approach being used to teach, in the understanding of what happens as one is teaching and the other is learning. The impossibility of following a prescribed guide book was not a hindrance; it was a transition into introducing only what is necessary at a particular moment in time, in guiding not dictating, in bringing out of the student that which is already there and has been learned during his lifetime, and in making the student aware of what is happening and of his capabilities.

During my teaching career, I have been overcome by this technique and the ease with which I was able to introduce students to English as a foreign language, or have illiterate farm workers begin reading in their native language. It was, and is still today, an indescribable feeling not only for me but for the students in class, who with little effort are able to take back with them so much achievement.

Though this happened over 40 years ago, the memories, the words, and the self confidence that Dr. Gattegno inspired have remained with me. His words, his melodious movements of the pointer, his agile use of his hands and fingers to elicit rhythm, the many models offered through the use of the rods, and the simple ways he made difficult phonemic sounds come so naturally; all this will never be forgotten. §

The Māori Revival

Te Ataarangi

Te Ataarangi is a language revitalization movement committed to the survival of the Māori language. Its immersion language-learning technique is modeled on Dr. Caleb Gattegno's the Silent Way, famously using the colored Cuisenaire Rods as a learning tool, and incorporating Māori values and customs.

> At the end of the 20 minute session I was elated. I had actually composed a number of sentences and I knew exactly what the function of each word was without any explanation.

Kāterina Te Heikōkō Mataira and Ngoingoi Pēwhairangi began developing Te Ataarangi during the late 1970s when research showed that the Māori language was dying. Designed as a community-based learning system for adult Māori, Te Ataarangi began delivering programs that increased fluency and cultural knowledge in 1979. People who completed Te Ataarangi programs became adept speakers of everyday Māori with a strengthened understanding of cultural identity, because successful language revitalization is based on whānau (family) and communities with initiatives that foster and promote inter-generational language transmission. Te Ataarangi now operates in two key areas: the re-establishment of language use in the home, and initiatives to increase the numbers of competent speakers and the number of speaker communities.

DR. MATAIRA MEETS DR. GATTEGNO IN FIJI

In 1973 while living in Fiji, Dr. Mataira enrolled in Fijian language classes at the local university. The method used was grammar/translation delivered through the medium of English, but Kāterina found she learnt more through conversing with the locals. She later met American Peace Corps students and was surprised at how fluent these young people were in the Fijian language. She learnt that they had acquired the language through an intensive 10 week course with Dr. Gattegno at the Language Institute in New York. Dr. Mataira decided to meet tutors from the Language Institute when they came to Fiji, and this is where she first experienced the Silent Way approach. She joined a class that included students from different countries with a variety of languages, and was introduced to teaching and learning languages using Cuisenaire Rods.

These colored rods, originally designed to teach basic arithmetic, were utilized to teach the students Japanese, and subsequently the students were required to teach some of their own languages. Dr. Mataira recalls:

> "What impressed me then about the Silent Way was the challenge it evoked. I was not being fed with a series of statements which I had to memorize and reproduce; I was being offered

2009 UNESCO Linguapax Award ceremony in which Dr. Mataira's lifelong work to revive the Māori language was recognized. From left to right: Hon Hekia Parata (Minister of Parliament, New Zealand), Dr. Kāterina Te Heikōkō Mataira, Dr. Miguel Angel Essomba (President of the Linguapax Institute), and Lyn Harrison (Board member of Te Ataarangi Trust).

(Te Ataarangi Cont'd)

minimal data in a contrived situational context involving the use of colored rods, and I had to use all my senses to derive meaning and form statements from that context. I had to take responsibility for my own learning. I could not lean on my fellow learners – they were not allowed to prompt me. I could not call on the tutor to provide answers for me – he would not. I could not dally for time expecting the tutor and group to lose patience and provide the answer for me – they just waited for my response. I had to get my wits together, I had to concentrate, I had to reflect. And given the time to do this, I found myself uttering sentences in this strange new language with relative ease. At the end of the 20 minute session I was elated. I had actually composed a number of sentences and I knew exactly what the function of each word was without any explanation." *The Effectiveness of the Silent Way Method in the Teaching of Māori as a Second Language," (1980).*

Upon her return to New Zealand, Dr. Mataira was offered a research fellows position at Waikato University and continued the development of this teaching methodology, which became the basis of her master of education thesis "The Effectiveness of the Silent Way Method in the Teaching of Māori as a Second Language."

As part of her research Dr. Mataira contacted Dr. Gattegno, who agreed to meet with her. Being friends of the owners of the New Zealand publishing company A.H. & A.W. Reed, Gattegno was familiar with the Māori language, and he offered his expertise to assist with the teaching of the Māori language in schools when he visited New Zealand. Dr. Mataira was unable to secure funding to meet with him, but Gattegno generously provided Dr. Mataira with all of his work regarding the Silent Way method to support her research.

Gattegno was not precious about his work and encouraged her to take from it what she thought would be appropriate for the Māori language. This eventually became the framework upon which the rākau (rod) method was developed. Limited resources are required to deliver this methodology, making it accessible in all environments.

Dr. Mataira appreciated that Gattegno's pedagogy fully encouraged diversity amongst the many languages he assisted, and that the approach could be adapted to suit and respect their unique cultures and nuances. Te Ataarangi is steeped in Māori culture, customs and the Māori world view, and although it has adopted Gattegno's principles, it is Māori in form and spirit. Te Ataarangi was seen to be one of the most significant programs to address adult Māori language learning during the infancy of the Māori language revitalization movement.

HONORARY DOCTORATE (1996), LINGUAPAX AWARD (2009), AND QUEEN'S BIRTHDAY HONOURS (2011)

Over the years, as a writer, artist, academic and Māori language pioneer, Dr. Mataira received numerous awards including an honorary doctorate from Waikato University. In 2009, she won the prestigious UNESCO Linguapax Award in recognition of her lifelong work to revive the Māori language. Dr. Mataira received the Linguapax Award at an official ceremony hosted at Parliament House in Wellington. The award is an international honor which recognizes the preservation and promotion of mother languages as essential vehicles of identity and cultural expression. This was the first time a New Zealander had been honored with the award.

In June 2011, shortly before her death, Dr. Mataira was awarded the highest honor in the Queen's Birthday Honours List, Dame Companion of the New Zealand Order of Merit as a tribute for her services to Māori language. The Honorable Dr. Pita Sharples commented that Dame Kāterina, of Ngati Porou, earned universal respect for the passion she helped generate in the revival of the Māori language.

In over 30 years since its inception, Te Ataarangi has taught thousands of adults to speak Māori. The continued support and development of a whole new generation of Māori language tutors has contributed to the revitalization of the Māori language for the future.

§

Whakarehurehu atu rā e kui
Whakawhiti atu ki ō mātua tīpuna
Waiho ake mātou ki muri nei haku ai
Pātukituki ai ngā manawa
Maimoa ai mōu … kia mahu ake rā
E ara anō ai ki te pīkau i te kaupapa
Kia kore koe e ngaro taku reo rangatira

Te Ataarangi, recognized for their work in the revival of Māori language and culture, adopts some of the principles of the Silent Way, including the use of rods to create linguistic situations. Here, students participate in workshops at the Te Ataarangi Language Revitalisation Conference held in 2008 in New Zealand.

Transferable Skills

Bill Robbins

I first encountered the Silent Way as a U.S. Peace Corps volunteer in Thailand in July, 1974 when one of the administration staff who had just returned from New York gave a demonstration using the charts and rods. I must have expressed an interest in what I saw because he loaned me the book *The Common Sense of Teaching Foreign Languages*. I really struggled with the concepts Dr. Gattegno presented; there was much I simply did not understand. However, one quote from the book still remains with me today, "In verbal relationships communication is almost a miracle." These words have helped guide me through a number of sticky situations, giving me the patience to focus on what is happening, and to try to find different ways of expressing myself or of understanding what has been said to me.

Unfortunately I had no access to any of the tools of the Silent Way while in Thailand. But I was intrigued, and after I returned, I spent several months in New York and took the opportunity to attend a seminar given by Dr. G, which gave me a more thorough contact with the approach and with the use of the tools — the charts, rods, pointer and drawings.

About a year later in 1977, when I went to Japan, I created my own Japanese Sound-Color Chart and Fidels to assist me in learning the Japanese sound system. However, once I had completed this task, I found I no longer needed the charts. I had already developed a quite acceptable level of skill in the sounds and melody of Japanese from the exercise, again confirming to me the validity of the approach. Soon after that, I started teaching at an institute that encouraged the exploration and use of non-mainstream approaches to language learning, the Silent Way being the primary one at that time. Through use of the tools, continued reading, and extensive discussions with colleagues also exploring the Silent Way, I continued to develop my understanding of this very powerful approach to the learning of languages. My conviction continued to strengthen that, when properly executed, this approach went far beyond other methods I had encountered in providing learners with the competence and confidence to be self sufficient in using the language. I saw how it put the responsibility for learning squarely on the learners' shoulders, while making the teacher responsible for guiding them along the way and actively staying out of the way of their learning.

> "I am continually aware that I am constantly learning, and as a result eagerly approach learning opportunities of all sorts…"

I later moved to Osaka where I began working with Fusako Allard toward enhancing our understanding of the principles of the approach. She sponsored a number of workshops by Dr. Gattegno over the years on a variety of topics to do with the Silent Way and the Science of Education, which were critical for me in extending my understanding and skill in working with learners. Eventually Ms. Allard developed the Japanese set of Silent Way charts in consultation with Dr. G.

One anecdote from my association with Ms. Allard rather dramatically illustrates the role of teacher and learner in this approach. Ms. Allard and another colleague had taken on the task of working with Vietnamese refugees, and felt that gaining a basic level of Vietnamese would enhance their own teaching. They knew that I had learned Vietnamese during my time in that country, and that I had developed a Vietnamese Sound-Color Chart, a Fidel and a partial set of Word Charts as a learning exercise for myself. They requested that I give them an introduction to Vietnamese, to which I agreed. I soon found myself in a position where my students were learning aspects of the language that I had absolutely no entry into. Four or five hundred years ago, French missionaries had established a Roman alphabet version of the Vietnamese language, which then became the standard written form throughout that country. Still, the smallest units of the language conveying meaning remained tied to the origins from which it came, the Chinese ideogram system. Since Japanese is rooted in the same system, and in fact continues to use an adaption of it today, the Japanese individuals I was teaching were able use this relationship to make links helpful to them in learning Vietnamese. They had taken on the responsibility of learners by pushing their own learning way beyond anything I was able to give them. The Silent Way made this possible.

I am recently retired, but my teaching career ended more than a decade ago when changes to the political landscape in Australia effectively ended any flexibility a teacher had in the language classroom to put something like the Silent Way into practice. I ended up operating a bookkeeping business for the last decade of my working life. Bookkeeping and the Silent Way – where is the link between those two, you ask? So did I.

A bookkeeper's job is to keep as accurate account of a business' finances as possible with the information supplied. I quickly became aware that many small business operators viewed the keeping of accounts as little more than a necessary and annoying evil in order to meet their tax obligations. I saw that I could do a lot for them by helping them become aware of what an accurate set of accounts could provide in the health of their business. In effect, I became my clients' teacher and they the learners. In this situation I did not have the authority of a classroom teacher, and had to find suitable ways to make them aware of how to use the tool of their accounts to benefit their businesses. I took on this task without presuming to myself or to them that I knew enough about their particular business to advise them in that regard. At the beginning this approach was anything but deliberate. It was more of an habitual response resulting from long-term contact with the principals of the Silent Way. It was only over time that I made myself aware of what I was doing, and then proceeded to deliberately refine my approach and my role. I made it my job to learn each of my clients so I could then find the most effective way of helping each individual use their accounting records most effectively for their business. After having worked with a given client for a period of time, the response was almost always very positive and sometimes downright enthusiastic.

> In verbal relationships communication is almost a miracle.

In one instance, at the end of the first month working for a new client, I asked the boss if he would like me to print out a profit and loss statement for him. His response was that I shouldn't bother. However, as I left that day, I slipped a printout on his desk. No mention of it was made at my next visit, but I continued to supply these monthly reports, until one month it slipped my mind – and I was severely reprimanded for not having left him the monthly report. I was delighted rather than distressed because it showed that the boss had indeed been examining the report and was discovering valuable information about his business. All I had done was supply the data in a format that could make him aware of critical aspects of his business. He did all the rest.

For me, attempting to affect the principles behind the Silent Way in the classroom has had the same effect in my life in general. I am continually aware that I am constantly learning, and as a result eagerly approach learning opportunities of all sorts, despite knowing that venturing into the unknown will inevitably bring uncertainty and errors on my part. One would think that at my age I would know better, but my life continues to be richer for it. §

Notes on C.G.'s work for circulation.

Caleb Gattegno L. ès Sc. D.E.S. Dr. Phil. M.A. D. ès L.

Founder of the British Association of Teachers of Mathematics (ATM 1953)
  " of the Belgian Association (ABPM 1952)
     each with its own journal still published
  " of the International Commission for the Study & Improvement
       of Teaching of Mathematics (ICSITM) 1951)
  " of Schools for the Future Inc USA 1965
  " of Educational Solutions Inc USA 1968
  " of The Silent Way Video Co Inc USA 1977

Originator of The Silent Way of Teaching Foreign Languages (1954-)
  of The uses of Cuisenaire rods in elementary math (1953-58)
  of The uses of J.L. Nicolet Animated Geometry films (1950-)
  of The uses of video for early childhood education (1969-)
     and for foreign languages (1977-)
  of uses of microcomputer in education (math, literacy,
     foreign languages) (1980-)
  of Words in color for teaching language arts to natives in English,
     French, Spanish and Ethiopian; Mandarin & other languages
  of Infused Reading through microcomputers in
     Spanish, French, Ethiopian and English & Japanese
     (the last two in preparation)

Creator of materials and techniques for uses of the above
  of the Geo-boards
  of the Folklore of Mathematics films
  of Absolute Visual Reading for the deaf
  of a new Braille
  of a new epistemology
  of the Science of Education based on awareness of awareness

Author of more than one hundred books, four hundred articles

Publisher of a current Newsletter (13 vols appeared to June 84), of a series
  of 65 career books "My Life and My Work" (1964-1981), of "The
  Common Sense of Teaching" series (1978-) of numerous monographs
  covering education, epistemology, psychology, health, children,
  stories, economics... a number of which exist in English,
  French, German, Hebrew, Italian, Portuguese and Spanish.

Worked in 48 countries since the end of World War II and met
  at workshops and seminars many thousands of educators.

Produced Silent Way classroom materials for twenty-eight languages,
  seven of them used to train Peace Corps volunteers.

Dr. Gattegno's handwritten C.V., from 1984, courtesy of Claude Arnould.

NOTES ON CG'S WORK FOR CIRCULATION

- Caleb Gattegno L. ès Sc. D.E.S. Dr. Phil. M.A. D. ès L.
- Founder of the British Association of Teachers of Mathematics (ATM 1952)
- Founder of the Belgian Association of Teachers of Mathematics (ABPM 1952) - each with its own journal still published
- Founder of the International Commission for the Study and Improvement of Teaching of Mathematics (ICSITM 1951)
- Founder of Schools for the Future Inc   USA   1965
- Founder of Educational Solutions Inc   USA   1968
- Founder of The Silent Way Video Co Inc USA   1977
- Originator of The Silent Way of Teaching Foreign Languages (1954)
- Originator of the uses of Cuisinaire Rods in elementary math (1953–58)
- Originator of the uses of J.L. Nicolet Animated Geometry films (1950–)
- Originator of the uses of video for early childhood education (1964–) and for foreign language (1977–)
- Originator of uses of microcomputer in education (math, literacy, foreign languages) (1980–)
- Originator of Words in Color for teaching language arts for natives in English, French, Spanish and Iñupiaq, Mandarin and other languages
- Originator of Infused Reading through microcomputers in Spanish, French, Iñupiaq and English and Japanese (last two in preparation)
- Creator of materials and techniques and courses of the above
- Creator of the Geoboards
- Creator of the Folklore of Mathematics films
- Creator of Absolute Visual Reading for the deaf
- Creator of a new Braille
- Creator of a new epistemology
- Creator of the Science of Education based on awareness of awareness
- Author of more than one hundred books, four hundred articles
- Publisher of a current Newsletter (5 times a year 13 vols appeared to June 84), of a series of 65 career books "My Life and My Work" (1964–1981), of "The Common Sense of Teaching" series (1973–), of numerous monographs covering education, epistemology, psychology, health, children; stories, economics . . . a number of which exist in English, French, German, Hebrew, Italian, Portuguese and Spanish
- Worked in 48 countries since the end of World War II and met at workshops and seminars many thousands of educators
- Produced Silent Way classroom materials for twenty-eight languages, seven of them used to train Peace Corps volunteers

Transcript of Dr. Gattegno's handwritten C.V. (Opposite page.)

Revolutionizing My Teaching By Doing the Opposite

Hugh Birdsall

I came into contact with Dr. Caleb Gattegno's work about 20 years ago and have been studying it ever since. At the time, I heard his approach referred to as the Silent Way. Later, I came to know it as The Subordination of Teaching to Learning. It literally revolutionized my teaching – that is, it turned it upside-down. Whatever I had been doing and thinking before, I started doing and thinking the opposite. In the process, my teaching improved, and my students became better learners. I began to feel it was my responsibility to share what I had learned with others.

Over the years, as I have become more fluent with the techniques and materials associated with Dr. Gattegno's approach, I have had the opportunity to share my understanding by presenting workshops on the Silent Way and Words in Color. To that end, with the help of some colleagues, I designed an introductory activity for Silent Way workshops. Through my description of this activity, I invite readers to experience vicariously some of the principles that continue to guide me in my ongoing learning of teaching. Perhaps readers will also gain some insight into the approach.

My purpose in designing the activity was to engage participants in a concrete language learning experience, through which they could perceive directly and reflect upon the principles that would drive the rest of the workshop. Now, having presented the activity, I have also discovered that the activity itself, and subsequent discussion of its impact, can spark enough interest in participants that they may examine the approach further on their own.

I started planning the activity by selecting five statements about human learning that I had come across while attending Silent Way workshops presented by Mrs. Shakti Gattegno, in New York City. The following are the statements I chose:

"Learners learn, not because they are taught, but when they mobilize themselves to learn."

"Meaning resides not in words but in situations."

"Learning requires time and varied practice."

"Learners build inner criteria for correctness."

"Mistakes are an integral part of learning."

To some, these statements might appear to be simple common sense, and indeed, Dr. Gattegno called The Subordination of Teaching to Learning a common sense approach. I have both observed and taught in many school settings over the years though, and I can attest that conventional wisdom has teachers acting as if their teaching caused their students to learn; as if teaching were merely a repeating pattern of presentation and standardized assessment; as if meaning could be derived from words alone and retained devoid of context; as if learning were not an internal process but simply an outcome of teaching; as if mistakes were evil things to be avoided at any cost. How then could I create conditions for teachers accustomed to the conventional wisdom to perceive directly the truth of the five statements I had chosen?

My strategy was to create a challenging linguistic puzzle for workshop participants to solve, with as little intervention from me as possible. So, to a group of language teachers I presented the following as a sentence in an unfamiliar language for them to translate: Sranréal ød tøn nréal asüécab yaht aré thgüét, tüb rahtér nahw yaht azilibøm savlasmaht øt nréal. (This was, in fact, a version of the first of my five selected statements about learning.) I asked them to examine the sentence for a couple of minutes and to raise hands if they had an idea what the English translation might be. Most participants were not able to figure this out initially. Those who did, I asked to remain silent and to use the subsequent activities to confirm or refute their preliminary interpretation. I put the sentence aside and gave them a series of challenges.

First, I put the participants in groups of four and gave each group an envelope with the following sentence on a card inside (cut into four or five pieces like a simplified jigsaw puzzle): Maening rasidas not in words but in situetions. I asked participants to put the pieces together, to translate the sentence, and to write down what they had learned about the language from this puzzle (in this case, the fact that /a/ and /e/ were exchanged for each other).

When each group had completed that task, I gave them a new envelope with a new challenge, and the same instructions: Laérnars büild innar critarié før cørractnass (/a/ and /e/ reversed and diacritical marks placed over /u/, /o/, and /e/).

Again, when each group was finished I handed them another envelope, again with the same instructions: Gninréal sariuqar amit dné dairév acitcérp (previous encoding and words reversed). My only intervention, other than letting them know that the instructions were the same, was to approach a group who were stuck on this particular challenge. In that case, when they asked for help, I put my index finger on the end of the first word and, without saying anything, drew an imaginary line from right to left. The group for which I performed this act, quickly figured out that they needed to read the words from right to left instead of from left to right.

Next, I gave each group an envelope with the original sentence for them to then translate with ease.

Finally, I presented the following English sentence: "Mistakes are an integral part of learning," and asked them to translate it into the language they had just figured out. (Sakétsim aré na lérgatni trap fo gninréal.) While a volunteer attempted to do this on a flipchart, the others worked on this individually.

During the activity, participants showed a lively interest in what they were doing, discussing what they were figuring out, listening in on the conversations of other groups, and showing increasing energy around the challenges as they progressed.

After the activity, I first asked for their feedback on their experience of the activity. This generated the following insights from the participants:

- We learned, but you didn't really teach us. We were doing it by ourselves.
- You gave us as much time as we needed, without pressuring us.
- We could help each other and even listen in on other groups' discussion without being called 'cheaters.'
- I felt lost at first, but quickly began to feel at ease.
- Each challenge was more complex than the previous challenges, but challenges were easier to meet, because we had learned how the code worked.

I asked them if they noticed any of the principles at work in the activity. They could identify specific examples of each principle as they had experienced it in the activity:

- We did the learning. You merely set up the situation for us to learn in.
- The meaning came from our experience, not from the words per se.
- Each new challenge gave us a slightly different kind of practice that enabled us to meet the original challenge eventually.
- As we worked our way through the challenges, more pieces of the code fell into place, and the more complex problems became easier to solve.
- When we had to translate from English to the other language, we made mistakes but were able to help each other fix them.

I then asked participants if they could picture themselves creating this kind of activity for their own students. Many of them thought they could.

As I reflect back on my presentation of this activity, a few additional points emerge. For example, I presented the most difficult challenge first, out of respect for participants' intelligence. While most

(Birdsall Cont'd)

could not figure it out, some could. Also, when one group got stuck, I intervened by giving a hint, without actually telling them the answer. There was always an information gap, no matter how small, that the participants had to bridge, but not so big as to be insurmountable. So, the challenge for me as a teacher is always to present the subject matter as a set of challenges, and to be looking for the right level and quality of challenge to present. This requires that I be willing to make mistakes and to work on them, just as I invite my students to make mistakes and to work on them. With both teacher and students functioning in this way, a special classroom culture develops; one built on mutual respect and concentrated engagement, with the human learning process at its center. While this may seem like a very time-consuming way to teach, as the new classroom culture develops, it becomes extremely efficient and self-sustaining.

Now, after 20 years, this is where I am in my learning of The Subordination of Teaching to Learning. I am certain of one thing – that tomorrow, next week, and next year – I will have learned more. §

Dr. Gattegno traveled the world eight times giving workshops and demonstrating his approach. (Educational Solutions file photo.)

> "This is the only attitude a scientist can adopt: "temporary evidence leads to temporary views" and *this* is a permanent maxim."
>
> - Dr. Caleb Gattegno

The Common Sense of Teaching Reading and Writing, Second Edition (2010), page 4.

Life is a Grand Experiment

Robert P. Echter

I spent 16 years with Caleb Gattegno, attending every workshop that I could manage, and a friendship ensued. I read everything he wrote in English and used his approaches for teaching mathematics, reading and writing, and languages with a very wide range of students – from ages four to 70, from kindergarten to college, and in special education, including talented and gifted. I developed and co-conducted local workshops and research-and-development grants, and spoke to large gatherings. No one in my life influenced me more, professionally. For a short while I represented his concern, Educational Solutions, in the Northeastern United States. I have spent many years in the New Haven, Connecticut public schools as a teacher trying to get his work implemented, studied, and adopted, with varying degrees of success and failure. I have also brought his work more fully to the attention of some nationally known educational players.

If you were not around in 1972 when I first became aware of the work of Caleb Gattegno, you probably do not have a sense of how wide an impact he was having. His book *Towards A Visual Culture: Educating Through Television* (1969) was one of the most esteemed and widely known on that topic. It was in paperback in the Harvard Book Store along with his *What We Owe Children* (1970). He also had *Pop Ups* on television for a while, and Action for Children's Television president Peggy Charren referred to his work as outstanding.

When I met Dr. Gattegno, affectionately known to his colleagues and friends as "Dr. G," I was on a quest to find the basis of a science of education. I did not know if I would find it in my lifetime. I had looked into the work of Jean Piaget, J. Krishnamurti and others. Piaget came to speak to us when I was an undergraduate, and I once inquired into teaching at a school that was to be run by the Krishnamurti Foundation in California. But it was at Educational Solutions in January of 1972, after a two-day workshop on mathematics Dr. Gattegno was conducting, that I found it. I immersed myself in every opportunity I could manage to study, try, report on, and share with others this work. I totally gave myself to it every way I could.

Shortly after they moved to 80 Fifth Avenue, I was truly surprised when I phoned Educational Solutions and Dr. Gattegno answered! That spoke volumes to me about him. When I asked him for his advice on working with aphasic and other children, he said that he had not worked with similar children, but that I should, "Work with their powers, not their handicaps."

Back in New Haven, CT where I was teaching at Benhaven, a school for autistic and brain-damaged children, I conducted a formal study with results that dramatically released the powers of the students to whom I applied his approaches. The results in one-year's time warranted the school sending me to deliver an invited address to The International Convention of the Association for Children With Learning Disabilities. I thought the results were so dramatic that I put off an invitation from Dr. Gattegno to consider a position at Educational Solutions, because I wanted to finish that work. I thought the world would sit up and take notice, but it did not. My dear friend and mentor, Louis Lerea, who was a consulting psycholinguist at the school, said to me that the greatest difficulty I would have would be getting people to believe what I reported. He had witnessed it on a biweekly basis, and had initially predicted that the materials such as the *Pop Ups* would be way too complicated for the students, in contrast to Dr. Gattegno's mantra to, "give them a banquet!"

Following this, in 1974, Dr. Gattegno came to visit me at Benhaven with Rosemarie March who was working on his biography. I also arranged for him to come and conduct workshops in New Haven at The Teacher Center. In addition, I employed his approaches in my work at the Goddard College Experimental Program in Further Education, with some dramatic results. During this time, the U.S. Office of Education supported pilot and replication studies of this work, and High School in the Community included it as a component in The National Diffusion Network project.

just by the energy sensed with a mechanical probe attached to their tibia (so that their pulse would not interfere). These were remarkable demonstrations, and used in a study, as always.

He many times referred to Michael Faraday and the psychologist Jean Emile Marcault with high esteem.

> "After premising that he had never said this to anyone before, he shared with us in a seminar that his overall view was that, 'Life is a grand experiment.'"

Dr. Gattegno let me record several seminars, and I have those, including one of the seminars he gave in New Haven; audios of virtually all his seminars in New York during those years were recorded too. His recorded work is truly very important, and I look forward to the public availability of his many first-hand documents, audio recordings, film and video, unpublished writings, and instruments he developed or had a hand in developing, but not yet marketed. Seeing and hearing him is much more than reading him.

After premising that he had never said this to anyone before, he shared with us in a seminar that his overall view was that, "Life is a grand experiment." Also in a seminar, he was once asked, if his pedagogical science were to be taken seriously and deliberately, how long would it take for mankind to get back on its sense? He hesitated and said, "A thousand years," paused and said, "but I am an optimist." His other sayings would come up now and then such as, "Truth has short legs." When he was asked about different psychologies, he said simply that there are either as many as there are people or there is one. In a few seminars, he demonstrated technologies that he had worked on with regard to locating acupuncture points, and to demonstrate the psychosomatic effect, whereby we could easily and readily read on a meter the imagining of someone ice skating on their dominant foot, non-dominant foot, clockwise and then counterclockwise

When asked in a seminar what he thought of Maria Montessori he said that she was helpful when he was clumsy. For clarification, he did not use this as a pejorative. He said on another occasion that, "Clumsy is at the beginning of learning anything." In fact, he speaks of her with respect and esteem in books, and many Montessori schoolteachers indicated to me that they warmly received his work. About Ogden Lindsley, the psychologist, he said that, "We are in the same place, back to back." He told me, that when Joan Cooney was seeking funding from the Carnegie Foundation for the Children's Television Workshop (Sesame Street) they told her to see him first. He said that he could not abide with her insufficient esteem for the powers of children by approaching them with commercial formats.

The last time that I saw him was the second day of the last workshop he gave in the United States, February 1988 on the Silent Way. At that time he introduced to us a revision of The Subordination of Teaching to Learning that he had come to during his recent travel. It was now amended as, "The Activity is the Product." It did not do away with the former, only heightened it. (I have that on audio.) We were planning to travel together on what was to be his next European tour. Normally he would walk home alone, but this time when I offered, he let me walk him home. It was startling how weak he was.

(Echter Cont'd)

That night my beloved mother had a heart attack and I did not return for the last day of the workshop. My brother still had to talk me out of going with Caleb to Europe. In the last months, I would speak with him on the phone a couple times a week. I called him from the hospital where both my mother and father were on the brink of living or dying, and knowing that he was dying, his having said so on many occasions, I told him how much I was going to miss him. He responded with candor and his typical wisdom, "You will put the energy someplace else."

That he was important to me is obvious. He might also have been one of the greatest scientists of his generation. He told of when he was being considered for the Princeton Institute of Advanced Study and he was denied in the final stage. He said that if he were studying ancient history instead of the dynamics of the mind it would have gone through. When I told this to my long and dear friend Seymour Sarason of Yale, he said that he was probably right. Seymour also said, before his own death, that Caleb had achieved what no other had in the field of education.

There are many more stories to tell and experiments to describe that had revolutionary results. My memories of this extraordinary man remain vivid.

Dr. Caleb Gattegno at a Silent Way workshop on August 30, 1987. (Photograph courtesy of Robert P. Echter.)

How Could I Prevent Turning Into A Teaching Zombie?

Dr. Patricia Benstein

Not many people start an interesting initial encounter in Hungarian, and then continue to take this relationship to another level in Chinese, and end up writing a Ph.D. about it. This is, however, the summary of my connection to Caleb Gattegno.

contrast to our teacher training at university, which emphasized communicative language learning with the teacher playing the role of entertainer, and whole sentences being practised by the students in order to help in the process of communication with native speakers. After these two significant experiences, I

> "I was fascinated by the quiet concentration in the room, and the tangible focus by even those who had no interest whatsoever in this unusual language."

While studying at Melbourne University to become a teacher, my classes were introduced to various teaching methodologies. As part of it, Andrew Weiler gave us a lesson in Hungarian using the Silent Way. I was fascinated by the quiet concentration in the room, and the tangible focus by even those who had no interest whatsoever in this unusual language. Ever since then I was hooked, not in the slightest suspecting where this fascination might lead.

It was a fortunate turn of events that resulted in me being able to learn Chinese the Silent Way. From the first lesson onwards, I had the same experience as with Hungarian, where there was such an exquisite, almost monastic calm concentration in our classroom while learning was taking place. It seemed such a stark

read more about Gattegno and the Silent Way but did not yet use it systematically in my own teaching at secondary schools or at university.

As often in my life, a turn of events happened one sunny morning in Perth while I was lecturing at the University of Western Australia. I taught these bright bushy-tailed students something about linguistics that I knew inside out, and caught myself looking out the window, dreaming about going to the beach instead of being in that room. All of a sudden, I realized that I was running on automatic, babbling on about my specialist field, pretending to be teaching while being non-present. I was shocked into realization that I had become a human robot.

That day became one of those significant times when

(Benstein Cont'd)

life gets challenged and turned on its head. I had become what I vowed I never wanted to be: a teacher who was absent-minded in class. I began asking myself how I could prevent turning into a teaching zombie, as I felt it was against my principles to ask my students to pay attention when I myself was not fully there. Was being there, even after years of doing the same thing over and over again, possible? When something has become second nature, when we know the material inside out, can we still be present? Being an idealist, I thought there must be a way to remain present and I was determined to find it.

I asked myself in the days after that shocking realization, when had I ever felt really 'there' – so fully concentrated that I would have wanted to stay in that place even if a bomb had been dropped next to me? And I remembered: the Hungarian and Chinese lessons that were taught in the Silent Way. I concluded that if I had felt so present as a student, the teachers must have felt present as well. And I wanted to find out more about the Subordination of Teaching to Learning.

A journey started with many twists and turns, but the end result was that I was offered a scholarship that only three students per year were offered – to study for a Ph.D. and to be financially supported for a minimum of three years. I had the choice to stay in Perth and study at UWA, or to move to Sydney to take up this challenge at the University of Sydney. Always open to new adventures, I decided for Sydney and moved yet again across the continent. My supervisor was the head of the Education Department and later on Vice President of Sydney University, Professor Ken Eltis. He had not heard of the Silent Way, but was interested, and I cannot thank him enough for letting me wander around in the maze of this unfamiliar territory while never losing trust in my capacity. I had to do four different types of literature reviews, because the Silent Way does not fit neatly into any one research category. I worked for a full three-and-a-half years on understanding Gattegno, on conducting a case study in Besançon with the support of master Silent Way teachers and their students, and on coming to

> "Being present to ourselves, to the people we are with, and the situations we are in, and to ever-changing energies inside and outside of us, can never become automatic."

a conclusion that has given me a tool that should ensure that my awakening experience and resulting question are no longer an issue.

In the context of this memoir, I would rather mention the effect his work has had on me as a person and as a professional lecturer. I am aware that mastery of any topic involves an integration of the skills that have become automated. We could not function very well in this world if we still had to remind ourselves of all the sequential steps that are involved in driving a car, for instance. There is a blessing in automated, integrated skills. However, being present to ourselves, to the people we are with, and the situations we are in, and to ever-changing energies inside and outside of us, can never become automatic. It is an ongoing field of rich exploration, and while I might be teaching the same thing as I have done before, the people, the place, and the energies in the room are never replicated. Pulling these elements into my awareness, and bringing such presence to the task at hand, so that I can enter together with my students the 'zone' or the sensation of 'flow' as Csíkszentmihályi put it, is what makes learning not only possible but also enjoyable.

I thank Caleb Gattegno and all the proponents of his Science of Education for first having exposed me to his insights, and then having nurtured and helped me along the way to implementing his Science of Education in my own life. I express my gratitude by passing on what has been given to me to my students in turn, which I assume, is what Gattegno would have wished for.

§

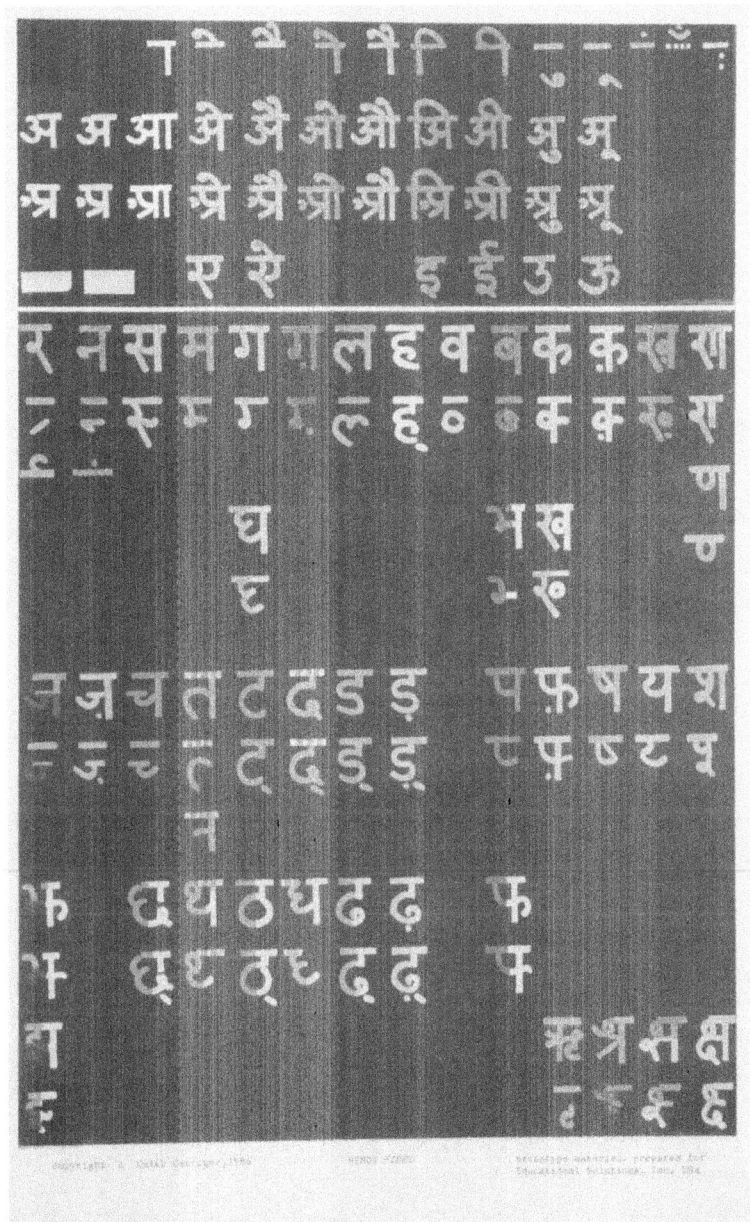

Prototype Hindi Fidel, hand-painted on cardboard, 1984.
©Educational Solutions Worldwide Inc.

Living, Learning, Teaching
En vivant, en apprenant, en enseignant

Brendan Marcus

LIVING

It's raining. I'm walking down the street and it's raining. I can tell it's raining because a short while ago I felt the first drops of rain on my cheek, on my nose. I then heard the sound of the water rattling on the ground, the cars, and some windows, getting louder; I now see the drops of rain. It's actually raining. In a few minutes I know my hood will be drenched and there will follow a wet sensation on my hair and on the nape of my neck. I'm aware that it's raining. But this very rich awareness happened because of that first awareness which were the drops on my face, followed by that second awareness, the sound of rain, confirmed by the blurring of the shapes on the street, preparing me for the growing weight of my hood and the wet sensation of my hair on my head.

LEARNING

"This just doesn't make any sense to me," says the nine-year-old little girl to whom I give after-school homework guidance twice a week. She's smart, she's one of the top pupils of the class, and she's serious, as in she expects something out of these evenings we spend together. "We did this in class today, and I don't know the answer to this exercise. The result from the calculator just doesn't make any sense to me." It is nine-year-old mathematics I say to myself, it shouldn't be a big deal, even though like many language teachers, and probably like many people in other professions too, I swore to myself after graduating high-school never have anything to do with mathematics in my adult life. "See, when I enter 0.5 divided by 2, I get 0.25! How is it possible that when I entered two digits (0.5) I get an extra one when I divided it by two? I should get the same number of digits or less!"

"Good question," I reply, "now summarize what you did in class today so I can see what the exercise is aiming at."

Buying time so that I can figure this out is what I am aiming at. Now, I'm sure the answer is right. But I can't figure out why I can not make sense of it for this little girl. I know the answer is right because that is what I learnt at school, or rather that is what I was told at school and, thank heavens, in this situation, remember. Why does half of 0.5 equal 0.25? What is it I don't see? Yet, if I know it but don't understand it, do I really know it? Did I really learn it?

I didn't want either to tell her that the answer was right and leave it at that, and turn her into an ignoramus like myself. Lately I had been working for a language center that used the Gattegno approach to language teaching, the oddly named Silent Way. At first, I didn't think much of it, but after observing an English workshop I had to admit it seemed like more fun than the textbook classes I had been doing since getting my degree in language teaching.

I started teaching the Silent Way, reading the literature, and therefore getting familiar in distinguishing know-hows from pieces of knowledge; the latter the basis of traditional education, the former what actually constitutes disciplines such as languages, reading and writing, and mathematics.

For Gattegno, these know-hows built themselves out of awarenesses which are granted to every human being. In fact, awarenesses are what constitute most of our lives, as when walking down the street we learn that it's raining.

The other novelty in using the Silent Way was that awarenesses about languages and language teaching were discovered through classroom work, by teaching, live in front of the students. I began unraveling one awareness after the other, as I was telling the students to say this rather than that, while asking myself why ever do we say this rather

and it was only by redoing the math in reverse that we uncovered what was hidden to us (0.25 x 2 = 0.50, and not 0.5, you vicious calculator!) and that we had both been led astray by the notation; a small awareness, yet essential in order to grasp the idea of division.

I had been lucky to come around so fast that time, but that day I found out that by working with awarenesses I had at hand a most powerful tool; a tool introduced to me by Gattegno, and grasped

> "My job is to trigger in each of them the necessary awarenesses to turn them into better mathematicians."

than that. The languages I was teaching showed new hidden meanings and a logic, building a system that could be easily learnt by anyone. A system that required many trials, feedbacks and practicing and not textbooks, the way every two-year-old learning his mother tongue figures it out. I learnt that every awareness in languages was derived from another awareness; and I had figured many of them out by myself. Could I do the same for mathematics?

I ask myself: "What is the awareness that eludes me so that I can be comfortable with this simple equality?" "Okay," I tell my nine-year-old accomplice, "let's break it down! Put it on paper without the calculator and let's see what we find."

TEACHING

We're a few years after this little panic-ridden episode and I am now facing a classroom of students ready to begin their mathematics lesson. I've changed jobs, and now besides languages I can teach reading and writing, computers, and yes, math. I've come a long way since asking that little girl what was 0.5 (the half of one, she replied) and what was 0.25 (the half of 0.5, according to the calculator she added smartly),

patiently through work with the Silent Way. A tool to discover truths for myself, and by myself, inciting me to question ordinary things, or what is held as obvious, and become more aware of the workings behind them. I felt I could learn anything. I started reading Gattegno's books about mathematics, and giving myself little challenges, gradually dismissing my past fears of mathematics.

Now facing this classroom anxious about new mathematical truths, I no more ask myself what it is I want to teach or share with them. It is clear to me now that my job is to trigger in each of them the necessary awarenesses to turn them into better mathematicians. I certainly won't achieve that by drills or rote learning. And in today's class, a young lady can hardly count correctly to 70, 80, 90 never mind 100. Well, I ask myself, what are the necessary awarenesses to master these numbers, and what are the challenges I can give her to acquire this mastery swiftly and humanely?

The awareness that I'm to work with awarenesses is what gives me the confidence to become a teacher for any willing person. I know now that Gattegno's gift will help us find out what work the day's topic requires so that the students can actually learn, and I become a better teacher.

En vivant, en apprenant, en enseignant

EN VIVANT

Il pleut. Je descends la rue et il pleut. Je peux dire qu'il pleut parce qu'il y a quelques instants, j'ai senti les premières gouttes de pluie sur ma joue, sur mon nez. J'ai ensuite entendu le cliquetis de l'eau sur le sol, les voitures, et sur une fenêtre, devenir plus intense; je vois les gouttes de pluie. Il pleut effectivement. Dans quelques minutes, je sais que ma capuche sera trempée et que suivra une sensation de mouillé sur mes cheveux et sur ma nuque. Je suis conscient qu'il pleut. Mais cette très riche prise de conscience s'est produite à cause de cette première prise de conscience qu'ont été les gouttes sur mon visage, suivie par une autre, celle du bruit de la pluie, confirmée par les formes troubles dans la rue, me préparant au poids croissant de ma capuche et à la sensation d'humidité de mes cheveux sur ma tête.

EN APPRENANT

"Ça n'a pas de sens pour moi", me dit la fillette de neuf ans, à qui je donne de l'aide aux devoirs après l'école deux fois par semaine. Elle est intelligente, elle est l'une des meilleurs élèves de sa classe, et elle est sérieuse, dans le sens où elle attend quelque chose de ces soirées que nous passons ensemble. "Nous l'avons fait en classe aujourd'hui, et je ne sais pas quoi répondre à cet exercice. Le résultat de la calculatrice n'a tout simplement pas de sens pour moi." Je me dis que ce sont des mathématiques pour des gamins de neuf ans et que ça ne devrait pas poser de gros problèmes, même si, comme de nombreux professeurs de langues, et probablement comme beaucoup de gens dans d'autres professions, je me suis juré après l'obtention de mon bac de ne jamais rien à voir avec les mathématiques dans ma vie d'adulte. "Vous voyez, quand je rentre 0,5 divisé par 2, j'obtiens 0,25! Comment est-il possible que lorsque j'entre deux chiffres (0,5) j'en obtiens un de plus alors que je l'ai divisé par deux, je devrais obtenir le même nombre de chiffres ou moins!" " Bonne question, je lui réponds, maintenant fais-moi un récapitulatif de ce que vous avez fait en classe aujourd'hui pour que je puisse voir l'objectif de cet exercice." Gagner du temps afin que je puisse comprendre ce que ça signifie est mon objectif. Maintenant, je suis sûr que la réponse est juste. Mais je ne sais pas pourquoi. Je sais que la réponse est juste parce que c'est ce que j'ai appris à l'école, ou plutôt "c'est ce qu'on m'a dit à l'école» et, Dieu merci, pour la situation dans laquelle je me trouve, ce dont je me souviens. Pourquoi la moitié de 0,5 est équivalente à 0,25 ? Qu'est-ce que je ne vois pas? Pourtant, si je connais la réponse mais sans comprendre pourquoi, la sais-je vraiment ? l'ai-je vraiment appris?

Je ne voulais pas lui dire que la réponse était juste et en rester là, et la transformer en un ignorant comme moi. Récemment, j'avais commencé à travailler pour un centre de langues qui a recours à l'approche Gattegno pour l'enseignement des langues, le curieusement nommé "Silent Way". Au début, je n'en pensais pas grand-chose, mais après avoir observé un stage d'anglais, j'ai dû admettre que c'était plus amusant que les cours avec manuels que j'avais donnés depuis l'obtention de mon diplôme d'enseignant de langues.

J'ai commencé à enseigner à le Silent Way, à lire les ouvrages qui y sont consacrés, et donc à me familiariser à la distinction entre les savoir-faire (qui constituent véritablement les matières comme les langues, la lecture et l'écriture, et les mathématiques) et les connaissances (la base de l'enseignement traditionnel). Ces savoir-faire se sont construits sur des prises de conscience accessibles à chaque être humain. En fait, ces prises de conscience sont ce qui constitue la plupart de nos vies, comme lorsque l'on marche dans la rue, on apprend qu'il pleut. L'autre nouveauté dans l'utilisation du Silent Way a été que les prises de conscience sur les langues et l'enseignement des langues ont été découvertes par le travail en classe, en enseignant, en direct devant les étudiants. Se dévoilant les unes après les autres tandis que je disais aux élèves de dire ceci plutôt que cela, tout en me demandant pourquoi on dit ceci plutôt que cela. Les langues que j'enseignais m'apparaissaient alors riches de nouvelles significations cachées et d'une logique,

(Marcus Cont)

présentant un système qui pourrait être facilement appris par n'importe qui. Un système qui a nécessité de nombreux essais, des feedbacks et de la pratique, comme tous les enfants de deux ans sur le chemin de la maîtrise de leur langue maternelle le savent bien, et non pas des manuels scolaires. J'ai appris que chaque prise de conscience dans les langues dérivait d'une autre prise de conscience, et que j'en avais trouvé beaucoup d'entre elles par moi-même. Pourrais-je faire de même pour les mathématiques?

Je me demandais quelle prise de conscience m'échappait pour que je puisse être à l'aise avec cette simple égalité. "Très bien, dis-je à ma complice de neuf ans, on va tout reprendre depuis le début ! Mettons-le sur papier sans la calculatrice et voyons ce que nous trouvons."

EN ENSEIGNANT

Nous sommes quelques années après cet épisode teinté de panique et je suis maintenant face à une classe d'étudiants prêts à commencer leur leçon de mathématiques. J'ai changé d'emploi, et maintenant en plus de l'enseignement des langues je peux dispenser des cours de lecture et d'écriture, d'informatique, et aussi, de maths. J'ai parcouru un long chemin depuis que j'ai demandé à cette petite fille ce qu'était 0,5 (la moitié de un, répondit-elle) et ce qu'était 0,25 (la moitié de 0,5 selon la calculatrice, a-t-elle ajouté malicieusement), et c'est seulement en refaisant les mathématiques à l'envers que nous avons découvert ce qui nous était caché (0,25 x 2 = 0,50, et non 0,5, saleté de calculatrice !) et que nous avions tous deux été égarés par la notation; une prise de conscience, petite mais essentielle pour saisir un principe de la division.

J'avais eu de la chance de m'en sortir aussi vite cette fois-là, mais je crois que ce jour-là j'avais découvert qu'en travaillant avec les prises de conscience j'avais sous la main un outil très puissant ; un outil qui m'avait été offert par Gattegno, et saisi patiemment au travers de mon travail avec le Silent Way. Un outil pour découvrir des vérités pour moi-même, et par moi-même, qui m'incitait à remettre en question des choses ordinaires, ou ce qui est considéré comme une évidence, et à devenir plus conscient des rouages qui s'y dissimulaient. Je sentais que je pouvais apprendre n'importe quoi. J'ai commencé à lire des livres Gattegno sur les mathématiques, et à me donner des petits défis, repoussant progressivement mes peurs mathématiques.

Face à cette classe impatiente de découvrir de nouvelles vérités mathématiques, je ne me demande plus ce que je veux enseigner ou partager avec eux. Il est clair pour moi maintenant que mon travail est de déclencher en chacun d'eux les prises de conscience nécessaires pour les transformer en meilleurs mathématiciens. Je ne vais certainement pas y parvenir en exercices répétitifs ou avec du par cœur. Et aujourd'hui est présente une jeune femme qui ne peut guère compter correctement autour de 70, 80, 90, sans parler de 100. Et bien, je me demande quelles sont les prises de conscience nécessaires à la maîtrise de ces nombres, et quels sont les défis que je peux lui donner afin d'acquérir cette maîtrise rapidement et humainement?

La prise de conscience qu'il faut travailler avec les prises de conscience est ce qui me donne la confiance nécessaire pour devenir enseignant à toute personne volontaire. Je sais maintenant que le don de Gattegno nous aidera à trouver quel travail faire pour que les élèves puissent réellement apprendre et que moi, je devienne un meilleur enseignant.

> Mon travail est de déclencher en chacun d'eux les prises de conscience nécessaires pour les transformer en meilleurs mathématiciens.

Used in the Silent Way approach for teaching foreign languages, this wall picture engages the students' powers of imagination and invites them to express their thoughts. What is important about these pictures is what is left out; the image is deliberately minimalist in order to encourage invention.

The Audacious Learner and Teacher in Me

Michiko Watabe

I learned the importance of observing my own learning and teaching from the Silent Way. Observing one has always led me to find something true about both. Here, as one example, I would like to share my experience of learning a word, and how I reflected that in my teaching.

I'm currently teaching eight Japanese adults using a textbook. As their English level is pretty high, I sometimes encounter words in the text that I don't know. Whenever this happens I feel embarrassed by the fact that I don't know our target words, and try very hard to learn them before introducing them to the class. A week ago, this happened again.

The word was "audacious." As soon as I met this unknown, I started exploring the word in regard to its pronunciation. The two syllables, "au-da," were unfamiliar sounds to me. I thought this uniqueness might help me to hang onto them. I pronounced the syllables several times aloud.

The definition of the word in a dictionary was, "Someone shows great courage or confidence in a way that is impressive or slightly shocking." I wondered if it had a negative connotation. The definition seemed vague to me. Another dictionary said "rude and insolent," which was of great help. I decided to keep that in mind and continue to search.

I moved on to its role in language. It's an adjective as the suffix "-ious" shows. Its word family should be "audaciously" and "audaciousness." I wondered about other forms. Does it have a verb form? I hypothesized that a verb form "auda" might exist, but it sounded strange. After that I checked the dictionary, and I found that there was just one more noun form, "audacity," and no verb forms.

Then, I proceeded to read the example uses: "the risks involved in such an audacious operation," and "audacious explorers." Both examples carried the image of taking risks. After checking more examples, I put the information down on one of my word cards I usually carry around with me. I use them not to mechanically memorize words, but to build a sense of each word through example sentences.

> One of the things I learned was that to retain a target, the students' production is far more important than the teacher's explanation.

(Watabe Cont'd)

Next, I looked for an example situation in which I could make a sentence. Just reading the examples does not help me acquire the target; I must produce sentences to learn the word. I remembered some news, and made a sentence, "When a woman fell from a platform just before a train came, a young man jumped to the rails and saved her. His audacious behavior was reported in newspapers and on TV." I hoped I used the word correctly. (I wished I could get someone's feedback on it.) I started thinking, "This 'audacious' sounds positive and impressive, but how about expressing the shades of slightly shocking, rude and insolent?" My study time was running out. I quickly thought of its synonyms; bold and courageous, and antonym; coward. Later, while fixing dinner, I came back to it to think again.

still needed to understand the meaning in depth and practice more. I decided to make some sentences and ask one of my colleagues for feedback on them. The sentences were: "Look at the audacious hair style that woman has!" "I don't like his audacious attitude," in a rude and a bit threatening way, and, "She is an audacious non-fiction writer. To write her book about the Japanese mafia, she worked at a bar run by the group to collect information." My colleague's feedback was that the first and second examples were okay. The third one was acceptable if the writer had gone through some dangers. Making sentences and getting her feedback really helped me deepen my understanding. I didn't ask her to explain the word; I only wanted to know if my sentences worked or not. If they didn't work, I was ready to struggle more. I

> "By making them experience how to learn effectively in everyday lessons, I expect them to become aware of how to learn."

Early the next morning, I tried to recall the word, but it didn't come back to me. Why? In my mind, only letters "a" and "cious" were floating along with the meanings; taking a risk, and bold. Thinking that I needed to make more associations with the pronunciation of the word, I left home and took a bus to work. On the bus, I looked at the word card. The sounds "au" and "da" were still very unfamiliar to me. "Au" is in "automatic" and "audio," and "da" has the "ei" sound as in "date" and "stage." After work, on my way home, I pronounced the word in my mind and checked the card. Finally, three days after I had encountered the word, the pronunciation started to come back without effort. Nothing is easy to learn!

The pronunciation problem was cleared up, but I

thought I could use this experience in my class.

My learning "audacious" continued and I was at the practice stage where I was building up the criteria of the word. I have come to be able to tell where I am in my learning process. With help from the Silent Way training workshops, and reading Dr. Gattegno's books, I have been trying to be an independent learner, not only related to language learning but in any kind of learning. Through observing my learning and that of various learners, I realized that independent learners can force their awareness by themselves in order to learn a target. They are aware of how learning takes place, and how to use themselves to learn. They can intentionally make themselves connect to their target until they master it.

I would like my students to become independent learners, hopefully in my class. By making them experience how to learn effectively in everyday lessons, I expect them to become aware of how to learn. How can I force them to become aware of it? My experiences as a learner back me up. As I cannot go into my students' minds and brains to see what is going on, I learn the way from observing myself as a leaner. One of the things I learned was that to retain a target, students' production is far more important than teachers' explanation.

Five days after I met the word 'audacious,' my class learned the word. No one knew the word. We started with pronunciation. I didn't model it; instead, I asked one of the students who had pronounced it correctly to model it. The other students quickly picked it up. We checked the meaning and example sentences in the textbook. Some were nodding, and some showed blank looks. One of them said, "Are brave and courageous similar to this word?" Some agreed. We looked at more examples from internet concordances. "He has an audacious plan to win the election." "He has risky tactics that ranged from audacious to outrageous."

Next, we looked at a photo of a snowboarder who was jumping high in the air. Using photos and images works well for me and many other learners for retaining vocabulary. I was hoping it would work here. One student made a sentence: "He is so audacious to snowboard like that. I like snowboarding, but I cannot do that." We worked on some other pictures including a picture of a woman with an audacious hair style. They explored what this word meant and how it was used in sentences.

After class, I looked back over their learning. Based on their production and feedback, I sensed that they had made a good start. However, I would never take it for granted that my students learned it as soon as the word was introduced. It took me two days to make its pronunciation settle in me. My class would continue practicing the word during the following lessons, but even after that, we would recycle it while studying other targets until the word flowed from them automatically.

During the next class, I showed them the photo of the woman with the audacious hair style again. I waited for six seconds expecting someone to come up with the word and make a sentence, but no one said anything. I decided to give the word since it was not a memory game. When I wrote the letter "a," one of the students said;

S1: "au…au…"

S2: "auda…"

S3,4,5: "audacious"

S1: "Ah, audacious!"

It was a nice example of group dynamics, but the students' feedback showed me that they needed more exposure to "audacious," which I already knew based on my own experience.

We started working on its word family, synonyms and antonyms. With my students' level, they should be able to guess at adverb and noun forms like I did myself. I waited for their responses, and they did well except for identifying "audacity." As for its synonyms and antonyms, they came up with "brave" and "timid," but not the "shameless, insolent, disrespectful" type of synonyms. They needed to work on that area more.

I recalled it was the same difficulty I had. The shade of meaning "shameless, insolent…" had slipped from my mind. What did I do to make them connect with me? I made sentences and asked my colleague if the sentences worked or not. Production and feedback was the key. Rather than giving explanation, I would provide more situations where they could make many sentences. My role is to give them feedback on whether their sentences work or not, like my colleague did to me. (I have to be ready for giving feedback!) We have class next week. I'll see how much my students have retained.

My learning experiences and teaching are like two sides of a coin. They help each other, and create synergy. If I hadn't met the Silent Way, I never would have known the depth to which they are related. I appreciate all the work Dr. Gattegno did, and the people who have helped me learn. Working on teaching and learning is now my life-long project.

From the Congo to the Bronx

Daniel Tamulonis

In the heart of Africa, then named Zaïre in 1971, there was talk of rods of different colors used to teach languages. I was a member of the U. S. Peace Corps, assigned to teach English as a Second Language to Zaïrian high school students. These young men and a few women had lived through Congo's upheaval in the 1960s and were now in their late teens and early 20s as they finished high school. I was just out of undergraduate school, their peer in age but certainly not in life experience, wondering how I could possibly use colored rods to teach English. As it turned out, due to an impossibly packed 12-week schedule, my training in the Silent Way of teaching was indefinitely postponed.

Fast-forward to 1987, New York City. John Fanselow introduces Kumiko Fujimura, his wife, to a tightly packed room of observers at Teachers College, Columbia University. She will be teaching me, and about 75 other people, Japanese the Silent Way during a weekend seminar. In the "response paper" I wrote to this experience, I made mention of the fact that there were so many people attending this workshop that many of us climbed the room's built-in cabinets to sit upon so we could see Kumiko in front of the striking, multi-colored charts of Hiragana Japanese characters. I had no idea what was ahead of me and wondered where the colored rods were, which was all I remembered of this Silent Way.

I had already heard the now-familiar mutterings of "How can someone teach a language silently?" However, since my classes with (and already lifelong admiration for!) Dr. Fanselow had begun, I felt anything he or his wife did could be nothing short of miraculous. Still, I was unprepared for the earth shifting that occurred beneath my soul as Kumiko silently and utterly unsmilingly introduced the sounds of Japanese. Before the morning session ended, I had climbed down off the cabinets and made my way to the front so that I could get as close as possible to what was happening. I laughed, I wept, I was moved and felt emotions I knew not from where as the hours passed and I learned to speak and understand Japanese. When others did not share my feelings, I retreated back into what I had learned and wondered all the more at what was happening to me.

I lived through the workshop in a trance, dumbly expressed my gratitude to Fujimura-san and went home to write my response. Although I could not quite figure how my emotions had gotten so involved, I knew that if I were going to teach, it would have to be the sort of teaching that would engage my students to the heightened degree that I had found myself while I was working with Kumiko. I wanted, in that moment, to return to Zaïre and re-do, to un-do, all the ego-centered and self-aggrandizing that I had inflicted on those extraordinary young Zaïrians in the name of teaching. I was fortunate to befriend both John Fanselow and Kumiko Fujimura and they gently tempered some of my hyperbolic responses to what I was experiencing. At the same time, they pushed me to study and continue investigating what had had such an effect on me.

Within the year, the great man had died and Shakti Gattegno, whom I had begun to work with, was telephoning me asking if I knew of someone at the *New York Times* who could help with the obituary. As it turned out, the then publicist at Teachers College, Roy Campbell, was a colleague and a concerned listener. He did know "someone" at the *Times*, and he was successful in securing Glenn Fowler's obituary of Dr. Gattegno, complete with photograph, into the paper, which was no small accomplishment.

> "Although I could not quite figure how my emotions had gotten so involved, I knew that if I were going to teach, it would have to be the sort of teaching that would engage my students to the heightened degree that I had found myself..."

Eventually, I found myself at 95 University Place, on an errand to purchase English language Silent Way materials for an outreach ESOL program I was then coordinating. The elevator opened directly into the offices of Educational Solutions. While picking up the materials, I was introduced to Dr. Gattegno. I was intimidated, but he seemed to take no notice and instead began at once to engage me in an intense conversation concerning the imminent and necessary consolidation of the countries of Europe into a unified whole. I felt I was in over my head with this discussion and found myself retreating. There was no escape; Dr. Gattegno declaimed his thesis full of energy, and directed it at me as though I were the person to make it a reality. After he had finished, and as my awestruck silence filled the office, he added in a dramatic afterthought that the various monies of Europe would be unified as well. This meeting with Dr. Gattegno was much on my mind when the European Union took its current name in 1993, and when the money followed in 1999.

My first teaching job where I began to use the Silent Way came a few years later, at the Riverside Language Program, housed in the church of the same name in upper Manhattan. The directors of the Program actively supported their cadre of teachers, allowing each teacher to implement her or his choice of teaching methodologies. I had dedicated, extraordinary colleagues experienced in the Silent Way – it was the best place to find my way with the approach and the materials.

I found a measure of success that first year but the real challenge came my second year, when the administration challenged me to take on one of the advanced classes, filled with mostly refugees from the former Soviet Union. These learners had a reputation for eating the instructors alive when they didn't get what they thought they needed. The focus would be on refining pronunciation and increasing comprehension and fluency. All my training had been working with beginning learners of English. The Subordination of Teaching to Learning would

(Tamulonis Cont'd)

truly have to guide me. Although the learners resisted, they still worked on the restricted exercises I gave them at first: making simple sentences based on objects they could see and gradually expanding these sentences into complicated strings of adjectives, adverbs and nouns, allowing the learners to play with the language even as they were forced to make sense

Paula Hajar, Arthur Powell, Ted Swartz, and the youngsters of the school to develop innumerable ideas for these sessions. This year, as I teach Kindergarten for the first time, I have been reading and re-reading Gattegno's *Now Johnny Can Do Arithmetic*. Here, Dr. Gattegno is more generous and dedicates an astounding eight pages to free play which here goes

> "We had feedback sessions regularly, many of which were filled with long silences, sighs and stares. Ultimately, these sessions became a part of the day we all anticipated."

of what they said. They made transcripts of short radio broadcasts and presented them. We played matching games with vocabulary, using science articles from newspapers and magazines. We had feedback sessions regularly, many of which were filled with long silences, sighs and stares. Ultimately, these sessions became a part of the day we all anticipated.

Another fast forward, this time to the Bronx, at the Bronx Charter School for Better Learning, an elementary (Kindergarten – Grade 5) school founded by a group of learning teachers committed to the approach. As one of the classroom teachers, I now had the opportunity to discover Gattegno Mathematics, as I had previously only concentrated on how to subordinate teaching to learning for second-language learners. While working with the first grade classes over the past several years, I have had the amazing opportunity to feel the earth move beneath my soul all over again. As the children investigate the rods and find their own way to play and manipulate them, their insights and challenges continue to amaze me.

In *Gattegno Mathematics Textbook 1*, the author specifies that "free play" with the rods comes first. In typical fashion, he indicates this in Part I of the book with the heading "Sessions of Free Play." This title page comprises the text for the entire chapter. The instructor, with his learners, of course, must supply the rest! I have had the good fortune to work with

under the heading, "Getting to Know the Material." With my Kindergarteners, I am constantly looking for ways for them to truly "get to know the material" so that it becomes part of their being. This is where again the earth moves for me while the five-year-olds take this spiritual seismic activity in stride.

At the same time, an even greater – yet equally exciting! – challenge than the study of mathematics has been investigating other school subjects: social studies, science, and the arts and finding how to subordinate the teaching of these subjects to the learning of them. Gattegno offers a few specifics in these areas, contained on a couple of pages in *What We Owe Children*, which are tantalizing starting points. One could take the idea of "getting to know the material" and use it as one begins to think about how best to implement the approach in these areas.

The school is well into its eighth year; the staff has grown and we have started several new initiatives, including an internship program. My journey from the Congo to the Bronx continues, filled with constant discoveries and new challenges. The U.S. Peace Corps once made much of one of their slogans: "This is the hardest job you will ever love." Certainly my years in the Congo validated the simple, realistic truth in that statement. The challenge of the work at the school is equally straightforward, difficult in the extreme, and at once easy to love.

§

Games of free play are often the starting point in Gattegno's mathematical pedagogy. Shown above, a student plays with the rods. (Educational Solutions file photo)

Leading Ways

Ghislaine Graf

Even though I met Dr. Caleb Gattegno and his unique contribution to teaching more than 40 years ago, I never feel like a veteran. The main reason comes from the fact that I had been looking for a real place to examine basics in learning, concerning children as much as adults, from my very early age.

When, in a small coffee shop in Geneva where he had invited me, Dr. Gattegno told me that my questions about the links between education and science corresponded with some of his own, I felt seriously recognized in my will to search. He then asked me to work with him at Educational Solutions in New York, especially on developing and expanding Words in Color in other languages than those already existing. I accepted and spent two years in New York. That was a period of personal investment for me. Everything I have done since then, back in Switzerland, teaching French and English according to the Silent Way – to schoolchildren, adults, executives, immigrants, and refugees, in the most varied settings and situations – as well as my work as a teacher trainer, has been built on that foundation.

From my first encounter with him, I was always struck by his attitude, choice, and technique to never answer questions by answers. "Q's and A's" were not his cup of tea. He loved opening Russian nesting dolls by throwing another question to your question, in order to make you think, analyze and discover the heart of the matter (if possible), by yourself. This turn of mind and then this habit of examining questions, and to remain with questions as truer companions, is certainly one of his best legacies to me, and most likely to more people than I can imagine. I learned to stop maintaining the illusion that one can solve a problem by erasing it.

A question does not have to be smart to be studied. It is a wonderful way to be kept both humble and bold. You may reject the formulation of the question anytime, if it is not relevant, without any damage, or you can start to perceive what is hiding underneath. The great by-product of questioning what seems invisible to others made Dr. G's search to understand the relationships between human powers and awareness a striking and continuous contribution to education.

The benefit of questioning leads to many hidden gifts, and one of them not to be neglected is the bag of mistakes we go on producing. As a child learning French spelling, I was taught not to make "faults," as misspellings were named – as if we were potentially criminals! Dr. G pointed out so well the distinctions between being wrong, and making mistakes, that to this day I am committed to deleting the word "fault" in all classrooms and in all learning places.

I appreciate the English word "mis-take" for its call to just take something else. "Un rien," a little nothing, as Dr. G baptized the minimum amount of energy to spend in order to modify a whole situation. "Un rien change tout, n'est-ce pas?" Then this "little nothing," a mistake, is the bridge that our mind can use to go from "not that" to "try differently."

How can one possibly assess the value of the powerful present Dr. Gattegno has offered educators of all kinds, by not repeating the most common trivial and ideological belief that mistakes are the result of our lack of attention? I learned from him that mistakes are to be welcomed as our best guides to knowledge.

Hundreds of students of mine have benefited from that knowledge and practice, in studying a language as much as in accepting to stop judging themselves, or others by the same token. It is constantly beneficial to me as well. It helps in considering gaps between mistakes and failures, and casting on the latter quite a different light and understanding. It reinforces one's courage and hope far more than one could ever think. It also gives justice to the sense of humor as being a wonderful help in renewing one's energy and ability to see another aspect of things. My only regret is that we did not collect the many jokes, plays on words, wonderful stories and sense of humor of Dr. G, to offer them as an important part of his teaching and maybe as a way of life for us too.

To me, it became a necessity to create specific seminars to show and share the amplitude of Dr. G's conceptual thinking, especially in continuing his work on what languages are about, and the human gift of language.

"Words, Words, Words!" From Shakespeare to Gattegno, what does language tell us, if not that words can be listened to, called to cast light on our search, and made into instruments of awareness? One of the best ways to do so is to use the process of defining words into a constant closer approach

> " I learned from him that mistakes are to be welcomed as our best guides to knowledge. "

Dr. G used to tease me a lot about my enthusiasm towards his materials and his educational approach, and my efforts to make them known and shared by many. He said that people needed decades to really understand what the Science of Education is all about. So what!

Since I have only this one existence, I have dedicated my time to creating space for other people to discover a real nourishment in the world of teaching and learning. If I still so appreciate how his role as a thinker and leader (though never a Guru I would have to obey!) gave such a powerful incentive to my own thinking and learning, I am even more grateful for his so-called philosophy and the scientific and intellectual instruments he made me understand and develop. For the last 20 years, I have been giving time and attention to the fact that teachers, psychologists, parents, and people moved by what education is asking of us today, are very thirsty to go beyond mere teaching methods or even the use of wonderful techniques. They express the need to be more in contact with fundamental research and understanding about different aspects of awareness.

towards meaningfulness. I profoundly know that the Silent Way is basically about that, as a tremendous tree, though its branches are not all perceived yet. It humbly goes from the discovery that "rod" means a little wooden block – to someone beginning to learn English – to the more precise and aware study, for all native speakers, of words such as intuition, energy, time, will, sleep, silence, or even education.

The incredible range of values to be opened by this care of language, oral and written, is infinite. For in today's world where so many people confuse collective attitudes with real knowledge, and tastes with enriched culture, it is essential to use an educational instrument available to everyone who speaks. And everyone who is able to witness and to explore with words the change and evolution of oneself. Can we feel the depth of that proposition valuable to each person, no matter his or her social position, everywhere in the world?

This humble but also great work creates beauty by relating the most personal intimate questions to universal ones.

§

Une enseignante française à Bobo Dioulasso

Geneviève Godard

Mon nom est Geneviève Godard, née en 1950 à Montpellier, France. J'ai grandi à Paris où j'ai passé un bac littéraire avant de faire des études d'allemand en France, à Münster en R.F.A et à Berlin-Est. Je suis restée trois ans en R.D.A. où j'ai aussi travaillé comme traductrice. A mon retour en France, j'ai enseigné l'allemand.

Après avoir quitté le système scolaire en 1990, je me suis mise à la recherche de solutions pour aider les enfants en difficultés scolaires. J'ai travaillé avec des orthophonistes et des spécialistes de l'audition pour élucider les questions relatives aux difficultés d'émission des sons, j'ai suivi des formations de pédagogie, de gestion mentale, etc.

C'est au cours de ces recherches que j'ai découvert la pédagogie Gattegno. Quelle découverte! Elle m'a ouvert tant de portes que je l'ai pratiquée pendant plusieurs années en remédiation individuelle ou collective chez des particuliers ou dans des écoles.

Enthousiasmée par cette pratique qui m'a permis d'aider de nombreux élèves du CP à l'université tant en lecture qu'en écriture, orthographe, expression française, apprentissage d'une leçon, reprise de confiance en soi, prise de conscience de ses capacités personnelles, etc., j'ai accepté de venir au Burkina Faso pour aider des enfants en lecture et en expression française.

Vu les bienfaits de cette approche pédagogique ici en Afrique, je n'ai eu de cesse de trouver un chemin pour apporter La Lecture en Couleurs au Burkina Faso, pays pauvre avec plus de 85% d'analphabètes.

Petit à petit, un projet est né porté par une association familiale et amicale : 'Dounia Don Kalan, savoir lire pour s'ouvrir à la vie' (DDK).

Installée à Bobo Dioulasso, j'ai commencé à travailler le dioula, langue parlée dans cette région, en faisant un tableau de rectangles de couleurs et un moulin à mots (qui complète 4 tableaux de mots en couleurs trop chers à éditer) pour les cours d'alphabétisation. Puis, j'ai travaillé sur le fulfuldé (langue des Peuhls) ainsi que le dagara. Pour ces deux langues, il existe aujourd'hui un tableau de rectangles de couleurs et un moulin à mots. Le mooré, langue du plateau central et de la ville de Ouagadougou, est en cours. Tout ce travail pourrait porter des fruits magnifiques, mais les formations en alphabétisation ne suivent pas par manque de financements. Aujourd'hui, trois alphabétiseurs seulement pratiquent encore La Lecture en Couleurs alors que 18 ont été formés en 2008.

A la demande de nombreux instituteurs, j'ai laissé momentanément l'alphabétisation pour me consacrer à des formations à la 'Lecture en Couleurs' pour les enseignants du primaire. A la demande de responsables de l'enseignement, plusieurs formations ont eu lieu. Actuellement, 49 instituteurs du CP1 au CE1 pratiquent 'La Lecture en Couleurs' dans leur classe, environ 4 700 enfants en bénéficient.

Ces formations ont pu avoir lieu grâce à une participation financière ponctuelle de la Région Rhône-Alpes, de la Francophonie et de la Fondation Dreyer. Mais pourront-elles continuer ? Nous ne le savons pas encore.

Il est reconnu que la difficulté majeure des enfants du Burkina Faso à l'école, c'est l'apprentissage de la lecture.

Les enfants de 6 ou 7 ans qui entrent à l'école n'ont pas eu la chance d'aller à la maternelle beaucoup trop chère pour la grande majorité. Ils ne connaissent que leur rue, les copains du quartier. Leurs jeux se sont limités aux cailloux, aux objets trouvés par terre et aux batailles entre eux. Pour les filles s'ajoute à cela le travail du transport de l'eau dont elles sont chargées très tôt ainsi que le balayage, la préparation des repas, la lessive et la garde des plus petits.

L'apprentissage de la lecture se fait en français, langue que les enfants ne parlent pas. La plupart du temps, leur enseignant (venu d'une autre région) ne parle pas la même langue qu'eux. Il existe plus de 60 langues au Burkina Faso sans compter les multiples dialectes.

L'enfant doit donc apprendre la lecture et le français sans avoir jamais eu aucune activité d'éveil. C'est pour cela qu'il existe un CP1 et un CP2.

Et pourtant, certaines classes comptent plus de 180 enfants. En moyenne, une classe rassemble entre 90 et 100 enfants dans la région où je me trouve.

Mon expérience prouve que le nombre n'est pas le problème. Les classes très chargées au-delà de 90 enfants sont animées par deux enseignants. Avec une bonne approche pédagogique (grâce à Caleb Gattegno) et une maîtrise du groupe, ils parviennent à ce que leurs élèves lisent et surtout comprennent ce qu'ils lisent, car 'lire, c'est comprendre' disait Caleb Gattegno.

J'ai un rêve : que tous les pays d'Afrique découvrent et pratiquent La Lecture en Couleurs et l'approche pédagogique initiée par Caleb Gattegno.

S'ajoute à cela une formation des maîtres réduite au minimum. Ouverte aux détenteurs du BEPC passé en fin de troisième, elle s'étend sur huit mois avec un temps de théorie et un temps de pratique dans les classes des enseignants accompagnateurs. Seule la réussite à un concours d'intégration passé après cette formation leur ouvrira définitivement la porte de l'enseignement.

Vu la situation, il m'a paru très important de permettre aux enseignants de compléter leur formation en les ouvrant à une approche pédagogique simple et peu coûteuse.

Voilà pourquoi, en accord avec les plus hauts responsables de l'enseignement au Burkina, j'ai adapté leur livre de lecture 'Lire au Burkina' à la pratique de 'La Lecture en Couleurs'. L'approche de la langue étrangère par les sons et les couleurs accompagnée des jeux de lecture qu'offre l'algèbre de la langue française, tout cela permet aux enfants d'apprendre à lire plus facilement et fait merveille dans les classes.

L'aspect sympathique et ludique de 'La Lecture en Couleurs' décide plus d'un à rester à l'école, car une des difficultés reste l'abandon précoce de l'école. Apprendre n'est plus une contrainte pour eux et la rigueur de l'apprentissage entre peu à peu dans leur vie. Un son mal prononcé change complètement le mot et donc le sens de toute la phrase. Grâce à la pratique des couleurs et du fidel, les enfants apprennent à se corriger eux-mêmes et petit à petit, à faire leurs prises de conscience.

L'enfant prend goût à la réussite. Il arrive à bien écrire parce qu'il a formé son oreille et sa bouche à bien prononcer les sons. En apprenant ainsi à articuler, la compréhension orale et la transcription écrite ne sont plus un problème.

Il découvre l'orthographe complexe du français au fur et à mesure des leçons en fabriquant avec ses camarades de classe le fidel qui correspond exactement à ce qu'il maîtrise. Une erreur devient une prise de conscience et plus une faute. Il ose participer, chercher des solutions aux défis qui lui sont lancés. Cette confiance lui ouvre un avenir possible. Il

(Godard Cont.)

devient vraiment acteur de son apprentissage. Peu de classes ici offrent une telle ouverture sur demain.

L'enseignant lui-même se détend, s'assure dans ses gestes et ses paroles. Bien que le passage de l'enseignement classique à La Lecture en Couleurs ne soit pas facile pour lui, il s'engage totalement dans cette nouvelle approche pédagogique en essayant de créer, d'inventer de nouveaux jeux de lecture, de trouver la façon d'aider les élèves en difficulté… Sa classe est dynamique et très participative. Il faut même parfois qu'il ralentisse le zèle de ses élèves.

Voilà ce que je vois dans les classes des écoles en ville et en brousse depuis que je travaille La Lecture en Couleurs au Burkina Faso.

Malgré les énormes difficultés d'organisation et de financement de ces formations, je sais que tous ces efforts ne sont pas vains et commencent à porter des fruits. Comment ne pas remercier Monsieur Gattegno pour son travail, tous ces outils qu'il nous a légués et la démarche pédagogique qu'ils sous-tendent.

La Lecture en Couleurs est née en Afrique. Il me semble qu'il est temps maintenant qu'elle apporte aux habitants de ces nombreux pays tous les bienfaits de cette approche pédagogique hors du commun.

J'ai un rêve : que tous les pays d'Afrique découvrent et pratiquent La Lecture en Couleurs et l'approche pédagogique initiée par Caleb Gattegno.

TRADUCTION EN DIOULA

O baara bɛɛ ka deen kɛ, nga a gwɛlɛya ye wariko ye. Ka kɛnyɛ n'o gwɛlɛ ya ye, mɔgɔ 18 ra minw ye kalan sɔrɔ 2008 ra, mɔgɔ 3 dama le bi seera k'o kalan bila baara ra. K'a ye ko lakɔkimɛtiri caama y'a lanyini ka kalan sɔrɔ, n wajibiya ra ka balikukalan bila gɛrɛnna dɔɔni, ka n nyɛ sin olu ka kalan dininman. Ka na se bii ma, ka taa bon fɔlɔ ka taga se bon 3 nan man, lakɔlimɛtiri 49 lo ye o kalankura sɔrɔ a ni o kalankura seera ka waliya denmisɛn 4 700 ra. O kalanw seera ka di Région Rhône-Alpes marala Faransi, tubabukanfɔlaw ka jɛn, a ni fɔndasiyɔn Dreyer sababu ra. O na se ka taga nyɛ wa ? A ma ole lɔn fɔlɔ

Burukina Faso, a lɔnna ko kalendenw caaman ka gwɛlɛya ye kalangwɛ le ye. San wɔrɔ walima san woronfila denmisɛnw caaman bi ta lakoli la kasɔrɔ u man matɛrinɛli kɛ, bari o sɔngɔn ka gwɛlɛ. Kinw kɔnɔn u ka tolow danan bɛrɛtolon ani minɛtɔmonintolon le ma. Musodenw bi sokɔnɔnbaraw fara u kan. Kalangwɛ bi kɛ tubabukan na ka sɔrɔ denmisɛnw tɛ u kan fɔ. Mɛtiri caaman fanan tɛ denmisɛnw ka kan fɔtaw mɛn, bari Burukina ka kan fɔtaw ka caa ni biwɔrɔ ye. O de ya to bon fɔlɔ ani bon filanan bi an ka lekɔli sow la.

Wagati min ka nyi ka ta ka kalan di mɛtiriw man fanan dɔgɔyara kasɛbɛ. O kalan sɔrɔli kɔfɛ fo i ka se sɔrɔ kɔrɔbɔli wɛrɛ laka sɔrɔ ka kɛ kalanfayɛ. Ka kɛnyɛ ni gwɛlɛyaw ye ne ya ye ko a kanyi kalan wɛrɛ dinin bina dɔ fara mɛtiriw ka kanlan sɔrɔta kan sɔngɔ nɔgɔman la. O sen fɛ le ne ye kalan nyɛmɔgɔbaw sɛgɛrɛ walisa ka se ka o ka kalangwɛgafe cogo kɛnyɛn ni nin kalankura ye. Kan wɛrɛ kalan ka tɛmɛ kannyɛw ani nyɛw fɛ, u ka fara kalangwɛtolonw kan, bi nɔgɔya.

Ne ka mara kɔnɔn, lakolidenw 90 wala 100 bi se ka sɔrɔ bon kelen kɔnɔ. N'ga ka kɛnyɛ ni nin fɛɛrɛ ye o min ye kalɛbu Gattegno ta ye lakɔlidenw caaya ti se kagwɛlɛ ya ye kalandi ra. Kamasɔrɔ i na fɔ kalɛbu Gattegno tun ba fɔ cogo min ko 'kalan ye famuyali ye' a fanan bi kɛ te kalandenw fɛ.

Kalankura nin nɔgɔya ni tolon min bɛ sɔrɔ a senkɔrɔ bi kalandenw jija ka ta nyɛ kalan na. Kalan tɛ jati diyagoyafen ye tun, nga a bi yelema ka kɛ i na fɔ olu yɛrɛ cogoya dɔ. Kalandenw bi o ka filiw latelen u yɛrɛ ma.

Den bi nɛgɛ sɛsɔrɔli kɔ. A bi sɛbɛli kɛ ka nyɛ, bari a tulo b'a mɛn ka nyɛ ani a da fana bi danyɛnw fɔ ka nyɛ. Gwɛlɛya te sɔrɔ danyɛw fɔcogo, u sɛbɛcogo n'u famuyali la tun. K'u to degeli la u bɛ tubabukan sɛbɛli gwɛlɛyaw ye, ka fɛrɛw sɔrɔ u yɛrɛw ma. O fana be bara nɔgɔya kalandiba ma hali ka sɔrɔ, ka kalandicogo kɔrɔ dabila kalandicogokura ye, u tɛ fɛnnɔgɔma ye. A fana bi ko caman dabɔ, minw ba kalan jidi. Lakolidenw bi niyɔrɔ ba ta kalan na.

Kabi ne ye nin kalan dabɔ Burukina Faso ne ka kɔrɔsili sera o kow le ma. Hali ka sɔrɔ gwɛlɛya beyi wariko ta fan fɛ, ne ya lɔn ko ni ko kɛtaw tɛ fu ye. Ani o daminɛnan ka den. Ora an ka foli bɛ Gattegno ye o baraw bɛ kosɔn. Nyɛkalankogwɛ bangera farafin na. Wagati nin jamanamɔgɔw k'o kalan nafa sɔrɔ

Ne ka nganiya filɛ : farafinajamanaw bɛ ka se ka nin nyɛkalankogwɛ lɔn ani ka bila barala, o min bɔra Kalɛbu Gattegno fɛ.

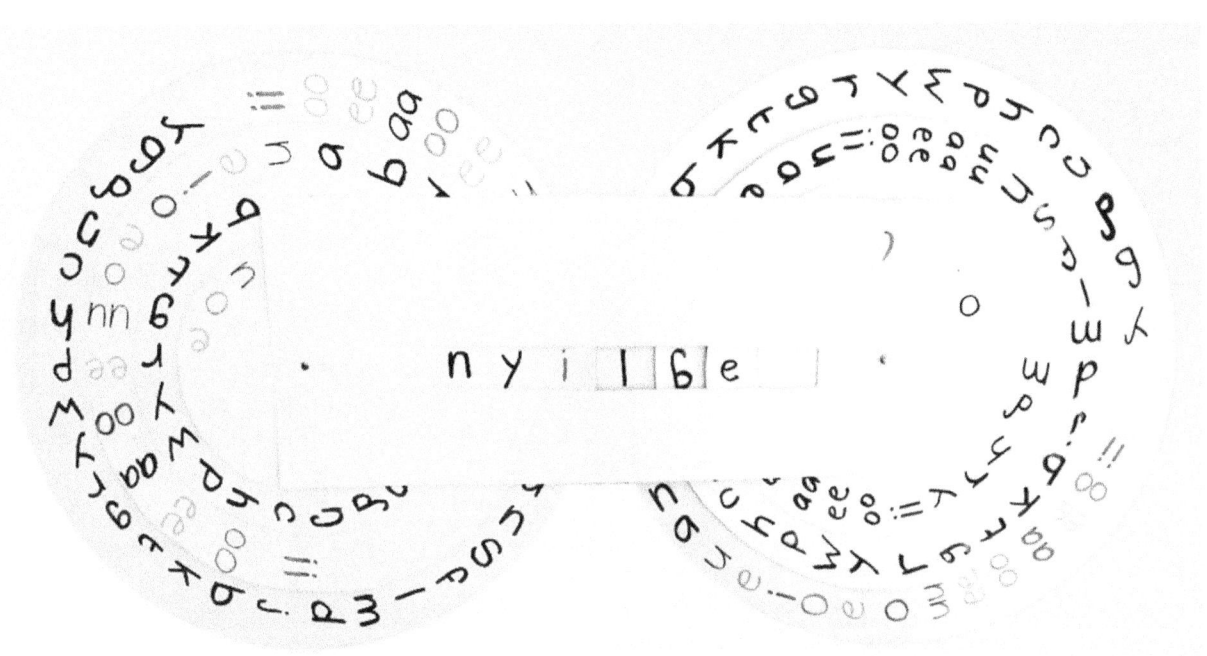

A Dioula word transformer, handmade by G. Godard and her colleagues in Bobo-Dioulasso, Burkina Faso. The original word transformer was invented by Dr. Gattegno as an instrument for inducing awareness of the "algebra" of a language, and allowing students to explore this algebra.

An Educational Awakening

David B. Davies

Religious believers invite unbelievers to find the God-shaped space – the sense of something missing – in their lives. The filling of that space produces the 'convert.' That is the nearest image I can find to describe my own first zeal for Silent Way teaching. I had always found teaching a difficult (though attractive) mystery, and was looking for a meaningful approach. I went to Cecilia Bartoli's Hastings seminar in January 1978 ready to be highly critical. The timetable was Friday evening, all day Saturday and most of Sunday. My memory is that she asked the group of about 30 a question about the fundamentals of teaching. Some tried to work on it; some thought she should be telling us about the Silent Way rather than asking. One person, asked to leave his prejudices outside, announced he'd TAKE them out, and left. (He reappeared at a Barcelona seminar some weeks later without explanation and with every appearance of the warmest friendship for Cecilia.) The Saturday evening, disillusioned, I phoned my wife and discussed leaving early. I didn't leave early. On the Sunday morning I woke with the realization that my disillusion had evaporated. I was ready to do anything Cecilia asked of me. My faith in the Silent Way was complete, although my understanding was zero. Starting to work on Italian was one of the most exciting moments of my learning to date. I was a 'convert,' with no explanation.

I had often been a bad student – the bane of many teachers' lives. Now it seemed that my resistance was somehow bypassed. Whether I could do the same for others was an open question. I left Hastings with my ears more open to my students than they had ever been – going into a classroom I knew, most strikingly, that I had never heard my students' voices in the same way.

In the ensuing years there have been experiences ranging from delightful to awful. Attempting unwillingly to teach an advanced lesson gave me the single worst experience of my teaching life. But I have learnt that I can teach well at elementary level, and have enjoyed classes filled with lightness and laughter.

My strength at conveying the splendors of the Silent Way to other teachers has been by proxy. My return to my school from the Hastings seminar ("Moses descending from Sinai, with tablets graven in color") was greeted with an instant rebuff by skeptical teachers. On the other hand, seminars I arranged, led by outsiders, sometimes struck a strong chord with one or two individuals. They never stayed around my school, so I hope they conveyed the good news elsewhere.

My own delight in Dr. Gattegno's work has been in learning creatively: that first experience of Italian; being a guinea pig for Dr. Gattegno demonstrating an introduction to calculus; his seminar in Paris on writing; learning French grammar from Maurice Laurent in Lyon; most dramatically, learning a little Turkish from a student whom I persuaded to let me organize the lessons using rods and creating our own Word Charts (no colors).

In retrospect, I wish I'd spent more time on learning, whether languages or maths. Somewhat late in life, I realize that my teaching has a place behind other highlights of my experience – first the joy of bursts of creativity during learning; then the witnessing of teachers at work: Dr. Gattegno, Cecilia Bartoli, Laura Guajardo, Roslyn Young, Barbara Villez, Fusako Allard – the list could go on and on.

Why did I become attached to Dr. Gattegno's ideas? My provisional answer is that the attraction lies in his uncompromising search for truth. There's a ruthlessness in it that I find irresistible. My greatest hope is that he will continue to infect the minds of others in the same way. Surely the Subordination of Teaching to Learning will in years to come gain worldwide currency as a common sense attitude, whether or not associated with the name of Caleb Gattegno. §

The Silent Way: A Pedagogy of Life

Dr. Marti Anderson

I met Caleb Gattegno in the fall of 1987 – in the final years of his life. This was my first introduction to the philosophy of the Silent Way and my teaching, and subsequently my approach to teacher training, was transformed because of it.

For more than 20 years, as a member of the School for International Training Master of Arts in Teaching faculty, I also had the enormous good fortune to work with Shakti Gattengno at least twice each year, as she carried on and further developed Caleb's work at SIT.

What I came to realize is that, for me, the Silent Way wasn't only about teaching language. It is a way of thinking about all my work as an educator. I came to think of myself as a Silent Way teacher trainer, working with teachers in similar ways as Gattegno would work with language learners. When I considered how to bring Gattegno's adage "do not do for the students what they can do for themselves" into my work as a teacher educator, I found that I approached the teachers in training in an entirely different manner. I was not the expert coming to impart my "wisdom." Rather, I was an observer of the teachers looking to understand what they are capable of. I would strive to start with where they are, not where I expected them to be. I would try to set challenges that would allow the teachers in training to work at the edge of their knowledge and experience.

"Only awareness is educable," Gattegno famously said. When one looks deeply at this statement it becomes clear that what we must do as educators is focus our students' attention. In my work training teachers, I found that understanding how to shine light on their teaching practice would allow them to become aware of themselves and to become truly reflective practitioners. No checklists of do's and don'ts are present in my work with teachers. Instead I find that I must look for processes, activities, and actions that help guide them into greater self-awareness. This is what will truly keep their teaching practice growing, transforming, and ever improving. It is always a challenge, but one that I embrace wholeheartedly.

When I became a parent, I realized that there were aspects of the Silent Way that found their way into my approach to parenting. I was a Silent Way mother as well. As such, when I would "subordinate teaching to learning," I would observe my children in their learning process and try to find ways to support them where they were, rather than where I thought they should be.

Gattegno's exhortation was that each of us should claim our own experience and learn from it. He would say, "Don't believe me. Try something that intrigues you and find out for yourself." So many of these ideas from the Silent Way intrigued me 24 years ago, and I continue to experiment and learn from them today.

The Silent Way is a philosophy and a pedagogy of life and a process for lifelong learning. §

Life Through a Silent Way Lens

Manuela Bartoli

When I first met Dr. Gattegno, many years ago, I could not imagine that it was one of those encounters that changes your life. I was working in a management school in Trento, as a staff coordinator and in management support. I was asked to film a seminar held by an expert in language teaching, Ms. Cecilia Bartoli. I still strongly remember the vivid impression I had, while filming, through the tiny hole of the steady cam. A strange colorful rectangular chart and a teacher interacting with two young students, using a pointer and making magic! They could utter English words with perfect English pronunciation, with no effort, while enjoying it. Moreover, on the desk, some little colored pieces of wood became people, numbers, days of the week, everything one can imagine and describe. I was amazed!

At the time, I thought my professional life would go on sitting at an office table, dealing with phone calls, scheduling, figures, and business correspondence. But that day something happened; I could not clearly explain what. I have loved English ever since my schooldays, but I had never even considered the possibility of teaching. I was probably too close to the time in school when I had to memorize tons of vocabulary by heart, and learn all the grammar rules, while translating every single sentence from Italian into English or German. What a stressful activity and a boring job to be a teacher, I thought!

I surely changed my mind during that seminar. I was puzzled, curious, and astonished. So I began to attend Silent Way seminars, and after a while, to teach English to a small group of friends. All the while I was reading Dr. Gattegno's books and realizing how his studies and works were precious for the education field.

> He was a master ahead of his time and his vast contributions have been the foundation for a new generation of teachers and learners.

Then, one day, he was invited to Trento to hold a seminar about the Silent Way and language teaching, and I had the opportunity to meet him.

His sharp look, his imposing bearing, or what seemed to be an "imposing bearing" to me, probably his age compared to mine, intimidated me a lot. But in a few minutes I was caught by his words, by his deep knowledge of the inner mechanisms that lead to the acquisition of one's mother tongue, as well as the natural capability of human beings to learn when engaged in a truly stimulating activity, on a human level based on their faculties, here and now.

At that moment it was very clear to me that teaching was what I wanted to do in life.

So I resigned, and as a freelance teacher I began to work for various companies and vocational training agencies around the province. Some years later I set up a small vocational training agency and I tried to involve young teachers in different projects, keeping in mind Dr. Gattegno's precious studies. Along my path I met thousands of grown-up students with different backgrounds, studying languages for a variety of personal and professional reasons as well as many teachers in charge of some courses our agency organized.

When I was worried about a new task as a language

teacher or I had to front a new target group, the Word Charts, the Fidel, the Sound-Color Charts, the drawings, or his books were there as invaluable tools from which getting new suggestions, games, and ideas steadily showed me and my staff the right way.

During my work with my students, my colleagues and, of course, my children and friends, Dr. Gattegno's Subordination of Teaching to Learning became clearer and clearer. The techniques I learned while watching Cecilia Bartoli, reading books, making hypothesis, trying, watching my students' progress, listening carefully to their feedback, feeling their joy in learning, and the light atmosphere in the word of children, and life on the whole – from an enlightening new perspective.

I understood that I am a student, a student of myself and/or of "my self," of my individual and collective functioning. The many mistakes I made have been a good track to start from, to search and learn, as well as being beside my students in their searching and learning process.

Dr. Gattegno's "suspension of judgment" helped me not to take things for granted, observing and listening carefully to my and other people's words and behaviors while trying to change perspectives in thinking.

They could utter English words with perfect English pronunciation, with no effort, while enjoying it.

class have allowed me to grow, to better myself as a teacher while getting a lot of motivation from the energy circulating during my "learning sessions."

I remember the many surprised, then happy, then satisfied faces of those who learnt English or Italian by working just a few hours together, and feeling independent at the same time.

No need to say how much I benefited from my colleagues' experiences during the various seminars in Italy and abroad, and from the discussions arousing pre and post seminars, sharing facts, ideas and opinions. Most of all I have enjoyed, and am still enjoying, the opportunity to work without feeling bored. Every new course, new group, or new company are a new adventure, a new land to be explored, thus giving me enthusiasm in my "discoveries." My students are an unbelievable source of doubts and intriguing questions, and make me love my job more every day.

My personal life also changed by looking at facts and phenomena, through Dr. Gattegno's books – his investigations on love, death, adolescence, the

His studies nurtured my interest in linguistics, and I can see a lot of his achievements on neurolinguistics now explained in academic brain studies through scans and the most up-to-date technologies.

At present, teaching Italian to people coming from all over the world, the Silent Way allows me to be more aware of their differences and similarities so to "let them learn" without interfering, and let them make their own learning experiences and me, my own new experiences as well.

Many things have changed from the time when I was at school, in many "learning environments," and as far as I am concerned, that has happened thanks to Dr. Gattegno, his foresight, his epistemological studies and his faith in science and human beings' capabilities.

He was a master ahead of his time and his vast contributions have been the foundation for a new generation of teachers and learners. I feel myself among them, grateful and happy of the little I have been able to learn and do. The "knowledge society" needs open minds, free teachers and lifelong enthusiastic learners.

§

The Silent Way in Hebrew

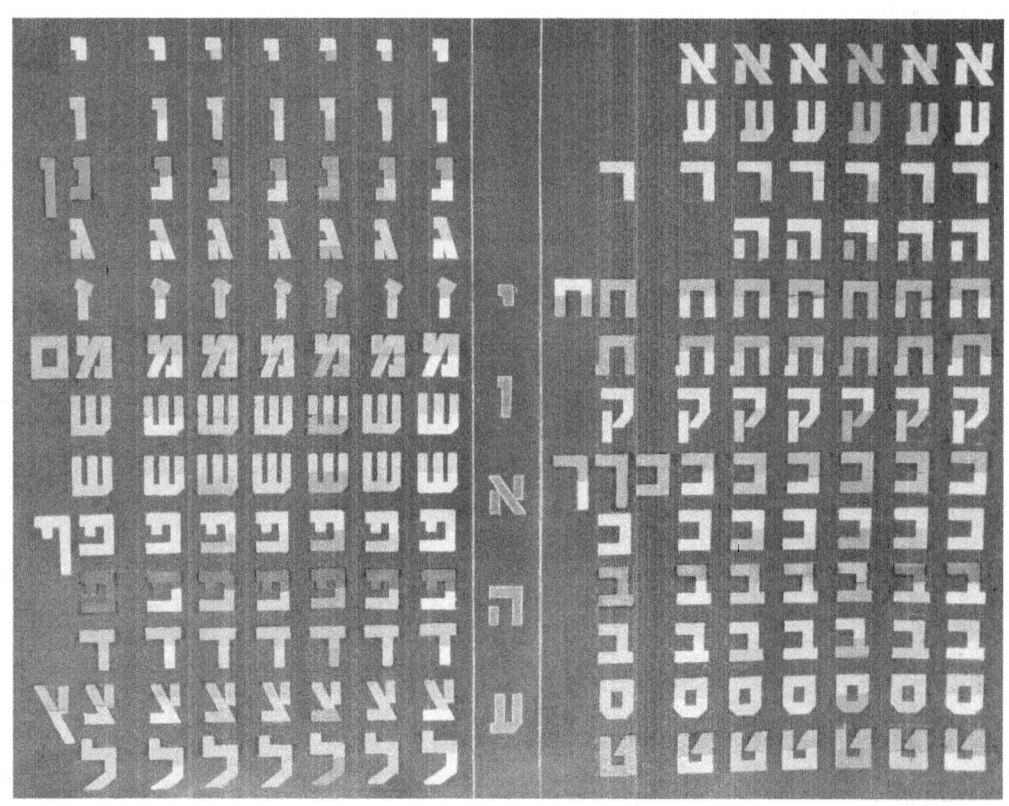

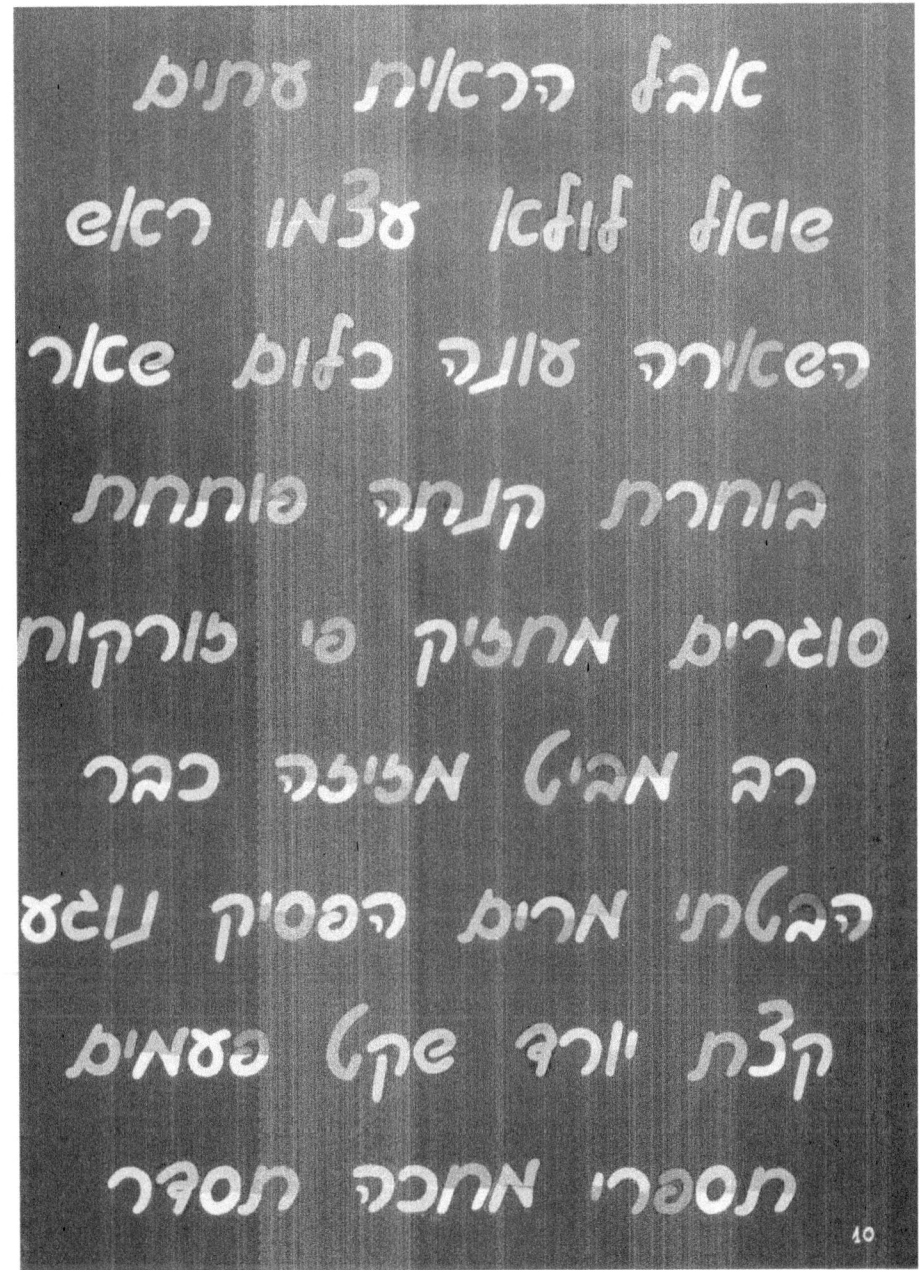

Throughout his career, Dr. Gattegno charted dozens of languages with the help of colleagues around the world. Many of these charts remain archived in their prototype form, which still lend valuable clues for future teaching and research in the language arts.

Above: Hebrew Chart 10, prototype, circa 1978. ©Educational Solutions Worldwide Inc.

Top Left: Hebrew Fidel in cursive, circa 1978. ©Educational Solutions Worldwide Inc.

Bottom Left: Hebrew Fidel, circa 1978. ©Educational Solutions Worldwide Inc.

Dr. Gattegno and the Riverside Language Program

P. Berman, L. Serota, N. Elliott, L. Pesce

The Riverside Language Program is a free intensive daytime ESOL program paid for by the government specifically for documented newly-arrived immigrant and refugee adults from around the world who have resettled in the New York metropolitan area. The founding directors were deeply inspired by the humanistic philosophies of Dr. Caleb Gattegno, and Father Charles Curran, and these philosophies have continued to influence our teaching staff. We are grateful as well to Dr. Earl Stevick who, in his keynote talks at International TESOL conferences and in his book *A Way and Ways*, introduced generations of ESOL teachers to these approaches. Since opening our doors in 1979 in rented space at the Riverside Church, we have worked with more than 20,000 adult learners from Asia, Africa, Central and South America and Europe. Our current staff includes eight teachers, two counselors, a language workshop coordinator, two executive directors, and an associate director; our two office managers and a data entry coordinator were former students at RLP. Most of our professional staff either trained directly with Dr. Gattegno or with someone who had trained with him; all of us have had the privilege in recent years to deepen our Silent Way understanding with Shakti Gattegno. We are committed to creating a learning-centered whole-person school for ESOL students and teachers-in-training.

PHYLLIS BERMAN
Co-Founder and Co-Executive Director RLP

Recently, a man from Bangladesh registered for our intensive daytime ESOL classes at the Riverside Language Program. His grammar was close to perfect, his vocabulary was rich, and his comprehension was strong, but it was almost impossible to understand him. I thought about Dr. Gattegno and his emphasis on pronunciation, stress, and intonation – what a gift his Sound-Color Charts are, distinguishing our letters and our sounds through the use of color. These charts simplify, for literate people, the process of learning to decode alphabets different from their own, and hopefully simplify the process of non-literate people learning to become literate.

> From Dr. G it became apparent that the best "curriculum" and "materials" for each student came not from the school system or the publishing companies, but from the students themselves.

I first encountered the Silent Way and Dr. Gattegno through Language Innovations, Inc. (LINC), a New York based professional organization of adult basic education teachers of ESOL and reading. Members of LINC had organized themselves for several reasons. One reason was because of the inherent "loneliness" of teachers, who were professionally alone in their classrooms with their students, without other colleagues (not supervisors!) to give them new ideas or feedback about what they were doing. Another reason was because the materials available for their adult students were limited, expensive, and quickly out-of-date.

To remedy the first concern, LINC held monthly meetings in which members shared ideas they were trying in their classes and materials they had created. To remedy the second concern, the organization began to "self-publish" inexpensively, and to make their own materials from students' own words, so that their students wouldn't have to lay out large sums of money for books that were quickly irrelevant.

Out of the monthly meetings came reports of new philosophies and approaches in the field of language learning, particularly whole-person, student-centered methods that arose in the 1960s. LINC organized workshops with some of these educational innovators such as the close-in staff associated with Father/Dr. Charles Curran (originator of Counseling Learning/ Community Language Learning), and encouraged one another to attend workshops at Columbia University's Teachers College and at Educational Solutions, where Dr. Caleb Gattegno was holding weekend workshops on the Silent Way.

With my LINC colleagues and other teachers, I spent many exciting weekends at Educational Solutions considering what worked for me as a learner, and what might work better for my high school, college, and ultimately, adult basic education ESOL students.

I have strong memories of those weekends. When we began each weekend, Dr. G would ask people to introduce themselves. If people said about themselves, "I've been teaching for 20 years," Dr. G would interrupt and say, "No, you've been teaching for one year and repeating the same things you did the first year 19 more times."

At the end of each weekend, Dr. G would ask people for their reflections – what they had learned. The idea that articulating what was new and valuable for you is central to an active learning experience was one of the first new practices I incorporated into my classes. Those reflections from learners also provided important information to teachers, who could then use what they were hearing from their students to reflect on what was and wasn't effective in their teaching. I also learned for myself, and in observing new teachers, that teachers shouldn't ask for reflection and feedback unless they are open to taking in without defensiveness what students had to say. Dr. G would say that the students were there to learn the subject, and the teacher was there to learn the students so as to serve their needs well.

Of course, the notion of silence – not a silent class as some people have misunderstood, but the silence of the teacher when students needed to practice – was central to Dr. G's teaching. Beyond the Cuisenaire Rods and the Fidels and Words in Color, we saw that teachers, listening to what their students were saying, could learn what students knew already, or what they needed to learn, or practice. From Dr. G it became apparent that the best "curriculum" and "materials" for each student came not from the school system or the publishing companies, but from the students themselves.

What those of us who became Silent Way practitioners also learned is that teachers don't need to teach what students already know and understand; we need to give opportunities for them to raise their awareness, develop their own criteria, and practice until they've attained mastery. However, we also can't assume that silence is an absolute principle: if students don't already know something, the teacher needs to set up clear examples that enable the students to figure out how our language works. Dr. G showed us that if a teacher demonstrates something just once, it raises the bar on students' attention; they can't afford to miss that one-time demonstration, whether it's the teacher or another student who is demonstrating.

Another one of Dr. G's teachings was about "ogdens" – the price each of us has to pay in order to learn something new. An ogden, we learned through trial and error, is the process of trial and error that requires

> It is the teacher's responsibility to create an atmosphere in class where mistakes are encouraged.

(RLP Cont'd)

us to make mistakes, just as we did as children learning to crawl, to walk, to talk. Mistakes are normal for children, but are sometimes more "costly" for adults who fear the humiliation of not knowing or getting it wrong. What that taught me is that it is the teacher's responsibility to create an atmosphere in class where mistakes are encouraged, active participation is essential, and shame is unhealthy for learning.

Even now, so many years later, I still see "experts" who believe that if you can create the perfect list of the most-used words in English, or create the perfect dialogues needed for all communications in English, or the perfect curriculum or syllabus with all the grammar of English, students should be able to master our language. We who have had the privilege of studying with Dr. G or with Shakti, his best teacher, or other brilliant Silent Way teachers, know how far off these ideas are from the sensitive, individual, relational process of learning.

LANE SEROTA
ESOL Teacher and Library
General Coordinator RLP

I first came in contact with Dr. Gattegno back in April 1976 when I was hired to fill an immediate opening in an NYC Adult Ed ESOL class whose previous teacher, as I was told, had recently begun working with her students using new materials as part of a new method, unfamiliar to me, called the Silent Way.

Feeling anxious and unprepared for the following Monday morning, I made inquiries and found a Silent Way workshop in Spanish Level 1 for which I could still sign up. It was being offered that very weekend at a place called Educational Solutions at 80 Fifth Avenue, and I hoped it could be of help. The experience I had in this 20-hour workshop, my first taste of the Silent Way, did help me relax that Monday morning as I went in to meet my new students. It also excited me so much as a learner that it launched me on a course of exploration into teaching and learning with Dr. Gattegno and Educational Solutions, which has led me on as a teacher all these years.

I remember at one of the many workshops I took with Dr. Gattegno, when he was asking the participants for feedback or comments, one of the participants after reflecting on several things that had been of value in the workshop, ended by saying: "But the big question for me as a teacher is: without a lesson plan or a curriculum, what is the first thing I have to do when I start up a new class? How can I know where to begin?" This is the question I had been worried about myself back on that Monday morning many years ago, when as a fairly new teacher I was about to step into a new class which had been working with a method I knew nothing about.

> It was not Dr. Gattegno's way to provide us with answers but to lead us through a process of exploration...

It was not Dr. Gattegno's way to provide us with answers but to lead us through a process of exploration where we would find good or right questions to ask ourselves, and come up with an answer that would lead us to the next good or right question, always on a search. The question this participant brought up was not what Dr. Gattegno considered to be a good or right question to be working on. "If you have to ask yourself that question, then maybe you shouldn't be in teaching. A better question to ask ourselves as teachers is: what do the students bring us? What learning did they already do as babies? Do we grant them this, that they have already acquired a first language on their own? Do we see that they come to us with powers and experience as natural learners, rather than as empty vessels? Do we see only the teachers as do-ers, or the students as do-ers? What does this mean for us all on day one?"

Over time and through much exploration, I came to see more and more clearly, and still remind myself, that on day one in each and every class my job is first to listen and receive what the students bring, knowing full well that if I do this they will show me what they need to work on. In each and every class this is my challenge: to find the "curriculum" in my students.

NORMA ELLIOTT
Associate Director RLP

If a person is lucky in life, we get to meet a genius. I certainly count Caleb Gattegno in that category. I think of what Walt Whitman wrote, "I don't need luck. I carry it around with me." I feel like I don't need a book of Gattegno's teachings. When I'm in the classroom, I carry around what I learned from his teachings.

And what did I learn?

1. There's no time like the present for a teaching moment. Work with what is in front of you. If a student says, "Can you borrow me your pen?" that's a perfect time for a lesson even if the unit on polite requests is two weeks into the future.

2. Why "teach" something to someone if they know it already? It's our job to find out what they know. We do that by listening and asking questions. Instead of explaining what the past tense is, create a situation and see if the students already know how to respond. And build from there.

3. We're aiming for absorption, not consumption. Language should become a part of us, not something that we intellectually know. Therefore, following a curriculum loses significance. To have language become a part of us, it takes as long as it takes.

And although charts and rods make for excellent tools, you don't need them to be a teacher who is awake and responsive in the classroom.

LIA PESCE
Language Workshop Coordinator and ESOL Teacher RLP

I regret never having had the chance to meet nor to work with Caleb Gattegno. Yet every time I step into the classroom, I am grateful to him for having shared with me his ideas, beliefs, and tenets about teaching and learning. Gattegno's Silent Way was, and continues to be, vital in the formation of my own philosophy of teaching and learning.

During my graduate school coursework, I had read theoretical studies written about the Silent Way, but it was truly introduced to me during my observations and subsequent internship at Riverside Language Program in New York City. I remember a great deal about the first time I observed a teacher whose philosophy includes the Silent Way. In Tom Miller's class, I witnessed the high level of musicality, energy, and autonomy emitted from students working towards acquiring the English language. And I quickly understood that the Silent Way is anything but silent.

I noticed that the teacher was like a coach to the students. He helped their bodies and minds to formulate and to practice various aspects of the English language. Yet all the while, the teacher remained mostly silent. For example, he presented a new sound from the Sound-Color Chart to the class. If a student needed to work on producing this sound, the teacher would only move his mouth or lips in order to show how the sound could be created. Yet it was the student who used his or her own criteria to decide on how to make the sound. The teacher did not need to overtly give the students any rules or guidelines. As time passed, the students were becoming increasingly more aware of the unique nuances of the English language. With the Silent Way, the students came to certain conclusions on their own and in their own time.

The teacher built subsequent parts of the lesson upon what the students were doing. Therefore, the students were able to guide the teacher in the direction that was best for them in that moment. I observed the teacher as a guide who was there to assist and to facilitate the students' language acquisition. But, the teacher did not impart all of his knowledge to the students. The teacher gave the students a piece of the pie and the students themselves created the whole. The students were autonomous, independent and responsible for their learning. It was all done at a pace that was appropriate for the students. It was exactly what they wanted and needed. The teaching was truly subordinate to learning, as per Gattegno's beliefs. Here, the students became their own teachers.

And now as a teacher myself, the Silent Way continues to help create the same opportunities for my students. In my classroom, I step back and watch my students work, shape, and mold their criteria and awareness of English to a new level. By subordinating my teaching to students' learning, I am ever more sensitive and responsive to these moments too. And I believe that Caleb Gattegno will forever remain an important part of all of these wonderful "ah-ha" moments that occur for my students and for many others. §

He Said Nothing, But I Understood Everything

Dr. Clifton de Cordoba

In the mid 1970's in California, a language-teacher colleague asked me one day if I'd like to go to a workshop led by a man who taught languages using colored rods. I laughed and said, "You're kidding." He wasn't.

> "I was, and continue to be, mesmerized by the intensity of his gentle guiding of students to learn languages."

The day of the workshop, the man, Dr. Gattegno, taught Japanese to a number of volunteers on a lecture hall platform. During the demonstration, he used colored rods and colored charts of Japanese script. He said nothing, but I understood everything.

I was, and continue to be, mesmerized by the intensity of his gentle guiding of students to learn languages by paying poker-game-like attention to gestures, props, changing relationships and changing perceptions of the props.

Subsequently, I attended many workshops led by Dr. G, as many affectionately called him, and by others familiar with his work: Cecilia Perrault and Shakti Gattegno. I became so interested in his approach to human learning that I even attended a workshop in Barcelona, Spain titled, The Mind Teaches the Brain.

In all my readings of and work with Dr. Gattegno – he graciously participated on my doctoral committee – I was struck by his ferocious belief in the natural power of human learning.

Many years have passed since that first Japanese lesson and many technological changes have taken place in the field of language instruction and first-language literacy. However, the power of learners to build their own inner criteria for what is correct, right and appropriate in a new language or modality – as with literacy students of a language they currently speak – remains a sleeping giant for the 21st Century.

The internet, properly programmed, is an untapped opportunity for current and future generations of teachers and learners to experience the natural power and speed of human learning that Dr. Gattegno tapped into. Speech recognition and mouse or touch screen technology will be able to create an explosion of excitement in language learning based on the ability of humans to retain meaningful experiences and associations. These developments will be a welcome relief to current computer-based language programs that rely chiefly on memory, disguised drills and fragmented content.

I see the same excitement potential for the teaching of mathematics, another focus of Dr. Gattegno's work. In fact, because of the increasing number of students who perform math and reading skills below grade level and the large number of adults in need of literacy and math skills to enter the labor force, the potential for an awakening, or educating awareness on a broad scale is huge.

I recall an image that Dr. Gattegno used to share in his workshops: those of us who were learning from him standing on his shoulders to see and affect the future. That would make us the awakened giants. §

Dr. Gattegno with friends. (Educational Solutions file photo.)

Caleb Gattegno, une expérience de maïeutique

Philippe Fagot

C'est en 1986, lorsque des séminaires de réflexion ont été organisés pour des participants non essentiellement enseignants que j'ai été amené à côtoyer le Silent Way et son créateur, Caleb Gattegno. D'emblée, par sa présence, par son écoute, par sa capacité à discerner des potentialités étonnantes chez ses interlocuteurs, ce fut une rencontre placée sous le signe d'une priorité à l'humain.

Lors des thèmes tels que « La génération de richesses », et surtout « La Conscience de la conscience », nos relations, nos échanges se sont affinés. Mes recherches sur la couleur portaient à cette période principalement sur des aspects scientifiques, dans une démarche de rationalité et d'objectivité. Lors des pauses, durant les moments où l'on pouvait échanger en face à face, seul à seul ce qui était rare car les participants ne lui laissaient que peu de répit, il ne manquait pas de m'interroger sur la nature de ces recherches, sur leurs vocations. Sa grande et profonde culture, sa curiosité, ses intérêts multiples et diversifiés étaient toujours vifs, et servaient une capacité d'écoute très fine.

A l'inverse, je lui confiai mes difficultés à pouvoir me dégager de ce qui était central alors dans mes préoccupations, entre autre la connotation des couleurs et de leurs significations, afin de m'en libérer pour pouvoir m'approcher de la didactique du Silent way.

Je ne participais pas à ces séminaires d'été pour maîtriser cette pédagogie, mais dans une perspective de développement personnel, dans le cadre d'une ouverture à d'autres dimensions humaines. Mes expériences antérieures me portaient à l'intériorisation, à cultiver via les langages non verbaux (gestuelle, posture corporelle, chorégraphie, la pratique équestre, mais aussi les expressions artistiques visuelles, la peinture), un intérêt sublimé pour la voie du silence. Quel terrain magnifique, magistral, qui a également inspiré, sous d'autres registres, le grand Miles Davis, que ce cheminement silencieux ! J'y trouvais, grâce à Caleb, grâce à sa faculté de mettre en situation les potentialités contenues en chacun de ses auditeurs sur des voies de la manifestation, de l'expression, de faire sortir le meilleur d'eux-mêmes, des réponses éloquentes à mes interrogations solitaires. Alors, cet écho a porté ses fruits dès lors qu'il m'a interpelé et m'a invité à passer de la méditation à l'action !

Je lui suis infiniment reconnaissant d'avoir pointé cette capacité de mutation, d'évolution, sans contrainte ni évaluation externe. Le sens de la liberté était, pour lui, l'une des valeurs primordiales, avec la tolérance et l'humilité. Ces trois facultés, entre autres, transparaissaient continuellement en ses propos, ainsi que dans l'attitude qu'il entretenait avec autrui.

Aujourd'hui, sans que ma pratique professorale pour différentes institutions universitaires et écoles supérieures, ainsi qu'en centres de formation pour adultes, n'applique une démarche directement issue de la pédagogie développée par Caleb Gattegno, elle n'en n'est pas moins héritière. L'imprégnation de l'esprit d'enseigneur que j'ai distingué de celui d'enseignant relève d'une véritable et puissante expérience de maïeutique au sens initial du terme. C'est une réelle joie que de voir s'éveiller les êtres en face de moi, de ne considérer que mon rôle n'est que celui d'un accompagnateur et rien d'autre, que les réponses sont déjà connues, mais qu'il suffit d'ordonner très modérément le cheminement pour accéder à leur reconnaissance.

Aujourd'hui, mes domaines de recherches sur la couleur se sont réorientés vers les sciences cognitives et les capacités insoupçonnées qu'offre l'incommensurable connectique neuronale. Mis aux services de la créativité et des métiers devant constamment innover, imaginer, remettre en questionnements continuels les savoirs acquis, ils m'amènent autant à repousser les connaissances de mes étudiants sur des pistes inconnues qu'à me nourrir de leurs propres observations et comportements. C'est en conséquence sur le plan du partage que se situe actuellement mon enseignement, un partage inégal je le concède, car je me limite à une transmission très économe de données pour un maximum de retours. Et cela correspond à une réponse personnelle à ce que m'a insufflé Caleb à l'oreille, sous les pins des Landes, à Carcans-Maubuisson, un jour d'été 1986. §

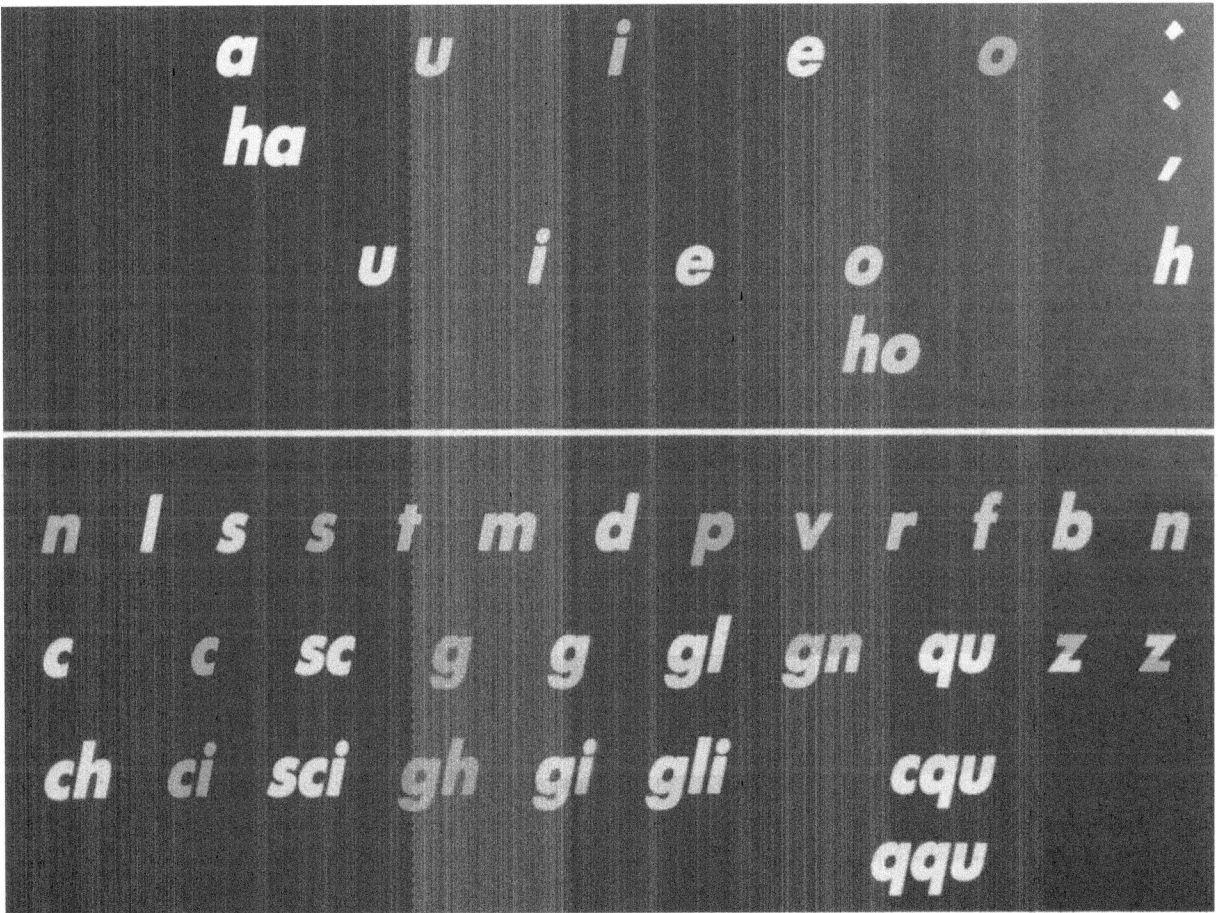

The Italian Fidel, originally printed in 1979 and revised in 1990. ©Educational Solutions Worldwide Inc.

The Heart of the Matter: Gattegno's Awareness of the Powers of Children

Laurinda Brown

It is 1972, an era of 'love, light, peace and happiness,' and I am deciding what to do after completing my university mathematics degree. At grammar school, mathematics was taught as a set of procedures. For me, these procedures linked and connected over time to create meaning, whereas for many of my classmates who were powerfully able to engage in critical debate exploring English literature, the subject was meaningless. The style of teaching was met with frustration, anger, and tears at various times, and of those 30 students in the top stream at the all-girls school, many failed their O-Level in the subject outright whilst getting 1's in some of their other subjects. I knew there had to be a different way of teaching mathematics.

I arrived at the University of Exeter for my one-year Post Graduate Certificate in Education (PGCE) course the following September to be met by a tutor, Dick Tahta, who in our first session encouraged us to work in pairs on a problem called 'Frogs.' The room was filled with equipment and resources, and we developed different ways to investigate and give insight into the structure of the problem. I found myself enjoying mathematics in a way I had forgotten throughout my degree. Another session I remember vividly was of playing a game called 'Racetrack,' using vectors to race around a track, simulating powerfully an actual Formula 1 race, screeching around bends – not having enough forward speed and drifting into the barrier whilst trying to kill the horizontal motion. Mathematics became visible and tangible and I now knew that, indeed, there were other ways to teach mathematics. Our handbook and reference for ideas for lessons became *Starting Points* by Banwell, Saunders and Tahta (CUP). There were also times sitting in a circle talking, and one day, we watched as a group, a film of a man called Dr. Gattegno teaching mathematics to young children using Cuisenaire Rods in a primary school in Montreal, Canada.

It is difficult to re-enter now the strength of my emotions on watching this film. I reacted strongly against what I saw. What I did not know at the time was that Dick Tahta had himself worked closely with Gattegno, and the styles of working that I had been experiencing at Exeter with the use of images and tangible resources such as Geoboards and Pegboards were directly linked to Gattegno's work. There is something in the contrast between my early 'hippy' values and Gattegno's taking of the responsibility position that I simply could not handle. I judged, and that judgment was to lead me to having nothing to do directly with Gattegno's work for many years. Of course, I was still working with Dick Tahta.

One day, Dick was visiting his PGCE students at the school where I taught mathematics and he came to work with me in a lesson. Afterwards, he said something like he enjoyed coming to see me teach knowing that I hadn't read anything by Gattegno because it gave him even more faith in the approaches, given where I was going with what I was doing. The effect of this comment was to provoke a move away from my own developing structures, to trying to link my language and practices to those of Gattegno. Initially it felt like everything fell apart – I couldn't be who I was, and the sorts of practices I was reading about were too far ahead for me to be able to 'do' what I imagined. Eventually things integrated and I was able to continue the work of subordinating my teaching to the learning of my students as I now could describe what I had been working on. I also became able to focus a class of students as well as run more workshop-style sessions.

When Dick Tahta formed the SubTLe (Subordination of Teaching to Learning) group, I became its treasurer and every year there were two or three meetings, usually in Bristol and Manchester, where we actively worked on learning, through teaching each other. Each year this group also hosted Gattegno for a seminar in Bristol lasting a few days. I was present at the 1988 ATM Easter Conference where Gattegno gave a moving talk a few months before he died. From this talk the following injunction stayed with me:

"People often say, 'I teach them but they don't learn.' Well, if you know that, stop teaching. (laughter) Not resign from your job: stop teaching in the way that doesn't reach people, and to understand what there is to do for you to become daily more skilled in helping these youngsters furnish their minds with things which are so elementary that, where they take five years today, I can do them in 18 months, sometimes less."

After Gattegno died, Dick Tahta, Dave Hewitt and I edited a collection of writings from *Mathematics Teaching* alongside an edited transcript of that final lecture to the ATM conference, in *A Gattegno Anthology*. The challenge of 'doing in 18 months' became transformed for me into questions, notably, what would be the minimal set of activities that I would offer in each year, which would span the syllabus and potentially go beyond it? What activities can I offer to year 7 (aged 11-12 years) students so that they are doing trigonometry?

As I re-watch the film of Gattegno teaching those young children, I see the use of resources, in this case Cuisenaire Rods, making mathematics visible and tangible. The children are working with fractions, and currently in the UK, the content of the lesson would be said to be level 7, where level 8 means that you could be taking a final examination in mathematics aged 16 and be doing well in it. The most powerful thing for me about Gattegno's work is that clearly he was able to teach in 18 months what most mathematics teachers work on for many years with their students. At the heart of the matter for me is Gattegno's awareness of the powers of children, written about in the classic *What We Owe Children*. His focus is on the children's learning as he teaches. What are these powers of children? I distil and paraphrase:

These functionings, the mental powers of children that can be brought into use by teachers are:

- The power of extraction, finding 'what is common among so large a range of variations.'
- The power to make transformations, based on the early use of language: 'This is my pen' to 'That is your pen.'
- Handling abstractions, evidenced by learning the meanings attached to words.
- Stressing and ignoring, without which 'we cannot see anything.'

Gattegno also has suggestions for how these powers can be 'used in the process of education':

- Students can notice differences and assimilate similarities, so ask them to tell you what distinctions they are making – what is the same? What is different?
- Students can use their power of imagery, so ask them to shut their eyes and respond with mental images to verbal statements.
- Students can generalize, given that algebra is a fundamental power of the mind (linked to abstraction).

As a teacher you work contingently to offer new challenges given what your students show you – there is always algebraic activity, often use of imagery and classification, the making of distinctions. These actions are so different from the classroom of my childhood where memorization and repetition were the ways in which we had to use ourselves in the lessons. I think that my classmates would have had a better relationship with mathematics if they had been allowed to use the whole of their selves.

Transformation: From Ideology to Science

Dr. Arthur B. Powell

Starting in 1971, as trite as this may sound in this volume, I began a profound transformative journey at the moment when I first became acquainted with the work and then the person of Caleb Gattegno. I transitioned from believing something is true to glimpsing and then beholding evidence to confirm its veracity. Starting in the late 1960s, I became politically active in anti-racist and anti-war movements and left-wing activities in my high school, and in communities in Brooklyn and Manhattan in New York City. My actions were informed by my belief that in the United States and elsewhere, unjust social conditions, not biology, prevented individuals and their communities from realizing their intellectual and economic potential.

Upon graduating from high school, I secured a year postponement of my admission to Hampshire College so that I could work with a community-based organization — The Dome Project — working with economically marginalized African-American and Latino students in a New York City middle school. These students were years behind in their reading and mathematics performances, and since they also presented behavioral issues, their school's principal allowed our organization to work with them during the school day, outside of school, in the basement of a local church. My colleagues and I had only the force of our personalities and belief in our ability to relate to the youngsters as our assurance that we could make a difference in the students' lives. However, we had no particular understanding of pedagogy beyond what we experienced as students — experiences that we criticized along lines informed by educational theorists such as G. Carter Wilson, Ivan Illich, and Paulo Freire.

We searched for help with our pedagogy. Somehow we found Educational Solutions, which, at that time, was on Fifth Avenue and 14th Street in New York City. There, my colleagues attended a mathematics workshop given by Marty Hoffman. After hearing about their experience and what they learned, I attended the next available workshop. It was on Words in Color and conducted by Jim McDowell. I experienced the use of two important principles: (1) use what you know to gain entry into what is new and (2) gain a lot from a little. I used the first principle to discover not only the correspondences amongst color, sign, and sound, but also began to understand how, at least with reading, learners could control of their learning. Beyond the specialized techniques of working with a pointer to tap out words, phrases, and sentences and to work on speed, rhythm, and melody, I also began to appreciate in yet only superficial ways Gattegno's notions of attention, awareness, and awareness of awareness.

Excited with the new world of learning that had opened up to me, I subsequently attended a mathematics workshop of David Wheeler's where, using Algebricks, I explored notions of algebra before arithmetic and employed the second important principal of gaining a lot from a little through attentive application of invariant aspects of situations created with rods. I also began to appreciate the complexity of teaching mathematics when, as a teacher, I had to attend to what my students do and to use their work as feedback on their functioning and as clues as to what next to invite them to do.

To further our abilities to use the Subordination of Teaching to Learning in reading and mathematics, our community-based organization contracted to have both Jim and Marty work with us at our site and with our students.

The following year, after I entered college, during a weekend break from classes, Marty and Jim invited me to attend a so-called "awareness workshop" that Dr. Gattegno was giving. I went, but felt nervous and awkward; I did not feel that I knew enough or had read enough about education to be able to gain much from the workshop. However, my trepidations were mitigated as I witnessed how Gattegno did not privilege so-called "expert" knowledge, but rather invited workshop participants to reflect on our lived experiences to gain entry into understanding how attention, awareness, and awareness of awareness function in our own past and present learning.

The work done in this workshop and subsequent ones triggered in me a desire to reflect on how to invite my students to mobilize their own attention, awareness, and awareness of awareness to engage in game-like activities so that they can build mathematical ideas for themselves. Importantly, through my participation in several of Gattegno's awareness workshops and my reading of *What We Owe Children* and *In the Beginning There Were No Words: The Universe of Babies*, I gradually shifted my approach to education from one based solely on an ideology of equality and equity, to one centered on an understanding of Gattegno's science of education.

This science posits the universality of the mental functionings that individuals develop to distinguish:

- among people and things in their environment,
- among noises heard and made to communicate simple and complex ideas,
- among other mental functionings such as ones used to speak, to walk, to run, and to climb,

which are not dependent on race or economic status. These very functionings can be employed to read, write, learn other languages, and do mathematics.

For me, this was a relief since I was able to move my educational practice from one based on ideology and hope, to one undergirded by scientific understanding. And, for me, being a mathematician, this was a more comfortable, rational position to be in. §

Dr. Gattegno working with teachers on the subordination of teaching to learning. (Published in *KWELI*, May 1970.)

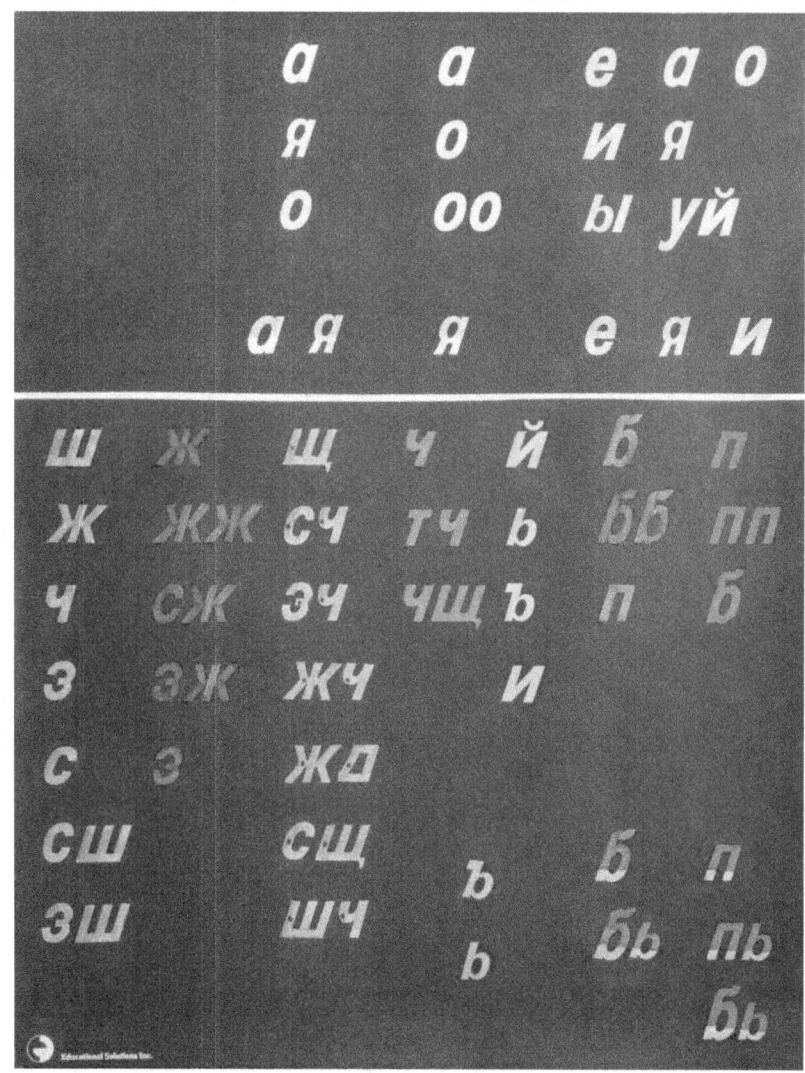

The Russian Fidel, chart 1 of 3, prototype stage, 1979. ©Educational Solutions Worldwide Inc.

Silent Way au Japon

Malik Berkane

Comment ai-je appris tout ce que je sais faire, et plus particulièrement ma langue maternelle que j'ai acquise sans la moindre souffrance, quel en avait été le ou les processus, et était-ce seulement une affaire d'imitation ? Cette question toute simple en apparence, je ne me l'étais jamais posée avant de m'intéresser à l'approche Gattegno. L'explication, l'imitation et la répétition étaient les seuls outils que je connaissais et que j'utilisais dans mes classes.

J'ai découvert le Silent Way il y a seize ans, et à un moment de ma vie professionnelle où j'avais la ferme intention d'arrêter l'enseignement du Français Langue Étrangère. À cette époque, j'avais pourtant à mon actif plus de dix années d'expérience dans ce domaine, mais les résultats qu'obtenait la grande majorité de mes étudiants me décevaient cruellement et entrer en classe était devenu une souffrance, et ce n'était pourtant, ni par manque de déploiement d'énergie, ni par manque de travail. Ceux qui savaient apprendre –ils n'étaient pas légion - arrivaient à tirer leur épingle du jeu et autant que faire se peut à progresser, quant aux autres, ils essayaient tant bien que mal de raccrocher les wagons mais pour – en règle générale – une bien piètre moisson, quand ils ne renonçaient tout simplement pas. Et j'avais l'amère sensation de faire un travail qui ne servait à rien ou presque. Je faisais cependant ce que j'avais appris à faire en observant les autres enseignants et ce que j'avais également appris en étudiant le FLE, et à cette époque, ça se résumait à : "de la grammaire, encore de la grammaire et toujours de la grammaire" Je m'évertuais donc à prêcher la grammaire et à en décliner à tour de bras ses règles opaques et quasi hermétiques à des personnes qui n'avaient pas dans leur langue maternelle d'équivalents en terme de métalangage grammatical et qui se devaient de dépenser une énergie folle pour mémoriser ces mots techniques qui ne servaient à rien, en tout cas pas à l'usage qu'ils voulaient –pour la plupart – faire de la langue française. Et quand j'observais leur désarroi, je leur disais que : "Les voies de la grammaire françaises sont parfois impénétrables".

Et j'en restais là, puisque de toute façon, tous les

> Tous les matériels Silent Way que Gattegno a mis au point permettent de forcer la présence des apprenants et de provoquer les prises de conscience nécessaires à leur compréhension et à leur progression.

enseignants que je côtoyais à Tokyo à cette époque faisaient la même chose que moi, voire pire. Pour les étudiants, réussir à apprendre le français dans de telles conditions et sans séjour linguistique dans un pays francophone, relevait de l'exploit.

Je dirige depuis 22 ans une école de français à Tokyo et le Silent Way est utilisé dans presque toutes les classes. J'ai actuellement une dizaine de cours sur les 60 que l'école compte hebdomadairement, et je totalise à ce jour plus de 15,000 heures de pratique avec le Silent Way. J'ai eu la chance de travailler avec

(Berkane Cont.)

des formateurs de grande qualité tels que Roslyn Young, Maurice Laurent, Fusako Allard, etc. et grâce à l'expérience acquise sur le terrain, j'ai pu, pas à pas, percevoir la pertinence, la profondeur et l'ampleur de l'héritage que nous a légué Caleb Gattegno tant sur le plan de la rigueur scientifique que sur le plan de la flexibilité des matériels dont nous disposons et dont l'usage est selon moi, extensible à "l'infini".

Ce que propose Gattegno sur la présence, les prises de conscience et les moyens de les forcer sont des outils précieux et d'une grande efficacité qui ont permis à bon nombre de mes étudiants d'obtenir des résultats sans aucune mesure avec ceux qu'ils obtenaient avec les méthodes dites classiques. Tous les matériels Silent Way que Gattegno a mis au point permettent de forcer la présence des apprenants et de provoquer les prises de conscience nécessaires à leur compréhension et à leur progression.

Le Moi, ses attributs, le psychisme, tout cela a été une révélation qui a bouleversé ma vision de mon métier d'enseignant et ma vie d'enseignant. Ces notions ne sont pas de vains délires théoriques, mais elles ont –et je peux l'observer tous les jours - une réelle place et une réelle existence dans la classe et dans les comportements des étudiants et dans ceux des enseignants. Et je suis parfaitement conscient aujourd'hui que c'est la connaissance de ce modèle qui me permet de mieux travailler sur les étudiants et de leur proposer les solutions les plus adéquates à leur apprentissage.

Dans notre école, et sans souci de prosélytisme, il est donné à n'importe quelle personne extérieure s'intéressant à l'enseignement du FLE, la possibilité d'observer des cours de Silent Way. Et mis à part quelques cas isolés (comme le jour où une spécialiste de FLE observant une de mes classes, ne voyait dans les pointeurs que des objets phaliques inutiles), les réactions sont quasiment unanimes. "Comment se fait-il que vos étudiants parlent autant et avec une si bonne prononciation ?" Les apprenants japonais étant de façon générale très passifs, les cours de FLE deviennent très fréquemment de longs monologues de l'enseignant, ponctués de temps à autre par quelques hochements de tête des étudiants. Malgré lui, le professeur tient presque toujours le premier rôle dans la classe et il lui est difficile d'amener les étudiants à prendre la parole. Chez nous, au contraire, les étudiants sont les acteurs principaux et l'enseignant quant à lui, n'a qu'un petit rôle de subalterne se résumant à donner les feed-backs nécessaires à la bonne marche de la classe. Et c'est pour cela que dans une classe de quatre-vingt-dix minutes, nos étudiants parlent quatre-vingt-dix pour cent du temps ce qui bien sûr ne manque pas de surprendre les observateurs.

Le travail que j'ai effectué jusqu'à aujourd'hui avec l'approche Gattegno m'a amené à porter un regard différent et conscient sur le fonctionnement de la langue française et à penser en matière de messages à donner à son interlocuteur plutôt qu'en termes de règles grammaticales et de métalangage. Ceci m'a amené à une tout autre vision de l'organisation de ma langue maternelle telle qu'elle s'impose à ses locuteurs, et à une réflexion sur les moyens dont je disposais pour forcer des prises de conscience liées aux usages. Quel message je veux donner quand j'utilise le passé composé, l'imparfait, le futur proche ? Quel message je veux donner quand j'utilise "je crois que", "je pense que", "je trouve que" ? Quel message je veux donner ou quelle partie de mon corps parle quand j'utilise "j'ai envie de", "j'ai besoin de", "je voudrais que", "j'aimerais que" etc. etc. etc. Et en était-il de même pour les autres langues ?

Si nos règles de grammaire découlent de l'usage, l'usage lui, découle de façon intrinsèque des besoins de transmettre des messages précis et "codés", eux-mêmes liés à des situations précises. Et si l'on considère que quelles que soient leurs sociétés, les hommes ont presque partout les mêmes besoins pour vivre leur vie, il devient possible de mettre en corrélation les façons de décliner ces besoins et d'en faire prendre conscience à nos étudiants.

La conscience et les prises de conscience sont des valeurs fondamentales sur lesquelles reposent l'approche Gattegno, et dont je suis tout à fait solidaire. Cependant, avancer sur le chemin de la conscience et chercher à savoir comment et pourquoi nous fonctionnons, agissons ou réagissons de telle ou telle façon dans telle ou telle situation de notre vie quotidienne, est une chose difficile à mettre en pratique. Il faut apprendre – et cela demande beaucoup de temps - à faire un tri nécessaire dans son psychisme pour arriver à réellement fonctionner avec soi-même sans être influencé par ce que nous avons stocké malgré nous dans notre psychisme et qui souvent nous empêche de voir la réalité de ce qui nous entoure. Savoir se défaire – ou pouvoir se servir de tremplin - de certains de ces automatismes psychiques qui nous ramènent souvent à la case départ, est je crois, une chose que peu de personnes arrivent vraiment à réaliser. Quoi qu'il en soit, si sur l'échelle de la conscience, personne n'a le pied sur la même marche et que du niveau ou l'on se trouve, on a tous une perception différente du monde et de soi-même, ce que je peux dire aujourd'hui, c'est que grâce au paradigme de Gattegno, j'ai l'impression d'avoir gravi quelques petites marches sur cette échelle. J'ai appris à me connaître en tant qu'enseignant et à connaître mes étudiants en tant qu'apprenants sans que cela soit bien sûr exhaustif et définitif. Et cela, pour mon plus grand bonheur et celui des trois cents étudiants qui fréquentent régulièrement notre établissement. J'aimerais ajouter aussi que si, libérer les étudiants de la tutelle du professeur est à mon sens l'épine dorsale de l'éducation, avec l'approche Gattegno, je sais que c'est réalisable.

Le seul problème auquel nous sommes souvent confrontés, et c'est un problème de taille, concerne la formation des enseignants à cette approche pédagogique. Et cela est malheureusement loin d'être une chose simple, car cette formation n'est possible que si les aspirants sont dans des dispositions propices à cette forme de travail qui nécessite un long et difficile apprentissage, et une remise en question permanente de ce que l'on est et de ce que l'on fait.

Mais le plus grand mal que je peux souhaiter à tout enseignant ou tout éducateur digne de ce nom et désireux d'aider ses élèves, c'est de tomber dans la marmite !

Primary mathematics using the original Numbers in Color math set. (Educational Solutions file photo.)

The Foundation of My Teaching:
A Belief in the Genius of Human Beings

Dr. Paula Hajar

I met Dr. Gattegno in the summer of 1970, a few months after I arrived in New York City. I was part of a group of recent college graduates who had come to New York to be part of Teachers Incorporated, a teacher-training project that was something like a precursor to Teach for America. The leaders of Teachers Inc. recognized Gattegno's genius, and as part of our summer training, signed the whole group and themselves up for a Silent Way weekend in Spanish. That's where I first met Gattegno, who was the instructor that weekend.

It was an intense and delightful experience, as he carefully built for us the structure of the language, piece by piece. I remember the last afternoon, when, in Spanish, Gattegno extended some sort of invitation to me personally (the specifics have faded). I answered, "No," and he replied "Lastima." Everyone burst out laughing. I think of the incident every time I hear or say the word "Lastima."

Scarcely a year later, I was the assistant in his son's first-grade classroom. The head teacher generously, or wisely, split the class in two and assigned to me all the students who could already read and do math – figuring, I suppose, that there'd be less harm done with the labor divided thus. My group included little Ashish, who I referred to as "the crown prince." I was terrified to teach the son of a man I so admired, worried that as a first-year teacher I could only disappoint Dr. Gattegno. Six-year-old Ashish, however, turned out to be a love, very pure, and in the diary I kept of the year, he figures prominently for his own sweet wit. (Once he told a classmate, whose last name was Best, "Michael, don't be surprised if sometimes I call you Michael Worst.")

> Everyone else, even my graduate school professors, seemed like fluff after Gattegno.

As I was in a "Gattegno school" (Horace Mann Lower School in Manhattan), that year I eventually began attending Educational Solutions math and language seminars, and Gattegno's monthly seminars on awareness. This went on for several years.

The awareness seminars showed me the human capacity for disciplined talk, and pretty much ruined me for whatever teachers and educational programs came later in my life – everyone else, even my graduate school professors, seemed like fluff after Gattegno. For a full weekend, which meant five hours on Friday night, 10 hours on Saturday and another 10 on Sunday, 25 to 30 people arrayed around a room with

Gattegno at a table at the front, would drill down on a single theme. Gattegno demanded that we work on ourselves in the moment, and this working on oneself in the moment became the pre-eminent tool for learning and for studying learning; referring to books that others might not have read was verboten, as it would put people on unequal footing.

Several things struck me about those experiences; first, how clairvoyant Gattegno was. His responses were often incomprehensible in the moment, and minutes or hours later his point would suddenly become brilliantly clear. It was as if he could see around corners. Second, how fully people gave themselves to the tasks Gattegno set. That kind of intense intellectual work created an amazing intimacy: I remember one Saturday afternoon looking up and around with a feeling of such love for my seminar buddies, and thinking I would like nothing better than the assurance that they would all attend my funeral. Third, how clear and prepared I would be on Monday morning when I went back to my students. After the intense listening of the weekend, I would be fully charged and aware of the "other(s)" in my classroom, highly attuned to them, and to staying out of the way of their learning.

One of the most moving awareness seminars was the one Gattegno held on the learning of babies, perhaps just after he had written *Universe of Babies*. I remember thinking that day how much I had missed about babies' cognitive activity and feeling sad almost to the point of tears about it. Here I was, cooing and burying my face in their soft downy curls while they were busy unpacking the mysteries of our language and teaching themselves everything they would need to know to progress into toddlerhood and beyond.

What I prize most from Gattegno is his belief in the inherent genius of human beings. It is a belief that I have tried to make the foundation of my own practice as an educator. It is what has kept me in the field, and has kept teaching fascinating.

> What I prize most from Gattegno is his belief in the inherent genius of human beings. It is a belief that I have tried to make the foundation of my own practice as an educator. It is what has kept me in the field, and has kept teaching fascinating.

It is amazing that someone with whom I spent relatively little time has had such a profound influence on my thinking for over 40 years. I never worked for Gattegno, never taught for him, was never a consultant in his organization, yet throughout my professional life, whether I was in a setting that was trying to use Gattegno's approach of subordinating teaching to learning or not, I have tried to stay with the practice and the belief in human capability. His approach became one I worked to learn, and then to practice, and then to promulgate. In graduate school I was impressive whenever I offered any of his ideas; as a new professor I astonished the unflappable by promoting his approach. In any administrative position I held, I tried to inject his philosophy into the professional development offerings. I measured every "great man" and "great woman" I met against Dr. G, and though many were entertaining, thoughtful, even brilliant, no one ever measured up. The mental challenges they set were nothing compared to those of Dr. Gattegno's awareness seminars long ago.

§

> "We are retaining systems and do not need to stress memorization as much as most teachers do. We hold better in our minds what we meet with awareness."
>
> - Dr. Caleb Gattegno

The Common Sense of Teaching Foreign Languages, Second Edition (2010), page 3.

A student learning using the original Numbers in Color math set. (Educational Solutions file photo.)

How Staying With a Question Pays Off

Maria Gagliardo

For 30 years, until 2004, I taught Spanish language and Latin American literature at Purchase College, SUNY. In everything I taught, I was guided by what for me are the two most important teachings of Dr. Gattegno, since they summarize a great deal of his educational philosophy:

- Only awareness is educable.
- Do not prepare a lesson, prepare yourself.

Applying these two concepts to the teaching of literature at the college level was my challenge, which I met with some success.

The first time I taught a college literature class, I realized that my most important job was to educate the students' awareness on the subject and that, to attempt to do that, I had to work on my own awareness of literature. I decided to transfer the educational philosophy behind the Silent Way and Words in Color to this new experience, putting to work what I had learned in so many seminars conducted by Dr. Gattegno at Educational Solutions in the '70s and '80s.

I started by posing a number of questions to myself, not aiming at getting the "right" answers but, instead, working on them through new questions which, in turn, would begin to create in me a state of peace; the process of continuous inquiry is so different from the emptiness of "right" dead-end answers. In 1975, in his introduction to the booklet on Leo Color, Dr. Gattegno asked important questions on reading. Two among them were especially helpful to me in developing my own questions: "What do we do when we read with different purposes?" and "How do we relate to poetry or to the sacred books?"

Equally helpful were, among others, the sections on Skills and on Understanding in Chapter 3 of *The Science of Education*. The difference between acquiring skills and working on understanding, which these sections make evident, helped me organize my thoughts and see more clearly what I needed to do for my students.

When I met that first literature course, I found out very soon that some of my students came with excellent reading skills, while others were but competent decoders and needed to become aware of themselves as readers. That is, as people who can make sense of what they read and reflect upon it, and who can draw conclusions related to the work and to its author, and feel comfortable interacting with both. Thus, I would ask my students some questions on which I had worked first, such as: What is literature? Do I know what the word means, or am I assuming that I know? If I am assuming, what is my assumption based on? Is literature fiction? Is it fantasy? Are they different? Is literature about reality? When is writing about reality different from reporting reality? If I collect information about a person and write it down, is the result a form of literature? What is a novel, a short story, an essay? How are they different from each other? What happens to me when I read? Do I read photographically and then think about what I read? Or do I think as I read? Do I "see" what the writer describes? Could I draw pictures of what I read?

Discussing questions such as these always results in a conversation about literature as a concept, as a creative process, as a task that requires purpose, discipline, mental, spiritual, and physical work. This discussion may take one class or several, depending on what the students bring with them. Once they are comfortable with this way of working on themselves and of staying with the question under consideration before rushing to give an answer, I would introduce a short piece of literature, generally a poem or a very short story, for example, the poem "Spinoza" by Jorge Luis Borges.

> Las traslúcidas manos del judío
> Labran en la penumbra los cristales
> Y la tarde que muere es miedo y frío,
> (Las tardes a las tardes son iguales.)
> Las manos y el espacio de jacinto
> Que palidece en el confín del Ghetto
> Casi no existen para el hombre quieto
> Que está soñando un claro laberinto.
> No lo turba la fama, ese reflejo
> De sueños en el sueño de otro espejo,
> Ni el temeroso amor de las doncellas.
> Libre de la metáfora y del mito
> Labra un arduo cristal: el infinito
> Mapa de Aquel que es todas Sus estrellas.

The title "Spinoza" was intriguing for students with little background in philosophy or the history of philosophy. Whose name was this? Was he a friend of the author, a famous person, a legendary hero? I would ask the students to leave it aside for a while and see if we could get some information on this person through reading the poem. First I asked them to read the poem silently and make a mental note of the punctuation marks. How were they connected to reading and understanding the poem? What is their function in each case? Since punctuation marks are the graphic representation of pauses and intonation in the spoken language, through this exercise the students were able to read the poem with the correct rhythm and melody, which helped them to understand a great deal more than they thought they did at first. My Silent Way training was instrumental at this stage.

As we went on reading the poem, the students realized that some research was required to make full sense of it. At this point their curiosity was fully awakened. By the third class on the poem, just by inquiring on their own on the implicated meaning of some of the words chosen by Borges to describe Spinoza, they could identify allusions and metaphors in the poem. They also learned who this philosopher was, when and where he lived, how he earned his living and what his relationship to women and to philosophy was. As a by-product, they also learned something about the philosophical wars of the 16th century. But the most important thing they learned, and the one that related directly with the course, was to appreciate the masterful and beautifully poetic use of language for which Borges is considered a great 20th century poet. They also learned that in poetry, as in many other things, beauty and economy can work together to great advantage.

For many years now I have thought that Borges and Dr. Gattegno were kindred souls in understanding the role of silence in creative work. One carefully chosen word can transmit more that many verses or wordy paragraphs. What Dr. Gattegno did with learners, Borges did with readers: he took what they brought with them into account. This too was what my students learned from the poem presented to them through my version of Dr. Gattegno's approach to educating awareness. All this was achieved through working on a very short poem using, as best I could, Dr. Gattegno's philosophy of education and teaching techniques. My role throughout was to speak only when truly needed, and to pose questions for discussion which would mobilize the students to work on themselves and on the material presented to them. With this approach, a literature course becomes an experience in educating awareness, which results in a better understanding of what is involved in reading and in appreciating literature.

As Dr. Gattegno used to say, "You don't need the rods or the charts to teach this way." I am convinced that he meant that any subject can be taught successfully using his educational philosophy. And he was right. §

Je n'imagine pas enseigner le français autrement

Maritée Juge

De la pédagogie Gattegno, j'ai une expérience assez courte, un an et demi à peine. Aussi mon témoignage ne sera-t-il pas celui de quelqu'un qui peut puiser dans sa pratique comme dans une réserve sans fond. Plutôt, j'aimerais parler de ces intuitions de base qui ont fait que j'ai naturellement embrassé cette approche. Un an et demi après, qu'en est-il de la promesse contenue dans la démarche de Caleb Gattegno ? Mes élèves y trouvent-ils leur compte ? Et moi ?....

Je ne suis pas enseignante de formation. Je viens du montage de cinéma, du journalisme et de la communication. Un peu touche à tout. Pourtant, lorsque Claudie Gattegno, m'a demandé pourquoi j'avais choisi d'enseigner le français à des étrangers, et pourquoi j'avais opté pour la pédagogie Gattegno, la connexion s'est aussitôt établie : quand on monte un film, on travaille sur deux tableaux à la fois, l'allusif et la précision. Il s'agit de guider le spectateur avec subtilité, de façon à ce qu'il suive commodément l'intrigue, mais en laissant suffisamment de champ à son imagination. C'est le paradoxe du spectateur d'être à la fois extrêmement passif et extrêmement actif, et il y a tout lieu de croire que plus un film est réussi et plus le spectateur devient actif, comme s'il fabriquait lui-même l'histoire … Même chose pour le journalisme : un bon article se doit d'être documenté, intelligent mais surtout pas ennuyeux.. De sorte qu'il va « titiller » le lecteur, lui offrir un espace personnel de réflexion et l'opportunité de rebondir vers des sujets connexes.

Même chose pour l'enseignement qui peut être assommant et induire beaucoup de passivité…ou inversement.

C'est cet « inversement » qui m'a plu dans l'approche Gattegno : la latitude offerte à l'élève de chercher et de découvrir par lui-même conjuguée à un guidage fin et à des outils formidablement bien pensés. En somme, la liberté jointe à l'efficacité, la créativité à la rigueur, l'intelligence à l'humanité profonde.

Tout cela est évidemment difficile à mettre en œuvre.

Je donne des cours de français à des jeunes de 15 à 18 ans, qui débarquent des quatre coins du monde (Afghanistan, Turquie, Tchétchènie, Géorgie, Algérie, Maroc…) pour se construire un avenir en France, car chez eux, c'est devenu impossible. Il y a aussi un groupe d'adultes, essentiellement des ressortissants de l'Union Européenne (Bulgares, Italiens, Lettons, Roumains…), qui sont là pour les mêmes raisons. Tous n'ont évidemment pas la même histoire, le même niveau d'études, ni le même rapport à l'école. Certains en gardent un bon souvenir, d'autres s'en méfient comme de la peste, d'autres encore, des Africains surtout, n'y sont jamais allés. Mais tous aiment apprendre. Et voilà où la pédagogie Gattegno les met sur pied d'égalité : ensemble ils cherchent, et comme il leur est demandé d'emprunter des chemins qui ne sont pas ceux de l'enseignement classique, ce ne sont pas forcément les plus lettrés qui trouvent les premiers…

J'utilise, comme tout le monde le « tableau des couleurs » et le « Fidel », géniales trouvailles de Caleb Gattegno en ce qui concerne l'enseignement des langues. Le premier représente toute les sons de la langue française sous forme de rectangles colorés. Le deuxième donne, pour chaque son, toutes les orthographes possibles. Ce sont des outils d'une rare efficacité en même temps que de puissants instruments de cohésion au sein de la classe.

J'ai longtemps hésité à affiché le Fidel, de peur de rebuter les élèves. A présent, je ne saurai m'en passer. La difficulté propre du français, y apparaît clairement : c'est l'écrit, puisque dans notre langue, ce qu'on écrit est toujours beaucoup plus compliqué que ce qu'on prononce. Et bien, au lieu de les rebuter, le Fidel les a captivés et il faut voir leur dextérité à passer de l'oral à l'écrit et vice-versa. Evidemment, leurs hypothèses ne sont pas toujours justes, mais l'important, c'est que l'esprit soit en mouvement – et le corps aussi, car ils se bousculent souvent pour aller pointer des mots ou des phrases !

le mot en entier. Puis il est passé au Fidel, où il a correctement orthographié « vendredi » avant de l'écrire au marqueur sur le tableau blanc. Et voilà. C'était un peu long mais, ce faisant, Mamadou a intégré des processus logiques fondamentaux. Quant aux autres, bien plus aguerris que lui, ils ont suivi ses pas avec une attention étonnante. Dans l'affaire, ils étaient acteurs autant que lui.

Rendre intéressantes des choses simples, claires des choses compliquées, tout en s'autorisant à tirer des bords vers des terrains de jeu moins évidents que la

> Rendre intéressantes des choses simples, claires des choses compliquées, tout en s'autorisant à tirer des bords vers des terrains de jeu moins évidents que la grammaire et le vocabulaire, c'est le challenge de cette approche.

Un exemple. Il y a quelques jours, je demande à Mamadou, un jeune Guinéen de 17 ans, de nous dire la date Réponse : vendredi 18 février 2011,. A l'oral, c'est parfait. Il se lève pour écrire au tableau ce qu'il vient d'énoncer, et là ça se gâte : « vendredi » devient « frndi ». Il faut savoir que Mamadou est analphabète : il lit et il écrit pour la première fois de sa vie, ici en France, dans une langue qui lui était, il y a peu, totalement inconnue. Qu'aurions-nous fait dans une configuration plus classique ? Probablement qu'un élève ou moi-même aurait écrit correctement « vendredi » au tableau, Mamadou aurait pris bonne note (?) et on serait passé au sujet suivant. Que s'est-il passé ce vendredi ? J'ai demandé à Mamadou de taper le mot dans ses mains. Il a tapé trois fois : « ven-dre-di ». Il a ensuite pointé sur le tableau des couleurs les trois rectangles correspondant aux voyelles sonores « en », « e », « i ». Puis il a pointé

grammaire et le vocabulaire, c'est le challenge de cette approche. Je me souviens qu'en fin de formation, Claudie Gattegno nous avait demandé de décliner toute une palette d'émotions sur une dizaine de mots. Histoire de donner vie à ce que nous disions. Et nous y avions trouvé grand plaisir.

Cependant, tout n'est pas toujours rose. Il y a des moments de flottement, voire d'égarement qui sont probablement des expériences désagréables partagées par tous les enseignants du monde, quelle que soit la méthode utilisée, et qui demandent d'incessants réajustements.

Ceci dit, je voudrais attirer l'attention sur le fait que la pédagogie Gattegno a l'immense intérêt de « créer du lien » entre les élèves - et entre les élèves et le professeur. Probablement parce qu'elle n'est pas conventionnelle et laisse donc libre cours à la vie. §

One of the seminars Dr. G led in the late '70s was called Towards a Theory of Human Relativity. Several years later, when this seminar was transcribed and published, it came out with the same title. He asked me, "Why did you use that title for the publication?" I told him, "That was the title you announced for the seminar!" "Yes, but that title was before the seminar took place. During the seminar, we were able to construct the theory, so the title of the publication should have been A Theory of Human Relativity. This incident confirmed my understanding of what he was doing during these seminars: he was honing his theories and stretching them to the limit, using the participants as a sounding board. The role of our group in France was to be as critical as possible. I saw over the years the results of this work. He would give the seminar, and a few months later, a newsletter or a book on the topic would appear.

- Dr. Roslyn Young

Dr. Roslyn Young (left), Dr. Gattegno, and colleagues at an informal gathering in Besançon, France, in the 1980s. (Photo courtesy of R. Young.)

A Mother and Daughter Story

Rachel Adams Goertel and Carole Adams

RACHEL

The Silent Way has the potential to raise consciousness in the lives of language teachers and learners worldwide. My excursion into the pedagogy of the Silent Way began 15 years ago, and Gattegno's Silent Way continues to be a guiding force in my approach to language teaching. The pedagogical implications of a method that grasps the essence of learning, discovery, and awareness is provocative. My journey commenced, quite appropriately, with the journey of my mother. Her personal relationship with Caleb Gattegno proved to be pivotal in my teaching philosophy.

CAROLE

There was about Caleb Gattegno what there is about some men — the power of presence: a face-to-face enigma, élan, charisma, simpatico. One of those words that expresses a quality you can't quite articulate, like an added dimension sticking to your tongue when you can't really say why you've become a disciple, a convert, or even just a schoolgirl with a crush. Some actors have had it, especially when they've embodied and emboldened a strong character: Brando in Streetcar; Olivier in anything. Churchill most certainly had it; he would walk into a room, talk would stop, and you could hear silence. Of course Gandhi (another teacher) possessed that power of presence. Crowds followed him, sat at his feet and took not only to heart, but into action his words of peaceful protest. I can't quite wrap my words around what it was about Dr. Gattegno that captivated and inspired people. Certainly the quality of his work, the depth of his knowledge, and his devotion to teachers like me were the foundation upon which the character and legend of the man was laid.

The beginning is always an easy place to start, but in all honesty I can't remember when I first heard of Caleb Gattegno. I do remember when his reputation engaged my imagination with intense interest. I was a graduate student at the School for International Training (SIT) in Vermont in the '80s. As part of our curriculum, Dr. Gattegno was scheduled to present a workshop. Rumors of what a Gattegno presentation entailed started circulating long before he arrived. Curiosity, anticipation, and excitement overtook the campus. We listened to those who knew him, had worked with him, or who had studied under him: there was great respect harnessed with trepidation, awe, and excited anticipation.

The day came. We had a distant glimpse of him across campus in the company of our professors. They were climbing a hill in the picturesque Vermont countryside. That night when we all came together, what had been said was true: he was like no one else. There was silence, time stopped, and our world in that room became Gattegno-centric. Perhaps we were there two hours, three, four — I'm not sure, but a framework constructed within me during that short period would stay the rest of my life to be the scaffolding for the making of a teacher. I would always see my students, myself, and the task at hand in a different light.

After I left SIT and heard that Dr. Gattegno was very ill and certainly his coming teaching days would be few, I moved quickly to register in one of his workshops in New York City. I had laughed with delight when I heard that the name of his school was Educational Solutions because I thought how badly teachers all needed an educational solution for the problems we faced in the classroom. When I called to register, a man answered. As we talked I realized that it was Dr. Gattegno himself and I would see, as time unfolded, that this was the way he ran his school. He was available. At the end of every call to Educational Solutions, Dr. Gattegno would question me personally. This time, he offered advice. I took it, as I would in future phone calls. In discussing

(Adams and Adams Goertel Cont'd.)

an inexpensive place to stay during his workshop, he said, "The Y has always been good to us." So, I booked a room at the Westside Y on 63rd Street.

These vignettes of phone calls remain fondly in my mind. Often I'd phone for items: a larger rod set, a pointer, a small word chart, and so on. Never did I leave the phone without Dr. Gattegno asking about my classes. Once I complained about a class I was teaching in rural, upstate New York: a one-room, three-hour, multilevel class with too many students. He openly listened to my further concerns: the class was multilingual — I had a large number of native Algonquians from Canada who spoke some French and a dialect of Ojibwa. They were coming to work at a local mink farm only during pelting season thus making it even harder to be successful with them. After intently listening, he responded, "I wish that were my class," a response that startled me. He took time to give me some pointers and to allow his enthusiasm to pass through the phone lines. I returned to my class deeply committed.

During another phone order, to encourage my efforts in acquiring a second language, Dr. Gattegno recounted a story of his racing up the stairs of an apartment house and greeting someone at the door in Basque, then up a flight offering another greeting in Spanish, and farther up the stairs extending another good-day in French. His point was it would be easier for me had I'd grown up speaking a number of languages, but I should persevere.

On another occasion, again on the phone, Dr. Gattegno asked me about my teaching. I told him I was unsure of myself when teaching with the Fidel Charts. His response was, "You must not be afraid to fail." His words and knowing how error is viewed in the Silent Way gave me the courage to fail and, with that, the power to succeed, sometimes.

RACHEL

"The Y?" I asked, incredulous. "We're going to New York City and staying at the Y?"

"Dr. Gattegno turned me on to it years ago. If it's good enough for Gattegno, it's good enough for us," replied my mother, whose footsteps I had followed to SIT for my Master's in Teaching and a career in ESOL.

It was the new millennium. We were headed for Columbia University where, coincidentally, we had both landed an interview for teaching an online ESL business program. Dr. Gattegno remained a guiding force in my mother's life and consequently, in mine too. In graduate school, by the time I was studying the Silent Way, the great master had passed away. I watched grainy videos of him, while in my mind, I vicariously experienced my mother's numerous personal interactions with the legend. I had even followed her to Besançon, France, where she studied French the Silent Way. Gattegno and his unique method had won my mother over and soon had me in his grasp.

Admittedly, I was hesitant to implement the Silent Way in my classroom, concerned I'd be challenged for using an approach that appeared nonsensical to some. I was an ESOL teacher in an elementary school in rural New York State. I had a class of about 12 students with four different languages, ages five through 10. I had nothing to lose, as these students were poor, minority, and had no support services for their native languages. Gattegno's adage rang clear in the back of my mind and was pressing forward every day: "I don't teach. I let them learn." I pulled out the Cuisenaire Rods my mother had given me and implemented the strategies I had learned bolstered by the enthusiasm of my mother's beliefs and Gattegno's guiding presence. The principal believed I was brainless, my colleagues thought I was archaic, and the parents thought I was a playmate, but my students thought I was wonderful. They eagerly engaged in the manipulation of the Cuisenaire Rods delighted as they forged through in a language that had been elusive. I smiled and knew the relationship my mother had forged with Caleb Gattegno had just been genuinely extended through me.

RACHEL & CAROLE

We remain confident about the future of language education for the linguistically and culturally diverse students seeking communicative competence. Methods such as Gattegno's Silent Way embody the essence of language acquisition: awareness and the belief that teaching is subordinate to learning. As teachers, if we pass on the legacy of Gattegno's ideals, others can effectively teach without uttering a word and learners can raise their voices in multilingual celebration.

The Summer with Dr. G

Jim Reed

I must have been 15 when I first met Caleb Gattegno. It was my first time abroad, a three-week holiday which he led at a country center near the Swiss town of Aarau. A teacher from my school took half a dozen of us on this educational trip. The other participants were French. We traveled via Paris, having a first experience of foreign food and wine. Garlic in the meat, garlic pervasive in the metro. That was 1952. In the two following years, I went on similar trips, one to southern Germany, the other to three centers in Belgium, Holland and the German Westerwald, always with international groups. It was particularly important at a time still so close to the Second Word War to be meeting and making friendships with Germans. The Gattegno daughters Alma and Lola always came along; on this last trip, Alma brought a fellow first-year student, Ann, from University College London, whom I have been married to now for 50 years.

All these holidays followed a similar pattern: we explored the immediate surroundings, had trips further afield, and – especially memorable – afternoon discussions which Dr. G chaired, asking some basic question that probed our understanding and attitudes to life. He was a born teacher. Why else would he have been running yet more educational courses in his free vacation time from the London University Institute of Education? I had some fine teachers at my school, but Dr. G was something different again. What sticks in my mind is not any one particular subject, but his style and method. He would sit with us all round him, his posture upright and slightly formal, speaking clearly and fluently with his still foreign accent. His approach was often teasing, provocative, designed to unsettle your assumptions and prejudices, very much the Socratic Method; serious but with an underlying humor, a sparkle of irony behind his glasses. Sometimes he would put you in the middle of the circle and get you to say something, answer some question, and then suggest something you'd revealed about yourself, your character, your outlook. Once he asked us to name some hope or ambition for the future. As already a lover of languages and literature, I said (perhaps not quite in these words) that I hoped one day to find a writer with a really convincing vision of life. I haven't been disappointed: Montaigne, Goethe, Kant, etc.

> "The most precious thing we had was self-awareness, the capacity to think about ourselves and what we were doing in a detached way, and that we should never let go of it."

Occasionally we rebelled – against the discipline of the timetable, or against some strange foreign food. To which his answer was always, with a smiling but firm intolerance of our intolerance, "Eat it and enjoy it!"

One other more serious thing sticks in my memory of what he said to us in those discussions: that the most precious thing we had was self-awareness, the capacity to think about ourselves and what we were doing in a detached way, and that we should never let go of it.

For all his teasing, he had a profound benevolent interest in young people, what they are made of, and what they might become. So it was entirely consistent, and only at first sight a surprise, when he became involved in a company bringing to Britain the revolutionary Cuisenaire Rods system for teaching mathematics in clear tangible form to the very young (during our Belgian week, we actually observed Georges Cuisenaire working with children too young, one would have thought, for the operations he was getting them to perform), and later promulgating equally imaginative new ideas of language-learning.

Caleb Gattegno aujourd'hui : quelques réflexions

Maurice Laurent

Depuis plus de dix ans, je n'enseigne plus, mais je suis encore et toujours en train d'essayer de promouvoir les idées et les solutions pédagogiques qu'un homme a commencé à proposer il y a plus d'un demi-siècle. Pourquoi ?

1. Le fait est que les progrès accomplis depuis plusieurs décennies en pédagogie sont si peu significatifs que les propositions de C. Gattegno demeurent pleinement pertinentes et porteuses d'espoir.

Chacun sait que les différentes enquêtes internationales comme Pisa ou les tests appliqués à tous les élèves dans les institutions scolaires montrent la pauvreté des résultats obtenus par beaucoup d'entre eux, en particulier dans les domaines essentiels de la lecture, de l'expression orale et écrite et des bases élémentaires en mathématiques.

Chacun peut constater le désarroi et la souffrance de quantité d'élèves en échec scolaire. Ils ont perdu confiance en eux et tout espoir en leur avenir : les comportements sociaux inadéquats et de plus en plus fréquents en témoignent.

N'importe qui est à même de reconnaître aussi que l'Ecole aggrave trop souvent la fracture sociale : la plupart des enfants des milieux défavorisés y échouent, parce qu'ils ne bénéficient pas d'un environnement qui puisse leur fournit en dehors de la classe l'aide nécessaire à leur réussite.

Or, des outils puissants existent, que C.G. a créés et/ou développés (La lecture en couleurs, Le Silentway, Les réglettes Cuisenaire, Les géoplans et les films mathématiques), mais qui ont encore trop peu droit de cité dans les milieux de l'éducation. Il convient donc de les faire connaître. De plus en plus de personnes s'y emploient un peu partout dans le monde, et ici, en France et en Suisse tout particulièrement.

Tous ces acteurs savent quel espoir représente la Subordination de l'Enseignement à l'Apprentissage, dont la pratique permet d'amener chaque élève à faire les prises de conscience nécessaires à tout apprentissage : si cette approche était étudiée, comprise et appliquée, l'Ecole pourrait conduire tout le monde à réussir les apprentissages fondamentaux et contribuerait à réduire en conséquence la fracture sociale dont souffrent de plus en plus nos sociétés dites évoluées.

Cet espoir n'est pas béat ; il trouve sa source dans le fait maintes fois démontré que l'utilisation correcte des outils existant permet aux maîtres des pratiques pédagogiques adaptées aux processus d'apprentissage, et aux élèves, respectés dans leur totalité et leur intégrité, de mettre en œuvre toutes leurs facultés pour apprendre, comme ils l'ont fait avant de fréquenter le système scolaire.

2. Un autre fait nous conduit aujourd'hui à vouloir faire connaître les travaux et les solutions de C.G. dans le domaine de l'éducation et nous amène à alimenter l'espoir que constituerait la mise œuvre de ses recherches : il est indéniable que ses intuitions, qui sont la base de son œuvre, n'ont jamais été prises en défaut par les avancées scientifiques réalisées depuis sa disparition. Trois exemples suffiront :

- Les résultats des travaux effectués en psychologie cognitive sur la conscience phonologique justifient largement les principes sur lesquels repose La lecture en couleurs (Voir en particulier : *Textes de base en psychologie, L'apprenti lecteur*, Delachaux et Niestlé 1989 : *Analyze segmentale et acquisition de la lecture*, Jesus Alegria & Jose Morais, *Conscience phonologique et acquisition de la langue écrite*, William E. Tunmer).
- Parmi les observations et les conclusions des chercheurs dans le même domaine, et qui s'appuient sur l'imagerie médicale, de nombreux faits déjà exposés par CG dans L'univers des Bébés (Voir en particulier : Les neurones de la

lecture, Stanislas Dehaene, Odile Jacob, 2007) se voient confirmés.
- L'œuvre aboutie de C.G. dans le domaine des mathématiques, exposée dans La conscience de la mathématisation, ne s'oppose en rien aux découvertes des neurosciences aujourd'hui (Voir en particulier : La bosse des maths, S. Dehaene, Odile Jacob, 2003.)

Je m'en réjouis, mais n'en suis pas étonné. Celles et ceux qui comme moi ont largement côtoyé C.G. savent à quel point il imposait une rigueur scientifique extrême à la réflexion, à lui-même comme aux autres. Mais, en échange, il accordait à chaque participant, comme à lui-même, le statut de chercheur. Je forme le vœu que de plus en plus de maîtres voient dans l'avenir leurs élèves comme C.G. voyait les siens, et utilisent ses outils pour avoir avec eux un dialogue du même type. C'est possible puisque grâce à lui ils existent ! Il convient donc, pour marquer le 100ème anniversaire de sa naissance, de demeurer optimiste et de poursuivre patiemment le travail de fourmi qui est le nôtre. Et la maxime de Guillaume d'Orange, au sujet de laquelle C.G. nous avait un jour proposé de réfléchir, demeure aussi pertinente que ses travaux demeurent modernes : Il n'est pas nécessaire d'espérer pour entreprendre, ni de réussir pour persévérer ! §

Gattegno's teaching approach advocated the use of well-crafted pedagogical challenges. For example, starting with the situation shown above, students would be asked to sort the rods by length or by color.

An Experiment in Humanizing Education

Ann Crary Evans

In 1967, three demonstration school districts in community control were set up in New York City. One of these districts was the I.S. 201 Complex in central Harlem, composed of the brand new, state-of-the-art Intermediate School 201 and its four feeder elementary schools, of which P.S.133 was one. The impetus for this experimental project, to be funded by the Ford Foundation, came from pressure by black parents to organize and run their own schools after the city's plan to integrate the new I.S. 201 had not taken place. The push for community control of black schools had evolved from failed demands of parents for integrated, quality education, to demands for community control of schools. In New York City, these protests had started in the mid '60s as the civil rights movement moved north challenging de facto segregation which was the norm.

At the same time as the I.S. 201 Complex was taking shape, and entirely by chance, the Center for Urban Education was looking for a big city public school willing to participate in a program testing Caleb Gattegno's approach to the teaching of reading and math. Someone suggested P.S.133. The Governing Board of the new experimental demonstration district was more than happy to accept the fully-funded project which included in-service training for teachers, funds for materials, and full-time consultants on site. At the time, the Complex was caught up in political battles defending community control and pedagogy had taken a back seat. The new acting principal of P.S.133 was supportive of the program, so, quietly and smoothly, the Gattegno Approach to reading and math was introduced into grades 1, 2, and 3 at P.S.133.

The 13 or so participating teachers were paid to attend an intensive two-week orientation led by Dr. Gattegno, which took place at the Day School at the Church of the Heavenly Rest in August 1968. For various reasons, three or four teachers opted out. The school year started in the midst of a city-wide teachers strike led by the United Federation of Teachers (UFT) who were protesting the "firing" of nine teachers in the other major demonstration district of Oceanhill-Brownsville in Brooklyn. The teachers had not been fired, but had simply been reassigned by their new Governing Board to other schools. Except for a handful of teachers supporting the strike, all the teachers in the I.S. 201 Complex were on the job, and the Gattegno program was under way at P.S.133.

During the first year of the program, three full-time consultants – Dee Hinman, Guy Gattegno (Dr. Gattegno's nephew), and Michler Bishop – were assigned to the school. They worked tirelessly at the school all day every day, moving from classroom to classroom, guiding teachers and helping us to absorb this radical new way of working with children. Dee Hinman and Guy Gattegno continued at the school full-time for the next two years.

I had been teaching fourth grade for four years at P.S.133 prior to the fall of 1968. For my first year of teaching and my third, I was assigned the "bottom" class on the grade. The students in these classes came to me in September not reading, and left in June not reading. I had received a master's degree in elementary education from Columbia Teachers College in 1964. I quickly found that the courses I had taken at Teachers College were irrelevant at best. At the school I found out that teaching and learning were subordinated to the maintenance of discipline. One of the few comments I received from my principal during my first year was when he passed by the room and didn't hear a sound, "If you can get them quiet like that, there's hope for you," he said.

When Gattegno came into the school, I fought to move from the fourth grade to the third grade to

"A teaching approach now being tried across the country appears to be having dramatic results."

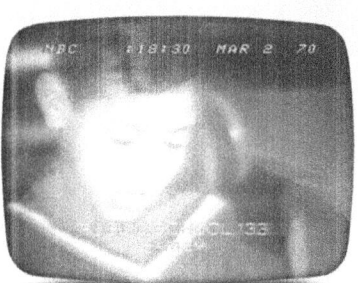
"Public School 133 - Harlem"

"Gattegno wants the teacher to stop telling the student everything and let the child figure things out for himself."

"[Gattegno's approach has] shown me what can be done."

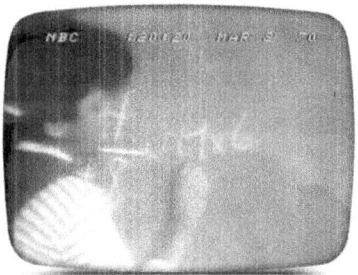
"There's never any question of 'can I learn this?' They know they can."

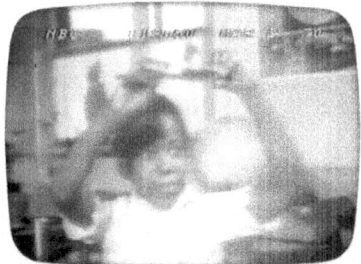
"Gattegno was a pioneer in the new math."

"Phil Brady - NBC News - New York"

Stills from "New Teaching Methods," a *Huntley Brinkley Report* news story from March 1970 discussing Dr. Gattegno's innovative approach to subordinating teaching to learning in a New York City public school.

participate in the program. How fortunate and relieved I felt to have this opportunity to become a teacher for the first time. Many of us came to feel that we were involved in a truly revolutionary educational experience with far-reaching implications and possibilities for the whole future of education.

The first few months were slow going, but by the end of the first year classrooms were filled with the Fidel, Word Charts, and the rods, and the Transformation Game was spilling over entire blackboards. There was an incredible feel in the air of excitement and possibility. We were experiencing a new way of working with children. And we were learning together at the same time – teachers and children discovering new links, new relationships, new confidence, and new independence. Everyone was changing, and this caused a fundamental change in the relationship between student and teacher. The relationship became closer and more human.

We were learning to start where we found each child and to build from there. We were made aware for the first time of the abilities and powers and gifts that children already "own" and bring to school. I remember a boy who was repeating third grade who, at the end of the year, could still not believe he was really reading because it just seemed too easy. After three years of failure, it just couldn't be possible that reading could be so easy. The same boy had the same experience with math.

Changes did not happen overnight. But it was with great anticipation that we started the second year eager to build on all that we had learned in the first. By the third year, other teachers asked to join the program. A kindergarten teacher, a fourth grade teacher, and teachers at I.S. 201 began using Gattegno Math or Words in Color. In the spring of the third year, citywide reading tests were given to the third grade. The results were clear proof of the success of the program. I wonder to this day how the city's school hierarchy failed to notice that here was a school where third graders were scoring at a tenth-grade reading level.

At the end of the three years, the principal of P.S.133 left to head a new school in the southeast Bronx where a Gattegno program was being set up in an open classroom environment. She took seven teachers from P.S.133 with her. The next year, seven more teachers left P.S.133 for other schools. I left to join Gattegno's staff as a reading consultant at Educational Solutions where I worked for three years. The principal who took over P.S.133 had not been involved with the Gattegno program and was not committed to continuing it.

Meanwhile the office at 12th St. and Broadway was a hub of activity with dozens of projects and seminars and workshops going on at once – a Silent Way workshop in Serbo-Croatian, Word Charts being prepared in Hindi, weekend seminars on whatever topic Dr. G was exploring at the time. In one project, Dr. G was involved in bringing together a group of western doctors and doctors of traditional Chinese medicine to discuss what each had to offer the other. It was at this time that many of us were introduced to Dr. John Shen, a master of Chinese medicine. He and Dr. G were the same age and Dr. G and a few of the rest of us continued to see him for many years until he returned to his native Shanghai in his early 90's.

At the same time as the Gattegno program was winding down at P.S.133, the demonstration districts in community control were being shut down. The UFT had won the battle. Community control was dead. A new structure of "decentralized" school boards dominated by the UFT took their place. The experiment in community control, however, will always be remembered as one brief, shining moment when the black and Hispanic community united to take charge of their own schools, and when education flourished as students and parents and teachers worked together in an atmosphere where the "humanization of education," as Dr. G called it, was taking place.

I disagree with those who dismiss the P.S.133 project as a failed project because it didn't last. I believe that it, too, will always remain as one brief, shining moment for those of us who were lucky enough to have passed through the school during those three years. I am convinced that the children who learned to read through Words in Color, and to do Gattegno Math, will carry with them always a knowledge of, and a confidence in, their own powers and abilities that they would not possess had they not encountered the genius and humanity of Dr. Gattegno and his work. All our lives are clearly richer for it.

Humanism in Language Teaching

Dr. Earl Stevick

Edited excerpts from *On Humanism in Language Teaching: Critical Perspectives.* (Oxford University Press, 1990.)

GATTEGNO'S SCIENCE OF EDUCATION AND THE HUMANISMS

It is not surprising that Caleb Gattegno's thinking holds great appeal for many people today. As one of his long-time students has put it:

> "'This descent of awareness into one person, and from him to others, and then to all, is another fact of awareness which is increasingly becoming collective every day.'"

"Dr. Gattegno [was] the only educator who constantly challenged me to be my best and then to become even better. His confidence in the learning powers he said we all possess was inspiring, and his ability to stimulate these powers in others was often uncanny."

In the practice of the leading exemplars of the Silent Way, students frequently have an experience of intense concentration, and of achieving, within a very short time, results that can only be described as amazing.

Gattegno was emphatically unwilling to be thought of as a philosopher. He variously described himself as a "scientist" and in private communication as just "a pedestrian technician," but one "who is not bound by any a priori, and is ready to alter radically his thinking if some evidence requires it." His aim was only "to put into circulation how I am educated by my contact with the challenges I encounter."

GATTEGNO'S VIEW OF HIMSELF

This leads us to the place Gattegno sees for himself in the process of collective evolution. In general, he points out that, "Some of us leave contributions in [various] realms, such as our works of art, our tools, our books, our organizations, etc."

Applying this to himself, he says that "I definitely knew myself as insignificant with respect to the totality of the universe. However . . . I could . . . gain some significance by making an original contribution to knowledge." His own original contribution is derived from his special gifts for self-observation and awareness: "For the moment only a small number of men have succeeded . . . [in acquiring] this knowledge of themselves as spiritual beings and as evolutionary energy . . ." Like any other evolutionary innovation, this knowledge can spread to succeeding generations:

"These are collective facts of awareness which had first to be found in individual awarenesses and made available to those others who would pay the price of obtaining them for themselves, and then were given to all for nothing, as a matter of course, as a birthright. This descent of awareness into *one person*, and from him to others, and then to all, is another fact of awareness which is increasingly becoming collective every day."

Gattegno appeared to view himself as such a person. Again: "The renewal of mankind takes place when someone finds in himself and his life a way of handling energy that integrates – by transcending it – what was available [before this discovery was made]. This vertical evolution has been at work . . . in the three realms of the cosmic, the vital, and the instinctual and many more times in the fourth realm of man. Today we are witnessing one more of these leaps."

At least in the Science of Education and at least today, Caleb Gattegno was such a 'someone.' He was first and foremost an educator, and:

"The educator . . . will not be discouraged by the traditional battles between the future which reaches out with its truth and the past which holds us back in the shape of organized bodies. He will make it known, loud and clear, that his experience assures him that he speaks of a sensible reality and that everyone can equally well assure himself of it. But if people refuse to follow him, *his* truth, which is *the* truth, will remain outside the awareness of those who refuse him credit and do not try in their turn to reach his level. All his actions will be based however on this truth . . ." [emphasis in original]

Gattegno commented a quarter of a century later: "I cannot consider that anyone will follow me. Certainly not at my request." [private communication]

OTHER PEOPLE'S VIEWS OF GATTEGNO

A number of people have said that Gattegno was 'overbearing,' even 'arrogant.' There is no denying that his manner in public appearances was often consistent with that description. There are two possible explanations here. The first might be that Gattegno simply lacked skill in interpersonal relations. After all, he was by his own description an introspective man, Kipling's 'cat that walked by himself,' unconcerned to please other people. Another guess is that Gattegno's sometimes abrasive public behavior was simply an expedient to ensure that people were both emotionally and intellectually involved with what he was doing in their presence. This second hypothesis receives support from two observations. One is that I have never heard of rude behavior in his face-to-face encounters with individuals who are not challenging his ideas. The other is that, in print, though he did not respond directly to criticism, neither did he reject it:

"I am, as a scientist, only concerned to speak about what I consider to be the truth in the matter. *My readers must judge me* mainly on whether I have departed from this imperative. [emphasis added]

"While I believe that [my] new approach has much to commend it, and while I very much hope that it will be given as fair a trial as my previous suggestions to colleagues in schools, I must point out that it is a one-man proposal based on one man's experience, *of necessity limited*, and that the most important contribution of this work is the opening of new vistas in education that should excite a new generation of people to investigate and *to experiment with what they find behind the doors that are now put ajar.*"

My personal experiences with Gattegno also support the second hypothesis. After reading the first draft of sections 6.1 to 6.6.1 of *On Humanism in Language Teaching*, Gattegno told me that, though my facts were essentially correct, he was disappointed that I had not provided my own 'creative reactions' to his thought [private communication]. I also know firsthand that he was quite gracious about accepting unsolicited criticism on matters not part of the substance of what he had written.

Here, then, is another myth-maker, but one who, as we have seen, explicitly invited criticism and testing. Quite possibly, on those occasions when he violated norms of polite society, he was simply continuing to exemplify, in ways that most people did not expect, the same teaching approach he was trying to convey to trainees: he was doing what he thought necessary in order to give his hearers a next to minimal something-to-work-with – something that would enable them to move themselves one step nearer to the goal they had in coming to his sessions, which was to find out what he had to contribute to their professional and personal resources.

Users of the Silent Way have varied greatly in their manner of dealing with others in the profession. Certainly some have shown 'the expulsive power of a new affection,' the zeal and intolerance that come naturally to those who are sure no one before them was right. But as with Counseling-Learning, we may hope that outsiders to this movement will not allow that to interfere either with practical or with intellectual investigation of the many potential values in Gattegno's work.

October 24, 1979

Dr. Earl Stevick
Foreign Service Institute
Department of State
Washington, D.C. 20520

Dear Earl:

I want to repeat that I was moved very deeply by your letter and the copy of the chapters of your new book which you cared to send me.

Rarely has anyone shown as much understanding of my work as you did. Although I contribute to the various fields of education I am considered an outsider because of my remaining aloof from the professional associations. You have found the door I use to show myself among colleagues in the various branches of education and accepted it as a legitimate entry. By your dedication to understanding what happened to me in this life, you gave yourself the right to present my work on language to our colleagues all over the world, and to help me to be understood by others. It is not the first time and it is the most thorough.

Shakti and I are most grateful. Although I do not hanker to be understood and did too little in that direction to complain that I am neglected, I feel gratified that there is someone of your stature who is prepared to do justice to my concentration on understanding knowing.

I am sending you texts of mine that you may not have, hoping they meet some of your questions still unresolved about my lighting of learning. Also a book (lent only) for the MY LIFE and MY WORK cooperation.

Yours,

Caleb Gattegno, Dr. Phil.
President

Letter from Dr. Gattegno to Dr. Earl Stevick, October 1979. (Reproduced courtesy of Dr. Stevick.)

The Silent Way in Japanese

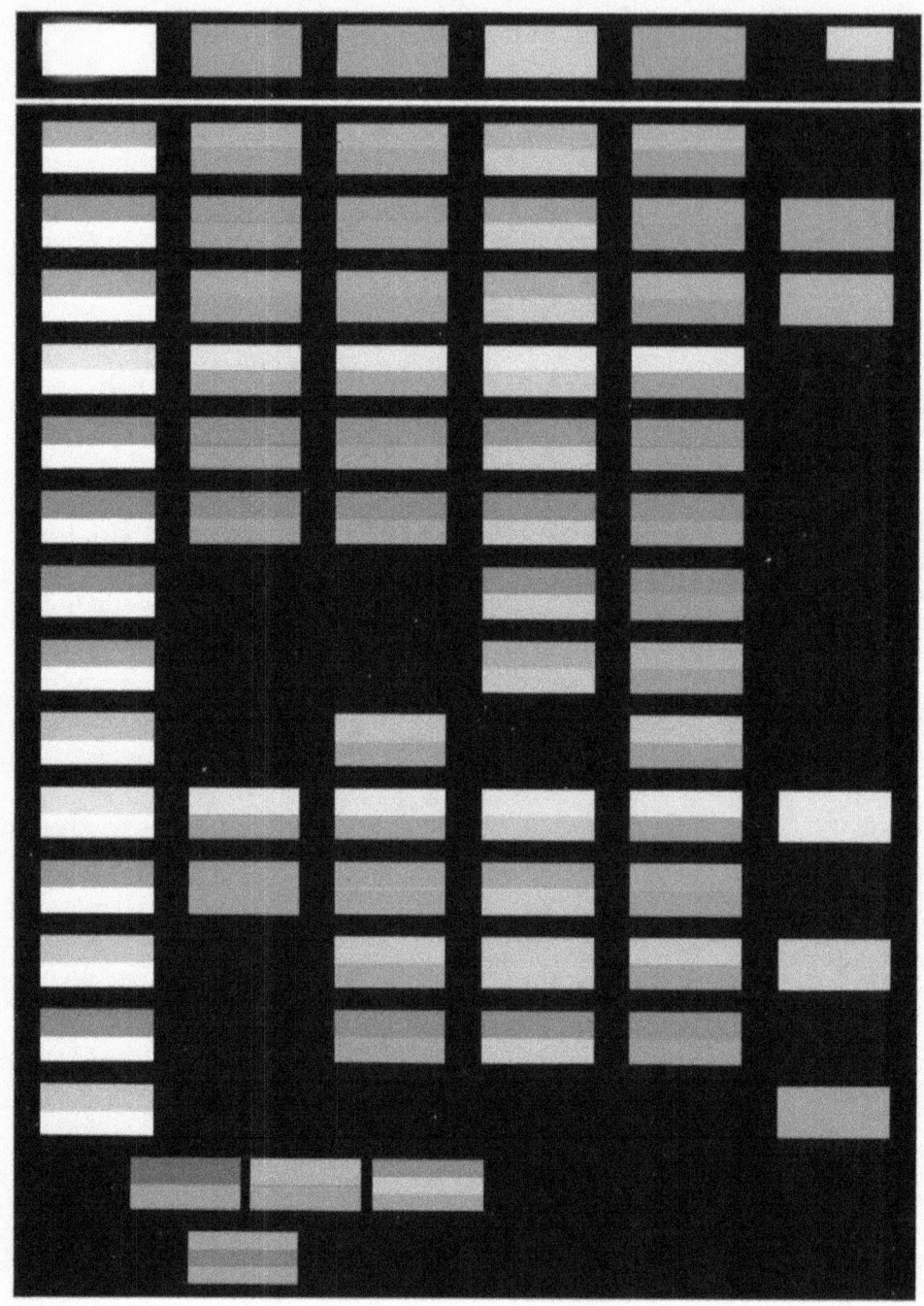

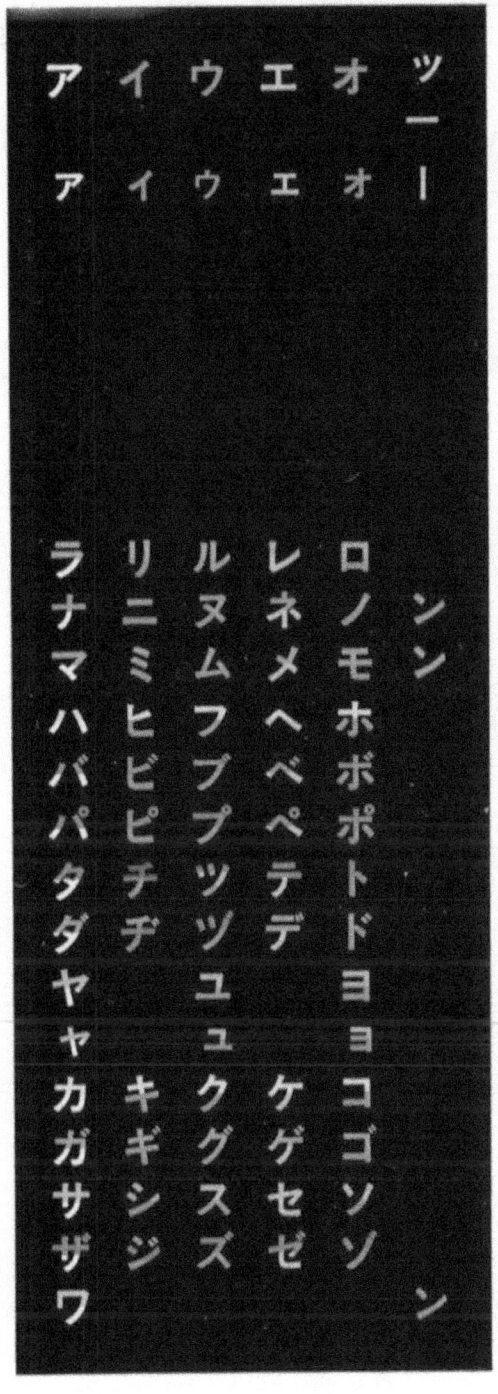
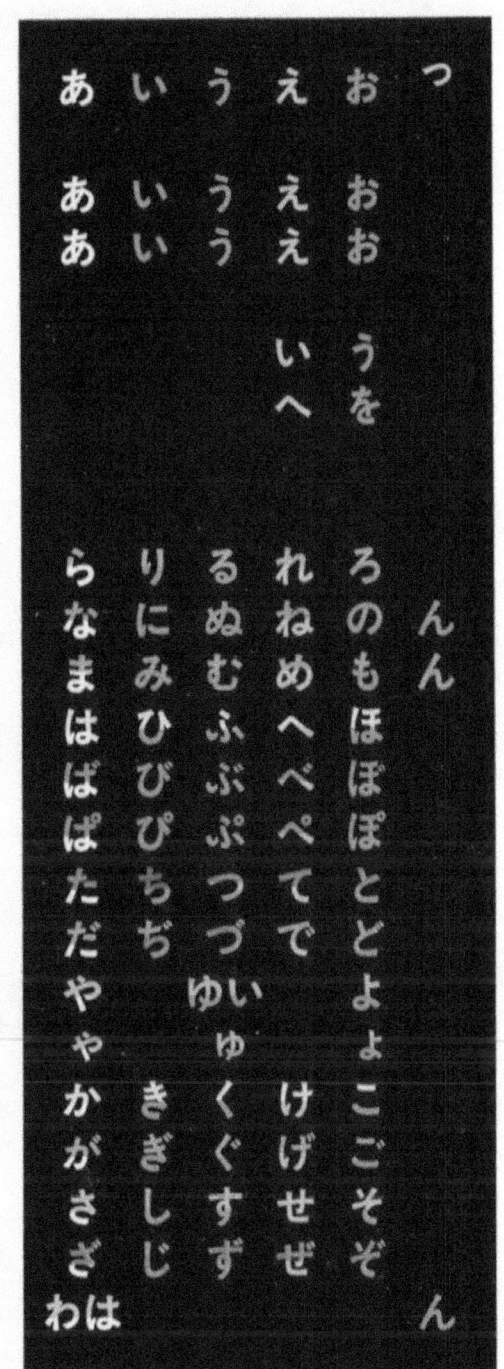

Above: Japanese Katakana Fidel # 1, 2, Japanese Hiragana Fidel # 1, 2. Printed in 1988 in Japan.
Left: Japanese Sound-Color Chart. Printed in 1988 in Japan.
©Educational Solutions Worldwide Inc.

Caleb Gattegno and the Well-Crafted Pedagogical Challenge

Eaton Donald

Significant, formative, defining experiences in one's life are easy to relive, as if the experiences happened just a moment prior, and yet can be paradoxically difficult to convey to others.

I was exposed to Gattegno's work when I was 27 years old, a full six years after his death. While living in Osaka, Japan, I had one of these formative, defining experiences learning Japanese from a remarkable group of teachers who were well versed in Gattegno's educational approach, and absolute master technicians in applying it. Almost everything they did was counter to all of my previous educational experiences. At no time did they attempt to "help" me or give me an answer. There was no homework, time pressure, or formalized tests. They did not lecture me or tell me how to do things. They embraced my mistakes. If they thought I could do better, they asked me, in a matter of fact way, to do so. This happened often enough, so I took it upon myself to try and do better before being asked. They pushed for perfection, but at all times respected my current level. I came to see that perfection for me was "that next level" and every time I achieved it, there was a new one to take the former's place. Even now, I believe I can do better. Not just with my Japanese language but with virtually all of my interests.

This experience marked a new beginning, which forever altered my understanding and relationship with my own successes and failures. I saw that on one level, both are simple forms of feedback from the involvements I undertook, but on another, I began to see the failures resident in each success as well as the successes that rode along in each failure. The more watchful, more perceptive, more aware person I was in the process of becoming welcomed both, such that the cultural judgments normally associated with success and failure became increasingly irrelevant while, paradoxically, my ability to judge was sharpened and honed.

I perceived vividly and brightly the mental machinery that powered my own evolution and learning at work. I got to know it better. I put it at the service of my curiosity and my need to know which felt a little like being able to fly after having lived gravity bound to the ground.

These teachers did something so unique that I feel a deep, personal responsibility to pass-on the essence of what they gave me.

It was the search for this "essence" that led me deeper into better understanding what, how, and why they did what they did, and directly into the ideas and proposals of Caleb Gattegno.

I started with Gattegno's books – *The Science of Education*, *The Mind Teaches the Brain*, and *The Universe of Babies* were the first followed over the next few years by virtually everything Gattegno had written in English. Many of these left me more confused after reading than before, since I found his writing did not give up its secrets easily.

It has now been more than 15 years since my study of Gattegno began and there is one word above all that strikes a chord with me and defines my understanding of his work. This word is 'challenge.' It is not that it appears that often, though it does, but certainly not as often as others like 'awareness,' or 'subordinating teaching to learning,' or the 'self,' or the 'psyche' etc. But for me, the concept of challenge is essential to understanding Gattegno. Why? Because in my own experience I have found that challenges induce the process of figuring out (i.e. they induce learning and the activation of awareness). Challenges serve to focus our actions, conceptions, trials, energy, attention, awareness etc. and bring out the most relevant aspects of our experience, to build upon and extend what we know. Challenges stimulate interest and nurture the need to know. Challenges set the right context for all of us to become producers of knowledge and skill rather than a consumer and memorizer of other people's knowledge, as is the norm in every school to which I have been exposed.

The exceptionally well-crafted pedagogical challenges, and the teaching materials which enabled their expression, together with the educators that helped guide the process when I learned to speak Japanese via Gattegno's Silent Way, helped me become progressively better (re-) acquainted with my ability to create my own knowledge and skill. I understand now that above all else, this was the essence of what these teachers gave me. I got to know and nurtured my capacity to perceive, to go slow, to exercise patience, to pose a question, to try it out, to analyze my mistakes, to take bold steps, and to watch myself and my awareness at work. I became a significantly better learner in part because I also became a significantly better and more conscious teacher of myself – I know my level and can propose challenges that are right for me and the situation.

It is my opinion that for educators, the magic is in finding the right challenge, and this is where their contribution is most significant. Should the challenge be too small, it may lead to very little figuring out, too big, an unwillingness to enter into it. The challenge must be just right. Just enough challenge to extend, and not too much to rebuff.

When I taught my six-year-old daughter to ride her bike, I put the challenge to her this way. First, I asked her to walk with me a few steps, and asked her if it was hard to balance. She said, "No it's easy." Next I told her that learning to ride a bike is like learning to walk, you must "find your balance." So we started and after a few attempts I asked her: "Think about what you just learned about your balance." Then I suggested we move from the grass, to the road. I gave her a little push and she rode about five meters, then about 10 and then 10 again, and again. Then I asked her: "Did you find your balance?" To which she replied: "Balancing is easy, stopping is hard," indicating that she was already on to the next challenge.

> "Challenges set the right context for all of us to become producers of knowledge and skill rather than a consumer and memorizer of other people's knowledge."

I agree with Gattegno when he says in the *Universe of Babies*, that "each of us has been the best teacher each of us has had." But it is also true that when you are lucky enough to have a teacher that presents well crafted challenges as their technique for subordinating teaching to learning, you might find yourself saying, "I feel like I did it (learned) myself, but that I could not have done it without you." Just as I did when I learned to speak Japanese with the laser focused challenges related to Gattegno's Silent Way for foreign languages.

My great fortune is the experience of being in a living laboratory of Gattegno's ideas set into motion, with me being both the subject and the observer. I have found the time spent trying to make sense of these ideas to be unusually rewarding. Lastly I feel an obligation to make the essence of Gattegno's work accessible to others, just as some have made it accessible to me. I feel optimistic and energized by this challenge which to date has been both an inspiring failure and success – exactly as it should be. §

A student using Words in Color for visual dictation, one of the many games and teaching techniques created by Dr. Gattegno. (*Del Norte Triplicate*, March 1971.)

> "Since knowing produces knowledge, but not the other way round, this book shows how everyone can be a producer rather than a consumer of mathematical knowledge."

— Dr. Caleb Gattegno

The Common Sense of Teaching Mathematics, Second Edition (2010), page 2.

Fractions Are Not Parts of Wholes

Dr. A. J. (Sandy) Dawson

It was a Friday night the fall of 1977 and I was headed to my first weekend workshop with Dr. Gattegno. I didn't know what to expect, even though I had been hanging around the Educational Solutions offices for a couple of months already.

Responding to encouragement from John Trivett and Jim McDowell, I had decided to take a sabbatical from my professional job in the Faculty of Education at Simon Fraser University in Vancouver, Canada, to go to New York and 'hang-out' in the Educational Solutions offices for a year. Dr. G had agreed to such an arrangement, making it clear that the company could not provide me with any financial support, but they would give me office space, and I would be welcome to attend all seminars and meetings. So on a cloudy, cold, rainy Friday afternoon there I was taking the RR subway line from Brooklyn Heights into the 14th Street exit to the 5th Avenue location of Educational Solutions. I was about to experience my first full weekend workshop with 'the man,' and I was more than a little nervous about what was to occur. The title of the seminar was Evolution and Memory.

The 50 or so people who signed up for the workshop gathered at 4:30 arranging themselves in a loose circle around the room. Subsequent to going around the circle so participants could introduce themselves, Dr. G talked at length for about an hour before taking a dinner break. He closed this first session of the workshop with the question: "Are you a rock?"

As I descended from the Educational Solutions offices in the building's creaky old elevator, I wondered what the hell kind of question was that? I had no idea how to even approach an answer, nor did I have any idea as to where Dr. G would go with such a question. Clearly, the question had an impact on me, because in my mind's eye I can still picture and hear Dr. G repeatedly saying, as his gaze swept around the circle making momentary eye-contact with each participant, "Are you a rock?"

As the weekend workshop progressed, I discovered that the "Are you a rock?" question was simply the first of a series of similar questions: "Are you an animal?" and, "Are you a plant?" were two other questions that followed during sessions on Saturday. Gradually, I came to the realization that Dr. G was leading us to an awareness of how each human being is all these things: a rock, an animal, a plant, and much more. Though reflection would lead one to recognize these aspects of all human beings, what Dr. G had done was to create a situation, an environment, where it was possible of participants to be 'aware that they were aware' of these human attributes. The knowledge of being all these things was always there, but perhaps not at a conscious level — an awareness of awareness level.

As the Saturday afternoon session was drawing to a close, Dr. G issued a challenge. He said that gaining an awareness takes only a slight shift of 'energy,' a small step. Going one step further to the level of being aware that one is aware takes another slight shift of 'energy.' The challenge he made for participants was to 'catch' themselves as that energy shift occurred, to notice when one moves from a state of not being aware to one of being aware, and, if possible, to capture what happened to cause the change of state from non-awareness to awareness. Dr. G contended that the amount of energy required to make such a shift was very small, that one could get 'a lot from a little' in terms of the energy needed to gain an awareness.

As I rode the RR train back to Brooklyn that Saturday afternoon, I tried to 'watch' how my body adjusted to the rocking-and-rolling of the subway car so that I could maintain my balance without hanging on to the overhead handholds: how my knees bent, how my center of gravity shifted, seemingly without conscious thought, and without a great deal of energy being expended. For the first time, I became aware of how my body 'automatically' adapted to the swinging and swaying of the subway train, and how little energy it took to accomplish this feat. Looking at the other train riders, I noted that some not only kept their balance without holding on to a pole or strap, they also managed to read the *NY Times*, turning pages, flipping from section to section, apparently oblivious to the constantly changing motion of the train. Of course, they were aware of that motion, but they weren't aware that they were aware, a subtle but important step in the education of one's own awareness.

I came away from the weekend with two insights that have been foundational to all the work I've done since. The first of these insights was the fact that learning — gaining an awareness — does not require a lot of energy *if* the essence of the concept or idea being taught is made available to learners in ways that they can grasp. The second of the insights follows from the first, namely, that identifying the essence of what is to be learnt is fundamental to effective teaching. 'Getting a lot from a little' was the phrase that Dr. G typically used to designate the first insight. The 'catching' of the essence has been called 'noticing' by John Mason. One has to 'note' the essential aspects of a concept before one can act upon and make use of the concept.

These insights are ones that I've since addressed in my professional role as a teacher educator of elementary school mathematics teachers. The workshop was the beginning of a 30+ year journey to educate my own awareness, and to seek out ways to assist others to educate their awareness.

One of the early elementary school mathematics situations in which I experienced this 'a lot from a little' was witnessing John Trivett work on fractions using the rods with a group of prospective elementary school teachers. John directed them to find a train of two rods both of the same color the length of which was equivalent to a single rod of another color. One participant offered, "Red is half of purple, light green is half of dark green, purple is half of brown, yellow is half of orange," at which point John said, "So where is the half? How can they all be a halves?" There was puzzlement among the group, because, some said, they are all halves but they are all different — how can this be, they queried.

> The challenge he made for participants was to 'catch' themselves as that energy shift occurred, to notice when one moves from a state of not being aware to one of being aware.

John had primed the participants for a new awareness, a new recognition, a new learning, which they had not quite reached. Jim McDowell often said that before learning there is often a time of confusion, and the participants in this situation were clearly experiencing confusion. After some spirited discussion among themselves in small groups, the spokesperson for one group said something like the following: "The half-ness is the result of a 'relationship' between the two rods of one color, on the one hand, and the rod of a single color, on the other hand. One rod is not 'part' of the other, but there is a relationship between the two." A second participant said, "Yeah, fractions are not parts of wholes. They are the relationship between one whole thing and another whole thing!" This was a new awareness for the speaker, and for many of the participants. The buzz went around the room: "Fractions are not parts of wholes — wow, maybe that's why kids have such trouble with fractions greater than one — what's the whole that a fraction greater than one could be a part of? Now, that's got to confuse kids." From my own experience, I can certainly agree with that statement.

I hope this example illustrates how for me at least, awarenesses gained from Dr. G have traveled well, and have provided opportunities for teachers of today to take different approaches to the teaching and learning of mathematics. §

A professional development workshop in Visible and Tangible Math conducted for teachers in Port au Prince, Haiti, in 2009. The workshop was sponsored by Elevating Learning Above Teaching (ELAT).

"Why Am I Doing This?"

Dr. Patrick Moran

It was 1973 in the auditorium at the School for International Training in Brattleboro, Vermont. I remember sitting in a circle in that large room filled with our MAT class and many outsiders, a Friday evening in the fall. Dr. Caleb Gattegno was sitting in the circle, in front of the blackboard. He had asked a question: "How do babies learn?" I think. He was eliciting answers from those with the courage to speak up. I say courage because whenever someone offered an answer, he would pick it apart, challenge the choice of words, point out flaws, and push people to say more. On the surface, it seemed very intimidating. In fact, a few of my classmates had already stormed out of the session. There was a moment of silence, and he looked at me.

Our eyes met, and he said, "You, sir, what do you have to say?"

I answered, very slowly, "It seems like you want people to pay attention to what they are saying."

"This is an observation," he answered, "can you say more? Why am I doing this?"

I understood his question, but I had no answer. I knew the answer was right in front of me, but I could not find it. I had no idea why he was asking everyone to pay attention to their words. "I don't know," I replied. Dr. Gattegno looked at me intently, and said, "Now you have something to work on."

This was my first experience with the power of a question, and of a response that put the responsibility on me to find the answer. I didn't know it at the time, but this exchange marked a transition for me, the beginning of a shift from teaching to learning. A shift from talking and entertaining to asking questions.

When I returned as a teacher in the MAT program at SIT in 1977, there were many more visits from Dr. Gattegno and in later years, Shakti Gattegno. Those of us who taught the language teaching methods course included the Silent Way, among other language teaching approaches. Dr. Gattegno would come to Brattleboro to do his Friday evening sessions followed by a full Saturday of demonstration lessons and discussions. I watched as he asked questions and studied the way that he responded to the students who answered. In my teaching, I modeled my own questions and responses on his way of working, though not with his intensity and rigor.

As the methods team, we purposefully used questions as a primary strategy for our work in teaching language teachers, as a means of evoking awareness. In the early years, we would jointly plan our lessons and articulate the questions to guide students through demonstration lessons, peer teaching, follow-up discussions, feedback, and ultimately, their own statements of teaching philosophy. We debated and discussed awareness. Some of us struggled mightily with Dr. Gattegno's writings on awareness. We did not find the same answers in his words. But we did manage to agree on the questions to ask and the need for students to find their own answers.

In the early 1980s, MAT faculty revised our MAT program handbook, which spelled out our educational philosophy and the organization of our competency statements for language teachers. We included awareness as an integral dimension in our program competency areas: knowledge, skills, attitudes, awareness. Since that time, educating awareness remains a central component of our training and education of language teachers.

Looking back now, I see how integral questions have become to my work with teachers.

When Dr. Gattegno said to me on that night when we first met, "Now you have something to work on," little did I know that I would spend my teaching career doing just that. §

Gattegno en Haïti

Raymonde Rocourt

J'avais toujours entendu parler du Dr. Caleb Gattegno par le biais de ma sœur aînée Gladys Doebeli-Héraux qui l'avait bien connu jusqu'à devenir Co-auteur du matériel d'enseignement de la « Lekti en koulè – Caleb Gattegno-Gladys Doebeli-Héraux ». C'est ainsi que lors de la visite de M. Gattegno en Haïti, je l'avais accueilli et hébergé dans ma maison, dans mon foyer le 4 janvier 1987.

C'était donc en 1987 que l'éminent professeur Caleb Gattegno voulut offrir son savoir au peuple haïtien alors analphabète à 90%. Il décida alors d'effectuer un voyage vers Haïti où il devait rencontrer le ministre de l'Éducation Nationale de l'époque pour lui présenter un projet de « Lecture » et du même coup, encourager la diffusion d'un apprentissage dynamique. Malheureusement pour les Haïtiens, le gouvernement en place à cette époque n'avait pas pour priorité d'éduquer cette nation voulant de préférence la garder non instruite. Moi-même, Haïtienne, j'en fus honteuse et bouleversée…

Ainsi, suite au refus du gouvernement haïtien de le recevoir, Dr. Caleb Gattegno a eu le désir d'apprendre à lire à ma servante en l'espace d'une semaine. Là commença mon émerveillement de cette personne inimaginable!

Une fois rentré à la maison, Dr. Gattegno transforma sa grande déception en un défi irréalisable à mes yeux. En un tour de mains, mon salon fut transformé en une vraie salle de classe ayant pour seule élève « Philocienne » et pour unique matériel didactique, les tableaux de lecture en couleurs. Les 26 tableaux du Français furent accrochés aux murs et hop ! les leçons de lecture commencèrent à un rythme progressif certes mais qui vite devint très rapide. En moyenne, Philocienne était en apprentissage pendant 7 à 8 leçons par jour. Des fois, Dr. Gattegno faisait davantage d'exercices avec elle selon la curiosité, l'enthousiasme, le plaisir de l'élève sur le visage de laquelle on pouvait constater et vivre « la soif d'apprendre ».

Ce « konbit » (terme créole employé pour exprimer l'idée d'une battue) comme on dit en Haïti prit fin dans une extase de toutes les parties concernées. Philocienne lisait partout au bout d'une semaine et elle pleura à chaudes larmes lors du départ du Dr. Gattegno. Lui, est parti de mon pays encore plus bouleversé de voir que les Haïtiens pourraient devenir d'excellents lecteurs au bout de 3 semaines à

> J'ai été épatée par sa façon de transmettre son savoir par la découverte en mettant de coté toute forme de répétition.

un mois, n'apprenant qu'à lire pendant ce temps…

Ce vécu a déclenché chez moi beaucoup d'admiration pour la personne que fut Dr. Caleb Gattegno. J'ai été épatée par sa façon de transmettre son savoir par la découverte en mettant de coté toute forme de répétition.

petits enfants possédaient un certain savoir dont je ne tenais nullement compte.

Gattegno m'a permis de découvrir les potentiels de chaque apprenant et il a déclenché en moi le désir d'accompagner ce petit être selon son rythme d'absorption des savoirs que j'ai à lui proposer.

> Gattegno m'a permis de découvrir les potentiels de chaque apprenant et il a déclenché en moi le désir d'accompagner ce petit être selon son rythme.

Au fils du temps, j'entendais Gladys, ma sœur, témoigner de plus en plus de ses propres expériences et de son parcours pédagogique fortement empreint de son vécu avec cet éminent psycho-pédagogue physicien. Petit à petit, je me suis intéressée à cette philosophie de l'apprentissage qui a changé radicalement ma propre perception de l'apprenant, celle de le regarder pour ce qu'il est et de l'accompagner dans son apprentissage.

Je viens d'une famille de pédagogues et c'est ainsi que depuis 1994, avec mes 2 sœurs aînées, nous avions conçu le projet d'ouvrir une école primaire « Gattegno » en Haïti. Ce projet devint réalité en septembre 1997. Notre institution scolaire nommée « Aux Alizes, la maison où l'on apprend » est une école primaire dans laquelle nous offrons un apprentissage dynamique par l'application des stratégies d'enseignement telles que proposées par Dr. Caleb Gattegno. Aux Alizés, nous utilisons aussi le matériel didactique créé par Dr. Caleb Gattegno pour l'enseignement de la « lecture » et « des mathématiques » avec les réglettes Cuisenaire comme support.

Honnêtement je peux dire que ma conception même de l'enseignement est toute autre aujourd'hui après 14 ans d'application du concept Gattegno en matière d'éducation. En effet, ma formation de base d'institutrice avait fait de moi quelqu'un qui ne tenait pas compte du vécu des enfants qui arrivaient en 1ere année primaire. Après 6 années de vie, ces

Il m'a aussi donné la possibilité d'éprouver de la joie à vivre l'acquisition du savoir avec mes apprenants et de constater combien gratifiant peut être un apprentissage solide, diffusé dans une ambiance de travail propice et stimulante.

Dr. Caleb Gattegno que j'ai eu la chance de connaitre, a su me montrer comment être en contrôle de soi face à des situations imprévues, surprenantes, décevantes et même déroutantes. De telles situations émergent souvent en salle de classe lorsque l'enseignant subordonne son savoir à l'apprentissage de l'apprenant !

Grâce aux techniques Gattegno, au sein de notre école, mes jeunes compatriotes haïtiens ont l'unique chance d'apprendre intelligemment à se connaitre eux-mêmes, de se découvrir capables d'accomplir avec succès une tâche donnée, de construire et d'entretenir leur propre estime et de s'approprier des manières d'être et des manières de faire qui les rendent des personnes autonomes, confiantes en leur devenir.

Dans un pays sous-développé comme Haïti, d'où je viens et où je réside ; un pays où les Haïtiens trainent dans « la négation », il est vital de promouvoir les techniques d'apprentissage Gattegno qui seules peuvent contribuer à une prise de conscience de soi pour un développement harmonieux des femmes et des hommes de cette nation. §

The Road to Inspired Teaching

Andrew Weiler

I came across the Silent Way when I first started teaching ESL in 1978, and I knew immediately that there was something special here, something out of the ordinary. I was not wrong.

The understandings and paradigm that gave birth to the Silent Way, as well as of course the approach itself, has enabled me to become the sort of teacher that I dreamt I could be. It has enabled me to transform every aspect of my teaching, so I now have the understanding, the tools, and the skills to provide the kind of input that enables my students to learn to be more – not just to get better improvements in their English, but also to become more powerful as learners.

I entered teaching having great hopes and aspirations built on the rhetoric of the alternative school movement in the '70s, but I soon fell to ground when I found that what I had at my disposal (a bunch of great sounding ideas) was patently inadequate for the tasks that faced me. What was available to me from any resource in those days was not enough to serve me or my students to get the results we wanted.

When I first attended a three-hour Silent Way class in Chinese, I was struck by the fact that the way I was being asked to work was so different, and yet refreshing. This experience prompted me to read Caleb Gattegno's writings, and from there I could see that his insights into learning had enabled him to create an approach to teaching that not only sounded good, but actually delivered the goods. He gave to those of us who knew that the thinking and practices in education were not providing results to the majority insights that have enabled a revolution within our classes.

His basic precept, coming out of his well-documented observations and analysis, that "only awareness is educable" is so profound that it turned my thinking upside down. It had me reassess everything that I did in my class and made me look more carefully at everything that I did with regards to my own learning.

> One of Dr. Gattegno's legacies has been to produce a system teachers can use to transform what they do, and continually improve on what they do.

The huge distinction with Gattegno's approach was the enormously deep vein and rich resources I could draw on. The approach was built on carefully laid foundations which could be used as a touchstone as I systematically reworked how I approached learning and teaching. The teaching tools which Gattegno created for the implementation of his new Silent Way approach educated both myself and my students alike, prompting my creativity, and encouraging attentiveness and creativity from my students as well. These tools in themselves continue to be an inspiration in my teaching, a characteristic that I have never noted in any other teaching tools that I have used.

Once I had done the preliminary work and study, carried out in my own classrooms in the main, I continually built on my understandings from these experiences, my unfolding awarenesses, and the experiences of my students. To this day, the process continues. Without the paradigm from which the Silent Way springs forth, none of this creative flowering would have been possible.

It's the common sense foundations which explain the nature of human learning, and a lot more than that, that gives the Silent Way of teaching foreign languages something which no other approach I have looked at comes close to. The way the approach was designed required me to build my understandings. The basic building blocks were provided, but in reality each Silent Way practitioner has to build the challenge and created the charts and taught the classes with the help of an Indonesian native speaker.

One of Dr. Gattegno's legacies has been to produce a system teachers can use to transform what they do, and continually improve on what they do. Every other teaching methodology I have come across provides teachers with understandings and tools, but seldom the means to improve on what they do, or inspire their students and colleagues to be better than they thought they could be. From the results that are evident in language schools that I have taught in, and been to around Australia, the need for an approach that can empower students and teachers alike is still as strong as ever.

> "The Silent Way 'forces' practitioners to be independent and creative, with one of the outcomes being that teachers end up feeling empowered, as I did, to construct what is needed."

their own understandings, otherwise the teaching soon runs out of puff. This is one of the beauties of the Silent Way – it is not possible to teach it without getting fully immersed in understanding learning, teaching, and language.

Early on in my forays into studying and teaching the Silent Way, I had the good fortune to meet Caleb Gattegno. His presence, his humanity, and his insights gave a depth and another dimension to the experiences that I had up to then, both as a teacher of English and as a student of a number of foreign languages taught via the Silent Way. With his encouragement, I created both Hungarian and Indonesian Fidels and Word Charts.

The Silent Way "forces" practitioners to be independent and creative, with one of the outcomes being that teachers end up feeling empowered, as I did, to construct what is needed. The Indonesian charts were actually made in response to a request from an Australian company requiring Indonesian for their engineers. Despite the fact that I knew no Indonesian when I began the project, I took on

Dr. Gattegno's contributions to teaching have considerably impacted the face of language teaching in all corners of the world, even if many teachers have no idea of the origins of what they do. For example, it is now readily accepted in language classrooms that students should be the ones doing the talking, not the teachers. I believe this view was never talked about prior to the advent of the Silent Way.

There have been periods where everyone was talking about independence and autonomy in students, but out of that dialogue there have been few substantive changes that have produced the desired results. Ideas are cheap as they say, and teachers need to be given the understandings and tools to not only transform their students, but also themselves.

This I believe is the area that needs the most amount of work still, the re-education of teachers so that they can become truly independent themselves, ready to embrace what they face without fear, and not be held back by the past. The Silent Way offers us a way to impart this to our students, and positions us as teachers ready to take it on for ourselves. §

Words in Color requires a high degree of student involvement, interaction and participation. Shown above is a group of students working on the first chart of five vowels with their teacher. (Educational Solutions file photo.)

A Man Ahead of His Time & Recuerdos Agradecidos

Laura Guajardo

I was lucky enough to meet Dr. Gattegno when I was not a teacher; I say this because I didn't have to change any habits, and I didn't have to defend any theories. Before becoming a language teacher, I attended several three-day intensive Italian courses. This experience was very fruitful; I learned Italian, I had a lot of fun, I observed myself as a learner, and it gave me confidence to go ahead and become a language teacher. So I just began teaching, suspending judgment and waiting to see what would happen.

I will never forget the first time I had to go teach Spanish to the big boss of a very important company near Paris. His secretary called the school at least three times before the classes began, asking to make sure they sent "a very good and responsible teacher," because her boss had no time to waste since he was doing a lot of traveling. As I entered the very fancy conference room my knees were shaking. When my student walked into the room, I introduced myself, put up my handmade rectangle chart, took out my pointer and began to work. When the class was over, my student was thrilled; he was reproducing short sentences in perfect Spanish, and he said it was a very interesting experience.

Then I began teaching groups with three days of full immersion every other week. The results and the feedback from the students were so good that other teachers, working for the same school but not using the Silent Way, came to observe my classes. They all said it was amazing, but at the same time most of them said it worked because Spanish was "similar" to French. Then I began teaching English and the "miracle" happened again. Some observers were convinced, but others were still resistant. When I talked about this to Dr. Gattegno, he mentioned that Piaget had boycotted him by saying, "Gattegno was born too early and his approaches regarding his way of teaching are ahead of his time."

For many years I taught all kinds of people: children, grown-ups, senior citizens, doctors, engineers, actors, and unemployed. I always learned a lot with my groups and the results were steadily good. And as more time went by, I ran into less resistant observers; so who knows, maybe Piaget was right after all. §

Recuerdos Agradecidos

Tuve la suerte de conocer al Doctor Gattegno cuando no era profesora de idiomas, digo esto porque no tuve que cambiar hábitos ni defender ninguna teoría. Su manera de enseñar me pareció muy lógica y tenia sentido. Antes de ser profesora de idiomas, participé en varios cursos intensivos de tres días de italiano. Esta experiencia fue muy fructífera, aprendí italiano, me divertí muchísimo, me observe como alumna y me dio la confianza para convertirme en profesora de idiomas. Entonces, empecé a enseñar suspendiendo el juicio y esperando ver lo que sucedería. Nunca se me va a olvidar la primera vez que tuve que darle a clases a un ejecutivo de alto rango de una compañía muy importante cerca de París. Su secretaría llamo a la escuela por lo menos tres veces antes de que las clases comenzaran para asegurarse de que mandaran "a una profesora muy buena y responsable pues su jefe no tenía tiempo que perder ya que viajaba mucho". Cuando entré a una sala de conferencias muy elegante, me temblaban las rodillas. Cuando mi alumno llegó, me presente, colgué mis rectángulos caseros (Los rectángulos de español no existen en la versión impresa), saqué mi puntero y empecé a trabajar. Cuando la clase terminó mi alumno estaba encantado, podía reproducir frases cortas en perfecto español y me dijo que era una experiencia muy interesante. Después comencé a enseñar grupos, tenían tres días de inmersión total cada dos semanas. Los resultados y la retroalimentación de parte de los alumnos fueron tan buenos que profesores que trabajaban en la misma escuela pero no usaban el "silentway" fueron a observar mis clases. Todos comentaron que era sorprendente pero al mismo tiempo casi todos dijeron que funcionaba porque el español era "similar" al francés. Después de esto comencé a enseñar inglés y el "milagro" volvió a suceder. Algunos observadores estuvieron convencidos pero otros todavía se resistían. Cuando platique sobre esto con el Doctor Gattegno el me comentó que Piaget lo había boicoteado diciendo que "Gattegno había nacido antes de tiempo y que su pedagogía era demasiado adelantada para esos momentos". Con el pasar de los años me cruce con observadores menos resistentes. Puede ser que a fin de cuentas Piaget haya tenido razón. Durante muchos años enseñé a toda clase de público, niños, adultos, personas de la tercera edad, doctores, ingenieros, desempleados, actores. Siempre aprendí mucho con mis alumnos y los resultados fueron muy buenos.

> 'Gattegno había nacido antes de tiempo y que su pedagogía era demasiado adelantada para esos momentos'

Hasta el día de hoy, mi vida profesional ha sido muy rica y satisfactoria tanto para mí como para mis alumnos, (puedo decir esto por la retroalimentación de los mismos. Algunos fueron mis alumnos hace más de veinte años y todavía estoy en contacto con varios). Nunca podré agradecerle al Doctor Gattegno suficientemente la influencia que tuvo en mi vida personal. Durante sus seminarios de verano en Europa, conocí a personas maravillosas. A algunas les tengo mucho cariño, otras se han convertido en amigos muy cercanos y hay muchas a las que admiro, pero lo que si es seguro es que aprendí algo de todas. Y aunque "la comunicación sea un milagro" la experiencia que adquirí durante ese tiempo ha hecho una gran diferencia en mi vida. Cuando mi esposo murió, leí su ensayo "Sobre la muerte" *y seria casi imposible para mi describir la serenidad que me dio.

Me da mucho ver que hay mucha gente en el mundo dispersando la pedagogía del Doctor Gattegno. En este mundo que va tan rápido utilizar los enfoques pedagógicos y los materiales del Doctor Gattegno que además de ser muy eficientes ayudan a ahorrar mucha energía y mucho tiempo y es esto lo que se necesita en el mundo actual.

§

To the Best of Our Abilities

Carol Rose

In 1970, after attending a seminar on Words in Color with Dr. Gattegno, I decided to buy the American English reading charts which I put up on the wall of my children's bedroom, one being almost five and the other almost four. I spent a few minutes showing the elder child about the colors, then left them alone. The elder had already developed a curiosity about how writing worked and it was very astonishing to observe over a few weeks that she was teaching herself to read, and furthermore was showing her little brother how to read. These two children became readers and good spellers at the same time. This far reaching event showed me the importance of the contribution of learning instruments which were appropriate to the specific knowledge desired. It was interesting to note that, once back in France, the first-grade teachers in one of the best schools in the country simply did not notice that the children were already competent readers.

Many years later, I was working as a psychologist at a children's service in a research project for non-readers. When I proposed the staff use Words in Color as the vehicle of instruction for these children, nine years old and above who 'never had learned to read,' it was in a spirit of testing whether these instruments accompanied by the requisite pedagogy of learning would function well with troubled children having severe learning difficulties. We were to learn that remediation, using Words in Color in specific ways, was extremely effective as was psychological help. Often the special utilization of only a few rectangles on the Sound-Color Chart, and keeping away from letters in the first session, managed to do what Caleb Gattegno termed "forcing awareness." Practically all of the children worked with became aware of how to read, but this development had never been seen before in the records of all the other similar children who had been treated over a 15-year period.

As for myself, Dr. Gattegno constantly pushed me to combat unfounded opinions and too-broad generalizations. He said once that after his death he would be known as 'a technician of education.' This, I suppose, referred to the instruments he devised and published. I have always felt that his theories about awareness, the structuring of knowledge within the brain which true learning affects, the nature of memory, and so on, go far beyond technical procedures.

Space does not permit me to continue the long iteration of the wisdoms he was able to pass along, which I have had the good fortune to be able to interpret and also pass along to others. His teachings have been active in me in most undertakings, and the reassurance that, "one can only do at any given moment whatever one is able to do," enables me to move ahead into new domains and to be patient with my own learning. §

> "Awareness is neither automatic nor constant. In fact, most people go through life only aware of a very small fraction of what could have struck them had they been uniformly and constantly watchful."

— Dr. Caleb Gattegno

The Science of Education – Part 1: Theoretical Considerations, Second Edition (2010), page 183.

Painting was one of Dr. Gattegno's many interests. Shown above is a painting from *The White Canary*, which was written and illustrated by Gattegno. (Educational Explorers, 1968, page 5.)

Two Simple Drawings
That Changed My Teaching Forever

Dr. Jane Orton

Illustration from *What We Owe Children: The Subordination of Teaching to Learning*, 1987.

"The Subordination of Teaching to Learning." The simplest exemplification of this maxim of Caleb Gattegno's teaching, which has served me in the 40-plus years since I encountered his work, has been the little pair of drawings that appear in *What We Owe Children*, a version of which is shown here. They remain one of the most effective means of touching awareness in the teachers I work with, both the Australians and the many others who were educated in an Asian country.

Within this milieu, comparing the drawings provides an immediate grasp of some of the key features of the very Western notion of 'learner-centered' rather than 'teacher-centered' teaching. For example, it shows in concrete terms how there can be roles for the teacher and the student that are separate and complementary, each with their own relationship to the content. They make clear that once a student is busy working, there is still real work for a teacher to do in observing and, when needed, in guiding. And it suggests that this will be done from the side, by asking a question, suggesting a pause and reconsideration, or other means that do not intrude the teacher between the learner and the content. Implicit in the second drawing is that the teacher will have done much analytical work on the content knowledge before the class, so that when it is presented to the student it can be tackled independently and will generate useful development. In providing all of this, the drawings shift the focus of teaching away from the content, and onto the learning and what the learners are doing with themselves. The teacher's job, and what student teachers need to learn, is to ask the right questions of the situation and to keep on asking them, and to notice the responses and design useful on-the-spot responses in turn.

The above are topics and propositions that are unpacked over hours of analysis of these drawings with teachers and student teachers. Not only do they represent a large piece of Caleb Gattegno's educational beliefs, but the apparent simplicity which masks the complexity and depth of knowledge

learner was himself. Someone who delighted in humor, especially verbal wit, he told me he had truly learned English during his first year in England by honing an existing formal base through listening to the *Goon Show* on BBC radio. At the start he had sat baffled, unable to understand a thing, while his local companions alternately chuckled and roared with laughter. It took a year to get there, but by the end of 12 months listening, observing society and himself, asking questions and entrusting himself to his sleep, he could understand the language and the references – and had become an avid, lasting, and highly metacognitively aware fan of the Goons.

> "...developments in cognitive science are confirming much that Gattegno proposed, and even more that he intuitively embedded in his resources and techniques."

and understanding exemplifies his immense capacity to move quickly and with ease back and forth across levels of abstraction; to represent complex wisdom in a concrete graspable form, or to deepen the knowledge of a superficial fact through to an encounter with a much more profound truth.

When I think back to the years I worked with Caleb Gattegno in New York (1969-1972), it is his voice endlessly posing questions that I at once hear in my memory: "Can we say…" he would begin, or, "In what way…" "How can we…." "Is it true? Is it true?" he would ask, with his thumb and index finger making a circle. Questioning was his approach to life and he posed questions as a way of dealing with events, from the most mundane matters of office management to major matters of intellectual consideration. With the question asked, there would then follow another instance of his most admirable attribute: patience. "Patience is not a virtue in education," he would remind us often, "it is a necessity!"

He practised what he preached, even when the

So it is not so surprising then that in my time at School for the Future and then Educational Solutions, staff meetings were held on Monday evenings in the Gattegno East 9th St. apartment, and largely consisted of watching the cutting edge, innovative comedy show *Laugh In* while being treated to fruit and oat muesli made by the boss. Gattegno particularly appreciated the show for the constant intelligence in the many jokes and physical presentations of two key factors that appear in all his own work: one, that transformation is the link among everything on the planet, and, two, that Homo ludens is a term of truth – sentient beings have a natural capacity for playfulness.

I first ever heard Gattegno pose a question at a weeklong workshop in Edinburgh in August 1969. He opened by asking in what ways it could be said that since his last such workshop in the UK some seven years before, the educational environment there was more open to the notion of subordinating teaching to learning, and to the understanding that only awareness is educable.

(Orton Cont'd)

One hundred years since his birth and more than 20 since his death, I find it is a question still worth pondering in relation to both the global educational environment and my local educational area.

Although there can be no simple answer, it is clear that there is no lessening of the need in every country for educating awareness. Today's advances in technology unwittingly reveal this need acutely. Gattegno was a pioneer in the adoption of technologies, using first film, later video, and eventually computers, and he was always elated at the power machines provided to present dynamic multifaceted representations and interactive virtual experiences. Yet although each technological advance has allowed teachers to show what earlier they could only dream of, today's results make it all the clearer that little is transparent to children without guidance, and that 'telling by showing' is not enough to arouse and engage most minds.

To harness the power of technology for educational purposes, teachers need their own awareness of what it means for a person to learn, plus the knowledge and skills – and the patience – to help bring it about in their students. Yet in so many places across the globe, contemporary teacher education programs are still largely superficial, crammed into a short year with little appreciation of the time and attention required to educate student teachers about educating awareness in their students, or of the value that would flow from such an investment.

Within education systems, problems are treated as needing essentially structural solutions, and discussions are often little more than arguments about money and resources. As a result, from the fundamentals of literacy and numeracy to consideration of the purpose of having a life, almost all societies continue to struggle to provide their children with an education that will allow them to develop the integrity and knowledge needed to shape worthwhile aims, and to grapple with and surmount the challenges they will face in working towards achieving them.

Amidst this potentially dispiriting course of events,

> 'Patience is not a virtue in education,' he would remind us often, 'it is a necessity!'

developments in cognitive science are confirming much that Gattegno proposed, and even more that he intuitively embedded in his resources and techniques. For example, the powerful role we now understand that kinesic support plays in achieving comprehensive and sustained learning confirms the value and efficacy of the work with rods in mathematics and the Silent Way.

As well, I remain as always very buoyed by the instant recognition by some student teachers and teachers that there is something excitingly 'real' about Gattegno's propositions and in the experience of his methods such as the Silent Way. For these people, especially the younger ones, the experience comes as a revelation, a sudden apprehension of new and greatly enriching new depths to teaching and living, which provides an enormous energy to go further. While the science catches up with the underlying assumptions, the responses of these people give evidence that the Subordination of Teaching to Learning remains a potentially vital and valued principle still. §

> "At every moment, there is experimentation – conscious, deliberate experimentation – so as to not assimilate wrongly what they can apprehend well. They observe carefully what people in the environment do before passing to a subsequent stage of their apprenticeship."

- Dr. Caleb Gattegno

Caleb Gattegno writing in *The Common Sense of Teaching Reading and Writing* on how babies learn to speak. (Second Edition, Page 35).

One-Minute Lessons Will Pop Up on Entire Network

For months now, on NBC's owned TV stations in New York and Cleveland, small fry watching Saturday-morning's cartoons and toy and cereal plugs have been getting something extra: one-minute doses of letter learning. Called "Pop Ups," the experimental spots—just eight in number—were devised by Dr. Caleb Gattegno, an Egyptian-born educator and author ("Toward a Visual Culture") and employ phonetics to instruct young viewers first in vowels, then consonants, and finally in oral sentences. Research has shown the spots are accomplishing their aim, NBC says, and, beginning Jan. 23, they'll be shown Saturday mornings on the entire network. Newer "Pop Ups" are planned on math and other subjects.

From *TV Guide*, written after the release of Pop Up and *Towards a Visual Culture*. (New York Metropolitan Edition, January 1971.)

Video stills from *Pop Up*, an expression of Dr. Gattegno's Words in Color approach to teaching reading, adapted for the medium of television. *Pop Up* originally aired on NBC in 1970.

Trois Enseignantes De Genève

A- L Ferro-Luzzi, A. Fayolle Dietl et R. Wisler

ANNA LAURA FERRO-LUZZI

Diplomée de physique à Rome, j'ai enseigné les mathématiques à l'Istituto Tecnico de Livorno pendant deux ans. En 1971, j'ai fait mes Etudes Pédagogiques Secondaires à Genève, puis j'ai assuré un poste de doyenne au Collège de la Golette à Meyrin. Depuis 1973, j'ai suivi régulièrement les séminaires que Caleb Gattegno a donnés à Genève à l'Ecole Internationale, puis les séminaires d'été en France. En 1986-87, lors d'une année sabbatique à New-York, j'ai approfondi ma recherche sur la pédagogie Gattegno.

J'étais dans l'enseignement des mathématiques et de la physique depuis quelques années et je commençais à avoir de sérieux doutes sur l'efficacité des différentes méthodes que j'avais essayées.

Bref j'étais en pleine crise quand le hasard m'a fait rencontrer le Dr. Gattegno.

La simple phrase "subordination de l'enseignement à l'apprentissage" a été pour moi une véritable révolution aussi bien sur le plan du travail que sur le plan personnel. Voici une petite anecdote que je n'oublierai pas:

J'étais chargée d'une classe d'accueil. Lisa était une jeune fille portugaise. A Genève depuis déjà quelques années, elle ne parlait pas encore le français, et même très mal sa langue maternelle, elle avait fait un amalgame entre les deux langues. Très peu scolarisée, elle ne dominait pas encore les quatre opérations en mathématiques. Elle a été la seule élève, parmi les centaines que j'ai côtoyés, dont je doutais des capacités intellectuelles.

Jérôme, un garçon russe hautement scolarisé, venait d'arriver en Suisse, et en plus de l'école obligatoire genevoise, il fréquentait régulièrement l'école russe. En mathématique, il connaissait les fonctions, les dérivés et les intégrales.

Je leur ai proposé de travailler avec les réglettes Cuisenaire (que le Dr. Gattegno a merveilleusement développées).

Jérôme participait de loin au travail et on voyait bien qu'il était presque fâché qu'on lui propose une activité si "puérile". Mais je vois encore son regard quand Lisa a dit d'un air très tranquille: « alors v (réglette verte) à la puissance cinq divisé par v à la puissance trois donne v à la puissance deux » et pendant qu'elle parlait, elle le montrait avec les tours des réglettes.

Jérôme savait tout ça, mais il ne l'avait jamais "vu".

ANNIE FAYOLLE DIETL

Après une maîtrise de langues de l'Université de Grenoble et un séjour en Allemagne, je suis arrivée à Genève en 1971 comme enseignante de français et d'allemand à des adolescents de 12 à 15 ans au Cycle d'Orientation, puis j'ai complété ma formation avec une licence d'allemand et de russe à l'Université de Genève. J'ai occupé ensuite le poste de Présidente du Groupe d'Allemand pendant 9 ans, puis j'ai continué de fonctionner comme membre et responsable de nombreuses commissions pédagogiques du Cycle d'Orientation, puis comme coordinatrice de recherche avec le Département d'allemand de l'Université de Genève sur les phases d'acquisition de la langue allemande, et, parallèlement, comme formatrice à l'Institut de Formation des Enseignants

Secondaires à Genève jusqu'en 2006.

C'est 1975 lors d'un séminaire d'italien "Silent Way" à Lyon avec Cecilia Bartoli que j'ai rencontré la pédagogie Gattegno et j'ai ensuite rencontré Caleb Gattegno lui-même l'année suivante à Lyon.

En 1982, lors d'une année passée à Cornell University, j'ai eu l'occasion de travailler avec lui à New-York à Educational Solutions.

De nombreux séminaires avec Caleb Gattegno sont venus s'ajouter ensuite, en France, et à Genève à l'Ecole Internationale.

En 1992, au bénéfice d'une année sabbatique, j'ai pu approfondir ma réflexion sur "Le jeu dans les apprentissages en langues" grâce à l'apport de la pédagogie Gattegno lors de séjours à Besançon à Une Ecole pour Demain, à Trento en particulier avec Rosaria dell'Eva, Cecilia Bartoli et à Osaka avec Fusako Allard.

Un peu plus tard, j'ai pu participer à la formation intensive donnée sur plusieurs années au CLA à Besançon.

J'aimais assister aux séminaires d'été, un petit groupe venait réfléchir avec C. Gattegno sur un sujet tel que "la mort" ou "l'amour". J'en repartais à la fois enrichie et troublée par les questions soulevées. Chaque fois, la construction qui s'élaborait du début à la fin m'émerveillait. Dans les discussions, Caleb Gattegno montrait une douceur et une patience doublées d'une intransigeance imperturbable, cela m'impressionnait. Le soir, dans les moments de détente, il aimait rire, chanter et raconter des blagues.

Je me souviens tout particulièrement d'un moment qui a eu des conséquences sur ma vie professionnelle. En effet, lorsque je l'interrogeais au début des années 80 sur le matériel d'allemand "Silent Way", il me répondit que le Fidel existait comme prototype, mais qu'il faudrait pouvoir le construire soi-même, car on ne pouvait pas l'imprimer, faute d'intéressés.

J'étais, je crois, à l'époque, une des rares à m'intéresser à l'allemand "Silent Way" avant que l'équipe de Trento ne réalise ce merveilleux travail qui a conduit à l'impression des tableaux. Ainsi en hiver 1983, Caleb Gattegno me donna rendez-vous au buffet de la gare de Genève entre deux trains, il me tendit un morceau de papier écrit au crayon. C'était le tableau des sons de l'allemand et le Fidel qu'il me confiait. "Voilà vous pourrez maintenant bricoler votre tableau d'allemand en cannibalisant des tableaux du français" dit-il.

Les élèves vous donnent leur temps, Que leur donnez-vous en échange?

J'ai utilisé mon "matériel-maison" plusieurs années, jusqu'en 1987 où le matériel officiel fut imprimé en Italie.

RENÉE WISLER

Après une formation d'institutrice (certificat d'aptitude pédagogique) j'ai enseigné pendant quinze ans dans l'enseignement primaire en France puis à l'école Française de Lausanne en Suisse. De 1971 à 1988, enseignante de français et d'histoire au Cycle d'Orientation de Genève, j'ai fait une formation en français langue étrangère au Centre de Linguistique Appliquée (CLA) de Besançon, langue que j'ai enseignée pendant dix ans en classe d'accueil à Genève.

PREMIÈRE RENCONTRE, PREMIER CHOC, PREMIÈRE CERTITUDE:

J'ai rencontré C. Gattegno pour la première fois lors d'un séminaire qu'il animait à Lyon sur la lecture en couleurs dans les années 80.

Je suis entrée dans la salle et j'ai vu le " Fidel ": un choc, une révélation! Comme si c'était ce que j'attendais, ce que je cherchais depuis longtemps. Aussitôt cet outil s'imposait à moi, il me restait à l'approfondir. Cette fascination, cette curiosité, suscitées par ce matériel, je les chaque fois observées chez les élèves. J'ai ensuite suivi de nombreux séminaires animés par Gattegno et ce fut chaque fois une remise en question et un nouvel élan.

En 2002, j'ai créé l'Association "Alphalire" à Entrechaux près de Vaison la Romaine, proposant des séminaires de formation à la pédagogie Gattegno en région PACA. Le public est essentiellement composé de bénévoles faisant de l'alphabétisation.

Deux questions:

- Comment enseigner le français langue étrangère dans une classe d'accueil? En effet toutes les méthodes sur le marché étaient conçues pour être utilisées en milieu captif avec une seule langue maternelle de référence.
- Comment alphabétiser en français langue étrangère les enfants ne sachant ni lire ni écrire dans leur propre langue?

Deuxième certitude:

Le "Silent Way" et la Lecture en couleurs sont les seules réponses possibles. Le "Silent Way", puisqu'il recrée la situation dans laquelle chacun s'est trouvé quand il a appris sa langue maternelle. L'apprenant est autonome et acteur de son apprentissage. La lecture en couleurs, puisqu'elle peut s'articuler au "Silent Way".

Une anecdote illustrant la puissance du matériel: un petit sri-lankais me prit un jour par la main pour me montrer ce qu'il venait de déchiffrer sur les tableaux, le mot "almanach" qu'il ne connaissait pas.

ENSEIGNER EN ÉQUIPE GATTEGNO EN CLASSE D'ACCEUIL

A Genève, la classe d'accueil dans l'enseignement publique est une structure regroupant des enfants étrangers de 12 à 15 ans, de nationalités différentes, de langues diverses et de milieux sociaux très variés, certains sont très mal scolarisés. Nous étions trois enseignantes de français, maths et allemand à enseigner dans cette classe. Convaincues de la pédagogie Gattegno, et confrontées à l'extrême hétérogénéité de ces groupes, nous avons décidé de relever les défis inhérents à cette classe spécifique d'adolescents, sur la base de plusieurs principes de départ:

- Utiliser le potentiel des élèves
- Appréhender l'apprentissage en s'appuyant sur la perception
- Créer des situations d'apprentissage concrètes, compréhensibles, accessibles et non ambiguës
- Rester dans une perspective de construction-recherche
- Observer l'apprentissage à l'oeuvre
- Respecter «La subordination de l'enseignement à l'apprentissage».

Utilisant la même approche dans les trois matières scolaires nous avons pu mesurer ce que l'on appelle «L'économie dans les apprentissages», voir progresser les élèves, prendre confiance en eux, se construire peu à peu, et nous pouvions constater que les notions du programme étaient largement dépassées.

En français et allemand, les élèves travaillaient dès le départ sur les sons communs aux deux langues, à l'aide des deux tableaux de rectangles, tandis que les sons spécifiques étaient travaillés à part.

Quant aux aspects fonctionnels et structuraux, ils intervenaient dans chacun des cours de langues. Chaque fois, et de même en mathématiques, l'accessibilité était garantie, et ainsi, les élèves avaient les moyens de progresser dans leur apprentissage, même les élèves les plus faibles.

Parallèlement à notre enseignement, désireuses de faire partager nos découvertes et expériences, nous avons organisé plusieurs fois des séminaires avec Caleb Gattegno.

Par la suite, nous avons mis en place une formation continue pour les enseignants de classe d'accueil avec le soutien du responsable de ces classes. Aujourd'hui, plusieurs classes travaillent encore avec la pédagogie Gattegno dans les classes d'accueil de l'Instruction Publique genevoise.

Pour nous, ce furent des années riches, encourageantes et passionnantes, tant sur le plan professionnel que sur le plan humain, et nous en sommes reconnaissantes.

Une phrase de C. Gattegno nous reste en mémoire:
«Les élèves vous donnent leur temps, Que leur donnez-vous en échange?»

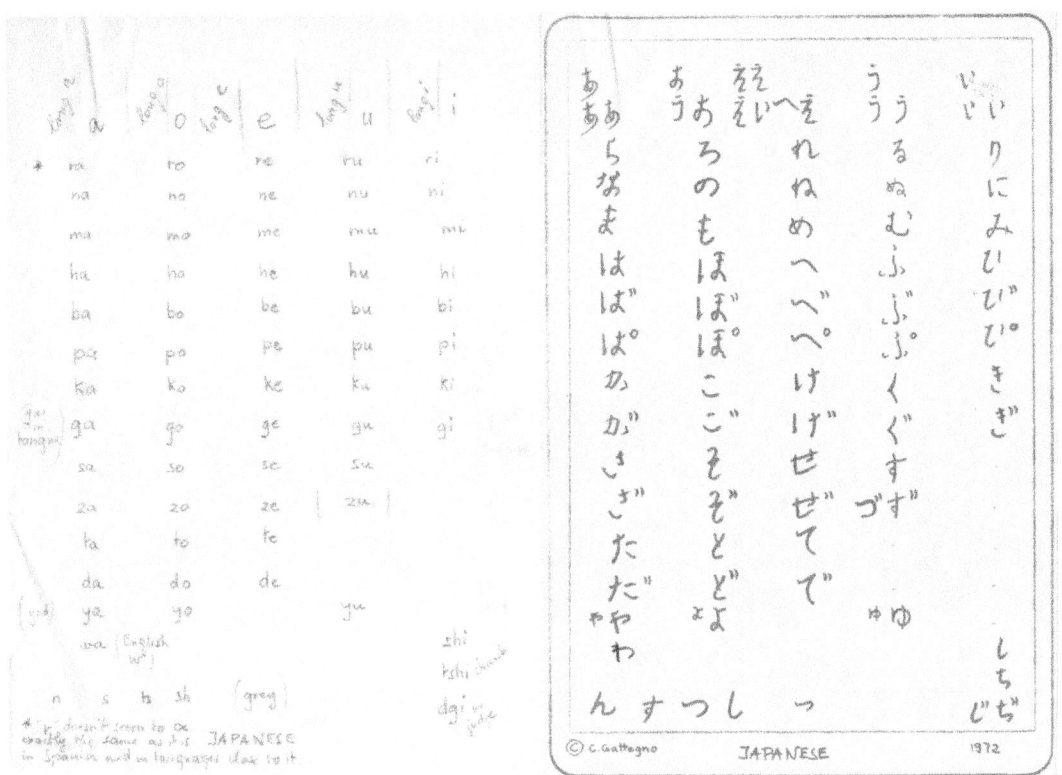

Hand-drawn Japanese Fidel. ©Educational Solutions Worldwide Inc.

Gattegno's technique for creating Fidels was meticulous and involved many stages of production. This hand-drawn Fidel was made in 1972, and can be overlain with the transparent sheet (right) to map out the sounds of each Japanese character.

The Fidel was a monumental achievement, unlike any other in language arts, then and now. It is the only instrument of its kind that seeks to panoramically represent all the sounds and spellings in a particular language. It represented a phenomenal amount of work to create one, particularly in non-phonetic languages like English and French. Secondly, Dr. Gattegno sought to make consistent the specific color representing a unique sound across all languages. The following images are from Gattegno's personal writings.

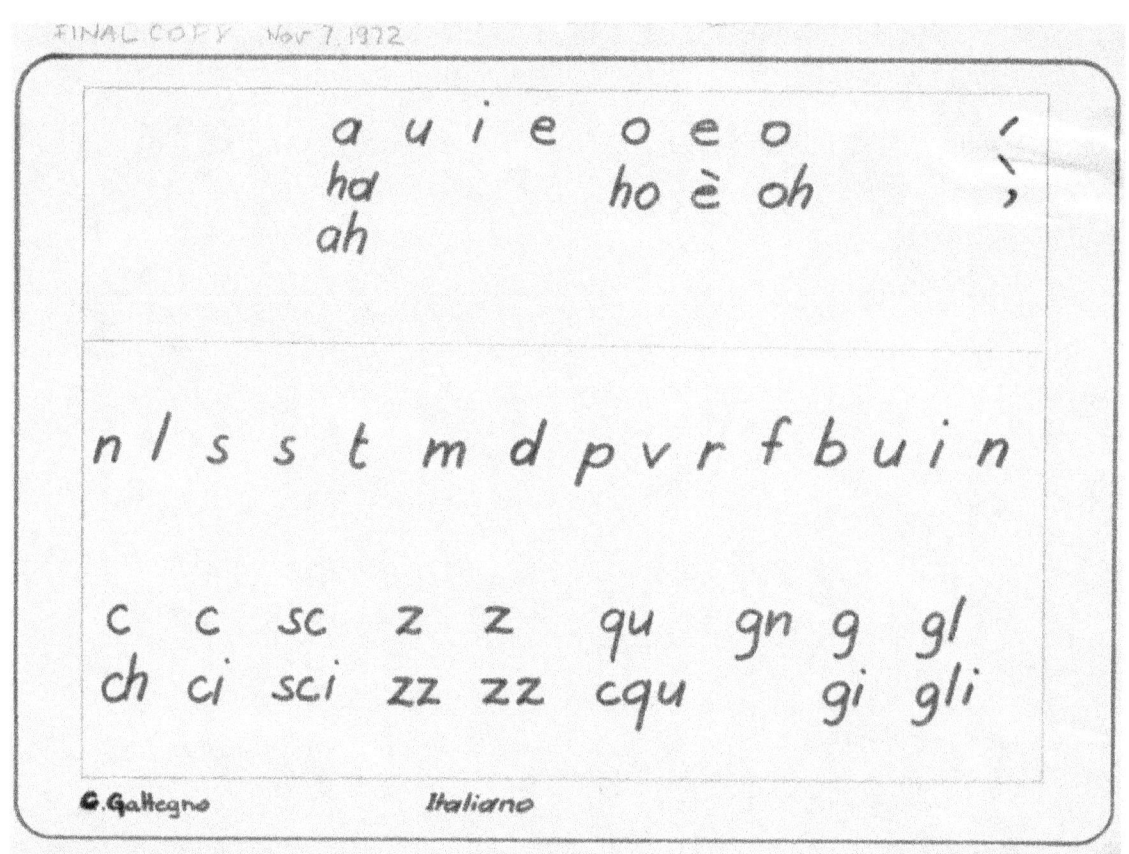

Hand-drawn Italian Fidel. ©Educational Solutions Worldwide Inc.

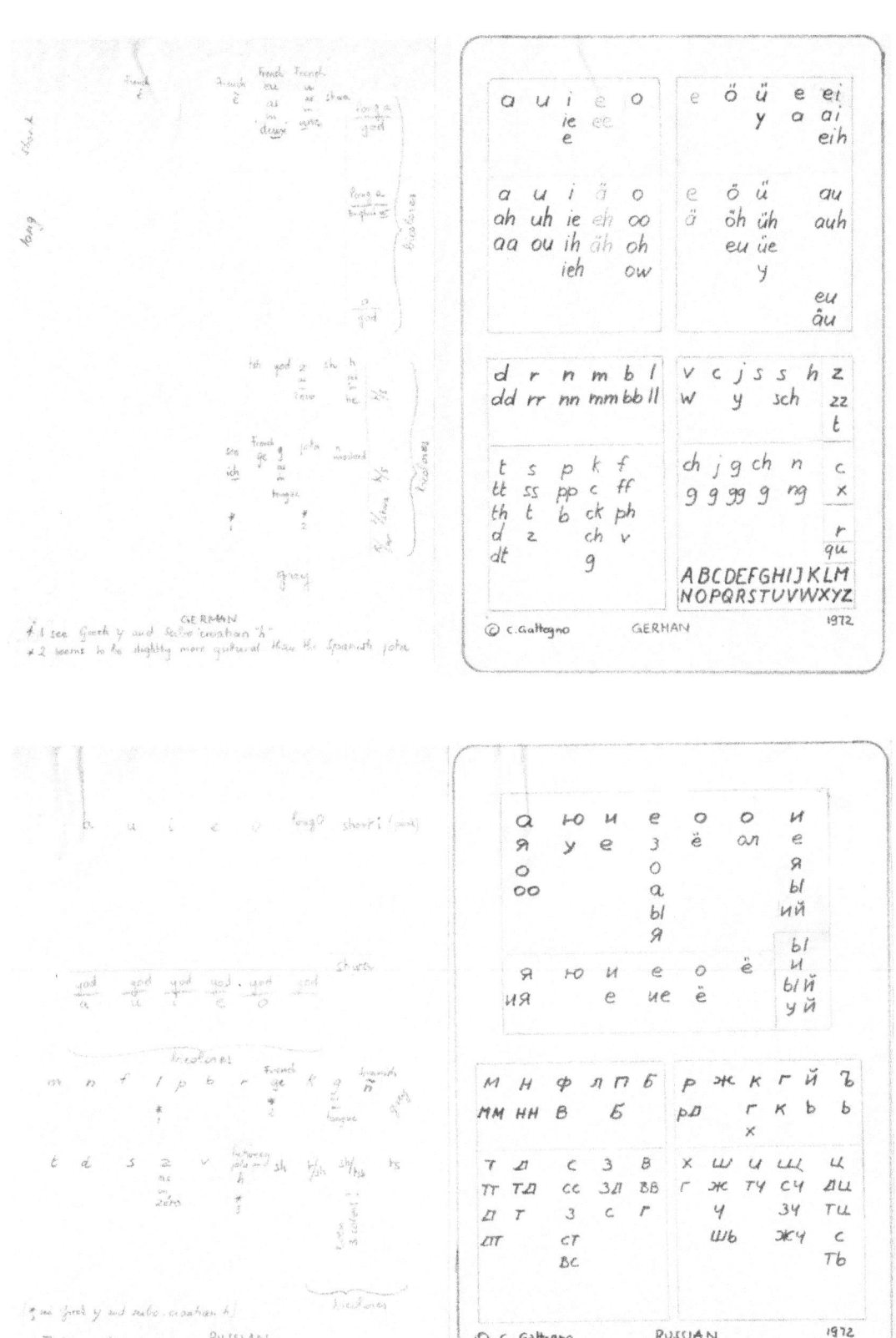

Hand-drawn German Fidel (above). ©Educational Solutions Worldwide Inc.
Hand-drawn Russian Fidel (below). ©Educational Solutions Worldwide Inc.

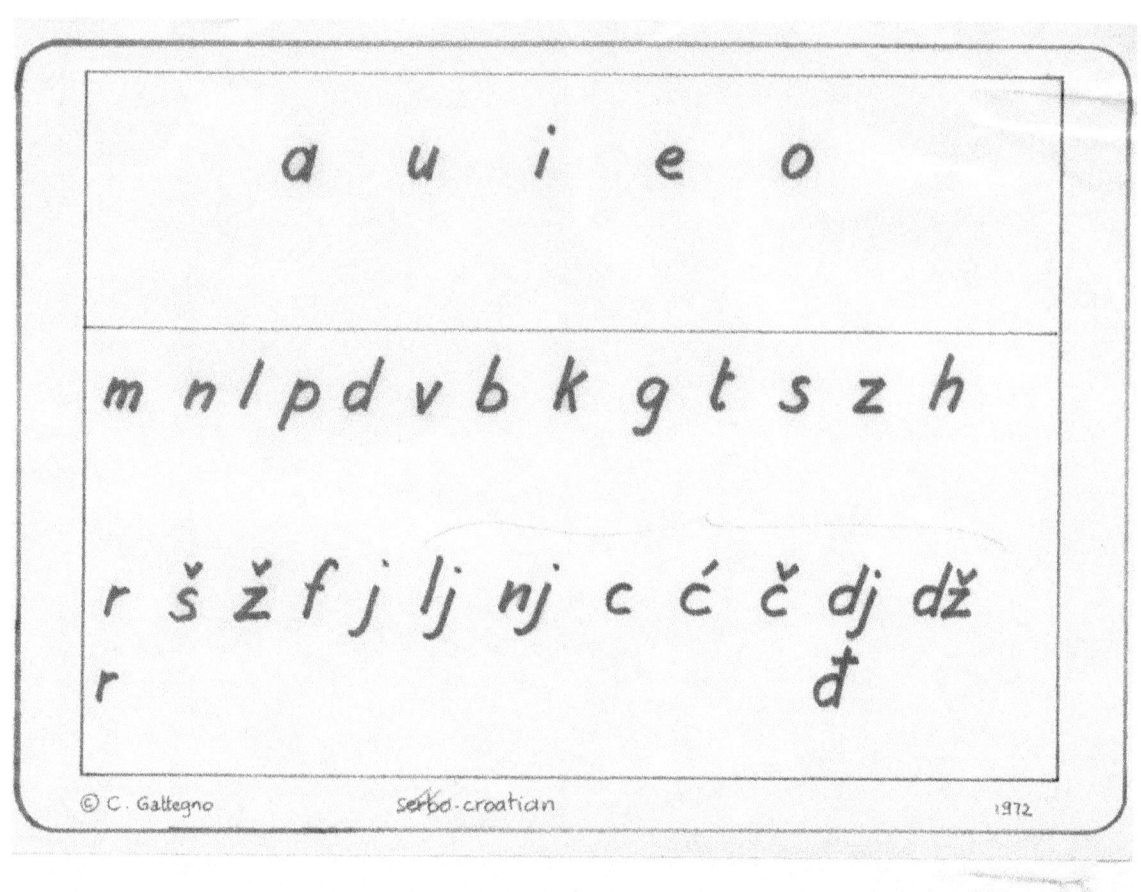
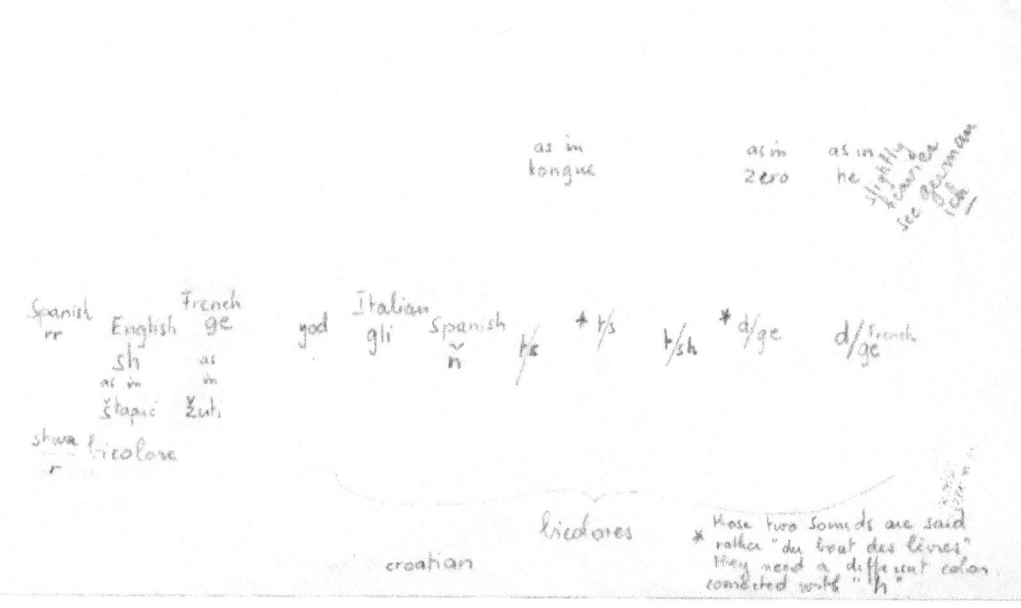

Hand-drawn Croatian Fidel. ©Educational Solutions Worldwide Inc.

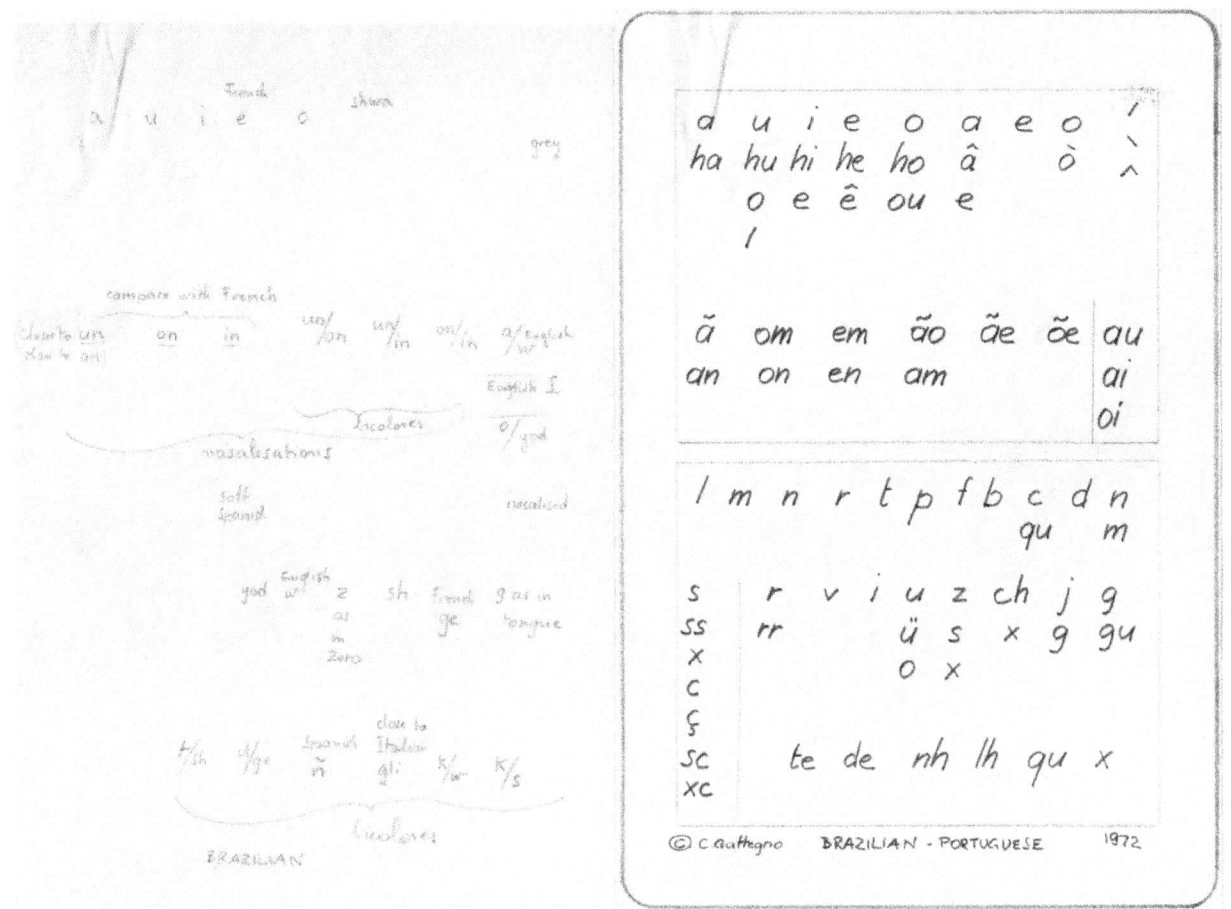

Hand-drawn Brazilian-Portuguese Fidel. ©Educational Solutions Worldwide Inc.

Reflections on Gattegno, Learning Lakota, and More

Dr. Jim Green

When I first began with the Jesuits in 1975, I had hopes of joining their work among the Lakota in South Dakota. I took American Indian language classes at the University of Minnesota that year, then, in 1979, when I first began work on the Pine Ridge reservation, I went to tribal college classes, worked through the latest books by two Colorado linguists, and lived with Victor Bull Bear and his family. In each case I learned a tremendous amount about Lakota cultural ways, but never found myself making any real progress in using the language. Finally, in 1982, not wanting to face another summer and little progress, I returned to the University of Minnesota and began looking through their collection of language methods. Everything in the collection seemed a reflection of the failed attempts I had made in the previous seven years. Then I came across a description of the Silent Way. The description of the Silent Way immediately connected with me and on an entirely different plane.

A small group of us adapted the Silent Way approach that summer, and when we found ourselves quickly communicating in sentences, we decided to contact Dr. Gattegno for further assistance. Of course we had no idea at the time that he had introduced the Silent Way to the Maori in New Zealand, or that he was currently working on a set of charts for the Inupiaq language in northern Alaska. But he agreed to work with us and somehow found time to develop the initial Silent Way charts for Lakota during the fall and spring of 1982-83.

> "...we had no idea at the time that he had introduced the Silent Way to the Maori in New Zealand, or that he was currently working on a set of charts for the Inupiaq language in northern Alaska."

I visited with him in New York to revise the initial charts in late spring of 1983. By then I had heard of his directness and his ability to immediately get to the heart of educational problems and find direct solutions for them; I found his ability very compelling, and his personality very likeable. I've always considered my relationship with him a real gift, but later that year it provided unexpected insight when a friend told me that the Maharishi Mahesh Yogi of Transcendental Meditation fame said he had once shared a cab with Dr. Gattegno and that there didn't seem to be enough room for anyone else in the cab. I only smiled.

I had a number of further interactions with Dr. Gattegno over the five years from 1983 to 1988. When he came out to Pine Ridge to conduct a training session in the summer of 1983, he clearly enjoyed his interaction with the Jesuits, nuns and volunteers who made up the learning group. As it turned out, however, the Lakota speakers at the training sessions had been taught to do most of the talking in the language classroom, and Caleb quickly found himself hemmed in by the cultural respect typically given to elders in American Indian culture. However, it didn't take him long to come up with a solution: "I'm an elder of sorts too," he told them, "So put up with me when I tell you, you need to stop talking!"

After the training session at Pine Ridge I began using the Silent Way materials, mostly with Lakota speakers but also at times with speakers of other American Indian languages. As a result, Dr. Gattegno was contacted by a group in northern Ontario in 1985 and asked to develop a set of Silent Way charts for Ojibwe. In talking with him about the project, I mentioned that the *Guinness Book of World Records* had once listed Ojibwe as the most difficult language in the world, and that I'd be interested in his response to that remarkable claim. Later he told me, with a sense of delight in his voice, he had never worked with a language that allowed so many variations in its structure. In fact, he said, it was as though Ojibwe didn't really have a set grammatical structure, but instead purposely allowed fluent speakers to rearrange words to communicate subtle meanings or to challenge other speakers to stay in the conversation. Over the years I've checked this assessment with Ojibwe speakers: the younger ones shake their heads, the older ones smile.

There was also the time when Caleb came to St. Paul, Minnesota in 1984, to conduct a Spanish Silent Way session for a group of young Jesuits in training. During the session I observed his obvious love for Spanish as he shared stories and sang songs. During the session, too, I saw him face the challenge of dealing with an individual who feigned defeat rather than face the challenge of learning in front of others. Caleb saw through the manufactured persona, as he always seemed to, and he kept up the pressure until the person opened to the learning. Meanwhile, though, several members of the individual's peer group showed resentment for Gattegno's refusing to honor the person's "weak learner" persona. There was not much to be said about the response, and he didn't, but I think he had hoped for better.

Later that evening, I found Caleb downstairs in the Jesuit library and invited him to take a look at *Insight*, a work by the Jesuit philosopher Bernard Lonergan. Lonergan, like Gattegno, identified awareness as the foundation of mathematics, education and science. Oddly, Lonergan, a fairly isolated and retiring thinker, had been on the cover of *Time Magazine* in 1970, though his perspective on genuinely innovative thought, including his own, was that it would be another 100-150 years before it was taken seriously. His perspective always reminded me of Gattegno's comment that "truth has short legs and is always arriving late and out of breath." When I stopped back in the library that evening, Caleb said to me, referring to Lonergan, "He knows what he's talking about."

Educational writing these days is attempting to follow the model of the natural sciences and claiming their "evidence-based" research to be the only writing worth taking seriously. Gattegno's work, in contrast, stands out as an immense struggle to provide a foundation for education as a human science. His *The Science of Education* is an attempt to develop the comprehensive set of terms and relations needed to ground education as a genuinely human science. If the theoretic differentiation of awareness emerged with the Greeks but only found its fuller expression in the scientific revolution many centuries later, it's likely that Gattegno's effort to give voice to a quite distinct differentiation of consciousness today will not come into its own immediately either.

In the last few years before his death, Caleb would sometimes telephone out of the blue, or so it seemed. He would ask questions about my work and my life, and sometimes about an article he had written for the newsletter. Of course I always regretted not having enough to say – who could take his work seriously and manage to keep up with him? – yet in those last visits I also felt an openness and interest on his part in just making contact and communicating. Although it is hardly possible to exaggerate the effect Dr. Gattegno has had in my personal and professional life, I'm especially grateful for those last few conversations. His life and work were marked by a constant and unremitting self-transcendence, every remarkable accomplishment serving only a temporary resting place. I like to think that his interest in making contact those last years came from a sense of fulfillment, an awareness of consolation that, if not entirely new, was flowing into his life and overflowed into ours. §

Gattegno's Body of Work: Providing Lessons For Life

Dr. Roann Altman

I never would have imagined that attending a seminar with Dr. Caleb Gattegno in 1979 would have such a profound effect on so many areas of my life for so many years. At the behest of a colleague, I agreed to take a break from touring Barcelona to learn Russian the Silent Way. I was in such awe of the man and this new way of learning languages that I enrolled in the remaining seminars in the series. What I learned that year, and in the years to follow, had an impact not only on my teaching but also on my entire professional (and I would venture to say even personal) life.

The basic message was simple — that only awareness is educable. But what did this mean? That awareness was at the foundation of everything we did. This principle shifted the focus from the content — the "what" of teaching, to the process — the "how" of learning. To learn as much as possible from this clearly wise man (certainly ahead of his time), I enrolled in many language, Silent Way, and Words in Color seminars, arranging many of the seminars to be presented in southern California.

In the beginning, I taught English as a second language using the Silent Way to entry-level college students. Over the years, although I was no longer using the rods and charts with my more advanced students, I noticed that I was still following many of the principles that I had learned from Dr. Gattegno. And they applied not just to classroom teaching but to coaching business professionals, to leading groups for personal growth, to designing courses and training programs – in fact, to almost every aspect of life. A look at some of Gattegno's basic principles for teaching language will reveal how far-reaching they are.

SUBORDINATION OF TEACHING TO LEARNING

This is the basic tenet of Gattegno's work in teaching languages. Yet how could this be if those entering the teaching profession do so in order to "teach"? Relinquishing the desire to be the one doing the work the students should be doing is crucial. That is where silence comes into play for teaching languages. The brilliance of the Silent Way lies in the rods and color-coded materials, which allow the teacher to step back, be silent, and elicit language from the students. Yet Gattegno insisted that the materials themselves were not the Silent Way; one could teach the Silent Way even without the materials. It was just a matter of allowing the students to do the work themselves.

The silence provides space for the students to talk and for the teacher to listen and know what the students need to work on next. I feel that silence and listening are key elements of my teaching and of who I am today. Allowing the students to inform the content of the course through their performance is something I build into each course I teach and each program I design. This flexibility is essential for keeping the course alive. Getting students to learn, from where they are, is more important than "covering" the stipulated material.

EXPECTING MUCH FROM OUR STUDENTS

Gattegno established several other principles that relate to how much we can expect from them. Students will be engaged when they are working on something that is at the right level for them, when the task is challenging — neither too easy nor too difficult. Lessons must be able to accommodate a range of abilities. Coaching requires custom-designed programs that will move the learner along quickly and efficiently. Programs must include tasks or projects that challenge everyone to work to the best of his or her ability.

When considering what constitutes a challenge, we also need to follow Gattegno's dictum of granting and not taking for granted. We must not do for the students what they can do themselves. We must not digest everything for them in advance. They need to discover what they can on their own: that's what makes the task challenging. Nor should we assume anything about their abilities to do — or not do — something. I have found it helpful to continually ask myself, "Am I sure?"

Gattegno also expected that students would be able to assess their own performance, that they would develop inner criteria for knowing when something was on target or not. The goal is not to spend valuable time and energy praising students for each little success but to find a way to let them know when their output needs adjustment. As a language learner myself, hearing frequent expressions of praise from a teacher is very distracting.

Gattegno took every opportunity to show his expectations of students. He once focused on a student hanging one of the Silent Way charts using too much tape. Gattegno drew the student's attention to the need to use a piece of masking tape that would just cover the plastic tape in each of the corners and extend enough to adhere to the board. The student immediately learned the level of awareness that was required of him.

LEARNING FROM OTHERS

When observing Silent Way classes for languages we already knew, we were guided to use a framework that included what the content of the lesson was, what the teacher did, and what the students did. This system focused our attention on different aspects of the lesson, without constraining us to look at very specific criteria. Whatever came into our awareness in these three areas could help direct us in our analysis of the lesson. I use a similar framework to this day when working with prospective teachers, as it provides a common language for talking about behavior in the classroom in a non-judgmental way.

> "The principles espoused by Caleb Gattegno apply to almost any learning situation — be it in the classroom or in life."

What is interesting about Gattegno's body of work is not just that it is timeless, providing lessons in so many areas of my life for so many years, but that it was ahead of its time. One prime example is the color-coded charts that are the foundation of the Silent Way. The words selected for the charts are based on the frequency list from the 1961 Brown Corpus. What an innovative idea to look at actual language to determine which words to teach! This approach to analyze language use has only recently come into vogue with the widespread development of corpora and the field of corpus linguistics.

The principles espoused by Caleb Gattegno apply to almost any learning situation — be it in the classroom or in life. They apply wherever awareness can be developed. A question arose just today in a group I work with about how to create learner autonomy. Indeed, this is the central question and one that Caleb Gattegno's insights can certainly help us answer.

§

> "What is it then, that will allow us to teach mathematics to anyone with a functioning mind and an inclination to learn? Simply, finding a way to make the learner aware of the powers of his mind — the powers he uses everyday..."
>
> - Dr. Caleb Gattegno

The Common Sense of Teaching Mathematics, Second Edition (2010), page 175.

A handmade Fidel drawn by a student learning to read. Words in Color, Gattegno's approach to teaching reading, encourages creativity, inventiveness, and play.

Ordinary Miracles

Claudie Gattegno

My sister and I are the only two French members of our Gattegno family. My father (Caleb's brother) left Egypt before the other members of my paternal family to come to France just before the war. Unfortunately, he was deported to Auschwitz when I was only two years old.

> "Instead of thinking that he was hopeless, as his teacher had kept saying to him all year, he realized on that day that he could use himself in an efficient way because he had the capacity to do so."

When I was about four, a gentleman came to collect us from the kindergarten. That was the first contact with my father's side of the family. I was very excited; I had the feeling on that day that life entered me. I clearly remember feeling that this family was mine, just as my uncle took my hand. Gaby, his first wife, and his daughters Alma and Lola were with him. They had just left Egypt to emigrate to England. I can never forget these very intense moments.

My second real meeting with Caleb Gattegno was when I listened to a radio broadcast on the *Radioscopy* program presented by Jacques Chancel in 1978. By the end of the interview, I was very taken with the remarks and the development of Gattegno's thinking.

The way he saw and talked about learning, his enthusiasm, and so many other things touched me very deeply. I wanted to learn more about it as I felt so close to what I had just heard.

Obviously, during the interview, I knew at once it was my uncle, as I straight away recognized his voice, but I wanted to go through the radio station to get in touch with him. I was not writing to my uncle, but to the person who was interviewed in that program.

He quickly replied and we met again.

We did not live in the same country, and he traveled a great deal. Because of that, we had not seen each other for several years. So it was in the '80s that my adventure began.

When my son Pascal was 14 years old, we attended a day of a seminar held at Aix-en-Provence. We three sat at the same table for lunch, and something happened which reveals a lot about Caleb Gattegno's pedagogic powers.

My uncle asked my son how his studies were going; he told him that he had difficulties in mathematics, and straight away Caleb Gattegno started working with him. Very shyly at first, Pascal answered all his questions and I could see, as he went on, Pascal's eyes get brighter and heard him answer spontaneously and joyously. That happened in the summer, it was holiday-time.

When school started again, Pascal had a very good mark in the first mathematics test. He had the same teacher as the previous year, and as he could not believe his eyes, he called me in to find out what had happened. I just told him that he had seen my uncle during the holidays and had been given an hour's lesson.

For Pascal, those moments turned out to be very important. Instead of thinking that he was hopeless, as his teacher had kept saying to him all year, he realized on that day that he could use himself in an efficient way because he had the capacity to do so. In a few minutes, he had gained self-confidence. It was miraculous.

that I could never have been able to start on this path without my own experiences, basic human ones. I do not mean theoretical knowledge.

It was as though I had always known I would find the answers to all my questions. These were: why is it that when we are little we have such great learning capabilities? Why do we lose them as we grow? Why is school not adapted to children's capabilities? Why do they allow us to get bored in school? And so on. The pedagogical approach as well as the pedagogical materials created by Caleb Gattegno made me search

"Why is school not adapted to children's capabilities?"

I participated in many seminars and then undertook a lot of deep work on myself. I had already started on this but the tools and insights which Gattegno had brought me allowed me to go further and much faster.

One needs to be ready for such work. His seminars were so rich, they opened up a significant field of study and allowed me to no longer be afraid, and to open up to any change of viewpoint.

What I was vaguely thinking about the power we have over ourselves, the importance of awarenesses which allow us to understand, and therefore solve difficult situations which we encounter and still move forward, became quite evident as I had more meetings with Caleb Gattegno. The baby's work and the hierarchy of learnings, and all he developed starting with his "model of man," led me to develop unsuspected competences.

From then on I began to look into pedagogical work, the deeper study of French, and the pedagogical materials created by Gattegno, because all of a sudden I felt the overwhelming urge to teach. I had the impression that all I had done so far had set me on this path which was mine.

At the time, my greatest awareness was telling myself

for other ways of knowing and naturally led me to share what to me seemed most important.

Working on knowing myself, what helped me most was to be aware of the Self and its attributes, on which we can act, on which I could act. I knew this because I had been through great adversity and had come out fairly well, but it only became clear after I worked with my uncle.

PEDAGOGY

After a few years working in seminars proposed and conducted by Caleb Gattegno, I felt that I was ready to teach and share what I had discovered. I became passionately engaged in the French language. The pedagogical materials were a gold mine for me. I had no wish to keep this treasure for myself.

I talked a lot with my uncle and we also corresponded often. He strongly encouraged me.

Before his death, we even had a project to teach French in Israel. He had laid the foundations for this with one of my cousins who, sadly, died in 1988 – a few months after Caleb.

The public I was interested in were those having difficulties. I therefore set out and started working

(Claudie Gattegno Cont'd.)

with different groups, mainly foreign ones, most of whom were illiterate people. I was convinced that everyone had the competences to be successful.

When I noted the pleasure of my trainees, when I saw how quickly these people learnt and gained self-confidence, when I heard them say "I am proud of myself," seeing the path they took after one or two courses (of four or eight months), all this really encouraged me to keep going.

French became my passion. Working on the sounds seemed the obvious way. Starting with little to build on leads to everything. When Gattegno says, "You cannot run before you can walk," it seems simple, yet this simple principle is not used to teach in our schools. All the children I came across or taught had learnt, or started learning, how to read from a text learnt by heart. For those who would, anyway, learn without a teacher, that is unimportant, but for the others, what a waste!

In my experience, whether working on French as a foreign language (with people who were literate in their country of origin) or on illiteracy (people who went to school, in France, but never managed to read and write much or at all), with foreign people with little or no schooling in their country of origin, or working with children having difficulties, I find that the Sound-Color Chart is the best tool.

This chart has always seemed magical to me; one can at the same time become aware of the sounds, and understand how French is built up by tackling the five algebraic operations which govern the language (addition, substitution, reversal, insertion and repetition). This chart allows us to see that with a small number of sounds (less than 40 in French), it is possible to read or say all the words in the language. This is, it seems to me, very reassuring for the learner.

It allows us to start the learning orally, whether for the spoken or the written language. It leads to the awarenesses needed to organize sounds, words and then sentences, as well as the awareness of the importance of pronunciation, rhythm, and the 'music' of the language before tackling the complexities of its spelling.

It also makes it possible to detect very quickly any problems of dyslexia, which is often found in illiterate people. As soon as this is evident, we can quickly bring in work on the order of sounds, by pointing to words and their reverse. This work is useful for the whole class, forcing the awareness that "lit" and "il" have the same number of sounds, but they are not in the same place in the word and incidentally that they do not have the same number of letters.

It allows us to use our perceptions. I see the sounds as I look at the chart, I hear them when I or others pronounce them, but I can also hear the sounds just by looking at the chart. The criteria are different for each person and that is what makes it such a powerful tool. The placing of the rectangles is also important. I have worked with color-blind students and asked them how they could point out the sounds. They all told me that their position guided them. Others said they counted from the first sound on the left.

How they do it is not so important, the fact remains that all seek and find their personal criteria to undertake efficiently the work suggested. The group helps to make each participant's acquisition quick and efficient because of the abundance each one brings. We tend to think that people who have had little or no education know nothing. The Gattegno Approach proves that is not so and sets these people up to be successful.

Finally, this chart puts everyone on the same level to start with and allows us educators to quickly judge what level the students are starting from.

Another important fact is that the learners notice from the very beginning that they are the ones working; they are the ones trying to produce the sounds, working on their sound-producing system, along with all the others. As each one encounters different problems, the teacher need only be the guide and mediator, not the model of the work being done.

I have trained many teachers and I can assert that they are much happier in their profession since they trained in the Gattegno Approach. They also know that the search is never completed, so they enjoy meeting with me or others to continue the work that is never fixed where education is concerned.

I do not think I need to say that the work I did with my uncle, and have kept doing since he died, has been a source of happiness. And that all this has changed who I am.

§

Dr. Caleb Gattegno in the city of Addis Ababa, Ethiopia. Gattegno went to Ethiopia on behalf of UNESCO to design and produce educational materials. Out of this experience, his core insights for Words in Color were developed. (Educational Solutions file photo.)

This Work Transformed Me
Ce travaille m'a transformé

Christiane Rozet

I became a schoolteacher because my father decided that this was the best career for me, and because at the time there were three months of holidays in the summer. For many years, I sold my time to the French state without any enthusiasm for the job. I was employed by National Education, but was certainly not a real educator until the day I met Caleb Gattegno and came into contact with his work.

I was teaching in a kindergarten with the children in the oldest age group. While never becoming a specialist in pedagogy, I gradually learnt to observe my young pupils and then, each year, discovered with pleasure children who were particularly gifted that I would never have noticed beforehand. Thanks to Gattegno, I was at last more present to the pupils than to the clock.

It was part of my job to prepare them for learning to read, and I saw how easy it was for them to learn not only to read but also to write with La Lecture en Couleurs (the French version of Words in Color). Some of them managed to make up short texts spontaneously, which they loved to illustrate.

In 1986, we found an old Apple II computer and were able to try out the Lecture Infuse software (the French version of Infused Reading). The experiment took place with 10 children from the top class and two from the next class down. They had between 45 and 50 minutes of work in all, in sessions of a few minutes spread out over a period of two weeks. They were tested two weeks later and none of the children could read. However, a few months afterwards, I realized that all the children from the top-level class could read, and a little later, the children from the next section down could also read. This showed that the software contained enough information for the children to have taught themselves to read in their own time.

In 1988, Raphael arrived in the school. He was considered to be autistic. I took him into my class and rapidly realized he had a passion for numbers.

> "I was at last more present to the pupils than to the clock."

He wrote them all the time, rather than drawing like the other children in the class. So I installed him in front of the old Apple computer, which by now lived in the classroom, and gave him the Visible and Tangible Maths software.

Raphael loved this program. He spent most of his time working on it. I loved watching him select the numbers to type with slow, very precise gestures, and seeing the joy on his face when the computer let him go on to the next item. This work transformed him. From being a sad, closed-up child, he became much more open, undertaking more activities, and positively joyful when the computer was on. He found in this software something which beautifully addressed the absolute he was in at that time. He could go along at his own pace, completely autonomously, far ahead of the others who were too young for such sport. When he went into primary school, he was tested and his level in maths was that of children aged 10 to 11. Thank you, Dr. Gattegno, on behalf of young Raphael!

It is thanks to Dr. Gattegno alone that someone as unmotivated as myself was able to become a teacher interested by her work, with the children, and keen to obtain the best results.

To begin with, I was quite reticent about attending Dr. Gattegno's seminars, fearing that they would be too intellectual for me, but I am now so pleased to have had the chance to meet him.

At first, I was put out by his way of working during the seminars, and I went to quite a few without really understanding the meaning of what he was saying. But I sensed the importance of his work enough to go back again. Since I need a long time to take things in, I gave myself the job of transcribing the seminars, and this gave me the time necessary to better understand his thinking and integrate it within me.

I also needed the courses given by colleagues who had been to most of his seminars, and who had worked a lot on his ideas themselves.

Now I get real pleasure from transcribing the seminars led by Dr. Gattegno, or his students, and preparing them for publication, while contributing in my own way to the life of Une Education Pour Demain.

Une Découverte Motivante

Devenue institutrice pour obéir à papa, et parce qu'il y avait à l'époque trois mois de vacances en été, c'est sans aucun enthousiasme que j'ai vendu mon temps à l'Education Nationale pendant des années. J'étais une employée du ministère de l'Education Nationale mais certainement pas une véritable éducatrice jusqu'au jour où j'ai rencontré Caleb Gattegno et son œuvre.

Professeur des écoles en Maternelle, j'avais choisi de travailler avec des enfants de grande section. Sans être pour autant devenue une spécialiste de la pédagogie, j'ai peu à peu commencé à observer mes petits élèves et c'est ainsi que, chaque année, j'ai découvert avec plaisir des enfants particulièrement doués que je n'aurais pas su reconnaître auparavant. Grâce à Gattegno, j'étais enfin plus présente à mes élèves qu'aux horaires.

J'ai eu envie de les préparer à l'apprentissage de la lecture et j'ai pu constater avec quelle facilité les enfants qui le voulaient pouvaient apprendre à lire et à écrire avec la Lecture en Couleurs. Certains sont même parvenus à composer spontanément de petits textes qu'ils se plaisaient à illustrer.

En 1986, nous avons déniché un ordinateur Apple IIe et nous avons pu essayer le logiciel Lecture Infuse. L'expérience a eu lieu avec dix enfants de la grande section et deux de la moyenne section. Ils ont eu entre quarante-cinq et cinquante minutes de travail par séquences de quelques minutes, espacées sur deux semaines. Testés deux semaines plus tard, aucun des enfants ne savait lire, mais quelques mois après, je me suis rendu compte que les enfants de la grande section savaient tous lire, et un peu plus tard encore, les enfants de la moyenne section aussi. Ainsi, nous avons pu démontrer que le logiciel contenait assez d'informations pour que les enfants apprennent à lire tout seuls.

En 1988, Raphaël est arrivé dans l'école. Il avait une réputation d'autiste. Je l'ai pris dans ma classe et rapidement, je me suis rendu compte qu'il était passionné par les chiffres ; il en écrivait à tout

(Rozet Cont.)

moment, plutôt que de faire des dessins comme les autres enfants.

Je l'ai donc installé devant le même vieil ordinateur, qui avait élu domicile dans ma classe, avec Visible and Tangible Maths. Raphaël a adoré ce programme. Il passait la plupart de son temps à y travailler. Je me régalais de le voir sélectionner les chiffres à inscrire avec des gestes d'une infinie précision, de la joie sur son visage en voyant l'ordinateur lui permettre d'avancer à la case suivante. Ce travail l'a transformé. D'un enfant renfermé et triste, il est devenu beaucoup plus ouvert, plus entreprenant, et franchement gai quand l'ordinateur était branché. Il trouvait dans ce programme quelque chose qui répondait très bien à son absolu du moment. Il pouvait avancer à sa propre vitesse en toute autonomie, loin devant les autres, trop jeunes pour de tels sports. Testé à son entrée en école primaire, il avait un niveau en mathématiques d'un enfant de 10 à 11 ans. Merci Gattegno de la part d'un petit Raphaël!

Si quelqu'un d'aussi peu motivée que moi au départ a pu devenir une enseignante intéressée par son travail avec les enfants et obtenir donc de meilleurs résultats, c'est uniquement grâce à Caleb Gattegno.

Quelque peu réticente au départ à assister à des séminaires animés par Gattegno, redoutant un travail trop « intellectuel », je me réjouis aujourd'hui d'avoir eu la chance de le rencontrer.

D'abord déroutée par sa façon de travailler pendant ses séminaires, j'ai assisté à un certain nombre de ces rencontres, sans bien comprendre alors le sens de ses paroles. Mais j'en subodorais suffisamment l'importance pour revenir la fois suivante. Ayant besoin d'un long laps de temps, je me suis attelée à la tâche de transcrire ces séminaires, ce qui me donnait le temps nécessaire pour mieux comprendre et intégrer la pensée de Gattegno.

Il m'a fallu aussi assister aux stages animés par des collègues qui ont suivi tous ces séminaires et ont fait un énorme travail sur eux-mêmes.

Maintenant c'est avec plaisir que je poursuis le travail de transcription et de mise en page des séminaires animés par Gattegno ou par ses élèves, tout en participant à ma façon à la vie de l'association Une Education pour Demain. §

> "The subordination of teaching to learning is the only way of handling the challenge of freeing students while ensuring that they learn by an economic exchange of their time for a maximum learning."
>
> - Dr. Caleb Gattegno

The Common Sense of Teaching Foreign Languages, Second Edition (2010), page 21.

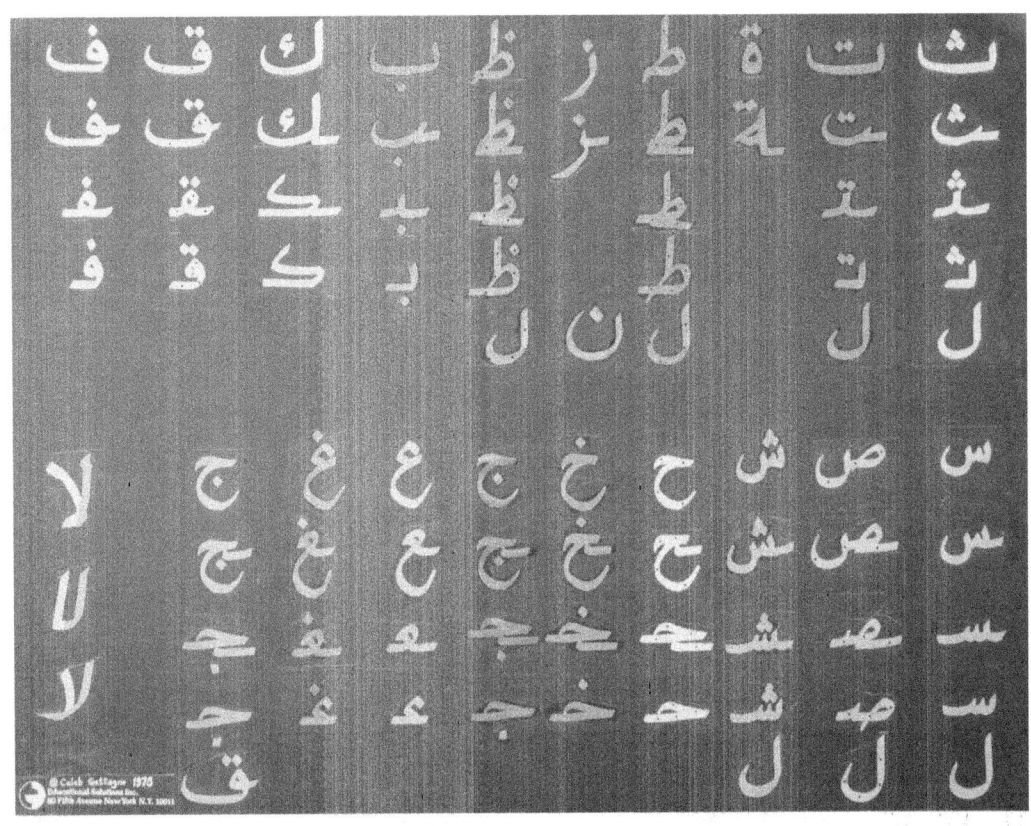

Prototype Arabic Fidel charts 1 & 2, hand-painted on cardboard in 1978. ©Educational Solutions Worldwide Inc.

Insights from Gattegno

Dr. Piers Messum

I attended three seminars given by Caleb Gattegno towards the end of his life, the first in Osaka in May 1986. I was teaching English there, but didn't imagine myself having any long term interest in teaching, and certainly not in teaching languages. I'd studied Latin, Ancient Greek, and French at school but hadn't enjoyed any of them, and my job was just a means by which I would live in Japan and have an adventure before settling into a 'proper' job, in business, back in the UK.

The seminar was entitled Who Cares About Health? In three days, Gattegno swept us through a history of energy in Western thought; through his model of self, psyche, soma, and affectivity, his proposals about sleep, development, the attributes of the self, and so on; and then on into health itself. I still have my notes; not made at the time, but made afterwards listening to the whole tape recording of the event which I didn't properly understand, but somehow realized was significant for me.

Since then, many things I have done have started with Gattegno's ideas, but I'm still most inspired by his model: his comprehensive, coherent and often lyrical account of humans and their activities described with the understanding that energy, energies and energy transactions are the underlying reality of everything. And I'm helped by the clear position he took that it was a model that would be superseded by more adequate ones in due course, and a model which was useful for what it can and does address but which does not either address or solve every problem we encounter when living a life. When I'm trying to regulate my feelings and emotions, I do not use Gattegno's model; when I'm trying to understand learning, development and much more, I do.

It seems to me that a large part of the variability we find in education must come from the degree to which a teacher can mentally take the part of each individual student in front of him, i.e. the extent to which the teacher can see how the student sees the world and can see what resources the student has available to meet what is at the moment unknown in that world. Technical knowledge about his subject and how it can be taught is needed as well, but to the extent that the teacher has insight into how his student is and can be, he is increasingly going to be in a position to subordinate his teaching to the learning of the student.

Insight into others – and insight that is useful and available in the moment – starts with self insight. That takes time and effort, but also, for most of us, some guidance from those who have worked on themselves before us. Gattegno's model provides a source of such guidance. It's a vision of being a human that has the qualities I mentioned before, and is also full of good questions and thoughtful answers to help our enquiry. This may mainly indicate my ignorance, but I am not aware of any other model of learning and the learner that is as complete as his. So my private hope is that his model might one day be commonplace as a way for us to understand ourselves. If it were, then I think the quality of education would be greatly raised.

The largest project I've undertaken was the research that I eventually published as a Ph.D. thesis. It was inspired by my experience of learning Japanese by the Silent Way in Fusako Allard's class in Osaka.

There I encountered the most curious, most counterintuitive aspect of Gattegno's approach to language teaching: the silence of the teacher. Fusako taught us Japanese pronunciation without, I think, ever uttering a sound in the language. This approach is shocking for teachers, but is not shocking at all for students as soon as they start to work this way. The silence of the teacher creates a safe space for them to experiment in, and Fusako made sure we used this to do the work necessary to create new, Japanese-speaking versions of ourselves. In fact, so inspiring was it to work this way that I can remember happily babbling to myself in Japanese on the way home from lessons.

I mentioned earlier that I hadn't enjoyed learning French at school. One moment in this, when I must have been about nine or 10, still stands out in my memory. That year we were played stories from daily life on a tape recorder and shown accompanying pictures projected from filmstrips. One episode was, I think, about Paul and his breakfast. As I recall, he put his bowl first au dessus de la table and then au dessous de la table. Well, I couldn't hear any difference between the sentences and certainly couldn't produce anything different when asked to repeat them. I was told to listen again carefully, I was played the sentences several times and nothing changed. I was baffled and, I think, a bit angry. We seemed to be being asked to do something impossible and absurd.

Learning to pronounce Japanese in a class with a diametrically opposing paradigm – not attempted mimicry but experimentation by the students with feedback from the teacher – led to none of this anger and confusion. It was also very successful. I enjoyed talking in Japanese, and my pronunciation was certainly better than that of my colleagues who had learnt in the usual way. But until one has had an experience like this it is difficult to imagine how it could work.

Anyway, when I decided to try teaching English by the Silent Way, in 1991, Roslyn Young recommended that I read some phonetics textbooks. I started to get the hang of phonemic analysis and so on, and I thought I was ready to start teaching until I came across a passage in *Teaching Foreign Languages in Schools* in which Gattegno pointed out the different demands that languages place on breath control. I must have missed that part of the textbooks completely. But when I returned to them, I discovered that none of them even considered this. Speech breathing was hardly mentioned.

I had already discovered some of the oddities that characterize English pronunciation, things that native speakers are completely unaware of but which mark the language out. The best-known one among learners of English is its so-called 'rhythm' which is so different from that of French, Japanese, and most other languages in the world, but there are quite a few other anomalous phenomena which are unexplained and which, in fact, many phoneticians don't even feel a need to try to explain. There is a rather despairing phrase in linguistics, "Speech is special," which refers to the fact that speech seems to break some basic psychological rules. Some linguists use this to let them off the hook of understanding basic speech phenomena: the easy way out is either to allow for everything to be arbitrary and to not require explanation, only description, or to posit magic 'modules' of the brain that take care of everything automatically.

With Gattegno's understanding of learning through awarenesses, in my mind, I could not accept any of this. I had a minor epiphany, and suddenly saw how a distinctive style of speech breathing in English might lead to the oddities of English phonetics. It took 10 or 15 minutes to sketch this out, and I've since spent the greater part of the last 20 years trying to make this sketch rigorous, to convince others and to apply the ideas to the teaching of pronunciation.

At the same time, I have been working on the question of whether Gattegno's Silent Way paradigm for pronunciation teaching also applies in some way to how infants learn to pronounce the sounds of their first language. And sure enough, it does. As he put it, during his final address to ATM in 1987, when talking about how children learn to speak:

"You are evading questions in saying, 'They do it by imitation.' By imitation, indeed. The greatest nonsense I ever heard, and everybody repeats it. It's absolutely wrong. No-one can learn to speak the mother tongue by imitation."

Such a small part of Gattegno's work, yet this idea has consumed such a large part of my life! §

It Takes the Time it Takes
何かをするのに　かかるだけの時間がかかる

Kazuko Shimizu

"Good morning, everyone! You have arrived safely without falling into a gutter nor getting hit by a car. I, too, came far from New York. I hope the precious time we are going to spend together will be fruitful."

Thus, Dr. Gattegno opened the May 1984 seminar in Osaka. This may not have been the exact wording, but the expression was so fresh to me that it made a deep impression. That day, I gained a new awareness on time – time in general, my time, and someone else's time – and the attitude toward valuing time and respecting it has been implanted in me. This new awareness became very helpful when I reflected upon each class I taught as a Japanese teacher. I would ask myself whether I wasted my students' time as well as my own, or whether I "was able to change my students' precious time into valuable experience." Not only in my classes but also in my daily life, I have valued and respected time ever since.

Around 1978, I learned from a friend who had been studying Japanese with Fusako Allard that there was a learning material which used colors, and one could teach pronunciation using it. As I was just beginning to teach Japanese using a conventional method, I hurriedly went to meet Fusako. This was my first encounter with the Silent Way.

There were several people related to Fusako's school, The Center, who were practicing the Silent Way, and some of them had been to New York to take Dr. G's seminars. I had always been envious of them as I was not able to go to New York with a young child.

There were many books written by Dr. G, as well as various learning materials, but I wanted to take the seminars given by the person who had written the books and developed the materials. I was very happy, therefore, when Fusako started inviting Dr. G to Osaka in 1984.

From then on, I was able to study in Dr. G's seminars on theory, and on various languages such as Spanish and Arabic, every year during the week of national holidays in May. In retrospect, the seminars made me feel that I was charged with a new energy, and was filled with ambition to try out different things. With less ability to comprehend English compared to today, I called upon all of my five senses, and tried to take in what was said in the session, and what was produced from the exchanges between Dr. G and the participants.

What I have learned from Dr. G's seminars, publications, and the learning materials such as charts and rods is unfathomable. Dr. G said, "I worked hard to invent these learning materials. You don't need, therefore, to work to make them. Take advantage of these things and achieve your own." He said, for instance, when you take the Word Charts, especially the first two or three, to a river and wash them out, what you get is the spirit of that language – the words needed to signify the specific behavior of that very language. I may have heard this second-hand from Fusako, but at any rate, I agreed with this view. Even now, I believe that it is possible for me to learn a language, any language, if I were given the Silent Way charts of that language, some rods, and a speaker of that language.

"Am I providing something useful for my students' learning utilizing the rods and charts properly?"

Among the learning materials of the Silent Way, the Sound-Color Charts and Fidels make the sounds and spellings of the target language visible and tangible, and the Word Charts and rods do the same for the structure, or grammar. It could be that only those who have experienced it can understand the power

> "Even now, I believe that it is possible for me to learn a language, any language, if I were given the Silent Way charts of that language, some rods, and a speaker of that language."

"It takes the time it takes." "Subordination of Teaching to Learning." "Suspension of judgment." "Only awareness is educable in man." "Meet the baby in you." There are many sayings that Dr. G has left. All of them are extremely useful not only in our classes but also in our daily lives.

When I am very busy with too many things to be taken care of, and get into a state of panic, I remember such sayings as "I am here and now," and "It takes the time it takes," and this awareness calms me. It also gives me the awareness of necessity to "suspend judgment" as I often try to judge things and people against my own yard-stick in my daily life. When I was teaching, his expressions helped me a great deal to check what I do in my classes or reflect on my classes. I would ask myself such questions as "Am I too hastily judging what comes out of my students?" "Am I interfering with my students' learning by intruding upon their time and space?" or

of the charts and the rods, which force the students' awareness towards the sound and the behavior of that language.

"Respect everyone's time – the students', your own, and the observers'"; "Take the time that is necessary, going along with the students' learning"; and for that, "Utter no unnecessary word." He was never preoccupied by such things as IQ which lead one to pre-judgment, but rather, Dr. G "knew the varied ability and possibility that each student brought, and using the rods provided the visible and tangible sources exactly appropriate for each student in front of him to learn the lesson," as John Holt witnessed.

I am ever so appreciative of the opportunity to learn from Dr. G in person, who showed me my own, and everybody else's, potential and made me aware of the means to activate it. I am also thankful to Fusako Allard who created that opportunity for me.

(Shimizu Cont'd.)
何かをするのに　かかるだけの時間がかかる

「今日はみなさん、溝にもはまらず、車にもぶつからず、私の講座にようこそ、来られました。私もはるばるニューヨークからやって来ました。皆さんと私の貴重な時間を大切にし、両方にとって、これからの時間が実り多いものになるよう願っています。」1984年の5月、大阪でのセミナーでガテーニョ先生(以下Dr. G)はそう告げました。言葉はこの通りではなかったかもしれませんが、この言葉は私には新鮮で印象深いものでした。この時から、時間、自分の時間、人の時間というものへの新たな認識ができ、それを大切にし、尊重するという考え方が私の中に植えつけられたように思います。

そして、当時の仕事であった日本語を教えるという場所で、生徒の時間、そして、自分の時間を無駄にしていないか、生徒の「時間を貴重な体験の数々に使えたか？」というのは一つずつのクラスを自分で振り返るときの役に立ちました。また、クラスだけでなく、日常の生活の中でも自分の時間はもとより人の時間も尊重し大切にするということはこのときから今までずっと私の中にあります。

1978年ころ、アラード房子さんに日本語を習っていた友人から、文字を色分けして発音も教える教材があると聞きました。当時、普通のやり方で日本語を教え始めていた私はさっそく房子さんに会いに行きました。これがサイレント・ウェイ(以下ＳＷ)との出会いです。

大阪にある房子さんの学校、語学文化協会の周りには、ＳＷを実践している人々がたくさんいました。そして、その人たちはNYまでDr. Gのセミナーを受けに行っていました。当時は子供も幼く、NYに行くことのできない私はいつも、皆のことをうらやましく思っていました。Dr. Gの本も色々あるし、教材もありましたが、それを開発した人のセミナーを受けてみたいとずっと思っていたのです。ですから、1984年から房子さんがDr. Gを大阪に招き始めたときは本当にうれしかったものです。

このとき以来、毎年5月の連休にDr. Gの理論のセミナーとスペイン語やアラビア語などの言語のクラスを習うことができるようになりました。今、このころのことを振り返ると

セッションのあとはエネルギーが充電されたように感じ、自分のクラスで試してみたいことでいっぱいになっていました。当時は今よりもずっと英語の理解力も悪かったのですが、とにかく体中すべてを耳にして、5感すべてを動員してセッションで話されること、参加者とのやりとりから生まれるものなど、すべてを受け止めようとしていたことが思い出されます。

Dr. Gのセミナー、著書、チャートや棒などの教材から学んだことは数知れません。Dr. Gは「私はこの教材を作りました。皆さんは教材を作り出す必要はないから、その分、この教材を活用し、さらにその上に自分たちのものを築いていってほしい」とも言われていました。「たとえば、英語という言語を川で選択すると最後に残るものがその言葉のスピリットだ」という言葉は房子さんから聞いたかもしれません。各言語の語彙のチャート、ことに最初の2～3枚のチャートにはそれぞれの言葉のスピリットすなわち、その言語特有の振る舞いに必要な単語でできていると思います。私は今でも何語でも、もし自分が習得したいと思えばSWのチャートと棒とその言語を話す人がそろえば可能だと思っています。

何かをするのに「かかるだけの時間がかかる」「教えることは習得することに従属する」

「判断を保留する」「教えられることは気づきだけ」「あなた方の中にいる赤ん坊の力に気づきなさい」などDr. Gの残した言葉はたくさんありますが、どれもクラスの中だけでなく日々の生活で役に立つことばかりです。

とても忙しく、たくさんのしなければならないことがあり、パニックになったとき、「今ここにいる」こと「かかるだけの時間がかかる」ことを思いだし、そのことに気がつくとパニック状態から抜け出すことができます。また、日常の生活ですぐに物事や人を自分の尺度で判断してしまいがちな私には「判断を保留する」ことがとても必要だと気づきます。

教えていたときも生徒から出てくることをすぐに判断していないか、生徒の時間と空間に侵入して学びを妨げてい

ないか、棒やチャートの活用で生徒の学びに役立つものを提供できているかなど、自分がクラスのなかでしていることをチェックしたり、自分のしたことを振り返ったりするときにこれらの言葉が教えることは大きいものでした。

SWの教材では、サウンド・カラー・チャートとフィデルで、ある言語の発音や綴りを「目に見え、さわれるもの」にし、語彙のチャートや棒で、その言語の構造、いわゆる文法を「目に見え、さわれるもの」にします。生徒がその言語の音やふるまい方に気づくより所となるチャートや棒の働きは体験した人にだけわかるのかもしれません。以下のレッスンの紹介は言語ではなく、算数のレッスンですが、底を流れる考え方は何も変わりません。

John Holt著のHow Children Failの中に1959年の10月にDr. GがNYのLesley Ellis Schoolで知恵遅れと言われている少年たち数名に棒を使って算数を教えた40分のクラスの記録があります。Johnはその中でとりわけ落ち着きなく、周りに対する警戒心でいっぱいの黒髪の少年をずっと観察していました。

Dr. Gは前置きも説明も何もなく、少年たちがすべきことを指示します。テーブルの真ん中に置かれた棒の山から、青い棒(9)を2本とり、2本の間に濃い緑色の棒(6)をはさむと、それと同じものを作るように少年たち指示、それから、濃い緑の上にできた空間にあてはまる棒を探すよう指示。皆は何度も何度もいろんな棒を試す作業を延々と続けます。そのあげくに薄い緑色(3)がその空間にあてはまることが皆にわかります。すると、Dr. Gは、自分のものを手に持ち、濃い緑(6)を振り落とし、今度は青(9)2本とそれにはさまれた薄い緑(3)の間にできた空間に何があてはまるか見つけるように指示。そして、全員がまた何度も何度も延々と違う棒をあてはめる作業を続けます。Dr. Gは全員が、あてはまる濃い緑(6)をみつけるまで見守ります。皆ができると、最初に戻ります。

このようなサイクルを少なくとも数回繰り返えすうち、黒髪の少年の中で腑に落ちたものがあったのでしょう。少年は喜びで震える手で自分がみつけた棒をあてはめると、「ぴったりだ、ぴったりだ!」と言いながら、周りにいる見学の人たちに見えるよう自分の4本の棒を持ち上げました。この後、色を変えて同じ課題が示されたとき、黒髪の少年はひとめぐりの作業で必要な棒をみつけ、前のときのように喜びで興奮することもなく静かで、自分の中に確信を持っているようでした。彼はもう知っているからです。

Dr. G自身がしたレッスンなので当たり前ですが、この40分のクラスにDr. Gが研究してきて伝えようとしていたことが凝縮されていると思います。「すべての人の時間、生徒、自分、見学者の時間を大切にし」、「生徒の習得の過程に寄り添いながら、必要で十分な時間をかけ」そのためには「不必要な言葉を発せず」、「知能指数などにとらわれ、やる前にできないだろうと判断することをせず」それ以上に「目の前にいる少年たちの中にある様々な能力と可能性を知っていて」、そのとき現在、少年たちが眼の前にある課題を習得するのにぴったりな「見ることができ、触れることができる」確かなよりどころを棒を使って提供しています。

自分を含め、自分と係わるすべての人が持っている可能性を見、各人にそなわっている能力を生かす手立てに気づかせてくれたDr.Gから実際に教えてもらう機会をもてたこと、その機会を作って下さったアラード房子さんに感謝する気持ちでいっぱいです。

§

> 何かをするのに「かかるだけの時間がかかる」「教えることは習得することに従属る」
>
> 「判断を保留する」「教えられることは気づきだけ」「あなた方の中にいる赤ん坊の力に気づきなさい 」

> "Without intuition no one could do more than respond timidly to discrete stimuli; with it, bolder, encompassing steps are in order."

— Dr. Caleb Gattegno

The Universe of Babies, Second Edition (2010), page 77.

Elementary school students working on the Fidel Phonic Code. Dr. Gattegno suggested the use of the pointer to help with focus and concentration.

Taking the Learner into Account:
An Effective Remedy for Becoming a Better Teacher

Wojciech Łukaszewicz

I am writing these words on a mid-winter Saturday evening in the city of Białystok, Poland, my hometown on the easternmost flank of the European Union. Just a couple hours ago, I ended a long talk on the phone with Roslyn, an Australian living and working in the heart of Europe, who, like me, is an English teacher. The conversation, though seemingly chaotic, had a sound reason and clear focal point throughout – it evolved around the ideas of an Egyptian-born scientist who had traveled the world and influenced, among many others, the two speakers on the phone at certain points in their lives. Reflecting on his ideas, I think of how ideas are born, developed, spread over time, and how they pull down various barriers and permeate the lives of individuals like Gattegno, Roslyn, and myself, in the span of roughly three generations.

Gattegno's 100th birth anniversary initially forces me to think in terms of ruthless chronology; in which case I am less fortunate in accessing and using his ideas than Roslyn, who had a chance to work with him in person. To me, she seems to be truly privileged to take the position of the middle generation, where both the past and future become dynamically connected. As we live our lives and do what we do, we inherit, adopt, and change ideas, but never really own them. In a sense, one is always in the position of an intermediary, and the awareness of this fact implies the right to modify, but also imposes the responsibilities of a mission. This is what Gattegno himself probably had in mind when he wrote about collective experiments.

I began teaching English in 1990, two years after Caleb Gattegno died. A number of teachers across the world, whose minds he had managed to ignite, had already been successful incorporating the Silent Way into their practice, and others were heroically switching to it from much less demanding domains. But it didn't cross my path then. There was not a single teacher around who could clearly show the power of the approach.

With hindsight, however, I recall a short period in the fledgling stage of my career when as a freelance teacher with next to no experience and scarce materials available, I followed intuitively, and only remotely, what Gattegno called "the common sense of teaching." The readiness to experiment and flexibly use my own and my students' mental and physical resources, take adventurous paths, improvise around problems as they aroused, and a genuine desire to invent effective techniques were all there, but the sound principles were missing. Sometimes a lesson would slip into drama, sometimes into Total Physical Response. Twenty years later, on seeing Glenys Hanson having her students usher each other along an imaginary line across the room to represent time expressions, I

> "In the pre-Gattegno years, what I took for granted was the physical presence of the learners, teacher, and language in the classroom."

was certain it was a chunk of my own lesson from the years before. Those were only Silent Way-like moments though, by no stretch of the imagination were they Silent Way lessons. I was not silent.

Years went by as I happily taught English to groups and individuals. Waving the flag of creativity became my obsession – I rejected coursebooks as schematic, avoided boredom in the classroom at all cost, and the hard drive of my computer was brimming with a multitude of materials, reinvented old recipes, and hundreds of "classic" lessons for any learner and level. I followed the latest trends, went to workshops and conferences, and took up teacher training in the hope to keep up the freshness of my teaching. Yet weariness, boredom, and routine were inevitably creeping in, and forced me to seek a remedy against the tired teacher syndrome.

The Silent Way was not meant to be such a remedy, but became one quite by accident. Before that happened, it appeared to me as a theory fossilized in books on linguistics rather than present day practice. Such a notion of it was about to be confirmed when I saw three different takes on the Silent Way by internationally renowned teacher trainers at workshops in 2008. To my dismay, those Jacks of all trades presented a few simplified and diluted knacks of the approach, which looked like jokes in the classroom. That was what I needed, a trigger to start an investigation of my own. Infallibly the internet helped, and gradually I managed to gather a number of pieces belonging to the picture puzzle called 'the Silent Way today.' The resources I found were telling me that there was something much more serious and substantial lurking behind. I tried and experimented with the groups I was teaching at the time, and my interest grew by the day. That nibbling lasted a year or so; to go one step further I urgently needed the know-how, and for that I did not really need to read Gattegno's books, but to talk to his disciples. One day in the winter of 2009, I picked up the phone and called Roslyn Young in Besançon, France.

That was when my true conversion began. Within a month, I got hold of all the charts and the Fidel. A box of wooden rods had already been my favorite toy for quite a while. Roslyn's role was pivotal all along, and I got a lot of support from other teachers at the 2010 summer workshop in France. Almost immediately after that, I was fortunate to start teaching a whole range of groups to whom I was eager to bring my newly revised confidence.

The transitions of the last two years have not made me a better teacher, or a dramatically different person; they have brought me to the stage where I can freely start evaluating all the previous stages in my 20 years of teaching. Indeed, the Silent Way frees me of the roles I was dutifully taking in the past: the expert, the controller, the guardian, the entertainer, the caregiver, you name them. More importantly, however, it helps my students to responsibly take the roles they often could not or did not take: the learner, the thinker, the risk-taker, the creator, or the peer. My silence has a two-fold effect – on the one hand, it enforces me to be with them when they are learning, on the other, it lets me distance myself from them and not interfere with the learning to take place. Of course, there are clashes and hindrances. Our insecurity could be stronger than the freedom to make mistakes, dependencies could get in the way, transference might reveal a certain dose of apathy, exasperation, or even aggression. A whole spectrum of old, deeply ingrained habits has to be faced and unlearned.

Like any theory that tries to encompass the complexity of human learning, the Silent Way has its own key notions. It would be unfair of me, a mere latest convert to it, to dwell on those notions here, while still coming to grips with the basic tenets. Personally, however, the notion of presence has taken an array of new meanings since I entered Gattegno's territories. In the pre-Gattegno years, what I took for granted was the physical presence of the learners, teacher, and language in the classroom. The language was presented, but learning was often missing. Now, when the board and materials are almost gone, the language comes to the fore as if out of nowhere, and is all that matters. At my disposal I have silence and gesture, which are new and far more intricate expressions of presence than spoken or written words. It is amazing how much nuanced human communication takes place and how high the level of involvement is.

In my beginner class, a young pregnant woman is genuinely worried by the fact she will miss classes for a week or two when the baby is born, and that her daughter will not be able to participate silently in the course anymore. What a tribute to her own commitment, and to Dr. Gattegno! §

A Father's Reading Laboratory

Michel Zobel

I met Caleb Gattegno for the first time in 1980, during a seminar he gave in France on computers and learning. That was 30 years ago. At that time, I was a skiing instructor. I wished to meet Caleb Gattegno after reading a very interesting article about him in the French magazine *Psychology*. Caleb Gattegno talked about his work on learning languages. He emphasized the importance of awarenesses and affectivity as ways of getting into learning. He presented the individual, the person, as a unity, with powers that enable him to be autonomous in his learning experiences. He took the example of the child, who learns by himself how to walk and how to speak his mother tongue without being taught.

I wondered how to build a bridge between the practice of teaching skiing and Caleb Gattegno's approach to learning.

When I first met him, after I told him I was teaching people how to ski, Caleb Gattegno, dressed in his traditional grey suit, crossed his arms and remained silent, facing me, for a few minutes. Then he started imagining, speaking aloud, how it would be possible to use the computer in learning to ski – he could not ski and considered the question most interesting. It was a new challenge! He told me: "We'll manage to work together on this question during the seminar and *you* will find solutions!"

This "*you* will find solutions!" thrown to me as a challenge, has accompanied me for the last 30 years, in my professional as well as private life. These words pushed me forward in my teaching experience and gradually allowed me to clarify and become conscious of Gattegno's assertion, which I heard so many times: "Only one thing can be educated in man – awareness!"

In this collective memoir, I would like to share my own experience as a father, accompanying my son, Nathanaël, from his first year at primary school on. He was six years old, then. Today, he is 12.

The way I accompanied him was greatly inspired by the direct contacts I had with Caleb Gattegno and his works, as well as with the people who worked with him for many years and who also produced very efficient tools. In passing, I would like to thank them all for allowing me to do such thorough work, based upon true, reliable and perceptible criteria, giving access to genuine Subordination of Teaching to Learning.

One day, at the beginning of the first year of primary school, Nathanaël came home from school, very proud, with an illustrated reading book under his arm. As soon as he arrived, he rushed to me and said: "Dad, I can read!" He immediately sat on the chair next to me and opened the book at the first page. He started telling me the story, his eyes turned towards the ceiling of the living-room, without even looking at the text printed on the page of the book. I discovered with astonishment that he knew the text by heart without reading it. I had to turn the pages of the book myself to be sure that what he was saying corresponded to the story written in the book. At the end of the story, he told me: "That's good, isn't it? You see, I can read!" Having a book open on his knees and being able to say all that was written corresponded to what he had seen his schoolteacher do during the morning reading lesson.

I was immediately aware that he had listened to the teacher so attentively while she was reading the story that he had retained the whole text he had listened to, even the slightest details. At that moment, I told myself: he has just shown me how he has managed to use his listening and retention powers to tell me the story he heard at school. As I noticed this, I told myself that my son had just demonstrated he was a very good listener and storyteller. Thus, it was very important for him to keep this listening ability alive at school, as it enabled him to retain so easily.

I had studied Caleb Gattegno's Words in Color and I knew that what he was doing was certainly not reading.

I wanted to avoid being an obstacle by creating confusion in him, so I did not tell him that reading was not repeating what you had heard, but decoding what was written on a page. I offered Nathanaël activities to allow him to discover and explore the French written language with the Words in Color tools. Of course, I called what we were doing together "games and discovery of sounds and colors with the use of signs," without referring to the learning of reading, which Nathanaël considered as an activity done exclusively at school with the teacher. I felt at peace with what he did at school, as I knew that at home he was doing very efficiently and successfully what had to be done about reading. Nathanaël named this activity "The Gattegno Method." I could see him exploring with great interest the various stages of learning to read, so well demonstrated by Caleb Gattegno.

My main concern, as a father guiding his son in his learning, was to avoid being an obstacle in his activity. I was careful to let Nathanaël fully benefit from these moments of exploration and experimentation in order to allow him to have the right awarenesses, and thus reach a good level of mastery in his activity and discover all the aspects required by the activity of reading.

I remember that I heard Caleb Gattegno say during a seminar: "As teachers, we shouldn't be obstacles for our pupils." I had the opportunity to transfer these words to my own experience as a father: "As parents, we shouldn't be obstacles for our children in their learning."

§

I Have Experienced the Gattegno Approach
Mon expérience avec l'approche Gattegno

Nathanaël Zobel

Let me introduce myself: my name is Nathanaël, I am 12 years old, and I live in France. I have a passion for music – I write songs, compose the music, sing, and play my own accompaniments on the piano. I love reading too, but what I enjoy most is writing – I have been writing novels since the age of nine. I also write poems and convey, through the words, my eagerness for traveling, and my dreams. My life is governed by the rhythms of my time at school, the most pleasant of times, from which I greatly benefit. And the approach created by Dr. Gattegno has been highly beneficial to me.

Indeed, at the age of six (i.e. my first year at primary school), I was initiated by my father into a learning method that was completely unknown to me, what I still call now "The Gattegno Method." From reading to arithmetic, this approach taught me so many things that represent an asset in my everyday life.

(Nathaniël Zobel Cont.)

I followed various courses in France and in Switzerland (mathematics, French grammar and spelling, English, Japanese, geography, history…), given by teachers who had worked with Dr. Gattegno for many years. And in passing, I would like to thank them for all that they taught me.

Before getting to know this way of working, I did not really feel, let's say… at ease in my work at school, and I came very close to being disgusted with school. But Dr. Gattegno's approach revealed in me a kind of facility for understanding and interpreting most of the aspects of the French language, and this allows me today to express myself quite easily, orally as well as in writing. As far as mathematics are concerned, they really frightened me before I was offered this learning method; sums were all mixed up in my mind. But rapidly, everything dropped into the right boxes in my mind, just like words placed in alphabetical order in a dictionary. I am telling you this to show you that Dr. Gattegno's work has made my life much easier.

I am talking about "The Gattegno Method" and you may wonder what I am talking about and how I was taught it. Well, one day, my father came back home with packets under his arm. I soon discovered, with astonishment, they contained mysterious black charts covered with words and squares in color. He taught me that each color corresponded to a sound of the French language and that, in that way, one could learn how to read, and even how to write. My great interest in this "funny way of learning" enabled me to go through all the levels of my schooling successfully, until today.

I was also greatly helped by the work with colored rods, developed by Dr. Gattegno. I benefitted, too, from the use of several learning software programs, based on Dr. Gattegno's work, for French as well as mathematics. Some of these are still greatly helpful to me.

Finally, what I want to tell you is that if I had not met this fabulous way of working, I would certainly not be writing what you are reading at the moment.

***

Mon expérience avec l'approche Gattegno

Je me présente : je m'appelle Nathanaël, j'ai douze ans, j'habite en France. Je suis passionné de musique (j'écris et je compose des chansons en m'accompagnant au piano), de lecture, mais surtout d'écriture, car depuis l'âge de neuf ans, j'écris des romans. J'écris aussi des poèmes, faisant passer dans les mots mes envies de voyages et de rêves… Ma vie est rythmée par une scolarité des plus agréables, que je mets à profit pour mon épanouissement général. Et l'approche de travail créée par le Dr. Gattegno m'a été grandement bénéfique.

En effet, depuis mes six ans (entrée au cours préparatoire, donc au primaire), mon père m'a initié à une méthode d'apprentissage qui m'était alors totalement inconnue, ce que j'appelle encore aujourd'hui « la méthode Gattegno ». De la lecture au calcul mental, cette approche m'a enseigné de nombreuses choses qui me sont un atout dans la vie de tous les jours.

J'ai suivi de nombreux et divers stages (mathématiques, grammaire française, orthographe, anglais, japonais, géographie, histoire…) en France et en Suisse, animés par des enseignants ayant travaillé de longues années avec le Dr. Gattegno. Et j'aimerais, par ailleurs, les remercier pour ce qu'ils ont pu m'apprendre.

Avant de connaître cette façon de travailler, j'étais, disons… très peu à l'aise dans mon travail scolaire et je suis passé à deux doigts d'être dégoûté de l'école. Mais l'approche du Dr. Gattegno a révélé en moi une certaine facilité à comprendre et interpréter la plupart des aspects de la langue française, ce qui m'amène aujourd'hui à avoir une certaine aisance dans ma façon de m'exprimer, que ce soit à l'oral ou à l'écrit. Pour ce qui est des mathématiques, j'en avais très peur avant que l'on me propose cette méthode d'apprentissage, les calculs s'embrouillaient dans ma tête… mais très vite, tout s'est classé dans mon cerveau, tels des mots placés dans l'ordre alphabétique dans un dictionnaire. Tout cela pour dire que le travail du Dr. Gattegno m'a nettement facilité la vie.

Je vous parle de la « Méthode Gattegno », et vous vous demandez peut être de quoi je parle et sous quelle forme on me l'a enseignée. Eh bien, un jour, mon père est arrivé à la maison, des paquets sous le bras. Je découvris bientôt qu'il s'agissait de mystérieux tableaux noirs recouverts de mots et de carrés en couleurs, à mon grand étonnement. Il m'apprit que chaque couleur correspondait à un son de la langue française et que de cette manière, on pouvait apprendre à lire, et même à écrire. Mon engouement pour cette « drôle de façon d'apprendre » me permit de gravir avec succès tous les échelons de mon parcours scolaire, jusqu'à aujourd'hui.

J'ai aussi été aidé par le travail avec les réglettes de couleurs, développé par le Dr. Gattegno. J'ai également bénéficié de plusieurs logiciels d'apprentissage, basés sur le travail du Dr. Gattegno, pour le français autant que pour les mathématiques et qui, pour certains, me servent encore aujourd'hui.

Enfin, tout cela pour vous dire que si je n'avais pas rencontré cette fabuleuse manière de travailler, je ne serais sûrement pas en train d'écrire ce que vous lisez en ce moment. §

A teacher works with a student using the *Word Building Book*, an early version of Words in Color. (Educational Solutions file photo.)

The Talk of the Town

Dr. Ubiratan D'Ambrosio

My first encounter with Caleb Gattegno goes back to the early '50s, while I was a student in pure mathematics at the University of São Paulo, Brazil. I was doing research on the boundary behavior of conformal maps, and the papers of Caleb Gattegno came to my attention. They were published in the prestigious *Transactions of the American Mathematical Society*, in co-authorship with the eminent Alexander Ostrowski, and they were basic references for my research. Thus, I became familiar with the mathematician Caleb Gattegno, indeed an interesting name. I learned he was from Egypt.

My second encounter was in different circumstances. After graduation, I developed much interest in mathematics education. One day, browsing at a bookshop in São Paulo, a paperback with a green cover, *L'Enseignement des mathématiques*, drew my attention. The book was published in 1955 and Caleb Gattegno was one of the authors. I was familiar with the work of the other authors and of their interest in education, but Caleb Gattegno was a surprise to me. He had helped me so much in complex analysis, but I did not know of his interest in mathematics education. I bought the book, which became an important reference for my work and I realized how deeply involved Gattegno was with mathematics education.

I learned of Caleb Gattegno's ideas on education and about the CIEAEM /Commisson Internationale pour l'Étude et l'Amélioration de l'Enseignement des Mathématiques (International Commission for the Study and the Improvement of the Teaching of Mathematics), created in 1950, on his initiative.

Some years later, in 1961, I read a small note saying that the educator Caleb Gattegno, the creator of the method Numbers in Color would visit Buenos Aires, by invitation of Professor Elsa Sabatiello. I was then living in Rio Claro, a small conservative town, not far from São Paulo, teaching at a new faculty of sciences with focus on preparing secondary school teachers. This institution is now the UNESP/Universidade Estadual Paulista, home of a most prestigious graduate program in mathematics education.

Rio Claro has the advantage of being close to the International Airport of Viracopos, a necessary scale, in the '60s, for all transatlantic flights. I saw an opportunity to meet, in person, the man whom I had encountered twice in my formative years and who had influenced me so much. I succeeded in finding his address and was bold enough to write him a letter, with an invitation to visit Rio Claro. I used a simple argument: since Buenos Aires to London was a very long trip and there was a necessary scale at Viracopos, maybe a two- or three-day sojourn in Rio Claro would be pleasant. And, being there, he might give a talk to our faculty and students. To my surprise, he promptly replied, welcoming the idea. An important factor was that his wife was pregnant and a rest on the way to Europe would be good for her health. This reply was, indeed, a most welcome notice.

We booked a room for our special guests in the modest Lider Hotel, at that time the best hotel in town. The hotel was situated in the central plaza of Rio Claro, the heart of the city, with centenary trees and a beautiful garden. I went to fetch Professor Gattegno and Mrs. Gattegno at the airport. This was for me an emotional encounter. He was very affable, and Mrs. Gattegno, a beautiful Indian young lady, Shakti Datta, was very charming. I drove to the hotel, they checked-in, and I told them that I would fetch them in the early evening for dinner at my home. Then, the big surprise! Gattegno told me they were vegetarians.

I went home and told Maria, my wife, the big surprise: they are vegetarians! Maria had cooked all day, preparing a special dinner, but all based in meat. Well, a new dinner was needed. She went to a market and rapidly prepared a new dinner, all vegetarian. I believe the Gattegnos liked it. It was a very pleasant evening.

The next day I went to fetch them up in the hotel and we went to the university. Gattegno gave a marvelous talk, introduced Numbers in Color to us, and even offered us a full set of wood colored rods and some books. He also showed us a movie, an 8mm roll, about geometry. The idea was to prove classical theorems about triangles with camera registered motions. I regard these movies as the prehistory of Cabri. He, very generously, offered the roll to us.

The next day, people in town were commenting on the big event: the presence of a real, authentic, Indian lady in town. The couple went for a walk in the park, just in front of the hotel. Everybody stared looking at this very odd couple. They had never seen in town a woman dressed in a sari. Everybody was commenting on this very special visit. Indeed, this was a very special moment for the town, for our faculty and students, and very special for me.

The next year, in 1962, I went to England and the Gattegnos invited me to their home in Reading. It was a pleasant reunion. I met the baby who had, in a certain way, visited us in Rio Claro the year before – Shakti Datta was pregnant with her. My memory is trustful – she was a beauty and the Gattegnos were so happy with her.

> "Caleb Gattegno's ideas are still very inspiring and to have met him was a remarkable experience in my life."

And this was my last contact with Caleb Gattegno. More recently, about 20 years ago, I became friend of three young mathematicians, Arthur Powell, Sandy Dawson, and Marty Hoffman, and found much affinity with their ideas. I discovered that the three were strong proponents of Gattegno's ideology. In fact, I asked them to convey my greeting to Mrs. Gattegno. She very kindly replied, sending a picture of herself. I knew that my good friend Bob Davis was also a friend and admirer of the work of Caleb Gattegno. This explains the sort of fraternity linking us all in a new concept of education.

I learned from Gattegno that love has a prominent place in education. Shakti Datta's book, *The Place of Love in Education*, which she kindly offered me in her visit to Rio Claro, in 1961, helped me to understand his position. Love in education leads children into their ways of being and to the joy of being creative. The proposal of Numbers in Colors is a way to realize this in elementary schools, and also favors creativity in more advanced levels of schooling.

Caleb Gattegno's ideas are still very inspiring and to have met him was a remarkable experience in my life.

Caleb Gattegno: As I Remember Him

Dr. Katherine A. Mitchell

While it is true that we are shaped by all the significant people and experiences in our lives, no one has had a greater impact on my life than Dr. Caleb Gattegno. I met Gattegno in July 1967 before my senior year in undergraduate school. He was one of the speakers at a world-wide education institute organized by the U.S. Office of Education and the Kettering Foundation. I had been invited to provide clerical assistance for that three-week seminar. During the seminar I participated in a French lesson taught by Dr. Gattegno. The experience was life changing. I left the hour-long demonstration believing that I had learned more French and had acquired a better feel for the language than I had achieved in three years of school instruction. I wondered how this was possible and who the teacher was. I also had the first thought that I might want to be a teacher if learning could be as effortless and engaging as what I had experienced with Dr. Gattegno.

I had several conversations with Dr. Gattegno during his time at the institute. He gave me a copy of *The Adolescent and His Will* which I read that summer. This book described me well, a person focused on my inner life and asking who I was and who I wanted to become. Reading this book and participating in the French lesson prompted me to earn credentials to teach during my final year of college. I sensed that learning more about Gattegno's work and learning to teach were the most compelling opportunities I had had to date.

This first encounter with Dr. Gattegno led me to a vocation in teaching. I attended a Words in Color seminar in the spring of 1968 and looked for a school where I could teach children to read with Words in Color. A school in Falls Church, Virginia, purchased one classroom set of Words in Color and assigned me to all the second and third graders who had not learned to read. That year all 17 students learned to read and visibly exhibited their new-found confidence. I also gained confidence in my calling to teach and in my passion for learning how to "subordinate teaching to learning," as Gattegno expressed it.

I joined Dr. Gattegno's staff the next year and spent 10 years in New York City at Educational Solutions. I taught first graders at Horace Mann Elementary School and worked with a faculty and administration dedicated to implementing Gattegno's work. Two years after that, I was one of three full-time consultants to the Twin Parks School in the Southeast Bronx. There I taught teachers and worked with the students who had stumped the reading specialists. In spite of a 60% turnover rate among students, we dramatically increased literacy rates from about 15% to 85% over a three-year period. Subsequently, experiences working with teachers across the United States, as well as in England, Switzerland, and Northern Africa, Arabic, Chinese, and other languages through Gattegno's Silent Way. In these settings I learned the importance of letting a problem dictate its solution; suspending my judgment rather than trying to force solutions; recognizing interferences to study such as preconceptions and prejudice; and allowing a topic to reveal its nature.

> "I left the hour-long demonstration believing that I had learned more French and had acquired a better feel for the language than I had achieved in three years of school instruction."

showed me that teachers were hungry for materials, techniques, and ways of working that would help them be more effective.

After 11 years of close work with Dr. G (as we affectionately called him), I knew that virtually any student who could speak and understand language could learn to read. I knew that teachers were developed, not born. I knew that far too many bright, committed people were dropping out of the teaching profession simply because they lacked the tools to deliver what they had hoped to deliver: learning and changed lives. And, I knew that I had to appeal to teachers' self-interest, because self-interest is a primary motivator for change. Working with teachers had become my life's work – a thoroughly joyful calling, a holy activity similar to prayer and worship.

A decade of study with Dr. Gattegno introduced me also to topics indirectly related to classroom life but central to shaping me into a broader, deeper person. At least once a month Educational Solutions hosted "awareness" seminars during which we studied topics as diverse as the mind, the brain, evolution, health, awareness, love, energy, affectivity, time, wealth, and ways of knowing. Several times a year I participated in workshops where I studied Spanish,

The awareness seminars showed me that Dr. Gattegno was a genius who had read much of the literature of the world. More important to me, someone neither exceptionally intellectual nor widely read, was Gattegno's approach to study. This approach drew largely upon participants' experiences. Participants' statements stood on their truth or, through examples and counter-examples, were rejected or refined. This way of working gave all participants access to the particular study and modeled for me how to approach any challenge.

A decade of work in awareness seminars and increasing familiarity with what Dr. Gattegno had written caused me to think of Dr. G as a renaissance man who knew how to let a rich affective life nurture his intellect. These qualities were especially visible in Dr. Gattegno's fictional writing. While teaching at Horace Mann, I read Gattegno's *Eight Tales* to my first graders. I remember being concerned that the tales might be over the heads of my students. Forty-one years later, however, I reconnected with one of those first graders. He remembered Dr. Gattegno and inquired about where he might get a copy of those "enchanted tales" to read to his six-year-old daughter.

Seized by a call to make a lasting contribution

(Mitchell Cont'd.)
to public education in my home state, I wrote a proposal in 1979 to eradicate illiteracy in Alabama. That proposal (which contained much of what Dr. Gattegno had taught me), and seeds sown through having previously taught teachers in Alabama to use the Educational Solutions Mini-Tests, prompted the Alabama Department of Education to hire me. I had to wait 18 years, however, to launch the literacy initiative envisioned in the proposal.

Comprehension." This presentation revealed that teachers faced only six interferences to reading comprehension. (They feared there were hundreds.) It was my way of making visible the precise challenge of learning to read well.

To this day I am overwhelmed with gratitude for the gifts that Dr. Gattegno gave me. I understand well the powerful impact of Gattegno's work on all

> "What makes you so excited about teaching children to read?" She replied: "Because they all learn!"

During my time in Alabama, Gattegno's influence was obvious in all areas of my work. What I had learned from helping to develop the Mini-Tests enabled me to educate an entire state about the appropriate view of high-stakes testing. I became an effective curriculum leader because of being acquainted with Gattegno's "open books" and because of Gattegno's insistence that the nature of any content area must dictate how it is best learned.

The highlight of my Alabama career, however, was the development of the Alabama Reading Initiative, a statewide effort that gained national acclaim and that is still being implemented successfully. Gattegno taught me that we need to work with allies if we are to lead large efforts with potentially big impacts. As a result, I proposed a team approach and involved people who knew how to secure funding, maneuver through bureaucracies, and publicize stunning results. Gattegno taught me that we must add our unique gifts to his foundational work to create materials and solutions that address immediate needs. In building the Alabama Reading Initiative, the most important product that I developed was a conceptual framework titled "Interferences to

contributors to this memoir, but can be surprised from time to time when I encounter strangers who have been similarly affected. For example, a few months ago I met a teacher from California who was visiting my neighbor. After a few minutes of conversation, I asked the visitor: "What makes you so excited about teaching children to read?" She replied: "Because they all learn!" "How do you reach them all?" I asked. She replied: "Well, about 30 years ago, someone came to our school and showed us a program called Words in Color." On another occasion I heard one of the most respected reading researchers in the United States advocate for reading programs that would support teachers while they learned how to teach reading. When asked if she had used a commercial program to teach reading when she was in the classroom, this researcher replied that she had learned much about teaching reading 30 years ago when she used a program called Words in Color.

I suspect that all who have experienced the power and efficacy of Dr. Caleb Gattegno's ideas and tools are hopeful about a future for education. How can those of us who were fortunate enough to work with him directly be sure that his work continues? What could we do collectively if we tried? §

Students learning to read, exploring the language in depth with Words in Color's transformation game. (*Del Norte Triplicate*, March 1971.)

" Dependence is what I want to reduce, and can reduce, in all my students, for I am aware of its paralyzing effects. "

- Dr. Caleb Gattegno

On Being Freer, Second Edition (2010), page 146.

Silence, apprentissage et méta-apprentissage

Dr. Michel Sagaz

Si l'on ne connaît pas ses concepts sous-jacents, on peut se méprendre sur la dénomination du Silent Way (l'Approche Silencieuse). On pourrait penser que l'enseignant ne parle pas. Or, ce n'est absolument pas le cas ; il parle :

- notamment lors des fréquents feedbacks qu'il donne aux apprenants ;
- le moins possible, pour allouer le plus de temps de parole aux apprenants ;
- mais il ne donne pas d'explications sur la langue cible ni de modèles que les apprenants répètent.

Dans le Silent Way, l'enseignant parle de façon essentielle, pour que son enseignement n'interfère pas avec l'apprentissage des apprenants. Il est considéré, à juste titre, que ceux qui apprennent doivent pratiquer, et donc bénéficier au maximum du temps de parole disponible. En ce sens, l'assertion de Cook dans son livre Second language learning and language teaching est étonnante: dans le cadre d'approches d'enseignement où les enseignants sont chargés de "distribuer la parole", ces derniers utiliseraient environ 70 % du temps de parole dans la classe. Le rôle du silence de l'enseignant est de faire en sorte que le temps de parole des apprenants soit également le plus profitable. Dans les mots de Patricia Benstein: «Silence allows the students to work and concentrate on what they do rather than on what the teacher does».

Selon les positions liées à le Silent Way la relation de cause à effet entre la réception d'explications/de règles sur la langue (enseignement déclaratif) et la possibilité de parler cette langue (savoir-faire) n'est pas avérée. L'alternative proposée est que, pour apprendre, les apprenants doivent faire des essais, et éventuellement les ajuster (notamment en fonction des feedbacks de l'enseignant) : on apprend en pratiquant (et en se trompant). Cette assertion consensuelle peut prêter à maintes interprétations. Dans le Silent Way, le silence de l'enseignant est l'un des garants de l'application de ce principe. Cette place accordée au silence met en exergue certains faits : enseigner une langue ne consiste pas à transmettre des connaissances mais à aider à faire acquérir des savoir-faire, l'acquisition de nouveaux savoir-faire demande de la pratique, les apprenants peuvent maîtriser la prononciation d'une langue étrangère autrement que par l'imitation de l'enseignant, par exemple.

Le point de vue cognitif renforce l'importance de la présence de temps de silence dans le déroulement même de l'apprentissage. Selon Trocmé-Fabre, le silence permettrait une meilleure qualité de l'intégration et du stockage des informations rencontrées :

«Dans un état de repos sensoriel, c'est-à-dire sans stimulation auditive, visuelle, ni tactile, et dans une position de détente, on note une augmentation d'activation de la partie frontale du cerveau [...]. Ceci représenterait [...] un état de vigilance ou de "conscience éveillé", permettant la programmation et la sélection des différents schémas de comportement, – au détriment, en quelque sorte, des aires motrices

The original French Fidel, printed in 1965 and subsequently updated in 1990 by Une Education Pour Demain (UEPD).

> It is in fact reasonable – and also important – to make students independent of their teachers and text books, autonomous in their work so that they sense their own initiative and see it at work at every stage, and responsible for everything they do – this being a separate awareness developing out of the other two.

— Dr. Caleb Gattegno

The Science of Education – Part 2B: The Awareness of Mathematization, Second Edition (2010) P 123.

(Sagaz Cont.)
et sensorielles qui seraient même, sans doute, "inhibées".

Que peut signifier une telle découverte pour ceux qui se préoccupent de l'acquisition et de l'intégration des connaissances ? Sans doute, une réflexion et une interrogation sur le rythme auquel sont soumis les apprenants […] lorsque l'information est donnée, envoyée, infligée, sans que la moindre pause ne soit ménagée, sans que le moindre temps d'intégration, de structuration, d'évocation ne soit prévu. Or […] les pauses structurantes sont indispensables à la formation des images mentales qui contribuent à la constitution de nos systèmes de références et de valeurs. » (1994 : 68)

D'un point de vue méthodologique, le silence représente également un paramètre important de l'enseignement. Dans son thèse de doctorat, Universaux dans l'enseignement et l'apprentissage de l'anglais et du français dans des situations pédagogiques diverses, Roslyn Young considère que le silence est un instrument à disposition de l'enseignant, dont il peut se servir avantageusement pour la gestion du cours et de son propre enseignement:

« Le silence oblige l'enseignant à réfléchir à chaque instant sur sa propre clarté, ce qui fait que la préparation de la classe change beaucoup. Le professeur doit toujours se demander comment trouver un moyen strictement non ambigu de présenter chaque situation. Pendant que la classe se déroule, il doit avoir comme souci constant la compréhension de ses élèves, non seulement des situations qu'il présente, mais de la langue qu'il y associe. »

Le silence ouvre à l'enseignant un espace de réflexion, lequel est crucial au vu de l'ensemble des paramètres qu'il doit gérer en temps réel, parmi lesquels :

Observer sa propre pratique dans le déroulement du cours :

- Est-ce que la situation qu'il propose pour aborder l'apprentissage d'une notion donnée est suffisamment claire ?
- Quels sont les éventuels problèmes de compréhension pour les apprenants qu'engendre ses actions ?
- Quel apprenant (plutôt qu'un autre) solliciter, et pourquoi ?

Observer ses apprenants en train de travailler :

- Pour évaluer un énoncé.
- Pour repérer les problèmes dans un énoncé.
- Pour évaluer la maîtrise par un apprenant d'un savoir-faire.

Anticiper la suite immédiate du cours :

- Vers quel matériau linguistique et/ou vers quelle activité faire évoluer le cours ?
- Quel feedback proposer pour tel problème en fonction de tel apprenant ?
- Quel support utiliser pour faire pratiquer tel savoir-faire ?

Un cours mené avec le Silent Way ne repose pas sur un scénario préétabli ; il se construit interaction par interaction. Il ne s'agit cependant pas d'improvisation pure de la part de l'enseignant : à l'instar de celles d'un comédien ou d'un musicien, l'improvisation d'un enseignant dépend de son expérience. Autrement dit, être silencieux n'équivaut pas ici simplement à se taire : face aux apprenants, le silence de l'enseignant ne peut jamais être un cache-misère pédagogique. Comme l'indique Benstein: «Used appropriately, silence can facilitate the learning process. Used inappropriately, the opposite effect of creating tensions in students is also a likely result » .

L'explicitation du rôle du silence dans la salle de classe illustre bien pourquoi on ne peut pas réduire le Silent Way à un ensemble de supports ou de techniques (= à une « méthode »).

Par là même, force est de constater que l'utilisation que font les enseignants du silence lui accorde une vraie valeur pédagogique. Ceci met ainsi en relief la pertinence potentielle de ce que ces enseignants disent dans la pratique de leur enseignement subordonné à l'apprentissage de leurs apprenants.
Nombre de ces interventions orales apparaissent dans le cadre d'un feedback que l'enseignant donne à la suite d'une production – le plus souvent dans le cas d'une aide à la correction. En effet, généralement, l'enseignant travaille avec les apprenants à partir de leurs propres productions. Or, quand un apprenant se trompe, il n'est d'ordinaire pas conscient du fait qu'il se trompe. S'il en est parfois conscient, il n'est pas nécessairement capable d'identifier son erreur

et de la corriger par lui-même. Ainsi, le rôle de l'enseignant est :

- de lui indiquer qu'il a fait une erreur ;
- de travailler avec lui à la localiser ;
- de l'aider à circonscrire le problème sous-jacent à cette erreur ;
- de lui proposer des activités susceptibles de résoudre ce problème.

travaille donc en conformité avec les potentialités des apprenants, et à deux niveaux :

- au niveau de la production formelle (de surface) ;
- au niveau de la démarche d'apprentissage (du méta-).

Nous sommes bien là dans l'ordre d'un travail sur soi : les apprenants prennent conscience de leurs fonctionnements dans l'apprentissage. L'enseignant vise l'activité humaine avant tout, car la langue cible – objet de l'apprentissage – n'est pas le produit de

> "L'utilisation que font les enseignants du silence lui accorde une vraie valeur pédagogique. Ceci met ainsi en relief la pertinence potentielle de ce que ces enseignants disent dans la pratique de leur enseignement subordonné à l'apprentissage de leurs apprenants."

La correction des erreurs est un point central dans l'enseignement-apprentissage d'une langue étrangère. La nature d'une erreur d'un apprenant, et donc la raison pour laquelle il la commet, peut provenir de diverses sources : état physio- et psychologique (fatigue, attention, motivation, etc.), représentation qu'il possède de la norme (linguistique, référentielle, socioculturelle, etc.) transgressée, etc. Deux erreurs identiques en surface peuvent ainsi être le résultat de deux problèmes différents. C'est pourquoi dans l'analyse et la compréhension des erreurs, on ne peut pas se fier seulement aux manifestations linguistiques de surface. On voit bien que l'intérêt de l'apprentissage (et la raison d'être de l'enseignement) n'est pas tant la correction de l'erreur en soi mais, au-delà, le diagnostic de sa source. L'apprenant concerné pourra ainsi agir sur la cause à l'origine de ce problème pour essayer d'y remédier. L'enseignant

l'apprentissage. Les apprenants n'apprennent pas (seulement) quelque chose mais (surtout) à faire quelque chose. En tant qu'objet de cet apprentissage, la langue cible n'est pas laissée pour compte, mais elle devient – de fait – un sous-produit de l'apprentissage – « by-product » en anglais.

Le deuxième niveau (méta-) transcende donc – tout en l'incluant – le premier (celui de la langue). Il s'agit d'un apprentissage de l'apprentissage, autrement dit d'un méta-apprentissage : l'apprenant opère une pratique qui est, à la fois, réflexive (méta-) et introspective, sur sa façon d'apprendre.

C'est notamment cette importance accordée aux processus d'apprentissage dans l'approche Silent Way qui révèle, dans le modèle de Gattegno, le rôle essentiel de l'activité des apprenants dans leur propre apprentissage.

§

Voices from AURAMA

A. Bregani, D. Cerretti, M-C Challandes, C. Delétra, B. Mesot, C. de Sybourg, M. Weinmann

In 1990, in order to meet a need expressed by people interested in education, teachers around Ghislaine Graf founded an association in Lausanne, Switzerland called Aurama – named according to the Greek etymology, meaning 'being watchful and attentive.' Since then, seminars have been held regularly, gathering people who are not attached to a figure of the past, but involved with the challenges of today.

ANNE BREGANI

To me, Caleb Gattegno's priceless contribution is mainly due to his determination to make what is invisible visible.

To create such a code as color rectangles to "read" sounds, in order to penetrate a language, was a work of genius. Not taking things for granted, Gattegno brought to the fore indisputable requirements of what languages – spoken as well as written – are about. Students and teachers have to accept them not as their personal preferences, but as the conventions a precise language demands. It is then within these references that the power of combinatory opens up a vast space, in which everyone may exercise his or her free expression.

Materials such as Words in Color and the Silent Way introduce almost immediately the words "yes" and "no" as an important indication of facing choice and liberty for every learner, and for me as a teacher as well! To acknowledge that a student may decide to accept a challenge or not also means each one of us remains in contact with oneself. It is sometimes necessary to take a small step, sometimes a jump, in order to explore our inner powers, whatever personal level we may be at.

I also learned to perceive mistakes and obstacles as dynamic elements in building up and nourishing my reflections. Then emotions that may arise at any time, even powerfully, no longer hinder our work, but give us the opportunity to work through difficulties, in a quieter flow. I am looking for that space of inner calm from where I can pay attention to what is new, with the question it carries: where is it leading me? Let's see.

I cannot help quoting Gattegno's own words: "Around the corner there is my guru: Life!"

DANIELA CERRETTI

About 18 years ago, I saw some charts in the classroom of a colleague of mine; I was intrigued by the beauty of this colored material, its unusual disposition of words, and its list of written forms. When I attended a lesson, I discovered, through the dance of a pointer, a new dynamic of colors and sounds giving access to speaking a language!

Moreover, everyone's intelligence and willingness were involved in the process.

This first impact the Silent Way had on me held in itself a whole set of beginnings that opened up new considerations about learning and education. They also brought me a clearer and beneficial lens on other aspects of life.

Thanks to the founders of Aurama, I have been able to know of Caleb Gattegno's work and to take part in seminars, becoming skilled with the materials, as well as participating in fundamental research.

Those moments devoted to studying within a group are very precious. I find a real similarity between the attention given to the deciphering of sounds – to be oriented – and the time spent on clarifying what is confused or ' confusing. This same momentum sustains distinctions between prejudging, making clear, and different forms of energy, to guide us towards building up criteria and awareness.

I am grateful for such seminars that open vast areas of thinking.

MARIE-CLAUDE CHALLANDES

The importance of knowing Caleb Gattegno's work makes me think of my teaching as a painter's art. To have attempted with so many brushstrokes to lead generations of children into reading or mathematics made me color and draw a whole landscape.

"Coming back to oneself is the most considerable enterprise," as Vietnamese writer Duong Thu Huong says. Remaining in contact with this awareness is still a real building site for me, for I see its efficiency.

I trust I may use the same accuracy of reading into myself as much as into others, and beyond words, capture signs of an intense and powerful work…

I trust I may continue to hope for a generation of children, not manipulated towards excessive use of technologies, but aware and awake…

I trust I may dare to believe that, as in mathematics, there are many possibilities for exploring the Science of Education, and that fields of experimentation are still to be discovered…

CATHERINE DELÉTRA

From 1973 to 1975, I lived the most beautiful years of my life. I was between five and seven years old, in first and second grades of primary-school. I was in Colette Rohrbach's classroom, at the International School of Geneva, Switzerland.

Colette had met Dr. Gattegno, and with him, La Lecture en Couleurs (Words in Color, in French) and his way of teaching mathematics. She was very inspired by them.

Colette was not teaching: she was learning with us, indeed guiding us on the way, our way in which she was included. She quietly let me learn, discover, inquire, change my mind. And yet all the knowledge always came naturally to all of us.

> "When I attended a lesson, I discovered, through the dance of a pointer, a new dynamic of colors and sounds giving access to speaking a language!"
>
> -D. Cerretti

The wonder of those years is not a mere memory, but it nourishes me today in my professional and private life.

BRIGITTE MESOT

While we settle down in a circle for our seminars, we are forming a kind of clock whose hands are moving to gather our energies and experiences. From our existence and from awareness, we are exploring different aspects of time, and studying fundamental questions.

Using Words in Color in a prison with an illiterate woman, I am moved by the way she creates inner criteria, giving breath to the written words as much as to her distressed life.

In front of the charts, I am requiring students to be present, and am responsible for offering every one of

(Aurama Cont'd)

I also learned to perceive mistakes and obstacles as dynamic elements in building up and nourishing my reflections.

them opportunities to be in contact with affective energy.

The attention given to precision, instigated by Gattegno and maintained by us, thanks to Ghislaine Graf, leads us in fact to understand our learning powers and to seek light, sweeping fears away. This study is guiding me in my whole life, as a wife, mother, woman and teacher.

Whomever I meet today, I attempt to have in mind and be aware that we all are, "Intelligence, Will and Sensitivity," thus defined by Gattegno's model. It is an irreversible knowledge that transforms one's life.

CAROLINE DE SYBOURG

I was already teaching illiterate people (not all French speakers), when I attended a seminar by Caleb Gattegno on Words in Color, in 1983, in Geneva.

The power and the beauty of his work, as well as their concomitant inner revolutions within oneself, impressed me indelibly.

Twenty-eight years later, as Head of Literacy and French FSL courses in a socio-cultural center of the city of Lausanne, I still feel the need to go in greater depth into teaching and learning defined by Caleb Gattegno. The passing of time has done nothing but amplify my quest and my interest!

The practice of continuous feedback, the attention given to the progression and evolution of each student, is the indispensable way to improve my accuracy in guiding them. Sometimes encumbered with traps and impediments, this complex task calls necessarily for richer questioning while constantly facing new situations. This work is paradoxically invigorating my energy, instead of wasting it. I even feel my whole lifetime will not be sufficient to accomplish it, for there is no end to such vastness of knowledge.

MAYA WEINMANN

I have never met Caleb Gattegno, but I discovered the Silent Way in 1994, watching a French course in Lausanne. Enthusiastically, I decided to get involved in this study and began teaching French to adults – all foreigners from varied backgrounds and social positions.

Little by little I found that this approach was not only very efficient in terms of teaching and learning languages, but that it applies to most studies. I never cease to marvel at the by-products it generates.

The educational approach, as well as the material of the Silent Way, are to me real signs of resistance against the galloping mercantilism of "new methods" – provided that they are submitted to careful and aware comprehension. Inviting and enabling all students to come into contact with themselves – here and now – is like "betting" they are able to learn and educate their true nature as well. This builds up a wonderful demonstration of respect and love.

I am finding this same fundamental attitude of respect, without complacency, in the Aurama seminars. There I am supplementing and nourishing my reflections and observations. Not only do I understand what "being aware" means, I have truly lived indelible experiences of awareness. Thanks to that work in progress, I feel more able to read and to welcome whatever is occurring in my life. §

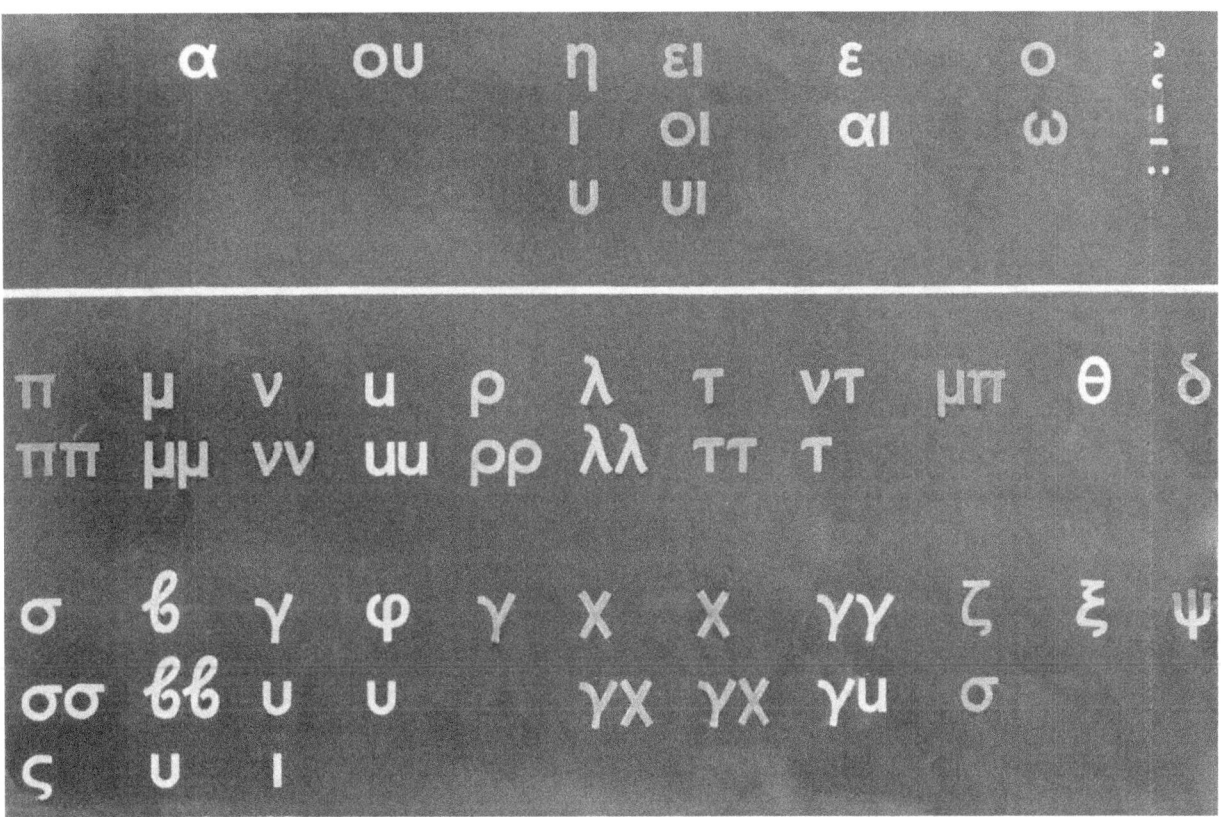

Prototype Greek Fidel, hand-painted on cardboard circa 1978. ©Educational Solutions Worldwide Inc.

My Personal Journey Towards Letting Go of "No"

Christian Duquesne

"No, no and no!"

In mid 1982, when Caroline Brandt advised me to meet Caleb Gattegno, I really had this "cri du coeur," as I had chosen to get away from the teaching profession for 10 years, and I didn't want to get back to it.

Caroline was obstinate and had another try. I was stubborn and refused point blank.

In 1985 she sent me a proposition for a seminar entitled "Generation of Wealth" in Carcans. As a young entrepreneur, I saw at that moment the opportunity to combine business with pleasure.

I met there Caleb Gattegno, quite inaccessible, the center of attraction of 60 persons. During the first three days, I felt suffocated: Caleb Gattegno talked about "awareness," "awareness of the awareness," and even "awareness of the awareness of the awareness"!

I still don't know why I didn't leave the conference.

At the fourth day, as far as I can remember, Caleb Gattegno asked me to volunteer to do an individual exercise with him after lunch. Why didn't I say "No!" again?

Before a group of about 30 persons, he gradually led me through a lesson of 10's complement mental arithmetic.

How did he get the insight that this part of basic knowledge had terrified me to such an extent since I was 13! It's a mystery.

But in the end, surprisingly, I came through and math was no longer unreachable for me from then onwards.

AWAKENING OF CONSCIOUSNESS

When I got past 25, my life was guided by my opposition to change and my comfortable refusal to take risks.

I now consider this "No" as a fear of life, and of the effort it implies.

Thanks to Caleb Gattegno and to the background he had developed around him, I lived and figured out what he meant by "forcing awareness."

In the course of time, my students – of all ages – have confirmed to me how mysterious, necessary and conclusive this step remains. Since then, I decided to know more about this "strange guy."

In 1986, at the seminar On Love in Chapeau-Cornu, I came across a synthesis of issues formulated in science and spirituality, through Caleb Gattegno's research.

Humility, exploration, rigour, research, respect of others, unsentimental compassion towards Man…

These 12 days were one of the brightest lessons in my whole life, completed by the seminar The Spiritual Disciplines that Help Us to Live in Summer 1987.

SCIENCE & SPIRITUALITY

Some people wanted to reduce Caleb Gattegno's universe of exploration to its sheer scientific dimension.

With the three seminars in summers '86 and '87 (On Being Freer, On Love, The Spiritual Disciplines...), bearing in mind his essay entitled *On Death*, Caleb Gattegno gave us a look at Man free from his beliefs of all kinds, by the power of the activity of his self and aiming at the unity of his components.

His suggestion of the quantum is, to my eyes, a guarantee of the continuity of individual energies expended to freedom of life. Then, it was time to act!

As I attended some seminars in Paris, Geneva, Besançon and Grenoble, more and more questions arose: What's my place in this symphony? How does one become efficient, and where?

By way of training, I firstly organized a Japanese Silent Way seminar with Fusako Allard in Paris.

Caleb Gattegno encouraged me to organize a second one, which I refused. He put his niece and me in "quarantine" for our laziness and lack of involvement!

THE CHALLENGE

On November 11, 1987, for his 76th birthday, Caleb Gattegno accepted an invitation to my home in Gif-sur-Yvette, near Paris, much to my delight, to celebrate his last birthday among some close friends.

I ran by him the vain attempt to create an organization that would aim at making his work durable. Probably infuriated by a flood of always well-meant technocratic propositions, Caleb Gattegno fell asleep at the table. And things didn't move any further!

Then came a strong moment for me: I went with him to Roissy airport in Paris for his return to New-York. We spent two hours together in the waiting room talking about the future. In these moments, he used to let the questions open, thus allowing anyone to enter a world whose evolution he anticipated. That day, he emphasized our meeting and encouraged me to explore his Science of Education in corporate environments. It took me 20 years to really understand the meaning of his proposition. I've now embarked on this project: Enterprise is one aspect of human reality among others that can be researched with the Science of Education, since it acts with Man, on Man, and in theory with and for Man.

Developing, with Caleb Gattegno, this Science of Education is for me a powerful vision of Man evolving towards his freedom.

SCIENCE OF EDUCATION APPLIED TO MANAGING

Not only did Caleb Gattegno contribute to reflection and help on evolution of awareness in schools, but also in all structures taking into account the living environment of human beings (family, social and economical life, enterprise/undertaking, etc.).

Our discussion in November 1987 allows me, even many years later, to implement a reflection on the Science of Education dedicated to "Homo Economicus" at work, aiming at a new vision that brings more justice and freedom, but also that generates greater wealths to discover and to produce.

In late July 1988, a few days after his last seminar in Grenoble, I went with Shakti Gattegno and his niece, Claudie, to the mortuary of the private hospital Geoffroy Saint Hilaire in Paris, where he had just died. Shakti asked me to witness the sealing of the coffin.

A few hours later, a pale sunbeam turned into millions of sparkling stars as his ashes were spread in the garden of Père Lachaise cemetery in Paris.

I thus learnt to use "Yes" as an answer.

All through my explorations, 22 years after, I'm still staying on course, modestly trying to contribute to more awareness in human life. I wish that all these energies, wherever they come from, would converge and lead Man to a higher awareness.

A Fascination with Pronunciation
発音の魅力

Junko Shinada

In May 1988, my husband and I participated in an English workshop offered in Tokyo, led by Dr. Gattegno. During the workshop I could feel that my way of learning English was developing aspects I had never experienced before. I became aware of these new aspects saying, "Oh, I see," and what I had thought I knew became dramatically changed.

During the session, Dr. Gattegno made Hideo pronounce the word 'live' repeatedly, but Dr. Gattegno only kept indicating to him that it was wrong, again and again. I knew that to be able to do so. I was absorbed in working on it. Suddenly I became aware that the correct 'l' had a sound which was not in the sound that I had believed was correct. Before removing the tip of the tongue off of the back side of my upper teeth to make 'l' sound with a breath, I noticed that there was another sound. All the students who could pronounce 'l' correctly used this sound. Then I tried it in the same way, adding the sound which was somewhat like a dog snarling. Dr. Gattegno said, "Yes." I don't remember how long I was grappling with making the 'l' sound. For me, this experience was meeting the Gattegno Approach.

> "Today I would say without hesitation, 'Yes, it was easy,' and move on to seek another challenge."

pronounce 'l' I had to put the tip of my tongue on the upper back part of my upper front teeth. I thought Hideo was articulating the sound faithfully in this way; I believed the sound was correct. Therefore, while sitting next to him, I could not understand why it was rejected. Then several others tried to pronounce 'live' and Dr. Gattegno accepted some of them. What's the difference? To my 'live,' he said, "No." I wanted to listen to the correct pronunciation as many times as possible, and to compare it to the wrong ones.

My desire was fulfilled easily and I was allowed to

To make the correct 'l' sound you need not only the forms of your lips and the position of your tongue. There are many other factors involved, such as the duration of a specific position of the tongue, and the way of the tongue movement. This process made my view of the pronunciation of a language change completely. After this experience, I became even more interested in teaching pronunciation as a Japanese language teacher. For example, when my students were having problems in pronunciation, I became able to consider many possible reasons for the issue. Moreover, I was convinced that students were able to become aware of those reasons by themselves. But the change that happened in me was not limited to this.

At the time, I was not able to account for what happened to me. But after this encounter I was driven to learn more about awarenesses. Other workshops were scheduled in Osaka a week later. I wanted to participate in some of them, but I was not able to afford the expense, as I had just started working. After the English workshop, I went to Dr. Gattegno to say thank you, and he asked me if I was coming to the workshops in Osaka – it was as if he had pierced my heart. I said, "I can't, because I'm too busy." Then he asked me back, "Money?" without a smile. I remember that I was very embarrassed, and I just answered him impromptu.

Dr. Gattegno spotted another lie of mine during the workshop, while we were working on spellings standing in front of the Fidel. Dr. Gattegno told me to point to the signs in 'elephant.' Before this, we worked on pronouncing 'elephant.' Thus, I was able to find its consisting sounds and I could tap its spelling with confidence. When I finished my task, Dr. Gattegno said to me, "That's right. It's easy." But for some reason I said, "No, it was difficult." Then he looked at me with eyes implying 'you're lying,' and said to me, "Tap it again then." I tapped it again feeling uncomfortable.

I should have accepted what I could do, but I chose to stay where I felt comfortable with what I had already done and accomplished. Today I would say without hesitation, "Yes, it was easy," and move on to seek another challenge.

The several days spent with Dr. Gattegno in May 1988 made my following days surprisingly rich. During the next 10 years or so, I participated annually in language and theory workshops offered by the Center and led either by Ms. Fusako Allard or Dr. Roslyn Young. The total number of hours of my participation has reached several hundred. As a result, I am able to describe how Dr. Gattegno and his approach have affected me. For all these years, I have been involved in the activities of the Gattegno Approach Study Group and Silent Way Tokyo, where my colleagues and I organize workshops and meetings in order to let many more people to know the Gattegno Approach.

発音の魅力

1988年の5月、私は、夫の英雄と共に東京で開催されたカレブ・ガテーニョ博士による英語のワークショップに参加した。そのワークショップで私は、英語の学習が私の中でそれまでとはまったく異なる様相で展開をするのを経験した。「ああそうか」と捉えたことが、それまで知っていると考えていたことの姿を大きく変えたのである。

英雄は"live"という単語の発音を何度も繰り返した。しかし、ガテーニョ博士は"No"と繰り返すばかりだった。"l"を発音するときは、舌先を上の前歯の裏側の上につける。私は英雄がそのとき私が知っていると思っていた"l"の発音方法で忠実に調音していると思った。だから、隣で聞いていてなぜいけないのか理解できなかった。それから、ほかの学習者が何人か"live"の発音を試みた。その中のいくつかの"live"に対して、ガテーニョ博士は"Yeah"と言った。どこが違うのだろうか。私が発音した"live"は"No"であった。私は、「正しい"live"の発音を何度も聞きたい。"No"とされる"live"と比べたい」という思いに駆られた。

その希望は簡単にかなえられ、心行くまで試すことが許された。夢中にそれだけに集中した。すると、ある瞬間、正しい"l"には、自分が考えていた"l"にない音が含まれていることに気がついた。"l"の音を出すために息と共に舌先を歯の裏から離す前に、少し違った音がするのである。正しく"l"を発音できる人の"l"には共通してその音がある。そこで、私も舌先を前歯の裏の上に押しつけながら、舌を離す前に同じような音を出してみた。「ウー」というような犬の唸り声のような音である。するとガテーニョ博士が"Yeah"と言ったのである。自分で"l"と格闘した時間はどれほどであったか覚えていないが、これが私にとってガテーニョ・アプローチとの出会いであった。

"l"の発音に必要なのは、舌の位置と唇の形だけではない。呼吸法とか継続時間とか、たくさんの要素が関わってい

る。言語の発音に対する自分の捉え方が完全に変わった。この経験の後で、私は日本語の教師として音声教育にそれまで以上に関心を持つようになった。学習者が日本語の発音がうまくできないとき、その原因としてたくさんのことが想像できるようになった。そして学習者自身がそれに気づけることを確信した。自分の中のこの変化は、もちろん音声のことだけにとどまらなかった。

当時は、今考えるようにその時の自分を説明することはできなかったが、その衝撃的な出会いから、さらなる新たな気づきを求めて学び続けたいという思いに駆られた。その一週間後に大阪でワークショップが予定されていたので、それにぜひ出たいと思ったが、まだ駆け出しの社会人だった私には経済的に厳しかった。ワークショップ終了後にガテーニョ博士にお礼を言いに行くと、博士は私の心の中を見透かすように「大阪のワークショップに来るのか」尋ねた。私がとっさに「来週は忙しく」と答えると、博士はニコリともせずに"Money?"と問い返した。博士の問いに取り繕って答えた自分がとても恥ずかしかったことを覚えている。

博士は、英語のワークショップの中で、学習者がフィデルの前に立って単語の綴りを指す作業をしていたときにも、私の嘘を見抜いた。私は"elephant"という単語の綴りを指して確認する役目を与えられた。その前に口頭で発音する練習をしていたときに、"elephant"の発音を構成する音がいくつあって、どれであるか、たくさんの気づきがあったので、自信をもって指すことができた。指し終わったとき、博士は私に「そうだ。簡単だろう」と言った。私は、まさしく簡単だったにもかかわらず「いえ、難しかった」と答えてしまった。すると博士は「この嘘つきめ」という目で私を見ながら「じゃあ、もう一度指しなさい」と言った。指しながら、私は居心地の悪さを感じた。

今の私は、この時の自分を説明することができる。自分の学びに適切に寄りそうことができなかったのだ。自分が何を知っていて、何を知らないのか、ありのままを受け入れて進んでいけばいいのに、既にできてしまったことにとどまって安心することを選んだのだ。今の私なら、迷わずに「簡単だった」と答えて、次の課題を探すだろう。

1988年5月、ガテーニョ博士と過ごした数日間は、その後の私の人生を驚くほど豊かなものにした。その翌年から10年あまりの間、アラード房子氏とロズリン・ヤング博士による言語や理論のワークショップに毎年参加した。その延べ時間は数百時間に及ぶ。現在、ガテーニョ博士によって自分に何が起きたのか、ことばで説明できるようになったのは、そのおかげである。この数年は共に学んだ仲間たちと、一人でも多くの人にガテーニョ・アプローチを知ってもらうために、研究会とワークショップの開催に関わっている。

> 学習者が日本語の発音がうまくできないとき、その原因としてたくさんのことが想像できるようになった。そして学習者自身がそれに気づけることを確信した。

An advertisement to "Learn English Through Television" with *The Silent Way Video Program* from the 1970s. This was an early experiment by Dr. Gattegno in using a visual medium for education. He foresaw that in the future much instruction would be delivered this way.

Sharing the Gift of Math, Learning and A Better Way to Teach

Dr. Joyce F. Baynes

I began to take a deep look at the teaching of mathematics when I was a student at the Harvard Graduate School of Education in 1968. We studied several of the reform programs of that era, utilized manipulatives, encouraged logical reasoning, accepted multiple ways to solve problems and gave voice to students so they could defend their solutions.

After graduation from HGSE, I taught mathematics at the Highland Park Free School in Roxbury, Massachusetts. The school was supported by the Ford Foundation with a grant written by parents who were dissatisfied with the Boston Public Schools. Concurrently, my good friend from undergraduate school, Marilyn Maye, was teaching in New York City under the tutelage of Education Solutions consultant, Marty Hoffman. Marilyn and I communicated regularly about the strategies and methods of Dr. Caleb Gattegno. Fortunately I was in a setting where I could develop my own curriculum, use the rods and Geoboards to teach nearly every aspect of elementary and middle school mathematics, and witness the joy that students expressed when they made "new" discoveries in numerical relationships. At Highland Park, I shared the knowledge that I gained from Marilyn Maye and Marty Hoffman with the teachers throughout the K-8 school. We spent hours after school, thinking about the meaning of subtraction and division and talking about Dr. Gattegno's ideas for teaching fractions and decimals. Difficulty with place value was never an issue with those teachers once they became comfortable composing and decomposing larger and larger numbers.

Marty Hoffman came to Boston and conducted a workshop for our staff — what an eye opener that was! The elementary school teachers, in particular, learned to use patterns in language to teach mathematics more effectively. For example, if two elephants plus three elephants results in five elephants, what would two sevenths plus three sevenths be? Only after several rounds of such dialogue would the children begin to write equations by simply translating their language sentences into mathematical symbols.

In 1976 I moved to New Jersey and accepted a position teaching mathematics at an independent school on the Upper East Side of Manhattan. The student population there was totally different from that of the community school in Roxbury. Nevertheless Dr. Gattegno's philosophy, strategies, and recommended manipulatives continued to guide my instruction. The concept of subordinating teaching to learning is universal; children of all ages, races, ethnicities and socioeconomic status learn at higher than expected levels when teachers apply this principle. At the Day School I was pleasantly surprised to meet Paula Hajar who was another proponent of Gattegno's work. We taught mathematics together to middle-grade students and had a wonderful time; the children, in turn, loved mathematics and truly thrived in the "Gattegno" environment. Marilyn Maye visited the school and was delighted to see the techniques that we had been discussing for several years being employed successfully in an entirely different setting.

In the late 1980s I moved into administration in three public school districts in New Jersey, first as a K-12 mathematics supervisor, then assistant superintendent for curriculum and instruction and finally finishing my career as a superintendent. During those nearly two decades I always sought mathematics programs and professional development opportunities that reflected the philosophy of Caleb Gattegno. I found that the developers of the University of Chicago projects respected the intelligence of children and created materials that gave students the power to accelerate in mathematics, unlike other lock-step instructional programs. Also, Paula Hajar worked with me for several years during my administration tenure. She interacted with teachers daily promoting the tenets of the Subordination of Teaching to Learning. Arthur Powell and Ted Swartz were amazing staff developers, both loyal followers of Dr. Gattegno.

Although the professional development workshops were well received by the teachers, they did not result in consistent and sustained changes in the classroom. Therefore, I relied on curriculum materials and insightful full-time administrators to obtain the transformation among staff that I desired. Marilyn was another guru who served as one of my administrators in North Jersey. Her skills in technology, mathematics, and evaluation were invaluable assets in her quest to educate children to be what she called "experts." As I look back at all of the Gattegno-trained people with whom I worked: Marilyn Maye, Marty Hoffman, Paula Hajar, Arthur Powell and Ted Swartz, I know that we achieved tremendous success but we craved and, some of us still do, to impact more students and more teachers with Caleb Gattegno's philosophy of education.

During the past decade, the standards movement has driven education in the United States. It is true that in mathematics and science, in particular, this country lags significantly behind other developed nations. Grade level standards, however, may be limiting to teachers and principals as they often require structured lesson plans that are tied to specific

> "The concept of subordinating teaching to learning is universal; children of all ages, races, ethnicities and socioeconomic status learn at higher than expected levels when teachers apply this principle."

standards. Gattegno's approach to mathematics requires some risk-taking on the part of the teacher and the student. For example, suppose a teacher asks her third graders to use the numbers 1, 2, 3, and 4 and any operations they choose to write expressions for each of the numbers 1 through 24. What a beautiful way for a teacher to assess her individual students' comfort with and mastery of numerical operations. The richness of mathematics that could come through the children's responses would give the teacher opportunities to discuss multiplication, division, exponentiation, order of operations, use of parentheses, etc. The normal textbook rarely uses this type of exercise that is not linked to a specific standard and the students' answers are so unpredictable. Yet, we want our children to take intellectual risks.

Fortunately, an increasing number of alternative and charter schools are free to use innovative, student-centered, experiential approaches to education. I support a charter school in the Bronx; this school was founded on the Subordination of Teaching to Learning principle. The children are happy and verbal, confident in themselves and in their knowledge, eager to try out new ideas and know that mistakes are simply more opportunities to learn. A bright light of learning shines in that school, a light that was ignited by Dr. Caleb Gattegno.

Small Vocabulary as a Big Idea!

Dr. Bob Coe

"What is educable in the learner?" This was one of the first questions Dr. Caleb Gattegno asked at a Silent Way seminar I attended in the New York offices of Educational Solutions in the early 1970s. Gattegno persisted. "Come now. You are all educators. What is educable in your students?" There was dead silence.

I had just returned from two years' study in Europe to my teaching post at the Pingry School, a private school then located in Elizabeth, New Jersey. Jim Karambelas, a good friend and colleague who taught Russian and French, had attended several of Gattegno's seminars while I was in Europe. "Bob, you've got to come along with me and meet 'Dr. G,'" Jim suggested. "He's a pretty amazing guy." Jim was not easily impressed, so I knew I had to learn more about this man who shared our professional passion for teaching foreign languages.

So here I was in my first Silent Way seminar, along with a group of fellow teachers from the New York metropolitan area, many of us experiencing our first contact with Gattegno. We had been trained at some of the finest colleges and universities in the world. "What is educable in the learner?" This was a key question, literally a gauntlet thrown down to challenge us. For me it was one of those pivotal moments – a turning point – that forever changed the way I viewed learning and teaching.

Gattegno challenged us to examine our core beliefs about human beings as learners, and specifically, what language-learning abilities and experience our students brought into the classroom. One of his basic beliefs was that, "Anyone who has learned to speak his mother tongue to an environmentally satisfactory level is endowed with mental powers that are, to say the least, sizeable." That was a revolutionary idea in those days, a radical departure from the views of language and language learning then in vogue.

Gattegno was fascinated by babies and especially by how they acquire their mother tongue. To the casual observer, learning one's native language seems effortless, because we all do it, but for Gattegno, learning one's mother tongue is an extremely complex process that demonstrates that babies are endowed with certain definable mental powers. Among them are:

- Extraction: the ability to isolate sounds and words from the flow of speech they hear.

- Transformations: the ability to use words in their proper context, pronouns and possessive adjectives, for example.

- Abstract thinking: the ability to attach meanings to words.

- Stressing and ignoring: the ability to focus on one attribute of something and not another.

- Sense of truth: a feedback mechanism that exists between utterances and hearing that permits a speaker to judge the rightness and correctness of an utterance.

Babies develop these abilities as they explore the mysteries of the mother tongue. These are powers of the mind that babies use to make neural connections and forge mental structures that are, in turn, integrated into the soma. Babies use these abilities to make sense of what they hear and see and, much like the persistent weightlifter who, over time, can lift heavier and heavier weights, are able to tackle ever more complex aspects of the mother tongue.

This task of organization and coordination does not exist when we are first born; we discover it in our crib, and we use it, practice it, refine it, and make it more powerful until it becomes an instrument for knowledge – knowledge that is meaningful within the criteria we have. Gattegno sums it up in this way:

"…to learn the mother tongue is an extraordinary achievement because it has been done without help from others and without the assistance of the tools which will be available at the end of the apprenticeship."

What are the implications, then, for the foreign language classroom? Gattegno recognizes that it is impossible to replicate the conditions of learning the mother tongue. It is possible, however, to create a learning environment in the foreign language class, albeit totally artificial, that challenges learners to make use of those same powerful functionings they developed and used when they learned their mother tongue.

In the initial phase of a Silent Way course, for example, Gattegno proposes that students learn what he calls a basic functional vocabulary, approximately 400 of the most frequently used words that, in turn, constitute a significant portion of just about any sample of the language studied. If we think of these words as the framework of a structure, we can appreciate their importance in learning a second language. The teacher uses the colored rods to create carefully controlled, unambiguous situations that, on the one hand, clearly illustrate the meanings of the basic functional vocabulary and, on the other, challenge the learners to use the mental powers they used to master their mother tongue.

Mastering these words enables the learners to create a large number of statements and thus gain an awareness of the spirit of the language with all the concomitant subtleties of pronunciation, stress, intonation, and inflexion. Gattegno refers to this as "much language with little vocabulary." It is an essential first step in second language acquisition. Once the learners have achieved a mastery of oral and written fluency in the basic functional vocabulary, they can proceed to more advanced levels of learning specialized vocabulary in accordance with their reasons for studying a second language.

To illustrate, let's say that the teacher, Ms. T, is sitting at a small table at the front of the classroom. She has six students sitting in pairs at three tables arranged in a semi-circle in front of her. She walks from table to table with a small box containing a set of colored rods.

"Take two red rods and give one to me. Put the other one here," or "Take four yellow rods; give two to her, one to him and keep the other one." She continues in this way testing the students' ability to understand and carry out her instructions. When she has finished she returns to her desk. Each of her students has one rod.

She takes a rod from the box and holds it up for her students to see. Then she says, "I have a black rod." She looks around at her students, waiting for them to join in.

Student A gets the idea and says, "I have a red rod," drawing on her linguistic experience to make the appropriate substitution.

Student B joins in: "I have a red rod." Ms. T looks at student B and realizes that Student B's rod is actually pink, not red. To the casual observer, Student B needs "to be corrected." Gattegno would insist instead that Student B needs to correct himself.

How can Ms. T do this? How can the teacher get the student to correct himself? She has a number of options. The first and most important is silence; simply look at Student B with a totally blank expression her face, expressing neither approval nor disapproval.

Student B may be waiting for Ms. T to supply and model the correct answer, but Ms. T doesn't. Initially, that silence can be awkward. After a few moments Ms. T has the option of continuing to wait or provide a clue. She might pretend to grab Student B's utterance out of the air and put it in his ear to get him to think about what he just said. She might hold up both a red rod and a pink one to show that there is a difference in both color and length, and then wait for Student B to correct himself, or she may ask other members of the class to join in and help.

Student B needs to listen to himself, to monitor what he just said, to become aware that what he said is not what he should have said, then make it right.

What is educable then in the learner is awareness, and the role of silence on the part of the teacher is essential in allowing that awareness to take place: to throw the learner back on himself and make him use those skills he developed during the learning of his mother tongue and take responsibility for his learning. This is precisely what Gattegno meant

(Coe Cont'd)

when he said, "I don't teach, I let them learn." And after all, isn't the proper role of language teachers to make themselves useless to their students?

In his preface to the first edition of *Teaching Foreign Languages in Schools the Silent Way*, published in 1963, Gattegno speaks of the Silent Way as one man's proposal based on one man's experience, "and that the most important contribution of this work is the opening of new vistas in education that should excite a new generation of people to investigate and to experiment with what they find behind the doors that are now put ajar."

The fact that 48 years later, in response to the call to honor him on the 100th anniversary of his birth, literally hundreds of teachers from around the world have come forth with their own personal reflections and analyses of his ideas is a fitting tribute to a man who has made a vast and invaluable contribution to the Science of Education.

It is my sincere hope that we have helped him open the door a bit wider. §

"I don't teach, I let them learn."

— Dr. Caleb Gattegno

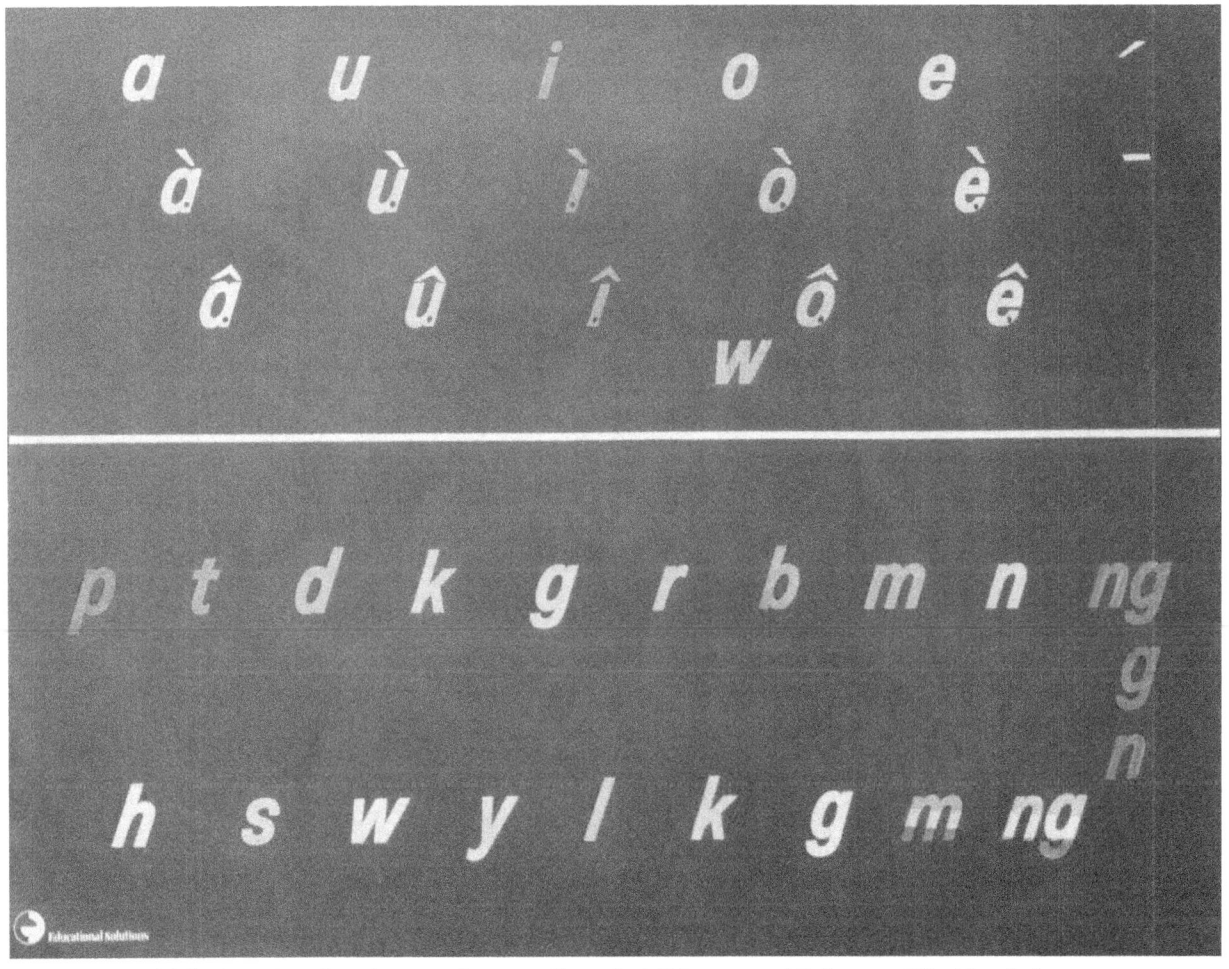

Prototype Fidel for Tagalog, hand-painted on cardboard. ©Educational Solutions Worldwide Inc.

A Less-Damaging Career

Donald Cherry

If it were not for the Silent Way I might have been a cook, and although I enjoy cooking, I am not particularly good at it. Fortunately, there is the Silent Way, and diners at the restaurant I never got around to opening may be thankful. I certainly am. Thankful, that is, for this teaching approach that made my job so much more interesting, and, keeping me out of the kitchen as it did, may have actually saved lives.

Before coming into contact with the Silent Way, I was slowly reinventing the wheel — well, more like trying to reinvent an entire automobile — and given perhaps a dozen lifetimes I might have come close to developing a teaching approach worthy of my students and interesting enough to keep me from poisoning the eating public. Thing is, I didn't have a dozen lifetimes and was in fact already halfway through the only one I had. So, while I was sitting in the teachers' lounge of a school in Osaka, Japan one day, appearing to search the pages of yet another desperately titled ESL textbook ("Let's Communicate!" or "Snappy Ideas for Sleepy Teachers") but secretly dreaming of what I would name my restaurant, a colleague sat beside me and asked if I was okay.

"You look like you're going to cry," he observed.

I would have unburdened my soul to this psychic young man, told him about how ineffective I felt my teaching was, confessed my sins, pleaded for absolution, or at the very least asked if he knew any good Turkish recipes as it seemed this was the direction my restaurant was heading. But there simply wasn't time.

"I have a class in half an hour. Got any ideas?"

And he quickly showed me a very simple way to work with students on English numbers. It was similar to the way I saw Caleb Gattegno work with students on a videotape I was to watch many years later. It felt right. It was in the direction my teaching seemed to be heading. It was simple, elegant, logical, and beautifully to-the-point. It was like a wheel on that automobile I was trying to reinvent. Well, maybe a spoke on a wheel.

More spokes and other bits came with my study at the School for International Training, and a great methodology teacher there, Bonnie Mennell. Then out of the blue came an entire car driven by Shakti Gattegno, and BAM! I spent an hour watching everyone around me speak Hindi while Ms. Gattegno pointed at some charts up front. I was hopelessly confused, even more confused when Ms. Gattegno had me come to the front and asked me to write my name using the Hindi script, and triply bewildered when I actually managed to write it. I'd like to say that at the moment of writing my name, the heavens opened up and I saw some sort of light, but to be honest I am to this day baffled by the experience.

Still a bit dazed and stumbling about, I ended up walking about one year later directly into the path

> "...there was no denying the effect it had on the students. They were on the edge of their seats..."

of yet another large vehicle, this one driven by Silent Way teacher John Beary.

BAM!

It was at Fusako Allard's wonderful Center for Language and Intercultural Learning in Osaka, or just "The Center" as everyone called it, where there was always some language course or theory workshop going on. John Beary was a regular there, doing five-day intensive English courses a couple times a year. I observed many of these courses. Unlike the lesson on English numbers my colleague had quickly described to me several years earlier, what John was doing seemed in some ways quite unlike the direction my teaching had been heading. Or so far in that direction that it fell right off the edge and out of sight.

But there was no denying the effect it had on the students. They were on the edge of their seats during those long, all-day intensive courses. So was I. I watched carefully, sometimes skeptically, sometimes confused, sometimes irritated, almost always intrigued, and I took notes. Then I went out and tortured, absolutely tortured, my students. So much so that I might have actually done less damage during that time as a cook.

I kept a journal during that time, mostly because I could not afford a good therapist. I wrote all kinds of things in it — problems I was having, descriptions of lessons I had taught and ideas for those I might teach, reflections on teaching and learning, and then every third or fourth page I'd write about some sort of awareness I felt I had. I drew a little picture of a light bulb next to these entries. You know, like the bulb that goes off over the heads of cartoon characters when they get an idea. Sometimes these awarenesses were as comical as cartoons. I would write something that seemed to suggest I had found some hidden secret, that my search and my work were over, that I had reached some end point, some sort of nirvana and could go make myself a sandwich and watch TV now. This would usually be followed a page or two later by a tortured entry written by someone obviously still struggling in a place nowhere near nirvana.

So why did I put myself through this? Why not pitch it all and just make that sandwich, flip on the TV?

> "... the approach freed me to be more observant and responsive to the always changing needs of students."

Here are a few theories:

- Pure stubbornness.

- Nothing in the fridge and nothing on TV.

- A fascination with the elegance of the Silent Way, the energy it is capable of charging the classroom with, the way it respects learners by treating them as complex, sophisticated learning beings and not parrots or monkeys (and poorly designed ones at that, incapable of flying or swinging from trees), the way the approach freed me to be more observant and responsive to the always changing needs of students.

- Pure stubbornness.

While not yet reaching enlightenment, I think I can now say with some confidence that I am probably a better teacher than cook. However, I am certainly not content to rest on my laurels, primarily because I don't have any, and I continue to learn from my students at Hiroshima International University and in the intensive ESL courses organized by Silent Way Tokyo. I even manage to learn a bit from my children who told me just the other day to put salt in the water when I boil broccoli.

§

Une rencontre avec Gattegno ou plus précisément avec sa pédagogie

Daniel Roder

Dans les années 1992, l'organisme de Formation que je dirigeais, INSEF Conseil, avait comme spécialité la remise à niveau des personnes dites « bas niveau de qualifications », cela consistait a traiter le problème d'analphabétisme et d'illettrisme.

Nos formations se déroulaient sur des durées de 500 à 900h avec des méthodes pédagogiques classiques, en tout cas rien de révolutionnaire sur le plan pédagogique et des techniques d'apprentissage.

Les résultats n'étaient pas probants sauf pour les apprenants totalement investis dans leur apprentissage, mais comme il y avait un consensus des institutions sur les modes opératoires, tout le monde s'en satisfaisait.

Au travers de différentes rencontres et par le plus grand des hasards, ma route a croisé la pédagogie Gattegno.

La première personne qui me l'a présentée m'a immédiatement emballé, j'ai tout de suite décelé quelque chose d'énorme qui allait changer la vie des personnes confrontées à la non maîtrise de la langue française. J'ai décidé d'orienter mon organisme de formation vers la mise sur le marché de la pédagogie Gattegno au bénéfice des publics analphabètes et illettrés.

Il m'a fallu environ 18 mois pour convaincre une institution et mettre en place une première formation d'alphabétisation au bénéfice d'ouvriers étrangers d'une entreprise sidérurgique.

C'est au cours de cette première opération que j'ai fait la connaissance de Claudie Gattegno qui était une des formatrices du groupe. J'ai assisté à une partie de la Formation, et bien évidemment j'ai été totalement conforté dans la nécessité de développer cette pédagogie non conventionnelle, mais ô combien efficace!

Cette approche pédagogique centrée sur l'amour de l'être humain est une démarche globale de prise en compte de l'Homme avec toutes les composantes émotionnelles liées au processus d'apprentissage : le plaisir d'apprendre et d'être l'acteur de ses apprentissages, la joie de découvrir, la joie de réussir, la joie de partager … Cela a été une révolution pour moi.

Je n'ai eu alors de cesse de promouvoir la pédagogie Gattegno, avec un certain succès je dois dire ; le Conseil Régional de Lorraine, l'Etat, de grandes Entreprises ont été nos clients.

Mon regard sur les modes d'apprentissage a changé depuis cette découverte, notamment sur la nécessité de faire émerger les prises de conscience qui solidifient le socle de l'apprentissage.

Il m'a fallu combattre des représentants des institutions dont le parti pris contre Gattegno était puissamment installé; ces organisations ne souffraient pas que l'on puisse apprendre autrement que de la manière dont ils avaient eux-mêmes décidé.

J'ai compris que cette opposition venait du fait que ce n'était pas une personne de l'institution qui la proposait, cela ne venait pas de l'une d'entre elles reconnu par elles.

Toutefois au bout de 10 ans de mise en œuvre j'ai été confronté à quelques freins qui ont ralenti le développement de Gattegno:

1. Les Formateurs; ils sont trop peu nombreux à avoir totalement intégré l'esprit de cette approche pédagogique.

> Nous mêmes avions engagé la formation de formateurs de 12 personnes, mais la remise en cause personnelle de «l'enseignant» était telle, que seules 4 personnes ont réellement enseigné avec le Dr. Gattegno.

2. La nécessité, pour une grande efficacité, de mettre en place un rythme d'apprentissage continu de 3 à 5 jours par semaine n'était pas aisé.

Ce rythme était possible pour les demandeurs d'emploi, mais pour les salariés des entreprises, libérer les gens de leur poste de travail posait de réels problèmes.

3. Nous avons constaté, en Lorraine, que les institutions qui luttent contre l'illettrisme, préfèrent travailler à leur rythme, avec des bénévoles et en cours du soir.

Les orientations politiques des collectivités qui financent ces formations (bien que les discours nationaux fassent toujours état de ce fléau) ont eu raison de notre détermination, et aujourd'hui elles ont délégué cette problématique à des associations de quartiers.

La proximité de la pédagogie Gattegno qui a été la mienne, a modifié mon regard sur nos capacités d'apprentissage et sur les problèmes des personnes illettrées.

Je les considère comme des gens normaux qui n'ont pas eu un environnement familial propice à l'éclosion des apprentissages de base et que l'école n'a pas su les mettre sur le chemin de la réussite.

La pédagogie Gattegno est la vraie solution pour réparer et recréer, en chacun, l'envie d'apprendre et donc de réussir. §

Educational Solutions file photo, 2010.

Education From My Father

Alma Arnould, née Gattegno

My contribution to *The Gattegno Effect* starts with early recollections of what it meant to be in my father's presence during my formative years.

EGYPT

My sister Lola and I had a very happy childhood, in spite of the upheaval of the Second World War. During that time, my father spent a lot of time with me and we often played. He always told me bedtime stories, fairy tales from different cultures, as well as the French classics – simplified so I could understand them. But he also made up his own stories, to suit my age as I grew up. I knew then that it wasn't the same, because he often forgot the names of the characters he was inventing for me. Before that, he never forgot the names of the characters from novels and plays. So already in the late 1930s and early 1940s, he had started on the stories he first published in French as the *Six contes pour enfants* (*Six Tales for Children*) to which he later added two more for the *Eight Tales*. He chose to publish our favorite stories.

His story-telling inspired me and I too entertained groups of children with magical tales, using their knowledge of the Egyptian environment to make the situations more real for them, including Arabic expressions in my English or French stories.

When I started at an English primary school, not knowing any of the language, I remember that I argued with the teacher showing me A for Apple, B for Bunny, C for Cat. I could not see the logic as "pomme" and "lapin" were pictured, C was valid for "chat." So I must already have been reading in French, and I suppose Dad helped me learn.

ENGLAND

After the war, Dad went to England to lecture at Liverpool University for a year and returned to take the family over in 1946. He was then a lecturer at London University. We were very suddenly uprooted and taken to a country still suffering from the privations of war, where children played in bombed sites. The whole environment was strange, the people and the language; though my sister and I spoke English well, the education system was different, friends difficult to find. We moved three times and went to different schools before we settled in Hampton Hill. He sent us to good schools, encouraging us to do well. Later he said to us, "I will leave you nothing but the education I am giving you," and so he helped me financially to obtain several qualifications I wanted after I left school.

When I think back on that stage of my life, I realize that I did not see all that much of my father. He was always busy, teaching during the weekdays and very often spending weekends writing many articles and books. He seemed to have them fully composed in his head, before he put pen to paper and just sat and wrote, then my mother typed out his work. He also had many visitors from different countries, mathematicians or scientists, so we knew that this was not quite a normal household. He was always very involved with children, and had a huge effect on any who came in contact with him, among them my teenaged friends, who envied us because they thought we were with him all the time.

He not only wrote his own books. He also translated two of Jean Piaget's books with our friend Mrs. F. Hodgson, and I often listened to them as they worked and considered how to convey Piaget's ideas in English. Mrs. Hodgson was a lecturer at the language education department of the University of London where Dad was in the mathematics department. She helped us to adjust to life in England and her library of English literature was a great source of enjoyment for me.

CAMPS

In 1947, Dad organized his first holiday camp for children in Neuilly, France. He had founded the Association Internationale pour l'Echange des Jeunes (International Association for the Exchange of Youth) to bring together children from different nationalities and social backgrounds during their school holidays. This was a cultural and educational period of two to four weeks, which allowed them to become friends, and for some this became a life-long friendship. The accommodation was often in famous places which were vacant at that time: boarding-schools, a castle, a convent, etc.

Initially, these camps were for children of our age, then the age level went up as we got older until we also had adults join us.

Dr. G ran most of them himself with other teachers helping, and later some groups were conducted by them, while he was with another group elsewhere. Lola and I attended one every year. Our French cousins also came to some of them, and have fond memories of that time.

We visited France, Belgium, Holland, Germany, Switzerland, Denmark with participants from several of these countries in each camp. One special holiday was in April 1951 at the Herzberg Volkshochschule near Aarau in Switzerland. It was combined with a seminar of mathematicians, scientists, and medical specialists, various groups holding their meetings at different times. But it allowed us younger people to come in contact with very interesting adults who were well-known in their own areas.

I met Claude, a Belgian student, in the summer of 1951 at a camp in Corsica. We married in Belgium in 1960. My father came to see us there about three times.

The last camp I remember was in Spain in 1955. Participants were students and adults from various professions and nationalities. We made a marvellous cultural tour of northern Spain and Madrid. It was there that another side of my father's concern for children became evident. A young and very gifted boy played the guitar for us and Dad decided to sponsor him, found him a teacher and for a few years helped him realize his potential.

Another example: at one camp a troubled young man asked if Dad could "be a sort of adopted father" to him. They corresponded for many years.

In Belgium, I was not involved in any of my father's work – I just heard about it, mainly the Cuisenaire Rods, his books, and approach for mathematics. We had met Georges Cuisenaire on one holiday and saw him again when Dad came to visit us in 1969.

AUSTRALIA

In Australia, not finding work translating or interpreting at the time, (though I did help out fellow-migrants), I decid)ed to teach, but needed a Diploma of Education. That was when I came across Dad's book *Teaching Foreign Languages in Schools the Silent Way*. As one of my projects that year, I taught French for several weeks in a primary school. Dad's approach seemed so obvious to me, that without any training, I set out to use the French charts we obtained. Twenty Grade 6 children volunteered and I taught them twice a week for a full hour, extending through their recess as they wanted to learn more, fascinated by the work they were doing.

Although I had to follow the secondary school programs, I still incorporated many aspects of the Silent Way into my teaching. When I had the only class of German, or French, I had more freedom. In lunch breaks, I taught Spanish to some students and teachers and the progress they made kept them coming in. My experience has been limited but very rewarding, as my students did not need to revise every year what was already theirs, they found languages easy. Whenever they worked in small groups, all speaking German (or French), they were involved and noisy, helping each other.

In 1980, I followed two one-week courses in New York on the Silent Way, which gave me more insight into my father's work. Because of the distance, I could only participate in one of his seminars in Sireuil, France in 1984 while on long-service leave. That was "Vivre à son sommet" (Living at your peak) which was for me a new view of his work.

In 1984 and 1987, Dr. G came to visit us and conducted seminars in Melbourne, which were well-attended and enlightening for many teachers.

What he wrote and proposed was so true, it should have been obvious to all. I read *The Universe of Babies* as I observed my daughter go through the stages he described. Small children keep at a task until it is mastered, then move on to the next task.

I have only touched on some of the impacts and experiences I had through my contact with Dr. G. I admired him and came to know his work mainly through his wonderful books.

§

Young Dr. Gattegno. (Educational Solutions file photo.)

The Silent Way Down Under
De Silent Way Downunder

Dr. Marietta Elliott-Kleerkoper

Reminiscences from Brunswick Language Centre, Melbourne, Australia

If there's something like a good virus, I was first 'infected' with the Silent Way while teaching in an English as a Foreign Language program at the University of California, Berkely. A colleague there, Deni Johnson Harding, was very much engaged with the approach. I began to try out aspects of what I understood to be the Silent Way and attended seminars and conferences on the practice, including a three-day seminar with Dr. Gattegno in New York.

Back in Australia, I began presenting teacher-training seminars. Gattegno was not well known here. Dr. Jane Orton and I teamed up and presented seminars to our teaching colleagues together in the late '70s and early '80s: and thus we in turn 'infected' our Australian colleagues. Some of them went on to develop innovative approaches of their own – you might call them 'mutations.' I recently went in search of them to gather their perspectives, from a distance of more than 25 years. First I spoke to Ruth Evans; she and Bill Cleland had developed the Topic Approach.

Brunswick Language Centre was one of a number of places offering a six-month intensive English course preparing students for mainstream schooling, and the Topic Approach was developed for this purpose. Content and language were arranged so that content was paired with specific language items. Science provided concrete visual material, which was vital especially for the beginner stages, and fulfilled a similar and complementary role to the rods.

I asked Ruth to reminisce about her and Bill's practice and how the Silent Way had influenced them in developing their approach. Whilst Bill used rods, Ruth says she never used them. So what did the Silent Way mean to her?

"Students were able to focus on what they were seeing; there was a mental connection between teachers and students. The silence improved concentration and processing. We were not crowding their minds in the initial stages. The rods or other visual objects provided an understanding of relationships and there was not too much stress on reproduction, especially in the early stages. Students would stay silent until they had internalized what was going on. We were getting from them what they knew instead of overloading them. Initially they need control, but as their knowledge builds up you can gradually loosen the constraints."

Within the Topic Approach, Ruth and Bill used other aids such as pictures and word cards, but with the same principles. Other influences were also integrated, such as the Communicative Approach (e.g. H.G. Widdowson) and Process Writing (e.g. Donald Graves).

Dr. Alan Williams did not come into direct contact with the Silent Way, never having attended a workshop, but was interested in developing the Topic Approach. He could see that the 'Visual Stage' in the Topic Approach had its origins in the Silent Way. He used the rods if the students were having trouble with a particular structure. He took care to transfer the knowledge gained from working with the rods to real life situations relating to the topics being taught, and to move from the micro-focus on phonemes and the sentence to real-life communication, using the Communicative Approach. However, we agreed, just like practising scales in music, micro-focus was

(Elliott-Kleerkoper Cont'd)

important. On teacher exchange in Canada, after witnessing a lesson using the rods, he bought his own, wooden set. (I too have a wooden set: we agreed plastic ones were definitely inferior.) As well as the rods, he found the charts useful for demonstrating the many different spellings for one particular sound.

Alan found the silence "a discipline imposed on talkative people to curb their chattiness. Bill would say after a 40 minute class: 'I only said eight words.'"

which was in part inspired by the Silent Way, as I wrote in a pamphlet for Child Migrant Education Services in 1982. My interpretation of the approach at the time was as follows:

> "Silence is a discipline which teachers impose upon themselves so that they do not intervene unnecessarily in the learning process. The responsibility upon the teacher is to present only the items which cannot be invented by the student – and to present only one item at a time.

'Students were able to focus on what they were seeing'

Alan said the Silent Way "was a framework that guides me rather than directs me."

Anna French, who took over Brunswick Language Centre when Bill left, was 'infected' when she attended one of my demonstrations to the Diploma of Education students at La Trobe University and a demonstration in Mandarin by Dr. Jane Orton:

> "I saw that you don't talk about language. You use it. The brain works it out. I was so impressed. I wanted to be able to do that. When I learnt Spanish through the Silent Way I became more confident – I knew that's how I wanted to learn a language. I still remember what I learnt.

> You have to have the courage to let the silence happen – they have to think. It can be difficult. It is important that correct pronunciation and grammar be insisted on: we don't want students speaking 'broken English.'

> I had to get custody of my face. I had to learn to gesture. It is very economical. I watched the machinery of the students' brains. I used to write down what students demonstrated they understood. You get to a comfort level with your idea of silence."

Researching at the Melbourne language center where Ruth and Bill were based, I was developing an approach to teaching writing in the second language

To present new items, unambiguous concrete non-verbal symbols are used. In Gattegno's case, the materials first used were Cuisenaire Rods … Writing is taught in the early stages through use of color-coded Word Charts … There is no need, however, to restrict oneself to the charts. My colleagues and I are using other materials in addition to those specifically labeled Silent Way, but our aim is to use these in as silent a way as possible; to guide without prescribing, not to be over-protective and to make our students as self-reliant as possible, as soon as possible."

It was remarkable that Ruth, Alan, Anna and myself still spoke with so much enthusiasm about our time at Brunswick Language Centre (known for its innovative practice at the time), even though, to the three of us who have retired (Alan lectures at the University of Melbourne), these concerns seemed distant. We each used the Silent Way in our own way, combining it with the best of other approaches, such as the Communicative Approach and Process Writing. In fact, the Topic Approach pre-dated the 'Genre' approach (e.g. J.R. Martin) by some years.

As Ruth said:

> "Provided we had an overarching concept of what we were doing and why we were doing it, there was no necessary conflict between the different approaches."

De Silent Way Downunder

Als er een goedaardige virus bestaat, ben ik met de SW 'besmet' terwijl ik in 1975 een paar maanden Engels voor buitenlanders doceerde aan de University of California, Berkely. Een enthousiaste collega, Deni Harding Johnson, bracht mij in aanraking met de methode. Ik begon de methode in te voeren en woonde conferenties bij, waaronder een congres onder de leiding van Gattegno zelf.

Omdat Gattegno in Australië toen nog niet bekend was, ben ik begonnen met de methode aan leraren en kwekelingen te demonstreren. Dr Jane Orton en ik presenteerden later samen. Sommige deelnemers hebben hun eigen innovaties, oftewel 'mutaties' ontwikkeld. Ik heb enige van hen opgezocht, om hun herinneringen over de SW, vanuit een afstand van meer dan 25 jaar, te verzamelen. Eerst sprak ik met Ruth Evans. Zij en Bill Cleland (helaas was het niet mogelijk om Bill te interviewen) hebben de 'Topic Approach' bedacht. (Cleland en Evans: Learning English through Topics about Australia: Longman Cheshire 1985).

Brunswick Language Centre was een school, waarvan er toen een aantal in Melbourne bestonden, die waren opgericht door de overheid met het doel immigrantenkinderen op het algemene onderwes voor te bereiden. De 'Topic Approach' (TA) was hierop gericht. Specifieke inhoud en taalelementen werden gecombineerd. De natuurwetenschap, met haar vele demonstraties, was bijzonder geschikt voor het beginstadium en het visueel materiaal was met de rol van de staafjes te vergelijken.

Ik vroeg Ruth welke invloed de SW op de ontwikkeling van de TA had uitgeoefend. Terwijl Bill wel de staafjes gebruikte, vond zij die te 'onpersoonlijk'. Zij zelf had zich nooit verdiept in de SW; ze had de principes van Bill overgenomen. Wat betekende de SW voor haar?

De leerlingen konden zich concentreren op dat wat ze voor zich zagen. Het zwijgen versterkte hun aandacht. Hun hersens waren niet overbelast in dit beginstadium. Met behulp van de staafjes konden ze de verhoudingen begrijpen. Er was niet te veel nadruk op uitspraak, vooral in het begin. De leerlingen zwegen totdat ze de taal hadden begrepen. Wij accepteerden het niveau van hun kennis. In het begin hebben ze veel leiding nodig, maar naarmate hun kennis zich opbouwt kunnen we die leiding langzamerhand afbouwen.

Als deel van de TA gebruikten Ruth en Bill verschillende hulpmiddelen, zoals beelden en woordkaartjes, in overeenstemming met dezelfde principes. Verdere methoden, zoals de 'Communicative Approach' (bijv. H.G, Widdowson) en 'Process Writing' (bijv. Donald Graves) werden ook deel van hun leerwijze.

Dr Alan Williams kwam in aanraking met de SW door zijn interesse voor de TA. Hij begreep dat de 'Visual Stage' in de TA zijn oorsprong in de SW had. Hij gebruikte de staafjes wanneer de leerlingen met een of ander taalelement moeite hadden. Voor hem was het belangrijk dat de praktijk niet tot de staafjes beperkt bleef, maar dat de grammaticale kennis op de alledaagse wereld werd toegepast en dat de oefening zo snel mogelijk in ware communicatie overging. Toch waren we het erover eens dat oefening een plaats had, net als bij het leren van een muziekinstrument. Na een bezoek aan Canada, waar hij een les met staafjes bijwoonde, kocht hij zijn eigen, houten stel. We waren het erover eens: hout is het beste!

Hij gebruikte de fonetische woordkaarten bij het demonstreren van Engelse orthografie, vooral van woorden die in het Engels dezelfde klank, maar een verschillende orthografic hebben.

Voor Alan was de het zwijgen:

…vooral voor spraakzame leraren een manier om hun spraakzaamheid te beteugelen. Bill zei dat hij soms, aan het einde van een les van 40 minuten, maar acht woorden gebruikt had.

Voor hem was de SW een handleiding, maar geen voorschrift.

Anna French nam de leiding van het Brunswick Language Centre na het vertrek van Bill over. Zij heeft de virus te pakken gekregen toen ze twee

(Elliott-Kleerkoper Cont'd)

'De leerlingen konden zich concentreren op dat wat ze voor zich zagen.'

workshops bijwoonde, een in het Mandarijns onder de leiding van Dr Jane Orton, de tweede geleid door mij.

Ik heb begrepen dat je niet over de taal spreekt, je gebruikt de taal. Ik was zeer onder de indruk. Ik wilde de methode zelf uitoefenen. Toen ik eenmaal zo Spaans geleerd had kreeg ik meer zelfvertrouwen. Ik herinner me nu nog wat ik geleerd heb.

Je hebt moed nodig om het stilzijn te aanvaarden en de leerlingen tijd te geven om na te denken. De juiste uitspraak is belangrijk. We willen niet, dat ze een gebrekkig Engels leren.

Ik moest op mijn gelaatsuitdrukking letten. Ik moest leren, geen overtollige gebaren te maken. Ik kon mijn leerlingen zien denken. Ik noteerde mijn observaties over hun taalkennis. Men voelt zich langzamerhand op zijn gemak met zijn eigen idee van stilzijn.

Gedurende mijn onderzoek op het Brunswick Language Centre was ik zelf bezig een methode voor het doceren van schrijven in een tweede taal te ontwikkelen. Mijn methode is gedeeltelijk gebaseerd op de SW (Students can write in their second language: an approach to writing in ESL classes: Child Migrant Education Services, Victoria, Australia, 1982). Ik citeer:

Het stilzijn is een discipline die leraren zich opleggen zodat ze niet onnodig in het proces ingrijpen. De leraar presenteert alleen die elementen die de leerling niet zelf kan bedenken en presenteert die één voor één. De concrete, visuele symbolen die Gattegno gebruikte waren de staafjes en de gekleurde fonetische woordkaarten. Mijn collega's en ik gebruiken nog ander materiaal, maar op een 'SW' manier. Dat houdt in: leiden, zonder strenge voorschriften op te leggen, niet te beschermend zijn en onze leerlingen bij te staan, zo snel mogelijk zelfstandig te worden.

Het is verbazingwekkend, dat Ruth, Alan, Anna en ik nog steeds met zo veel enthousiasme praten over die tijd op het Brunswick Language Centre, een school die bekend was voor innovatie, al waren Anna, Ruth en ik al met pensioen en kwamen deze kwesties uit het verre verleden. Wij hebben de SW ieder op onze eigen manier gebruikt, en de methode gecombineerd met andere, zoals de 'Communicative Approach' en 'Process Writing.' De TA was zelfs een voorloper van de 'Genre' (bijv. John Martin) methode.

Zoals Ruth het uitdrukt:

Als je weet, hoe het geheel in elkaar past, kun je de verschillende methodes zonder tegenstrijdigheid gebruiken.

§

Three Lessons Learned From
An Uncompromising Man

Dr. Theodore Swartz

' I create the best instrument I can. People will do what they want with it.'

The year was 1977. I had just returned from a business trip to Dallas, Texas and was sitting at a table, having lunch with Dr. Gattegno and several other of his Educational Solutions employees. Young, enthusiastic, and proud of a significant sale of materials, I boasted that on the plane ride back to New York City, I read a complete book.

Without a moment's pause, Dr. Gattegno quipped mildly in his clipped British accent, "The last time I was on a plane, I wrote a book."

Humbling moments like that remain vivid. Also, deeply appreciated.

On another occasion in the late '70s, Dr. Gattegno had recently completed a revamping of Words in Color, including the placement of perhaps 50% more content on each of the Word Charts. A couple of us who had been trying to sell the program and train teachers to use it told him, "Teachers will complain there are too many words, and they won't like it. They already find the Word Charts confusing at first." He responded, "I don't know. I haven't met that many teachers." That from a man who worked closely with thousands of teachers all over the globe, countless more than his staff collectively had encountered. He added, "I create the best instrument I can. People will do what they want with it."

For me, there are three lessons learned that are directly linked to Gattegno's rich contribution to the improvement of education. First, to permit his extensive legacy of articles and books, Gattegno was sufficiently clear about the nature of the challenge of serving learning. He was facile in expressing his understanding of that challenge and how to address it because he discovered that only awareness is educable in man. Everything flowed from that.

A second lesson is that commonly held beliefs require close scrutiny, even when they appear to be supported by shared experience. Gattegno knew that convictions, no matter how widely held, are subject to revision and that what seem to be sufficient data may very well be sorely inadequate, certainly subject to the limitations of the observers and their methods of analysis.

Third, valid contributions to a field of study as wide and complex as education require decisions that are not distracted by commercial interest. In particular, educational publishers who design and market materials based on their analysis of what will sell easily may generate wealth for company owners or shareholders, but they are therefore prepared to compromise the integrity of their products. Gattegno steadfastly refused to make such compromises. He instead was guided by a trust that teachers have the capacity to identify those approaches that best meet the needs of their students, even when such approaches demand deep, sometimes disconcerting introspection and continuous self-scrutiny. Teachers may not always do so, but Gattegno knew they can, and that it serves their self-interest.

It is no surprise that the best advice he could give one of his young, ardent admirers some 40 years ago was an unexpected, handwritten note on which he had transcribed the attributed words of a 16th century king, William the Introspective: "To act there is no need for hope and to persevere, no need of success." His steadfast determination and sense of purpose, perhaps even more than his extraordinary intellect, led to an opus that is as vital and worthy of serious study today as it was decades ago, maybe more so. §

Primary school classroom using Words in Color. (Educational Solutions file photo.)

Seeing 'I' to 'I'

Steve Hirschhorn

I would have liked to start this piece with any other word than "I" but it is a challenge too great for me. The reason for this is that Dr. Caleb Gattegno influenced me, my career, my students and probably my students' students; therefore "I" was the student and "I" is also the teacher. "I" is central to the whole experience of learning to learn and becoming aware of oneself as a learner and teacher; in short without "I," there is no "we" and "we" is the basis of classroom interaction.

My first introduction to Dr. G's work was at the school in Hastings, Sussex where I trained to be a language teacher. There I encountered such inspirational figures as Allan Brammell and Adrian Underhill, both at that time delving into alternatives to traditional teaching and learning. They encouraged an investigation into approaches which put the learner in the center of the teaching / learning dialogue, and through them I discovered the Silent Way and the extraordinary work of Caleb Gattegno.

A few years later, in the early '80s, I attended a Silent Way teacher training course with Dr. G in London, and those five days were to create the foundations of my career as a teacher who put the Subordination of Teaching to Learning at the top of the agenda.

For a while I taught what one might describe as "pure" Silent Way – closely following the advice and guidance of its creator. Later, I developed a more individual and personal style as I grew in confidence and experience. Throughout the whole process, I somehow managed to maintain contact with Dr. G, attending workshops with him, inviting him to give workshops at my own school, and on one memorable occasion, watching him work with a group of mathematicians in Bristol.

This was memorable because I am no mathematician – in fact, I am close to innumerate! And yet, Dr. G managed to keep these high-powered mathematicians happy while also teaching me something! By the end of the day, I had learnt some fairly irrelevant (for me) things about factors and integers, but much more importantly, I had watched a true master teacher in action. Since that day, I have felt that my challenge as a teacher must be to embrace all my students to ensure that even those who may not yet have the ability of the strongest, have the chance to flourish.

During my master's program, I wrote a paper on the use of the rods in revealing grammar. My tutor, who clearly had no idea how they might be used, and no belief in anything other than explanation, continually commented in the margins, "But how will students know how to do this?" She could not conceive of the extraordinary way in which learners respond to the rods, and how they will react to the challenge of small pieces of colored wood. I did later offer to run a demo lesson so that she could experience them, but she declined.

(Hirschhorn Cont'd)

This refusal by many academics to be engaged with anything but the mainstream also brings to mind the conference I organized in the mid '90s, which examined the many gifts Gattegno had offered to our profession. An old friend who worked for a university on the English south coast said he couldn't come because his head of department "didn't like Gattegno." There is no doubt that Dr. G wasn't universally understood or accepted, and that, in a sense, increases my gratitude for having been able to appreciate the valuable gifts he bestowed on us. I have been proud to pass some of his gifts on to others, and to challenge academics to open their minds.

I have spent some years now developing the use of the rods as a major language teaching aid, and introducing new teachers to them as well. They form a mainstay of my teaching, and both new and more experienced teachers are usually awed by their simplicity of use, accessibility, and the language that can be generated with them. All of this is excellent, but without the underlying philosophy proposed by Dr. G, the rods become just another classroom tool, indeed, in the wrong hands they can be disastrous – they are after all just little pieces of colored wood. What brings them to life is that which teacher and students invest in them, and how that investment is performed.

Dr. G's own didactic approach when demonstrating or talking about the Silent Way allowed for misinterpretations and misunderstandings to occur – I am quite sure he knew this and felt that if one couldn't work out the basics, one probably had no business taking his ideas forward. The result though was that some adopted Silent Way (or so they thought) without really having invested sufficiently to understand the underlying meaning of it.

The notion of "silence" for example was much misunderstood by some who thought it was the point of Silent Way, but of course it wasn't. If anything, the term "way" holds more weight than "silent" since it provides clear differentiation between "method," "approach," and "technique" – it is not only a "way" but the common sense way! And in answer to those who questioned him on the purpose of the famous silence, Dr. G on one occasion explained, "Why should I speak when my students can?" I use the term "explain" loosely, you understand! In the '80s, I believe there were those who called themselves Silent Way teachers who simply used the rods and didn't speak, but of course any approach is liable to misinterpretation.

Over the years, I packed and unpacked things which Dr. G. wrote until I managed to encapsulate what I felt was the essence of his teachings into something which I could handle and pass on: these are Dr. G's principles but I call them the Four Principles of "I," since they revolve around each learner recognizing his and her own uniqueness and value as a member of a learning group.

Those four principles are: Independence, Autonomy, Responsibility, and Awareness, and here is my interpretation of them:

The value of Independence suggests that "I" can be my own person, can be self-reliant, but can also depend on others. "I" can be challenged and choose to accept or not, can respond or not – "I" have freedom to decide.

Autonomy means that "I" can do the learning – the teacher can't "learn" me and "I" can go the way which seems most interesting to me.

Responsibility tells me that "I" have a duty to myself to be the best learner possible, a duty to my peers to support and assist, and a duty to my teacher to offer the best responses "I" can find.

Awareness grows as soon as "I" become aware! Part of my life as a learner is to develop my own awareness of "I" in all kinds of roles as well as being aware of my peers and their successes and challenges. "I" can nurture multiple awarenesses.

These things may be basic to many readers, but to me they form a contract between myself and my teacher, or myself and my learners, and they are notions which I could not have formulated without the special intervention of Dr. G.

His memory is embodied for me in a thousand magical moments of high-quality learning and realization, but also the quick wit he sometimes allowed himself. Some smart alec asked at the end of a workshop: "Dr. Gattegno, why is it that your English is not perfect?" the Master thought for a moment "Because," he responded, "I didn't have the benefit of myself as a teacher." §

A "Maverick" Among Thinkers

Dr. Alvino Fantini

"... it was an intense, stimulating, and exciting time during which we had the luxury of exploring a reconceptualization of language education with some of the best minds of the time."

It was sometime in the late 1960s when I first heard the name Caleb Gattegno. A friend mentioned him to me after she had seen him on a TV feature that only lasted a few minutes, but one that caught her interest in his brief presentation that involved, in her words, the use of "colored sticks" and various colored Word Charts. At that time, I was director of foreign language programs for my organization, then called The Experiment in International Living (now World Learning), an international educational exchange organization, and I was also responsible for the language component of several Peace Corps training projects being conducted on the former Sandanona Estate outside of Brattleboro, Vermont (later the SIT Graduate Institute).

We were happily and successfully (we thought) into an audio-lingual approach to teaching at that time, achieving great success in teaching a variety of languages for the Peace Corps – from Portuguese to Turkish to Gujarati – and others contracted out to The Experiment. Using this new approach, in great contrast to the traditional grammar-translation method, we had now worked with about 50 languages at that time.

Yet, I was intrigued with what I heard and I contacted Dr. Gattegno and invited him up to our center, probably about 1966 or so, to learn more about the Silent Way. We were also searching for better ways, and I wanted to see how we might incorporate this

(Fantini Cont'd)

new method into both our extensive and intensive language programs. Intensive language programs included about eight hours of classroom instruction and other interactive activities each day, such as cocktail parties in the target language, roleplays, simulations, and the like.

Dr. Gattegno made his appearance in our old "carriage" house-barn where he stood in front of about 80 trainers and instructors, after being introduced, and said nothing. A long pause ensued. As the tension mounted, one individual in the audience finally blurted out to him: "Well, what are you here for?" to which he responded: "Ah, finally a question. If you don't ask any questions, there is little to learn." Since Dr. Gattegno also ignored the microphone set out for him, another person then added, "Could you please use the mic!" To which he responded: "You are going into the field where there will be no microphones; learn to use your own ears." And so it started, or rather ended, right there!

Most of those in attendance refused to stay and began to file out of the room. In an attempt to make best use of his visit, I convened a smaller group. We met separately and engaged directly with Dr. Gattegno in his inimitable manner and style. And of course we were sometimes confused, often challenged, but mostly fascinated. At the end of his visit, I proposed using the Silent Way on a pilot basis with some groups and continue the audio-lingual approach with others, in an attempt to make some comparisons. Dr. Gattegno did not agree with this idea, and so things stalled. For a while.

The experience lingered with me and I was determined to learn more, so I later attended a course in French at Schools for the Future in New York City. Clearly, the Silent Way was different, innovative, and exciting. About a year later, an administrative decision was made to begin a Master of Arts in Teaching Languages (MAT) program at our newly founded institution. For this reason, we decided to search out and invite as many "mavericks" in the language field that we could think of – people who were asking important questions, and finding better ways to teach languages and prepare language educators. Of course we remembered Dr. Gattegno and included him along with about 15 other educators, all doing innovative and important things in language teaching, albeit not always well recognized at that time – people like Earl Stevick, John Rassias, and Carl Pond.

We secluded ourselves in an old "stone garage" for an entire week where we discussed and planned our graduate program to prepare language teachers. Our focus question was: What makes effective language teachers, and how can we best prepare them, given the current status of foreign language teaching? Needless to say, it was an intense, stimulating, and exciting time during which we had the luxury of exploring a reconceptualization of language education with some of the best minds of the time. The result was the development of our MAT Program which was launched in 1969 and continues to this day, more than 40 years later. Many of the participants in that think tank were so invested in our efforts that they continued on as members of our MAT Advisory Board, and returned frequently as lecturers and workshop deliverers over many years. Dr. Gattegno was among them, and continued returning several times each year until his death – after which his wife, Shakti, continued to contribute to these connections with our institution.

Clearly, Dr. Gattegno had an immense impact not only on our program and our approach to language education, but on the field of language education in general. As a result, he influenced countless numbers of our students, and thousands of others as well. Today, language education is moving in still expanding directions – where proficiency, communicative abilities, developing intercultural competencies, are all important aspects of our work. In this post-methodological era, emphasis has shifted to helping educators to develop their own personal approach to language teaching, as appropriate to the needs of each context and situation. Dr. Gattegno's ideas and publications regarding education go beyond specific methodologies, and provoke questions about the educational process, and interactions between teachers and students.

Looking back and looking forward, his contributions to our profession are profound and he remains an important educator whose efforts survive through their influence in the work of countless educators. §

Un plaisir pour la vie

Alain L'Hôte

Je n'ai que très peu travaillé avec Caleb Gattegno. La dernière fois, c'était lors des deux derniers stages qu'il a animés consécutivement en 1988, en France, au Col de Porte. Il s'agissait de *Le mystère de la communication* et *Des mathématiques*.

J'ai toujours le souvenir très présent d'une partie de mon feed-back à la fin du premier stage. Je peux le reformuler comme suit.

Pendant mes jeunes années, j'avais fait du travail avec un groupe de recherche et d'actions non-violentes. J'étais heureux des actions que nous menions, mais insatisfait du travail de recherche : je voyais bien que l'on n'était pas non-violent mais que l'on ne pouvait être que sur le chemin de la non-violence. Et je voyais aussi qu'aucun outil ne m'était adapté pour progresser, tous semblaient me demander courage démesuré et transpiration.

Ce n'est qu'avec Caleb Gattegno, pendant ce premier stage, que j'ai réellement entrevu qu'il était possible de travailler sur moi, sans l'interférence du jugement ou de la morale, sans rien qui ressemble à une religion.

J'entrevoyais des outils pour travailler sur moi, mais aussi sur mon enseignement.

C'était tout nouveau pour moi de voir que travailler sur soi, entrer dans un problème – d'enseignement ou autre – et mettre en œuvre des actions appropriées pouvaient être unis dans une même vision.

Le plus réjouissant était que les outils semblaient être à portée de mains, même si je ne les cernais pas vraiment.

Je me souviens que cette découverte m'avait mis dans un état de satisfaction profonde. Enfin, j'étais équipé pour un bout de chemin. Il ne restait qu'à travailler.

Au niveau pédagogique, j'ai très vite été séduit par la base scientifique de cette approche et par la liberté qu'elle donne, y compris la liberté de se l'approprier à son rythme.

J'ai souvent rencontré des enseignants, surpris devant le matériel, me dire "Ça doit être compliqué d'enseigner avec ce matériel. Et les enfants, ils s'en sortent ?"

Mes réponses données à ceux qui avaient envie de se lancer ont invariablement été :

- Si tu fais confiance aux enfants, tu n'as pas de souci à te faire. Je ne dis pas cela par croyance, mais par expérience.

- Il faut simplement les regarder travailler et changer nos propositions d'exercice en fonction de leurs réactions. Mais il faut le faire minute après minute, c'est un entraînement.

- Et puis nous avons un garde-fou qui est le guide de l'enseignant : il faut le lire et le relire.

Ce qui est beau, c'est que ces premiers outils sont accessibles à tous. Ils transforment le métier d'enseignant en enseignant chercheur qui sait se faire surprendre, qui tous les jours découvre. Un plaisir pour la vie.

> "If ever we can re-educate ourselves to the point that we can live without expectation but not without drive, without investment but not without commitment, without ambition but not without resolution, without egocentricity but not without presence, we shall know that there cannot be any fear left in us that our actions will let us down. We shall know ourselves as free from the recurrence of the thing we labeled failure, which made us prefer to avoid it rather than face it."

— Dr. Caleb Gattegno

On Being Freer, Second Edition (2010), page 180.

Cover image for *Towards a Visual Culture* (1969, Discus Books).

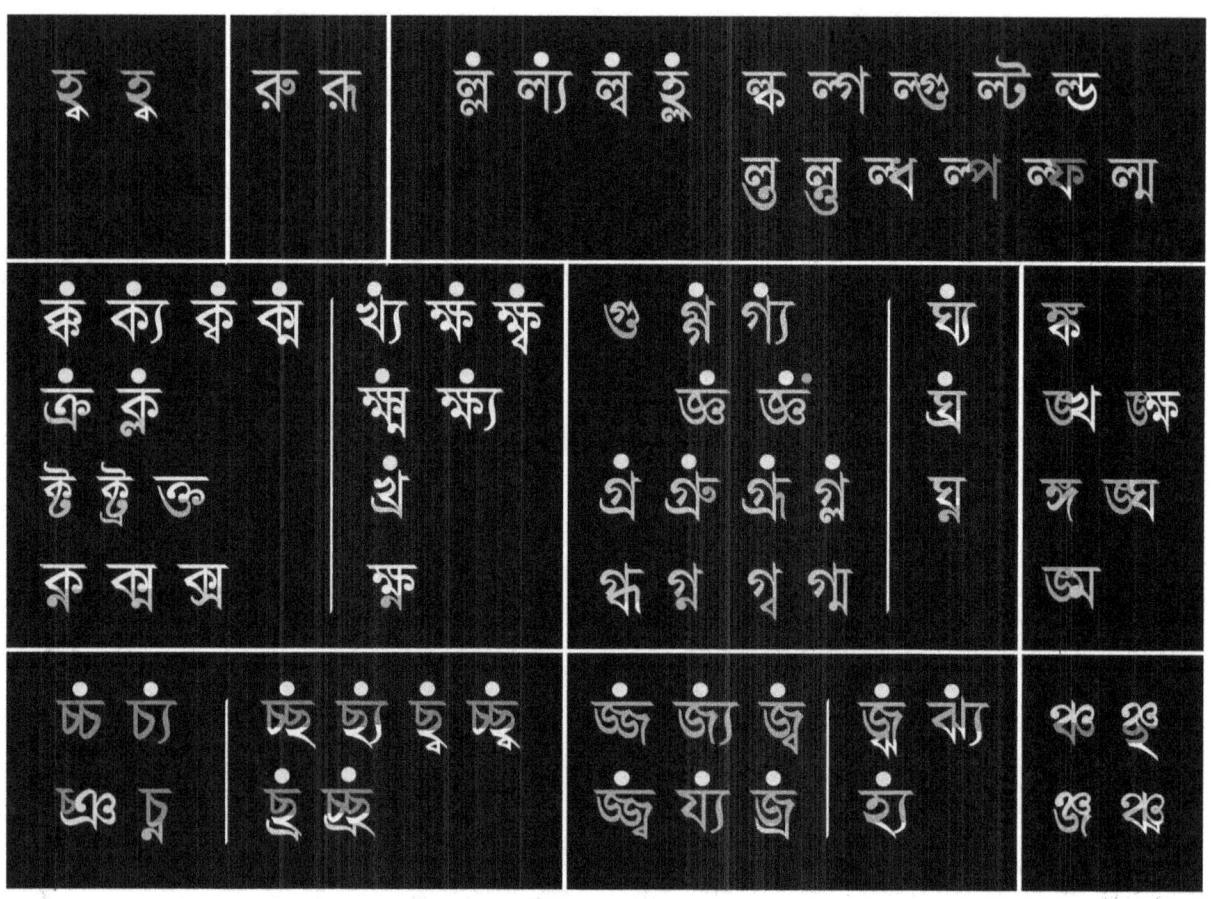

Bangla Fidel representing complex consonnants, chart 1 of 3, created by Masayuki Onishi.

The Real Learning: Educating My Self

Noriko Ogino

The Gattegno Approach has been like an art of living to me. It guides me to resolve questions by observing myself, while considering the attributes of the self. I realize that I have changed a lot since I became involved in the study of this approach.

My first encounter with the Silent Way was in 1987 when Dr. Gattegno did a demonstration at SIT (School for International Training), where I was studying in the MAT program. When the English Sound-Color Chart was presented in class, I thought it was a unique way of teaching sounds, but I felt discouraged by the thought of memorizing all of the corresponding sounds and rectangles.

Then, after I finished my academic year at SIT, I had an opportunity to attend an English the Silent Way workshop offered by the Center, in Osaka, directed by Ms. Fusako Allard. The whole workshop had a great impact on me, and I became aware that I had hardly heard the voice of Mr. John Beary, the instructor. Although I learned a lot, and was concentrating very hard, the way of learning was very enjoyable. How was it possible?

I began to wonder about the theory behind the way Mr. Beary taught us, so I started participating in some theory workshops, in addition to the language workshops offered by the Center. At one of the workshops, Dr. Roslyn Young spoke about the self and its attributes. The attributes of the self cannot be acquired from the environment or "learned," and the self is there from the quantum moment when the process of a human life starts. I was awestruck when I heard this.

Then I realized that this was something I had been searching to learn for years. I had a good career at the time, but somehow I was not content, and I had been searching for something from which I was able to be absorbed. Even though I had tried a few things, I didn't make any significant encounters until I heard of the self and its attributes. In addition, I was also very much impressed when I read the *Universe of Babies* by Gattegno, translated into Japanese by Prof. Sumio Tsuchiya. Both the principles of the self and its attributes, and the *Universe of Babies*, were talking about me – and they were universal. This was how I had been behaving, and this meant that every one of us is standing on common ground.

I became aware that the self's attributes were something you were able to educate. This meant to me that I was able to educate any of the attributes, and maybe educating my own attributes was what you could call "the real learning."

I have read more of Gattegno's writings, but they are really difficult to understand. Nevertheless, I'm excited while I'm reading his work and I feel that he really understands the truth. The truth to me has to be simple, functioning, and beautiful. I feel I must be encountering the truth while I am reading his writings, even though my comprehension is poor.

Thanks to Ms. Allard's devoted contribution to the Gattegno Approach and the Silent Way for all these years, I was able to find what I really wanted to do. I will continue to be involved in the study of the Gattegno Approach and the Silent Way to make my life happier, since I have my own laboratory with me wherever I am!

Approaching the Approach
L'évolution d'une approche

Isabelle Luter Doussain

I discovered Caleb Gattegno's approach to teaching late, during the second period of my professional career, around six years ago. I'd gone from law to linguistics – returned to school and studied at the Sorbonne University, and found myself in a whole new profession: FSL teacher (French as a second language).

The linguistics courses were interesting, but they nevertheless left me feeling a bit confused, so I was counting on putting the different teaching methods and theories taught at the university into practice, in order to reinforce my knowledge.

I thus began to teach using different methods, but this didn't satisfy me. Something was missing; I was unhappy with the relationship between the teacher and learner, and the manner in which I was conveying knowledge.

The traditional classroom situation, with the good teacher and the good or poor students, struck me as completely outmoded. I felt the need for a different kind of contact, a different form of communication with them.

Then I heard people talking about a certain Caleb Gattegno. I was intrigued by what I heard. I happened to work with some students in a training center who were having problems and were working on improving their level of French through his teaching methods.

The learning tools I discovered were rather atypical, very different from everything I had used up until then. The stress was on learning, I could observe the students making rapid progress, and above all, they were relaxed and happy to learn. I wanted to know more.

I located an association in Besançon called Une Education Pour Demain (or An Education for the Future – UEPD) focused on preserving and promulgating the resources and works of Caleb Gattegno. This association also organizes initiation and training sessions throughout the year. I was to pursue my training there later and participate in these sessions led by extraordinary teachers (Roslyn Young, Maurice Laurent, and others), advocates of Caleb Gattegno's teaching approach. But Besançon was far from home, so I began looking for teacher training closer to the Paris area where I live.

Then I happened to meet Gattegno's niece Claudie, and her husband, Jean-Jacques, both passionate about their work and possessing vast experience with all sorts of learners.

They had a training center in the Paris suburb of Montreuil. They became my guides. Claudie trains teachers following her uncle's approach to learning. I took a training course; it was very intense and deeply gratifying.

I began reading Caleb Gattegno's work; I learned about him, his great voyages in the realm of science, particularly mathematics, psychology and linguistics. I listened to him speak through his writings, his words – transcriptions of his conferences, and certain books.

I followed one of Claudie's many invaluable suggestions: I found other associations where teacher-guides use this approach. I observed them as they taught. It's very important to watch other teachers working. We all have our own personalities, emotions, and ways of doing things. We need to observe, and also to be observed to consolidate our training, our ideas, and practices.

I discovered teaching resources, tables, colors,

a fantastic group dynamic, action, sharing, and above all the teacher's role as a guide. A veritable laboratory where everyone is searching, discovering, advancing together. Something magical took place. It was the students who were discovering, practicing, mastering and marveling at the learning process. They learned themselves, with just our guidance.

view of teaching, of my role as a teacher.

Before, I thought I could transmit knowledge to my students, using teaching resources that are too often based on memorization rather than learning.

Who are my students? People who are either beginning to learn or trying to perfect their

> "Something was missing; I was unhappy with the relationship between the teacher and learner, and the manner in which I was conveying knowledge."

It was no longer the good teacher transmitting knowledge; the teacher was guiding the student on the road to discovery and awareness. It was no longer the good or bad student; it was the student who was discovering and learning in his own way, at his own rhythm.

Each student is different, thus there is no longer a single method for the teacher to utilize and transmit, but "the" method adapted to the student. The teacher's role, his task, is to accompany the learner along the right path so that the learner becomes aware of his capabilities, his ability to change, and to remain autonomous.

Another of Claudie's invaluable suggestions: the need for those of us who are new to this approach to learning to share our experiences. We, the new practitioners, as a result find a place to meet and try to get together on a regular basis. We exchange stories, we talk about our difficulties and successes, our different ways of "approaching this approach," this teaching-learning experience.

I have discovered an approach to learning where respect for the learner prevails. "A realization, an awakening…" these magic words changed my whole

knowledge of French, some having been to school, others not; adults in difficult situations, some with varying degrees of physical or mental disabilities; French and foreign learners – each group is different.

A variety of teaching methods have been elaborated to address these groups, and they should be recognized for their merits, for the improvements that have been achieved and the linguistic research that has been a result. Each represents a specific view of teaching and an educational value that shouldn't be discounted. I believe that we need to remain receptive to the changes and evolution in this field.

In the beginning, even Caleb Gattegno needed to explore these methods, to study them, criticize or adapt them, according to what interested him or not, before he arrived at his own personal vision, his approach, the finalization of his endeavors.

Today, I can happily say that Caleb Gattegno's work on education and learning is fundamental, and for me, the most enriching in terms of his understanding of people and his concept of the learning process.

It is thanks to his work that my general approach to teaching and my job as a teacher has evolved.

(Luter-Doussain Cont.)

L'évolution d'une approche

J'ai découvert l'approche pédagogique de Caleb Gattegno tardivement, dans ma seconde vie professionnelle. Il y a à peine 6 années.

Du droit, je passe à la linguistique. Je me recycle professionnellement. Une formation universitaire à la Sorbonne, et me voilà avec un nouveau métier en poche : professeur de Fle (Français Langue Etrangère).

Ma formation en linguistique, intéressante, me laisse néanmoins un peu perplexe et je mise sur la pratique pour conforter mes positions relatives aux différentes pédagogies et conceptions de l'apprentissage abordées à l'université.

Je pratique donc et utilise différentes méthodes pédagogiques. Mais je reste sur ma faim, quelque chose me manque. Je ne suis pas tout à fait satisfaite du rapport entre l'enseignant et l'apprenant, de la manière de transmettre les/mes connaissances.

La situation de classe, avec le bon professeur et les bons ou mauvais élèves, me semble dépassée. J'ai envie d'un autre contact, d'une autre communication avec eux.

Et puis, j'entends parler de ce Monsieur « Caleb Gattegno ». Je suis intriguée.

Dans un centre de formation, je rencontre des élèves en difficultés qui font de la remise à niveau de français en utilisant son approche pédagogique.

Je découvre des outils quelques peu atypiques et très éloignés de ce que j'ai utilisé jusque-là. L'apprentissage est dominant, je les vois progresser rapidement, et surtout, je les vois à l'aise et heureux d'apprendre. Je veux en savoir plus.

Je découvre l'association « une éducation pour demain » (l'UEPD) à Besançon, détenteur et conservateur des outils et des écrits de Caleb Gattegno. Cette association organise aussi des formations et stages d'initiation, échelonnés sur l'année. Je compléterai d'ailleurs ensuite, mon expérience en participant à ces stages, animés par de grands formateurs, proches de Caleb Gattegno, dont Roslyn Young et Maurice Laurent.

Mais, Besançon est loin, et je recherche une formation de formateurs possible près de chez moi, en Ile-de-France.

Enfin, par chance, je rencontre sa nièce, Claudie Gattegno et son mari, Jean-Jacques.

Tous les deux passionnés, et surtout riches d'expériences nombreuses et diverses avec toutes sortes de publics d'apprenants.

Ils pratiquent dans leur centre de formation à Montreuil. Ils me guident. Claudie forme des formateurs à l'approche pédagogique de son oncle. Je participe donc à une formation, intense et très enrichissante.

Et puis, je le lis, lui, Caleb Gattegno … Je le découvre, grand voyageur au pays des sciences en général et plus particulièrement des mathématiques, de la psychologie, et de la linguistique. Je l'écoute à travers ses lignes, ses mots …dans les retranscriptions de ses conférences, dans certains de ses livres.

Je suis un des nombreux et précieux conseils de Claudie : je vais à la rencontre d'autres associations où ces guides professeurs pratiquent cette approche. Je les observe sur le terrain.

C'est très important de voir d'autres professeurs pratiquer. Nous avons chacun notre personnalité, nos émotions, notre façon de faire. Il faut observer et aussi se faire observer.

Cela complète notre formation, nos réflexions, nos pratiques.

Je découvre des outils pédagogiques, des tableaux, des couleurs, une dynamique de groupe fantastique, de l'action, de la participation, et surtout le rôle de guide du professeur. Un vrai laboratoire ou tout le monde cherche, trouve, avance ensemble. Une magie s'opère.

C'est l'élève qui découvre, s'étonne, pratique, maîtrise. Il apprend par lui-même, juste guidé. Il n'y a plus le bon professeur qui transmet, il y a un professeur qui guide l'élève sur le chemin de la découverte, de la prise de conscience. Il n'y a plus le bon ou le mauvais élève, il y a un élève qui, à sa manière, à sa vitesse, découvre et apprend.

Chaque élève est différent, donc le professeur n'a plus une seule façon de faire, de transmettre, mais « la » façon qui convient à l'élève. C'est son rôle et son devoir, de trouver le bon chemin qui mènera l'apprenant à prendre conscience de ses possibilités,

langue française, certaines ayant été scolarisées, d'autres pas ; avec des adultes en difficultés, certains ayant des handicaps, physiques ou mentaux, plus ou moins graves.

Apprenants français ou étrangers, chaque public est différent.

> « C'est l'élève qui découvre, s'étonne, pratique, maîtrise. Il apprend par lui-même, juste guidé. Il n'y a plus le bon professeur qui transmet, il y a un professeur qui guide l'élève sur le chemin de la découverte, de la prise de conscience. »

de sa capacité de changer, de la possibilité de rester autonome.

Autre conseil précieux de Claudie, il faut échanger, entre ceux qui découvrent et pratiquent cette approche pédagogique. Donc, nous, les nouveaux pratiquants, nous trouvons un lieu, et essayons de nous réunir régulièrement. Nous échangeons, nous exposons nos facilités, nos difficultés, nos différentes façons « d'approcher cette approche », cet enseignement - apprentissage.

J'ai découvert un enseignement où le respect de l'autre, celui qui apprend, est dominant.

« La prise de conscience », ces mots magiques ont changé ma vision pédagogique et mon rôle de professeur.

Avant, je pensais pouvoir transmettre à mes élèves, mes connaissances en utilisant des pédagogies basées malheureusement un peu trop souvent, plus sur la mémoire que sur l'apprentissage.

Qui sont mes élèves ? Je suis en contact avec des personnes qui découvrent ou perfectionnent la

Des méthodes d'enseignements nombreuses et variées essayent de s'adapter à ces publics.

Elles ont le mérite d'exister, de vouloir s'améliorer, de faire l'objet de recherches linguistiques. Chacune a une vision spécifique de l'enseignement et un intérêt pédagogique qu'il ne faut pas renier. Je pense qu'il faut toujours rester à l'écoute de l'évolution de la pédagogie.

Caleb Gattegno lui aussi, au début, a dû les découvrir, les étudier, les malmener et/ou les transformer, en fonction de ce qui l'intéressait ou pas dans chacune d'elles, avant d'aboutir à sa vision personnelle, à son approche, à la finalisation de ses travaux.

Actuellement, je peux dire avec bonheur, que les travaux de Caleb Gattegno sur l'éducation et l'apprentissage sont les principaux, et pour moi, les plus riches, tant au niveau de la connaissance de l'être humain qu'au niveau de la conception de l'enseignement.

Ils ont fait évoluer mon approche pédagogique en général et mon métier d'enseignante en particulier. §

The original Sound-Color Chart, shown here, is used for work on pronunciation of sounds and words. Each color represents a sound. Rectangles with two colors are a blend of two sounds. This chart helps with pronunciation because students are not distracted by the shape of a letter, and perhaps how that letter is read in their native language. (Educational Solutions file photo, 2010.)

"Have You Ever Thought You Might Be Boring?"

Donald Freeman

I first met Caleb Gattegno in 1974 at a seminar on the Silent Way. I was a new high school language teacher, and I thought I knew my way around the classroom. But all that was challenged in both immediate and indelible ways that Friday evening when we were taught — or rather learned — some Mandarin Chinese. The immediate impact of the experience, and the two days that followed, left my head spinning. It was as exhilarating as it was unnerving — a teacher who didn't model; students who created new language out of sounds and shaped it with criteria that they themselves discerned from their activity with little blocks of wood. And there were the technologies: the colored rods, the somewhat mystical charts, and the conductor's baton, that extendable silver pointer, which somehow wove everything together.

The indelible impact came from the experience, but more so from the pithy statements that seemed to fall like hailstones throughout the seminar. These statements, or aphorisms, became the building blocks of another way of thinking about learning and teaching. Often over the last 25 years, I have wondered at how durable and fruitful these aphorisms have been. What is it about a string of words that sparks such a radically different way of thinking and acting as a teacher? From that first seminar, I remember the syntactically awkward statement, "I can't eat and you get fat," that captured for me the teacher's silent and parsimonious work in relation to what felt like our constant flailing around as students. The words stayed with me from that first encounter, appearing at the most unexpected times to recalibrate my own work.

As I say, I am not sure why these short statements have had such power in influencing my development, first as a language teacher and later as a language teacher educator. But they have and do; their generative power remains almost as intriguing to me as the ideas themselves. Take the statement "Words don't have meaning," which at once distills the nature of language and exposes the intellectual sloppiness of a lot of constructivist thinking. Now when I hear elementary teacher candidates talk about "children as sense-makers," I wonder how deeply they have grasped this notion of what the learner actually does in using language to make sense. Or the statement "We are all lived by our preconceptions," which pinpoints for me a basic challenge in approaching a phenomenon in education to try and study it, a challenge that is inherent in all research. In the end, good research has to be a constant interplay of expectation, anticipation, and responding to what is in front of you, and this calls on the researcher to be open to his or her preconceptions. This process of remaining open to what we assume is probably one of the toughest research skills to engage in.

Of all these aphorisms, there is one that seems to resurface most often; it is something between an old friend and painful annoyance. It came along on another Friday evening; in fact it was the opening question of a seminar. We were seated in a large irregular circle, waiting for things to start. Dr. Gattegno came in, took a seat, and looked around at each of us rather intently. Then he asked, "Have you ever thought you might be boring?" That challenge — which came as a sort of social affront — opened up a line of thinking about how the teachers' ideas and efforts intersect (and at times interfere) with what students are doing to learn. For me, the aphorism became a fulcrum that shifted the focus from what matters and makes sense to me as the teacher to how those things could potentially be useful, or not, to my students in their learning. I began to realize that I can only work with what I know, but how I use what I know needs to depend on the student.

(Freeman Cont'd)

It is this power of aphorism that I have come back to time-and-again in Gattegno's work. Clearly, the words alone are not what make the difference. After all, I know "Words don't have meaning." So it must be something more, something that has to do with how these aphoristic statements distill elements of a particular moment of experience into an awareness. And to carry that awareness around, like a card in your wallet, the distillation needs to have a form. The words of the aphorism are the form, like grains of experience. They are generative because they refer simultaneously to the experience from which they derive and to the awareness that will carry them into new situations.

For more than 20 years, with good colleagues at the School of International Training, we built an approach to language teacher preparation that was profoundly shaped by Gattegno's ideas. Although we each recalled slightly different statements (or differing experiences of the same statement), there was sufficient overlap and commonality that these aphorisms became some of the key social facts of our work together. Hearing or saying them was one thing; acting on them was another. Therein, I think, lies the power and the benefit of these aphorisms; how can we teach students or prepare teachers with these facts in mind? Now, in a university school of education where we are preparing new teachers across a range of school subjects, I see how important these 'aphoristic facts' can be. Without them, there is little in common that anchors the work of learning to teach. Ideas can float freely, without reference to experience, like what Gattegno used to call derisively "café conversation." Engaging this type of sloppy talk and thinking is hard and ongoing work. But it is very worth doing, because there is an element of mis-education, when new teachers leave their professional preparation without having being pushed to seriously consider that they "… might be boring." §

The Portuguese Fidel, prototype stage (hand-colored letters). ©Educational Solutions Worldwide Inc.

Le rôle que Caleb Gattegno peut jouer au Burkina Faso

Soré Hadara

Je suis animateur de langue. Je faisais de l'enseignement classique dans des centres d'alphabétisation lorsque j'ai rencontré le travail du Dr Gattegno. C'est à ce moment-là que j'ai pris conscience de certaines étapes dans l'apprentissage telles que : c'est un processus basé sur une succession de prises de conscience et c'est l'apprenant lui-même qui crée son apprentissage.

J'ai pris conscience aussi que la base de l'approche pédagogique du Dr Gattegno repose sur le principe de la subordination de l'enseignement à l'apprentissage.

Enfin je peux dire, grâce à l'approche pédagogique du Dr Gattegno, que l'apprentissage n'est pas un transfert de connaissances, mais un espace dynamique et interactif qui suscite le désir et le plaisir d'apprendre et réveille l'estime de soi et la confiance, facteurs nécessaires à un développement durable tant sur le plan culturel social, économique et humain.

La situation au niveau de l'illettrisme au Burkina Faso n'est pas en recul par manque de structure et de personnels qualifiés. La plupart des personnes que j'ai rencontrées qui sont restées illettrées ont eu des difficultés avec le système éducatif basé sur la place de la mémoire dans l'apprentissage.

Le plus grand problème dans l'éducation au Burkina Faso pour les enfants qui restent à l'école est qu'ils sont confrontés à la méthode mixte, c'est-à-dire la méthode globale et la méthode syllabique.

En ce qui concerne les enfants qui quittent l'école avant la fin de la scolarité, la plupart n'arrivent pas à apprendre à lire plus tard parce qu'ils ont subi une éducation basée sur la mémoire; donc en quittant l'école, quelque temps plus tard, cette place est occupée par une autre activité et ce qu'ils ont appris tombe dans l'oubli.

Je pense que Gattegno peut apporter :

- l'outil.
- la qualification du corps enseignant
- l'autonomie de la méthode.

> "... l'apprentissage n'est pas un transfert de connaissance, mais un espace dynamique et interactif qui suscite le désir et le plaisir d'apprendre"

De toutes les formations que j'ai réussies lorsque j'ai pris contact avec l'outil, j'ai retrouvé la confiance en moi et l'envie de partager ce que je sais avec les autres, ce qui fait que je suis plus enthousiaste lorsque je vois mon niveau d'animation et je constate que je n'ai pas eu une vraie formation, je sens que là j'ai quelque chose d'important en ma possession. Je ne pourrais pas dire autre chose, sinon de dire que tout le programme et l'outil mis en place par Le Docteur Gattegno à une place importante dans mon pays.

Le travail du Dr Gattegno a changé ma vie et je me sens privilégié en tant qu'animateur en langue. Je suis arrivé à développer le comte en Dioula et en faire des mots. Cela m'a fait découvrir ma langue.

Présentement, je continue dans ce sens-là avec l'assurance que j'ai dans ma possession un outil formidable et une approche pédagogique particulièrement performante.

My Time with Dr. G and His Overwhelming Flow of Creativity

Michael J. Hollyfield

I first met Dr. Gattegno in June 1961, when I was 26 years old. The following year I attended a five-day course he gave, and shortly after that he invited me to join his expanding company. I was offered a job as a demonstrator, with my territory being the South East of England. At that time the company was overwhelmed with requests from schools for instruction using the Cuisenaire Rods.

Organising and giving courses was my initial function. Soon after, my family and I moved to Reading (Reading was the original home of the Cuisenaire Company), which enabled me to take on additional work in the office. I also became Dr. G's chauffeur, driving him to the numerous meetings and courses he was giving. On the way back to Reading it was feedback; me giving feedback on what I had learned at the course, and Dr. G giving his response by discreetly falling asleep after my first few minutes. However, as I came to appreciate, I was exceptionally privileged to have spent so much time with this remarkable man during the years he lived in Reading.

He came across as a mild and gentle person with an old fashioned courtesy about him. He did not accept unjustified familiarity – he declined first name terms unless he knew one well enough. The question "Am I welcome?" was his way of inviting himself to a discussion or other activity that happened to be ongoing. He publicly asserted, "Humility is my strongest suit," but his presence exuded something intangible yet unmistakable. He fiercely contested pre-conceived ideas and fought courageously for what he knew to be valid. In fact, his forthright and challenging outspokenness was frequently confused for rudeness by those who made the error of imagining themselves to be personally attacked when their counter arguments were analyzed and dismissed.

Looking back – which I haven't done until embarking on writing this – I remember what a full and busy time it was. The shabby building at 11 Crown Street that housed the still small company was in fact buzzing with activity, and the influence of Gattegno, the benefits of his writings, and the materials he published were already making their impact in classrooms and amongst teachers in many countries.

The first years of the '60s were amazing. The publishing company Educational Explorers Ltd. was formed, and a group of new people joined, some fresh from university, who were to be involved in great new projects. First, Words in Color in two versions – British English and American English; then the Silent Way for both versions of English, followed by the French and Spanish versions. Next, a new career series of books *My Life and My Work* launched. Soon after began a project of new animated mathematics films designed by Dr. G and created under his supervision. The overwhelming flow of creativity from him was staggering. Just as impressive was the thoroughness and the critical examination he brought to all these projects. We were all at different times and according to our different abilities, invited to contribute. Whilst all this was going on, Dr. G was at the same time working with colleagues in California for the U.S. editions. Remembering those years reminds me of how committed we all were. We worked weekends and evenings and I believe all, like me, loved every minute of it.

Dr. G had traveled widely and worked in numerous countries introducing the Cuisenaire-Gattegno method of teaching mathematics. His work established the Cuisenaire Rods as the most widely known of the new materials for teaching mathematics appearing in schools during the '50s and '60s. He also established agents and sister companies in the countries he visited.

Those of us who were already visiting schools and meeting teachers were expected to add *Words in Colour* (published 1962) to our portfolios. Our involvement in the creation of the literacy materials was an education in the technical and philosophical aspects of his work, but we had little first-hand experience of how these projects would actually be received or used in classrooms. To remedy this, we knew we had to educate ourselves in the practical use of Words in Color in order to have valid experience to offer when assisting others. We established the Reading reading clinic and invited parents to let us help their children who were having problems with reading. This was an excellent way to observe what happens for learners when Words in Color is the activity. We mostly worked one-to-one, it not being practical at this stage to arrange classes.

One of our students was a 13 year-old, brought to us by his probation officer, who believed that learning to read would help the boy in question – Robert – overcome his behavior problems. Robert's time with us was memorable for me not only because of his progress, nor only because after a while he brought a friend, another non-reader, and instilled in him the 'rules of the game' that he had learned to abide by: no helping – let him do it himself, don't ask if you are right – make sure, and so on. It was great to see. However, it was neither of these outcomes that impressed me most. It was what happened after the pupils returned to school. That first day of the new term I received a call from the deputy head of Robert's school asking, "What have you done with Robert?" Robert had scored 100% in a spelling test, having refused to attempt any spelling tests until that day. Sadly, the school did not seek to have us help them to adopt Words in Color for their non-readers. The school's request was only, "Can we send our non-readers to you?"

But Robert taught me how to appreciate what Dr. G had built into Words in Color. I learned how accessible Words in Color was to a learner reader. I began to understand how not to interfere whilst he did his work; that waiting quietly and not impatiently does help; that very soon your student just does not want your help, only the necessary 'teacher inputs' at each new stage of the task. Through this activity I came to appreciate Words in Color as a scientifically co-ordinated 'program' of materials and activities designed perfectly for the task. Word charts, Fidels, primer books, the Word Building Book and the worksheets each link to one another as progress is made, each new word chart being the key mover in this progress; the supporting materials widening the area of the study and building reading confidence in the learners.

Working with Words in Color led me to recognise what I think is key in Gattegno's work. His study of how children learn and his appreciation of their will and capacity to overcome the most demanding of tasks is implicit in these materials. Learners are invited to engage in games which make no unreasonable demands on memory, do not encourage guessing, and which free learners from their teachers.

No matter how profound and philosophical the ideas behind the materials are, it is in their apparent simplicity that his genius is evident. In creating what he once described as "the whole of English in one panoramic view," the English Fidel was a mammoth undertaking. Each phoneme and grapheme of the language analyzed, and organized into colored columns. The English Fidel is uncluttered and uncomplicated. A tool that learner readers have easy access to, and which serves them well in their getting to know thoroughly the written form of their language.

I remember Dr. G with great affection. He was always generous and he gave much of himself to those who worked with him, to all who attended his seminars, and especially to the children he worked with when teaching. His energy was infectious. Years later as he neared the end of his life, he continued working at the same pace. He was writing, addressing meetings of teachers, and leading seminars up until a few days before his death. I don't feel he has received the recognition his contributions deserve, but I believe that as time goes by, his work will continue to influence what goes on in classrooms around the world and in this way enhance the lives of learners lucky enough to be exposed to his work. He would not have sought more than this.

§

Student learning to read, exploring the language in depth with Words in Color.

> "Only awareness is educable"
>
> — Dr. Caleb Gattegno

I Went Looking for a Match And Found a Volcano

Yoko Yasuda

When I first heard the phrases "the Silent Way" and "Gattegno Approach," Dr. Gattegno had already passed away. I learned about Gattegno by listening to Fusako Allard and Dr. Roslyn Young talk about what he used to say. Because of their detailed insights, I felt I could draw his picture in my mind. These people who had worked with Dr. G made me believe that his Science of Education was a gift that had been passed down through generations.

I met the Silent Way in 1993, in the middle of my 20s. The Center, which was literally the educational diffuser of the Silent Way and Gattegno Approach in Japan, held a workshop about teaching Japanese with the Silent Way. It is clear to me now that my life changed during this workshop.

All of the topics we covered during Fusako's workshop were very big "questions" related to universally human characteristics, and we couldn't jump to any rapid conclusions. The workshop was for Japanese teacher-training, but the contents went far beyond language teaching, and were more interesting and exciting than expected.

The questions were: What is learning? What am I made of? How have I been learning? And so on.

Fusako said, "The world is full of unknown, and we know a very little part of it. Gattegno said we don't tear down unknown to known."

For me, Dr. Gattegno's theory was full of riddles and shocks. For example, the question about what I did in my sleep made me realize that I sleep for one third of my life because my sleep is on the same line as the system of a baby, who sleeps, and learns, so much.

My way of looking at human beings was gradually and totally changed. I didn't know, however, how his theory was related to teaching languages. It was like my search for a box of matches had led me to a volcano. I learned that learning is related to existence.

After that, according to some advice, I took a Silent Way English course taught by John Beary. I was surprised that the teacher kept really silent, yet we were all able to precisely pronounce English sounds as he tapped the color chart. I found that my "thinking" was a very small part of my capacity and that the ability of awareness was a greater power. I realized that I (as a human) have a lot of types of abilities besides thinking, and I can use them. This kind of learning takes place when the teacher considers not only their students' language, but their existence too.

There was an unforgettable incident during Mr. Beary's workshop. I was supposed say a phrase with "at" in it. But the word never hit me. There was just the world of me and rods. I tried to say everything I saw, one by one. The teacher pointed his finger strongly at the end of the rod and in my mind there was just "the end." And John forced me to say something. I was looking at the place he pointed. I gave up and just looked at the space between his finger and the end of the rods. Then suddenly "AT" hit me as if the word was visible!

My prejudice that I need to memorize when and where English prepositions should be used was torn down. I came to know that each word has very precise contextual meaning. This still affects my teaching and learning.

I attended these workshops as often as I could. The insights they gave me helped me to meet the challenges I encountered in my daily life. Especially during the five years I was learning with Dr. Roslyn

Young, who had been introduced to me by Fusako, as it was very big process for me. Dr. Young trained me to use the theory of Dr. G by using my whole existence, not just my mind.

I told her that the period of being a baby was unrelatable to me, because I couldn't remember that far back. As my learning progressed, I became able to think freshly about myself as being in the same universe as a baby.

How do we use a tool, which is to observe one's self, for the future? The answer we got was this: to use the tool itself is training to use it.

In the process of my quest, I was frustrated and sometimes interrupted teachers by saying silly things. I think I was in a process of experimenting with I, myself, as a working laboratory.

To use the Gattegno Approach is to use myself practically in this world. That's why I work with "myself" as a laboratory – observing myself makes me able to shatter unconscious beliefs. This frees me to accept myself as an existence which is renewing itself for the future. I have been tied to a root of learning since I started to exist in this world, I am independent, and I meet the future every minute of life. What a great freedom I have! I can feel myself as a free existence full of potential while being in contact with this real world.

We did practical work with Dr. Young to convert the time scale from the Big Bang to now into one hour. We calculated many big numbers with calculators and finally we got to feel like we were touching the time.

We learned "here and now" with our experiences to realize that we change infinite time into our experiences. I thought about a human being as a pure learning system and how its power could face any kind of matter in the future.

I was relieved and felt free when I could understand that people can change, and in fact we cannot be the same as before. And this freedom is what Dr. G taught me.

§

A still from *Mathematics At Your Fingertips*, an award-winning film produced in 1961 showing Dr. Gattegno teaching in elementary school classes in Montreal, Quebec. (©National Film Board of Canada.)

Ignoring the Threat of Violence for the Hope of Becoming a Better Teacher

Esaie Pierre

We all heard the buzzing somewhere in the distance. Soon Dr. Arthur Powell's attempts to speak over the noise were pointless. He was losing. He had to wait until the noise passed to continue the workshop. Minutes later the buzzing started anew. We knew Arthur would be forced to stop again.

> "After four days of being challenged to rethink their teaching methods, the teachers and administrators seemed to have concluded that the potential violence surrounding Aristide's return, was outweighed by their need to complete the training."

The buzz we were hearing in our wall-less, rooftop classroom was from several helicopters flying above us. The noise of the copters underlined the fact that the entire country had been abuzz with the news that Jean-Bertrand Aristide would return to Haiti today at noon. There was a very real possibility that one wrong word from Aristide would send the entire country into an uncontrolled frenzy of frustration and anger.

At our mathematics workshop on the rooftop, one of our colleagues from the US felt that we should end the workshop early allowing the participants to make their way home and avoid harm in the event of violence. Arthur selected to let the participants decide. He was willing to continue the workshop, however, anyone who wanted to leave was free to do so. After the announcement and a few minutes of talking among themselves no one moved.

This was day 5 of a five-day seminar on the teaching of mathematics, and teaching approaches in general.

After four days of being challenged to rethink their teaching methods, the teachers and administrators seemed to have concluded that the potential violence surrounding Aristide's return was outweighed by their need to complete the training. They wanted to gain the knowledge that they knew they needed to empower their students to be better learners and better at mathematics.

During the workshop, Arthur demonstrated how rods of varying lengths could be used to teach mathematics in a visible and tangible way. Through our discussions, the teachers began to redefine their role as a facilitator of their students' learning, rather than the source of knowledge asking them to recite rote information. After our discussion of the theory of the Subordination of Teaching to Learning, the teachers became convinced that their students had enormous capacity to understand mathematics like mathematicians, and that by using these techniques, the teachers could help make this type of deeper learning happen.

One teacher, inspired by the workshop, commented that by using the rods and teaching with this new approach, she will be able to unleash the engineering ability that she knows is dormant in her students.

As the latest flock of helicopters disappeared, the teachers, by their actions, were saying that on this last day of the workshop, no buzz or fear of vilience was going stop them from gaining the knowledge that they needed to be better teachers to their students. Despite the uncertainty that surrounded Aristide's return to Haiti, they were not going cower by letting the past control them. They were not going to live in the fear that comes with not knowing. They had found a source of knowledge, which they knew would positively impact their students' futures. The fear of personal harm was not going to stop them from gaining the knowledge they needed to release the potential of their students' futures. §

Teacher training workshop in Gattegno math.

Witnessing the Truth
En témoin de la vérité

Jean-Jacques Dutrait

It was only in 1989 that I came across Caleb Gattegno's ideas, and this was for me a life-changing event. Of course, I had never met him; I didn't even know he had existed until this very moment. It was just by chance that I had met his niece, Claudie, a short while before through a mutual friend, and our paths crossed through our activities.

On a spring day that year, I was having lunch in a restaurant with Claudie and a small group of her friends. Claudie started explaining and describing the features of the famous Lecture en Couleurs (Words in Color), and the Silent Way, and how it was possible to learn a language or even several languages quickly. Her way of explaining (as she could not demonstrate this in a restaurant environment) seemed to me so enlightening that I was greatly moved, so much so that I can still remember now precisely the moment when something in my life was turned around.

What had made the biggest impression on me was that what she was saying was deeply touching matters in me, and I could see the truth in it all.

Looking back now, I think that was the moment I understood, at the time in a more or less confused way, that it is possible to discover and see new horizons and create fields of investigation hitherto unsuspected, by just displacing very slightly our thoughts, our mind, our viewpoint.

From that day on, I asked her for more information so that I could proceed further and understand better what had so deeply affected me. She suggested I attend a class she was giving in a distant Paris suburb.

I joined a group of a dozen adults, mostly foreign women, who spoke very little French or spoke it badly, who as children had rarely been to school or not at all.

What struck me from the beginning was how very attentive they all became as Claudie started pointing to words on the colored charts. They all wanted to answer, make attempts, and suggest new elements so as to check the correctness of their suggestions. Each one corrected or suggested to others what she had understood or had just discovered – all of it in a happy and relaxed, yet very attentive and studious atmosphere.

I was discovering all this to my utter amazement.

A gentleman of about 55 had come to the color chart and Claudie undertook to make him pronounce sounds that were obviously not in his language. This took about 20 minutes, during which time Claudie made him work on where to place these sounds in his mouth, and on the rhythm he needed to be able to pronounce them. This went on without respite until it was all considered right.

At first, I was observing the excellence of the teacher who was doing her utmost to lead her student to produce the correct sounds, but as it went on, the student found it hard to reach the required objectives and I began to feel for this relatively older person. He showed signs of fatigue but he was not giving up. I thought he would get annoyed and throw it all up, maybe even attack the teacher, especially in his position as nearly the only man in a class full of women.

Claudie was not giving up; I was getting more and more anxious about how things would turn out.

Then I noticed the rest of the group. Far from wanting to make fun of him as I imagined they would, they were hanging on his lips as though to breathe into him the energy he needed to help him succeed.

Finally, the man managed to pronounce correctly and the whole group greeted this with cheering before Claudie had accepted it.

All this was most perplexing for me: how could people who were in the same position as this man know if the answer was right or wrong?

curriculum. Claudie made them work on the color chart, something they obviously enjoyed very much. They would line up so that each could point on the chart and certainly not miss his turn, all except for one, who chose to sit under a table and was clearly involved in other activities.

I wondered why she did not tell him to come along like all the others and do the required work. He stayed under the table for about half an hour, then as she asked a question, he shook himself and leapt up from under the table, to point on the chart at the correct answer. I was dumbfounded, but I did notice that he never returned under the table.

I later noted that long periods are not needed to give

> " ... it is possible to discover and see new horizons and create fields of investigation hitherto unsuspected, by just displacing very slightly our thoughts, our mind, our viewpoint. "

The class continued normally but just as active and good-humored.

At the end when everyone got up to leave, this man came to Claudie and wanted to say things to her which he had difficulty expressing in French and finally said to her: "Thank you, madame. Because of you I will not need to take any medicine tonight; I will sleep well." His face was transformed, radiant as he left.

The work that Claudie was engaged in at the time, with children who had great problems at school, first left me very confused, then fascinated me. She worked with a group of six or seven children who were falling badly behind at school. They were between seven and 11 years old and, according to their parents, could not learn and follow the school

these children self-confidence and make it possible for them to go back to a normal school situation.

These anecdotes were basic to my becoming involved in searching out the work and thinking of Caleb Gattegno. Later, I joined training sessions with Claudie and at the same time I started reading all of Dr. Gattegno's books. I also went through the seminars, which are hard to read, but in which one finds transcribed pages of Dr. Gattegno's very words, which deeply affect me and bring me back to the feelings I had when I first encountered his thinking and his work. They so dazzlingly lead you to admit the truth which is probably universal to human consciousness.

Being an architect at the time, I was asked to give a series of architecture lectures at the Ecole Spéciale d'Architecture (Special Architecture School) in Paris. I decided straight away to see if I could organize my lectures using what I had learned from Dr. Gattegno's work. I was only a beginner in pedagogy, but I was determined to make my students work through the Silent Way approach.

So I let my third year students put together the course themselves, based on their knowledge, on documents or themes that I set before them. This quite surprised them as it obviously disturbed their habits which, for some, meant they had a nap at the beginning of the afternoon. Of course, this required that they work and be active, so that a certain number of students did not come back to this optional lecture. But at least half never missed a lecture and asked if I could be part of the jury for their diploma.

A few years later I married Claudie, changed profession, and we created our own education center in Seine-Saint-Denis. Every year, we took in adults who had many problems due to life itself, the lack of education, or their ignorance of the French language.

Besides the obvious pleasure these people felt while working with us, the results obtained surprise me to this day; we had a large number who after one or two courses of four or eight months were able to return to an active life, others found their dignity to face all sorts of problems, and others started reading books. Even now, we still get news of our students who went on to other things and thank "Gattegno" for giving their life meaning.

After many years of working with these people, and seeing the results obtained on the human level – open-mindedness, tolerance, returning to a social and professional life – as well as acquiring knowledge which allows them to lead a full life, I can say that, beyond the personal satisfaction which I managed to gain from my second profession, there are universal elements to be found in the work that Caleb Gattegno tried to pass on through unconventional ways, which were in keeping with his thought processes, but which just have to be exploited, and more deeply applied and spread in different realms of human thought and activity.

To do so, one has to change one's viewpoint, have a different way of looking, and that is probably the most difficult of all.

En témoin de la vérité

C'est en 1989 que la pensée de Caleb Gattegno est arrivée jusqu'à moi et cet événement devait changer toute ma vie. Bien sûr, je n'avais jamais rencontré Caleb Gattegno, ignorant même son existence jusqu'à ce moment-là. Par un grand hasard, j'avais connu sa nièce, Claudie, peu de temps auparavant grâce à un ami commun et à nos activités qui se sont croisées.

Un jour de printemps de cette année, nous déjeunions au restaurant, Claudie et un petit groupe de ses amis. Claudie entreprit donc de raconter, expliquer, décrire en quoi consistait la fameuse Lecture en Couleurs et le Silent Way, comment on pouvait apprendre rapidement à parler une langue et même plusieurs. Sa manière d'expliquer (puisqu'elle ne pouvait faire de démonstration dans la salle de restaurant) me parut si lumineuse que je fus profondément touché et bouleversé au point de me souvenir encore précisément aujourd'hui de ce moment où quelque chose a basculé irrémédiablement dans ma vie.

Ce qui m'avait le plus impressionné, c'était que ce qu'elle disait touchait des choses très profondes en moi et que je pouvais en reconnaître la vérité.

Avec le recul, je pense que c'est à partir de cet instant que je compris, plus ou moins confusément à l'époque, qu'en déplaçant même très légèrement la pensée, l'esprit ou le regard on pouvait découvrir, voir d'autres horizons et créer des champs d'investigation insoupçonnés jusque-là.

A partir de ce jour, je me suis enquis auprès d'elle d'autres informations et renseignements me permettant d'aller plus loin et de comprendre ce qui m'avait si profondément touché.

Elle m'a proposé d'assister à un cours qu'elle donnait dans une lointaine banlieue de la région parisienne.

Je suis arrivé dans un groupe d'une douzaine d'adultes, des femmes en grande majorité, d'origine étrangère, parlant mal ou très mal le français, très peu ou pas scolarisés dans leur enfance.

Ce qui m'a frappé au départ, c'était la très grande attention de toutes les personnes présentes, dès que Claudie a commencé à pointer des mots sur le tableau de couleurs. Toutes voulaient répondre, s'essayer et proposer des éléments nouveaux afin de vérifier la justesse de leurs propositions et chacune se corrigeait ou proposait aux autres ce qu'elle avait compris ou venait de découvrir, tout cela dans une ambiance joyeuse et décontractée, mais très studieuse et attentive.

Je découvrais tout cela et mon étonnement était total.

montrait des signes de fatigue, mais ne renonçait pas et je pensais qu'il allait s'énerver et envoyer tout en l'air et peut-être agresser la maîtresse, surtout dans la situation où il se trouvait, presque le seul homme devant une assemblée de femmes.

Claudie ne renonçait pas, je devenais de plus en plus inquiet pour la tournure qu'allaient prendre les événements. Alors j'observais le reste du groupe qui, bien loin de vouloir se moquer, comme je me l'imaginais, était suspendu aux lèvres de ce monsieur comme pour lui insuffler l'énergie qui pourrait l'aider à réussir.

Enfin l'homme finit par prononcer juste et fut salué

> " Il y a dans l'œuvre [de] Caleb Gattegno (…) des universaux qui ne demandent qu'à être exploités, approfondis dans leurs applications et étendus dans différents domaines de la pensée et des activités humaines. "

Un monsieur âgé d'environ 55 ans est arrivé devant le tableau de couleurs et Claudie entreprit de lui faire prononcer des sons que, bien évidemment, il n'avait pas dans sa langue. Ce travail dura une bonne vingtaine de minutes, au cours duquel Claudie le fit travailler sur le placement de ces sons dans la bouche, le rythme dans lequel il fallait les émettre pour être prononçables pour lui et ceci inlassablement jusqu'à ce que tout ceci soit reconnu juste.

Au début, je voyais l'excellence de la maîtresse qui faisait tout son possible pour amener son élève à produire juste, mais le temps passant l'élève avait bien du mal à atteindre les objectifs fixés et je me mis à souffrir pour cet élève relativement âgé. Il

par le reste du groupe par des acclamations, avant même que Claudie n'acquiesce.

Ceci me plongea dans une grande perplexité : comment des personnes qui étaient dans la même situation que ce monsieur pouvaient-elles savoir si la réponse était juste ou non ?

Le cours continua normalement, mais toujours aussi actif et plein de bonne humeur. A la fin, lorsque tout le monde se leva pour partir, ce monsieur vint vers Claudie et voulait lui dire des choses qui avaient bien du mal à être formulées en français et finalement lui dit : « merci madame, grâce à vous je n'aurai pas besoin de prendre des médicaments ce soir, je vais bien dormir »… Son visage était transformé, radieux et il s'en alla.

Le travail que Claudie menait à l'époque, avec des enfants en grandes difficultés scolaires, me plongea d'abord dans une grande perplexité, puis me fascina. Elle avait un groupe de six ou sept enfants qui tous accumulaient des retards scolaires importants. Ils avaient entre sept et onze ans et, au dire des parents, ne pouvaient apprendre et suivre les programmes scolaires.

Claudie les faisait travailler sur le tableau de couleurs, ce que visiblement ils adoraient faire. Ils se mettaient en file, pour chacun venir pointer sur ce tableau et surtout ne pas rater son tour… sauf un qui avait choisi de s'installer sous une table et qui visiblement vaquait à d'autres occupations. Je me demandais pourquoi elle ne lui disait pas de venir, comme tous les autres, exécuter le travail demandé. Il resta sous la table pendant peut-être une demi-heure puis à une question qu'elle posa, il s'ébroua, bondit de sous la table et vint pointer au tableau la bonne réponse. J'étais éberlué, mais j'ai pu remarquer que plus jamais il n'est retourné sous la table.

Je constatai plus tard qu'il n'était pas nécessaire de temps très longs pour remettre ces enfants d'aplomb et leur permettre de réintégrer les cursus scolaires.

Ces anecdotes sont restées fondatrices dans mon engagement à découvrir le travail et la pensée de Caleb Gattegno. Par la suite, je suivis une formation avec Claudie et parallèlement j'entrepris la lecture de l'ensemble des ouvrages de C. Gattegno. J'entrepris également celle des séminaires dont la lecture est certes fastidieuse, mais dans lesquels on trouve des pages transcrivant les paroles de C. Gattegno qui me touchent au plus profond et me remettent dans l'état que j'ai ressenti lors de mes premiers contacts avec sa pensée et son travail. Elles sont d'une fulgurance qui force à en reconnaître la vérité probablement universelle à l'ensemble des consciences humaines.

Etant architecte à l'époque, il se trouva que l'on me proposa de donner des cours d'architecture à l'Ecole Spéciale d'Architecture à Paris. Je décidai aussitôt de voir si je pouvais construire mes cours en utilisant ce que je connaissais du travail de C. Gattegno. J'étais novice dans le domaine de la pédagogie, mais je résolus de faire travailler mes étudiants de manière Silent Way.

J'amenai mes élèves de 3e année à construire le cours eux-mêmes à partir de leurs connaissances, sur des documents ou des thèmes que je leur livrais. Cela les surprit beaucoup, car visiblement cela dérangeait leurs habitudes qui, pour certains, étaient de faire la sieste au début de l'après-midi. Evidemment cela leur demandait d'être actifs et de travailler, si bien qu'un certain nombre d'élèves n'est pas revenu dans ce cours optionnel, mais une bonne moitié n'a jamais raté un seul cours. D'autres m'ont demandé de faire partie de leur jury de diplôme.

Quelques années après j'ai épousé Claudie, j'ai changé de métier et nous avons créé notre centre de formation en Seine-Saint-Denis. Nous avons reçu chaque année des personnes adultes en grandes difficultés dues à la vie elle-même, à l'absence d'instruction ou à la méconnaissance de la langue française.

Outre le plaisir évident que ces personnes ont pris en travaillant avec nous, les résultats que nous avons obtenus me surprennent encore aujourd'hui, car nous avons eu une très forte proportion de personnes qui à la suite d'un ou deux stages de quatre mois se sont réinsérées dans la vie active, d'autres qui ont retrouvé leur dignité face à des problèmes de tous ordres, d'autres qui se sont mises à lire des livres… Nous avons encore aujourd'hui des nouvelles de quelques personnes qui ont continué leur chemin et qui remercient « Gattegno » d'avoir donné un sens à leur vie.

Après de nombreuses années de travail avec ces personnes, et au vu des résultats que nous avons obtenus tant sur le plan humain - ouverture d'esprit, tolérance, réinsertion dans la vie professionnelle et sociale - que sur celui des acquisitions de connaissances ouvrant sur la capacité à conduire sa vie, je me dis qu'au-delà des satisfactions personnelles que j'ai pu retirer de mon second métier, il y a dans l'œuvre que Caleb Gattegno a tenté de transmettre par des voies non conventionnelles, mais conformes à sa manière de penser, des universaux qui ne demandent qu'à être exploités, approfondis dans leurs applications et étendus dans différents domaines de la pensée et des activités humaines. Pour cela, il faut changer de point de vue, regarder autrement et c'est peut-être ce qui est le plus difficile à faire.

§

Dr. Caleb Gattegno, who wrote prolifically throughout his career, is shown here editing a rough draft of one of his books. (Educational Solutions file photo.)

Caleb Gattegno, Scientist: A Learner Remembers

Stephen DeGiulio

I encountered Caleb Gattegno's Science of Education as an undergraduate in 1971. I had always disliked school, but loved to learn about the world through the senses, something forbidden in school where we had to sit in chairs and contemplate black-and-white pages and the backs of our classmates' heads.

Professor Bob Perrault's class was another world, meeting for eight hours at a stretch, after which we went our own ways for a few weeks before regrouping for another day long class. In those few hours I learned more about myself, learning, language, my classmates, and my teacher than in all my previous schooling, with the main lesson a total surprise — I realized that teaching was what I wanted to do, because it is coextensive with learning, when subordinated to it.

I would never have dreamt of doing to others what my teachers had done to me — waste my time and try to disable my native ability to learn so I would fit into a worker-ant social slot. What I learned in those few days about Gattegno's scientific approach was to respect every learner's autonomy and intelligence and free them to direct their own learning toward their own ends. I immediately took this into local schools as a K-12 substitute teacher of all subjects, and found it easy to establish that I am there to learn with the learners, not to oppress them, and that they are full of enthusiasm and good ideas about how to learn.

Of course, substitute teachers operate below the administration's radar. The schools where I subbed ignored me as long as no one got hurt or disturbed the regular teachers. Thus I had the freedom to toss out the conventional cruelty and discipline of schooling and let each day and each child take its course, feeding them games, facts, and ideas to help them master skills and acquire knowledge through engaging play — something I would not have been allowed to do as a fulltime teacher. I had no students with control or behavioral problems, though often given classes considered "the worst." I was a beginner, and not very creative or knowledgeable, but most of the ideas and energy came from the children themselves, so I could relax, observe, and enjoy with them, bringing what I learned one day into the next day's classes.

Finishing up my B.A., I needed some boring "education" courses to get a teacher's license, but I often skipped those classes so I could spend more time teaching, and found it easy to pass the university's exams with what I was learning from my experiences on the front line.

As a substitute teacher, I couldn't use the Gattegno materials I was learning about, but I applied Gattegno's principles with whatever was available — chalk, talk, pencils, paper, hearts, and minds. There was no need to control or direct, no need to praise or reward — more than anything, these children and teens, freed by principles of learning that respect their essential nature, were like volcanoes of creative affect and intellect who gave me a chance to learn by including me in their learners' world. It was as if the sterile school walls disappeared and we were out in borderless nature. And, because the regular teacher found her room and students in good shape the next day, I was frequently called back to the same schools. Forty years later, I still remember those hours and those children.

Meanwhile, I read Gattegno's *What We Owe Children* and *Towards a Visual Culture*, and attended a Words in Color workshop. The following year, with a fresh teaching license, I asked Gattegno how I could learn more. He pointed me to a public junior high school on New York's upper west side where Educational Solutions was providing support to a literacy program for immigrant kids. I signed on to a team with two experienced Words in Color teachers, entitling me to attend weekend workshops and seminars conducted by Gattegno and others at Educational Solutions.

Partway through a Silent Way seminar conducted by Gattegno, something happened that brought the education of awareness into focus. Gattegno realized that one participant was experiencing a block. He dropped the Silent Way altogether, and appeared completely fascinated with her efforts. Leaving the other participants to observe, he began to elicit some math concepts from her using the Algebricks that had been serving as realia for the Silent Way. This got her involved with learning rather than with being blocked. That moment is when I saw that the way to free learners is to free oneself to interact with others in the moment — and that no curriculum, no method, no theory is more important. In fact, when we attempt to follow a curriculum, employ a method, or apply a theory, we are engaging in cognitive activity (mental manipulation of past thoughts, images, etc.), and we can't do this without losing our awareness of what is happening within ourselves and with learners, here and now. Our choice is either to impose the dead past on the living present, and accept very poor learning results, or to drop the past and accompany the learners into the future, without any guide or plan.

Gattegno offered this opportunity — really, a privilege — to thousands who came to see him teach — an opportunity to observe learning naked of any theory or method, with the teacher subordinating his work entirely so the learners (and the teacher) could grow. During the years I participated in Gattegno's New York workshops and seminars, the majority of those who attended appeared unprepared to observe without bias; yet, they also seemed to be positively moved, very often by a specific interaction with Gattegno, who never addressed a group, but always a room full of individuals, making the principle that all learning is individual and constantly visible.

One such "interaction" was key for me. During one of Gattegno's awareness seminars, I remarked that we are better off working with whatever facts we can find, without resorting to beliefs. Gattegno paused and fixed me with a look whose intensity I can never forget; then, with perhaps the shadow of a smile, he said: "I'll watch you."

What Gattegno did was to charge me, by a pause and a powerful look, to take myself seriously — to accept the responsibility to live by my own light, however dim, and cultivate it.

Gattegno worked tirelessly to bring this to all, especially to the young, whose oppression by the

> "I would never have dreamt of doing to others what my teachers had done to me — waste my time and try to disable my native ability to learn."

hegemony of modern schooling — virtually identical the world over — remains invisible to most adults, who were formed by the same system. *The Universe of Babies*, *Know Your Children As They Are*, *What We Owe Children*, and *The Adolescent and His Self* are too poetic, and at the same time too scientific for most of today's harried and compromised scholars and scientists. "Truth has short legs," Gattegno would sometimes say, "it travels slowly."

***

Gattegno taught a series of demonstration classes at Staten Island Community College to urban college students who were poorly prepared for the traditional curriculum and struggling with jobs and family responsibilities while trying to get an education. A teacher who was inspired by observing Gattegno, but frustrated at his own, less successful efforts, asked him, "How do you get them to respect you?" The answer came in a very quiet voice, "By being someone they respect."

§

Working on the Edge of Discomfort:
Threads of a Complex Journey into Awareness

Chris Breen

Five scenes containing themes of learning, community, maths, and awareness paint a quick picture of some moments on the journey that I have taken since first being exposed to Caleb Gattegno's ideas.

It's a journey that has very much been rooted in the tremendous challenges of the political struggles of South Africa. It has been a teaching journey that has always seemed to be on an edge, challenging the accepted norms and paradigms of education and society. On the road, I have depended on the support and insight of other wonderful similarly-influenced fellow travelers such as Europe Singh, Tony Brown, Dave Hewitt, Laurinda Brown, John Mason, David Pimm, and Sandy Dawson. My challenge has been to frame my work so that it is in service of the learner rather than my teaching. I have felt an urgency that requires me to take the risk to step into the unknown and ask the questions that I believe are right and to unreservedly believe in the potential of each learner. I have tried to see the absolute brilliance that exists in each person who comes to me having learned to speak (as learned from *What We Owe Children*) and to appreciate the power of imagination rather than that of memory. These powerful threads have their roots in the Science of Education.

A CLASSROOM IN EXETER UNIVERSITY 1974

I enter the lecture room as a young South African maths teacher studying abroad for the first time at Exeter University. The lecturer, Dennis Crawforth, asks the class what we have each been doing since the last time we met, and then sits comfortably in silence until someone speaks. A little later he picks up a Geoboard and moves an elastic band around the nails asking, what do you notice? Again he waits and insists that someone answers.

A SEMINAR ROOM IN SOUTH ENGLAND 1975

The Exeter Maths education Masters group have traveled to attend a seminar given by Caleb Gattegno. He talks about awareness and mathematics and then asks us to do some work. It is not a soothing experience as he keeps each one of us on edge with provocative and challenging questions. But we work and there are many "Aha!" moments in the room. I am intrigued and buy some books, rods and films and return to South Africa to explore these ideas and way of teaching.

A UNIVERSITY HOSTEL ROOM IN LONDON 1992

There's a knock on the door of my room, and two excited strangers burst in and want to shake my hand. It's my first conference abroad as the academic boycott has been in place ever since I started lecturing, but an exception has been made for this Political Dimensions of Mathematics Education conference. The two strangers, Arthur Powell and Marty Hoffman, have just been reading the conference proceedings and have noticed that I have also been strongly influenced by, and quote, Caleb Gattegno's work. After the conference, they insist I drive down to Wiltshire to meet Dick Tahta – the way to his home is signposted with banners that read "Only Awareness is Educable." Dick becomes a hugely significant influence in my life.

A QUAD IN THE EDUCATION BUILDING 1995

Dick Tahta is my guest in Cape Town and is running a workshop for a group of mathematics educators who are working with teachers in township schools. Apartheid has only recently come to an end, and the success of the first elections has created a buzz. We have watched one of the Nicolet films and are now constructing our own understandings by creating the geometric movement using people. A vantage point a couple of floors above the quad gives a bird's eye view of the shapes being generated by our movements.

awareness and knowing. I live in a country where the miracle of the peaceful transition from the apartheid era has seen more people become aware of the outer visible forms of judgment and oppression and seemingly less aware of the actions that still maintain these constructs.

> "I choose to work in a different way where I try to set up a paradoxical place of safety that sits right on an edge of discomfort."

A LECTURE THEATRE IN CAPE TOWN 2011

It's late afternoon in the middle of a four-hour session on business numeracy that I am giving to a group of junior managers at the Business School. In earlier sessions they have spoken about their past experiences of school maths with a great deal of fear and sadness. We are constructing number sequences by building shapes with matchsticks and paying attention to what we can see we are doing as we work. As we work on our images, I talk about geometry being "an awareness of imagery." We are working on an edge of discomfort as I challenge each person to name what it is they see and then to move onto a big picture where they can generalize what they see. We start talking about x's as we move onto algebra as "the dynamics of their imagery."

REFLECTIONS ON THE JOURNEY

I only met Caleb Gattegno once and much of the story I know about him relies on stories from Dick and the lovingly captured scripts of his working weekends on a variety of topics. But I believe there are some core features of my current work and beliefs that owe an enormous amount to this man.

The last classroom scene I depicted describes a moment in the only mathematics class I still teach. In 2008, I decided to leave mathematics education and I now teach topics such as "error and illusion," "complexity and diversity," "personal leadership," and "decision-making in the moment" in the field of executive education. In my teaching in the corporate world, I experience familiar certainties of self that, to me, stem from an education system that has foregrounded results and knowledge rather than

In this environment, I am deeply concerned about the damage done by our over-exposure to this dominant paradigm and what others have called our "self-deception." Many of my colleagues have established ways of working that create safe containers for participants and they invite them to work at particular activities and choose the way in which they want to be exposed to new ideas and change.

I choose to work in a different way where I try to set up a paradoxical place of safety that sits right on an edge of discomfort. It's a place where I aim to work in real time, real life and then hold a mirror up to challenge/question events and ideas as they unfold. In doing this, my aim is to explore how we can become more aware of our actions in the moment and their effect on others through our interactions and feedback from these same "others." It is a scary place to work and requires me to continually work on myself to ensure that I prioritize learning and compassion for the learner. It is an approach that requires me to let go of any stake in being liked by all participants. It requires me to be willing to go to the learning edge and challenge the learner to take a next step. I have to be able to handle the discomfort of that edge in silence with full presence. And I have to find the courage to do this continually each time I enter a classroom and encounter new challenges.

I think that Caleb would understand exactly what I am talking about in describing this life journey, as my path to this way of being a teacher received an enormous boost when I met him and his work and later interacted with the community of wonderful people who had been similarly influenced. §

Where do Good Results Come From?

Dr. Bruce Ballard

I've always been easily seduced by good results, much to my detriment. Because I witness so many positive outcomes when I'm in a classroom that uses Dr. Gattegno's pedagogy, I tend not to dive below the surface to ponder what's really happening. I get a thrill watching another teacher work, and as a teacher myself I can easily coast on effective techniques and materials.

> "I began to see that a teacher could rely on the students to do astonishing things if the teacher set the situation up clearly enough, then stepped out of the way...The students are far more brilliant than the teacher."

For example, when I was teaching English at a university in South Korea in the 1970s, I attended a Silent Way workshop in Seoul where I learned how to use the Cuisenaire Rods to clarify the difference between the articles 'a' and 'the.' The exercise seemed powerful and clear cut. The next week in my university class I tried it with my students. I set up the same situation with the rods, tapped out words I had written randomly on the blackboard, and did not speak myself. As the lesson progressed, some of the students became entranced: they got dazed looks in their eyes as they incessantly, and of their own free will, repeated the phrases and sentences, experimenting and self correcting with little or no prompting from me. It was like magic. It seemed that for the first time they and I were clear about how these two tiny English words worked (Korean has no equivalents for 'a' and 'the'). And I saw that by teaching this way, the center of attention was not on me the teacher, but on a situation that the students perceived and on how they were using themselves. It was one of the first times where I had the freedom to just observe students in the process of learning.

But that's as far as I took the analysis then. The surface was so simple and appealing, the results so startling. How often did that happen going forward, when I watched Dr. Gattegno or one of his impressive colleagues work with learners, and after an hour or more of awareness exercises the learners were doing and saying things an observer would never have dreamed possible? How often does this happen today, in my work training primary school teachers to use Words in Color, when we see kindergarten and first grade students making huge leaps in their learning?

I could never hope to see inside Dr. Gattegno's mind, and understanding his books is a long and difficult process – they're not easy reads! However, I began to see that a teacher could rely on the students to do astonishing things if the teacher set the situation up clearly enough, then stepped out of the way. I created, then started to believe in my own mantra: The students are far more brilliant than the teacher. I saw again and again how smart the students were if I or another teacher I was observing did the right things.

In 1999 I started working with one of Dr. Gattegno's former colleagues, Shasha (Charlotte) Balfour. We taught business writing courses in the financial services industry, primarily at Fortune 100 investment banks in the USA and overseas. Shasha had already developed much of the curriculum by applying Gattegno's Subordination of Teaching to Learning to basic awarenesses about business writing.

The participants were usually equities analysts who wrote about topics I did not understand well. Part of the reason I couldn't understand their writing was that they structured the information so poorly, but also I could claim almost no knowledge of the subject matter. I learned not to let that bother me, but just to work with them on their relationship with the reader. To be precise, they needed to stop writing from their perspective as a writer/researcher, and start writing from the reader's state of mind. The awareness exercises I learned from Shasha seduced most of the participants into making that leap. A few hours into the course I would ask them to revise sections of their job-related reports and emails, which they had sent me in advance. Typically, the rewrites showed a dramatic shift.

Here's an example that may make sense to a general reader. A junior analyst in an Asian country I was visiting had been asked by her boss, the head of equities research, to investigate a problem with the power supply in the country's northern provinces. Her boss had heard something was amiss, and he wanted to know what to tell his clients if they asked him about the immediate outlook.

The analyst, a young woman new on the job, did the research and sent him this email. (Note: I've changed the names of specific companies, but otherwise the email is real.)

Power Supply to the Northern Provinces

Among all the independent power producers that were approved previously, only Apex Power and Zynergy are up and running. Apex Power has 1000MW capacity but is now only generating 500MW to NatPower because of residents' protest on the power transmission line setup. It is assumed that a similar problem will occur with other independents and delay the expected commercial run. Consequently, Sunshine Group's Zynergy seems like it could be the solution for the power shortage in the northern provinces by transmitting power from the center of the country (where it is located) to the north (if NatPower can resolve the transmission problem from the center to the north). However, it should be noted that Zynergy has five coal-fired units, each with a capacity of 650MW, only three of which obtained approval during the Ministry's First Solicitation, while the rest were installed without the authority's permission. Another issue is that all power-generating units in Zynergy are coal-fired, which might violate the government's emission control objectives in the future.

When she included this email as part of the work-related writing she sent me before the course, I could see that it was a big tangled jungle of information. I felt any reader would have to read through it a few times to get on top of her message. It was probably also unclear to her boss.

In the workshop, however, after a few hours of awareness exercises about how she could work with the reader's mind, she took the email back and rewrote it like this:

Power Supply to the Northern Provinces

The power supply delivered by the independent power producers (IPPs) to the northern provinces could be lower than planned. This is because:

• Residents are protesting. Among Ministry-approved IPPs, only Apex Power and Zynergy are up and running. For the other IPPs, residents are blocking construction. Although Apex Power has 1000MW capacity, it now generates

(Bruce Ballard Cont'd)

only half that amount because citizens object to how the power lines were set up.

• Not all of Zynergy's units received government approval. Every Zynergy plant is coal-fired, which may violate the government's future emission control standards. Only three of Zynergy's five units obtained Ministry approval in the First Solicitation. The rest were installed without permission.

I could never have predicted such a change, and even she was surprised at the transformation. During a feedback session she asked, "Is it really OK to write to my boss like this?" Her boss, who was sitting in on the course, said, "This is exactly how I want you to write."

When I look over all that I've written here, I come up with a few conclusions. First, I've been extremely fortunate to have encountered the Subordination of Teaching to Learning early in my teaching career, and to have worked with Dr. Gattegno and his colleagues full time. This has allowed me to witness many astounding results in a wide variety of classrooms. I also realize anew that working on awareness is the way to go. I recall what I read in the teacher's notes for the Mini-Tests that Educational Solutions produced over 30 years ago. "In developing this kit, we kept in mind the two stages that are involved in learning any skill: developing awarenesses and then gaining facility in those awarenesses. Our first responsibility, then, is to set up situations which force awareness." §

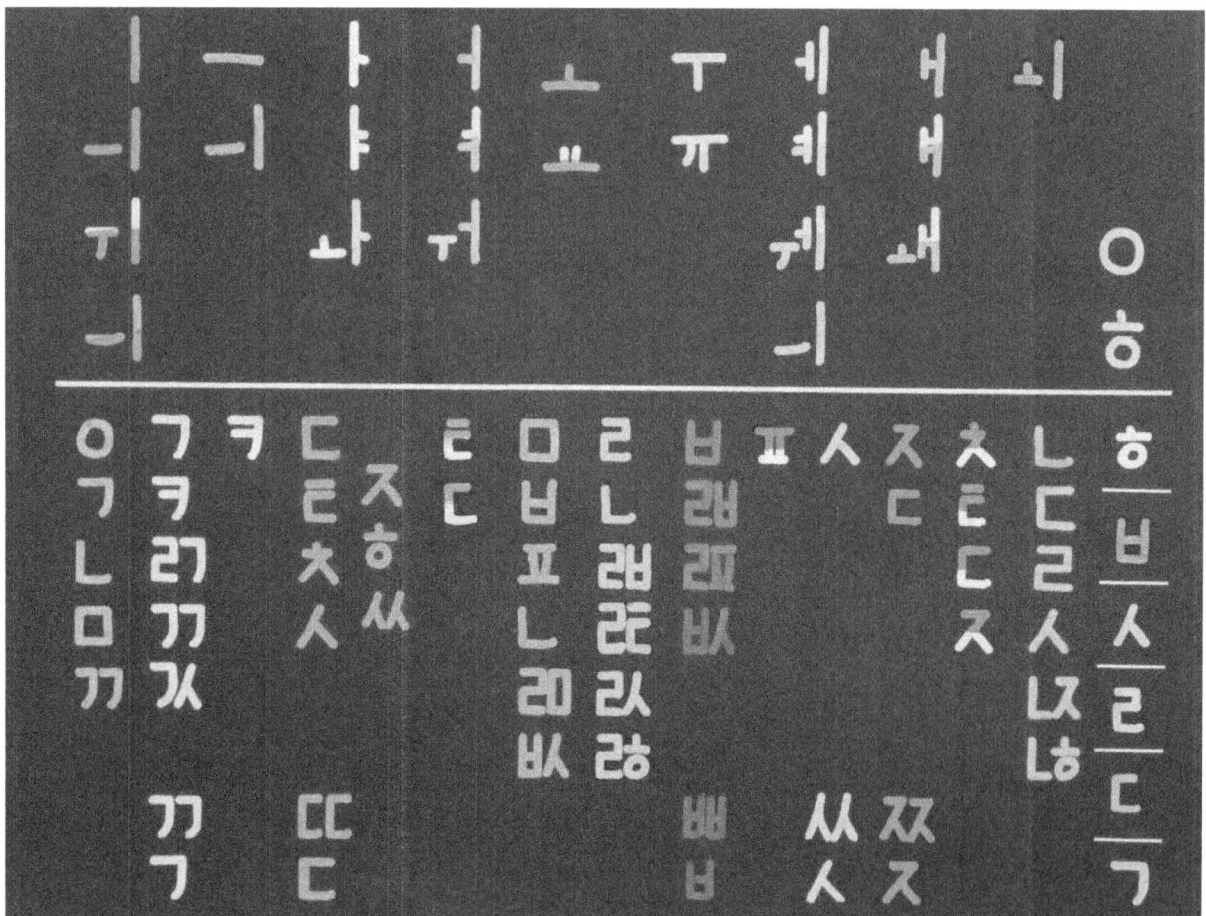

Above: Korean Fidel, 1978 prototype. ©Educational Solutions Worldwide Inc.

Right: Korean Word Chart 11, 1978 prototype. ©Educational Solutions Worldwide Inc.

가족 애기 아버지 아들 시
할머니 오빠 아주머니
동생 할아버지 딸 어른
아이 자매 녀 형제 친척
형 누나 주인 부모 손자
친구 아저씨 인 조카
가끔 지난 이젠 중 지금
아까 작년 곧 초순 잠깐

In the Midst of a Whirlwind

Dr. Masayuki Onishi

My first encounter with the Silent Way took place in October 1988. At that time I was traveling with my wife and son in the USA. My wife and I had been disappointed with the standard educational options in Japan and set out to find a place suitable for our son's education. On the way we stayed at our friends' home in Albuquerque, New Mexico and visited a small alternative school called Little Earth School in Santa Fe.

We borrowed our friend's car to drive the highway to Santa Fe. It was a glorious morning. The sky was crystal clear and the sunlight was showering everywhere. When we arrived at the school, we were invited to join a Spanish-language class where a young Hispanic teacher was teaching a dozen or so seven- or eight-year-old students.

Two rectangular charts were hanging behind the teacher. One of them had small rectangles, and the other Spanish words, all in different colors, neatly printed against a black background. In front of the teacher was a box of small wooden rods of different lengths painted in 10 different colors; later we learned that they are called Cuisenaire Rods. She would take some rods out of the box, and while showing them to the children, tap the colored rectangles and the words printed on the charts. As though enticed by a wand of a magician, the children pronounced some sounds or words. After this process was repeated several times, she handed some of the rods to the children, again tapping on the charts. Gradually the children started to pass the rods to each other and form sentences for themselves. It was a thrilling game and I could feel the energy flowing smoothly between the teacher and the children in the room. We were in the midst of the whirlwind of this flowing energy, and the class hour passed very quickly.

The teacher told us later that this teaching method is called the Silent Way. She showed us other materials for teaching geometry, and wrote down for us the address of the New York center of Educational Solutions on a small slip of paper.

A month later we went to New York, stayed in a small room at a YMCA surrounded by skyscrapers, and started to explore the city. One day we visited the center. We were cordially received by Shakti Gattegno who had been running the center since Dr. Gattegno had passed away earlier that year. She showed us various teaching materials and explained how to use them. My son immediately started to play with rods, and a box of Cuisenaire Rods and a green book titled *Arithmestics* was his companion for the rest of our travels. In the center I saw, among other things, charts of the Hindi language hanging on the wall. The image of these charts stayed deep inside me for a long time, and stimulated me to make my own charts for the Bengali language 20 years later.

At the time of our visit to New York, we had already decided to move to Australia via Japan. Shakti told us that there was a center in Osaka, and that there were also a few Silent Way teachers working in Melbourne, and kindly gave us the information we would need in order to contact them.

We went back to Japan in December of that year and stayed in Osaka for a few weeks before setting out for Canberra. We visited the Centre in Osaka and got acquainted with Fusako Allard and other staff members there. The Centre was very active, and Fusako was busy finalizing the Japanese language materials she and her colleagues had been developing for two decades. Luckily they organized a two-day workshop on teaching Japanese and English while we were in Osaka, and I decided to take part in it.

The workshop was run by Fusako and John Beary. On the second day of the course John had a session demonstrating how to teach the pronunciation of American English. He chose two Japanese participants — a lady teacher of English and myself — as the target students. He taught us the sounds and rhythms of the language using a "Sound-Color Chart" with a pointer. Each of the 58 rectangles printed in various colors against a black background represented a phoneme or a phone of English. He tapped the rectangles one after another and invited us to produce the sounds represented by the combination of these rectangles. He himself didn't produce any sound, but he gave us cues by the movement of his lips and tongue, and/or his hands. The movement of the pointer was too fast for me to remember the correspondence between the color and the sound, so I soon gave up trying to memorize the links and let my brain work more freely. A lady sitting beside me was apparently unwilling to relax in this way and subsequently withdrew from the session.

I felt as if I had entered into Alice's Wonderland. The colors of the rectangles indicated by the pointer came into my sight one after another and my vocal organs were formed into particular shapes and produced some sounds which resounded in my brain. In the next moment they left some traces in the depths of my consciousness and disappeared. As this process was repeated, the association of the color and the sound became more and more automatic, the energy started to form a natural flow so that I felt that I was swimming in currents of intertwined color and sound — and then suddenly the session was finished. I was shocked to find that a 45 minute language lesson could trigger such an intense inner experience in the learner.

"I was shocked to find that a 45 minute language lesson could trigger such an intense inner experience in the learner."

Soon after the workshop we moved to Canberra to start a new life. I visited Melbourne and attended a few workshops organized by the teachers there, such as Andrew Weiler, Alma Arnould, Bill Robbins, and Jane Orton. In the meantime, a full set of Japanese charts were published in Osaka. I decided to organize a Japanese Silent Way course at our home, and invited Fusako to Canberra. It was in one of the sessions of this course that Fusako pushed me to take over ...

At present I teach Japanese, Bengali, and English in spare moments from my research work. During my field research in Papua New Guinea and India, I sometimes help people develop literacy materials for minority languages which haven't yet established adequate writing systems. I also occasionally teach the pronunciation of English, German, and French for Japanese students who sing classical songs. In any of these occasions, what I have learned by teaching and taking part in Silent Way courses is an invaluable asset.

> " Babies are at peace with change simply because they perceive it as the basis of reality. "

— Dr. Caleb Gattegno

The Universe of Babies, Second Edition (2010), page 83.

Educational Solutions file photo, 2010.

Some Facts of Awareness

Allen Rozelle

I learned these facts of awareness working with Caleb Gattegno:

1. Words have no meaning.
2. You cannot force awareness in readers through writing.

So the question becomes: why write anything about Caleb Gattegno on the occasion of the 100th anniversary of his birth?

Memory 1: I am sitting in my office at the IBM-France English Language Program in Paris one late-summer afternoon in 1971. Catherine, who resigned her teaching position a month or so earlier to move to Tunisia, walks in unexpectedly. Chit-chat follows briefly. Then, she tells me that she had an unbelievable experience while she was visiting friends in New York: a Chinese-language workshop with something called the Silent Way invented by some guy named Gattegno. She announces she wants to show it to anyone still around the office.

Reluctantly, as it's time to go have a beer at the cafe, I gather up a few colleagues and find an empty classroom. Sitting around a big conference table, we listen as Catherine explains she is going to teach us Chinese, saying words only once, and that we will find ourselves thinking, speaking and understanding everything directly in Chinese as we go along. As we grumble awkward agreement, she sets a small, plastic box on the table and opens it. Inside are neatly arranged compartments of little colored blocks of different lengths.

She takes one out, holds it up for everyone to see and says something strange. Then she puts it down, holds up a block of a different color and repeats the strange utterance, which I notice begins with "mu." She repeats the process with a third color, and I understand "mu tiao." I realize that I have heard the same utterance in the three situations. When she does it for the fourth time but doesn't speak, some of us offer our version of "mu tiao." She points to one of us and asks us to say it the way he or she has. We practice. Then she goes back through the first three blocks to let us practice a bit more, sometimes pointing to the person we're supposed to copy. I participate willingly, trying to correct myself and realizing simultaneously that the "word" seems to mean block to me. She continues, using blocks of colors and lengths we haven't seen, and the "word" comes back each time. We gain familiarity.

Then, she picks up a red block, strokes the side with her finger and says what I hear as "hong." Someone tries to say it. Catherine makes gestures indicating that the utterance is not complete. Someone tries, "hong mu tiao." Without comment, Catherine puts the red block down and picks up another one, which she strokes with her finger. She looks at us and says, "lan." Someone says, "lan mu tiao." Catherine picks up the red block, and we try "hong mu tiao" again. She shows us the blue block, and we say, "lan mu tiao." While I am doing this, I am aware that we are working on the colors of the blocks and that while relaxed, I am very attentive to what the other colleagues are saying. The utterances I want to make come spontaneously when I see Catherine hold up a block.

As we continue to work through the blocks faster and faster, people make mistakes, and someone chimes in to correct them while everyone laughs with the confusion. I am very aware that I am working directly in what Catherine says is Chinese, and thoroughly enjoying the experience.

My memory and awareness of this simple, easy-going, afternoon lesson, which continued for some time that day and the direction of which many of you can imagine, form the basis on which I have built my understanding of The Subordination of Teaching to Learning and most of my professional career since then. It did not come from reading one of Dr. Gattegno's books, which I only encountered in 1973 when I met the man himself. However, reading his works later and working with him and many, many others on awareness and learning have permitted me to deepen my understanding and add to my appreciation of that afternoon experience. Hats off to Catherine, Dr. G, those many others and me!

Some six years later, Dr. G and I were chatting in Paris. I had resigned from IBM to work with him on what became the Silent Way Video Project. He told me his wife, Shakti, was concerned that he had overly influenced me into giving up a secure position for a very uncertain project. I told him not to worry, that he and his work had shown me a way to live my professional life joyously.

Memory 2: I am sitting with Dr. G and several colleagues in a classroom at the International School of Geneva in the winter of 1980. They have just attended a disastrous English lesson I gave to a class of third graders. In a deep hole of "despond," I am desperate for feedback and *answers*!

Dr. G: "You're boring them. You don't vary the activities enough. You have to learn how to play their games the way they do. If you want to become a good teacher and have the will to do so, you will succeed, but it will take you 19 years." Thanks…

Once again, no book was involved even though I had already devoured *Teaching Foreign Languages in Schools* and *The Common Sense of Teaching Foreign Languages*. I had also attended numerous workshops, observed wonderful fellow teachers and taught adults for several years.

In such situations as mine, Dr. G used remarks the way he used a pointer to correct intonation in language work: banging on the wall chart! Only in this case, it was the wall of my mind. It took me three years to *begin* correcting the situation although perhaps knowing you're a lousy teacher is a variation of Teaching Level 0. I'm a slow learner so I had lots of time to read his books again, observe colleagues' classes and take seminars. The resulting osmosis certainly must have helped, but I have to say I had no awareness of it until something, and I still don't know what, finally clicked.

So why contribute to a collective memoir of Caleb Gattegno? What might my words and written text bring to a new teacher looking into The Subordination of Teaching to Learning, or even an experienced teacher who's fallen into a hole similar to mine? Perhaps, it's the similarity of holes or that holes exist at all, from which with time and energy one can extract oneself. After all, Gattegno never promised us a rose garden. I perceived one myself all on my own when I took my first lesson with Catherine. I just forgot to notice the thorns, ignorant, of course, of the ones Gattegno would add himself to my perception and awareness as time went by.

Perhaps, it's to say that the primeval beauty one spots at the outset is there to be discovered. Having some "supreme being" follow you around the garden telling you you're naked and pointing out the potholes in your mind might also help. However, you have to learn to dress and avoid the holes yourself, and it takes the time it takes, each of us being unique.

Perhaps, it's to offer those swift enough to reach awareness directly through written texts another opportunity to do so. It does provide a shortcut and savings on workshops.

Certainly, it's a possible source of inspiration, which served me well until awareness could catch up. Inspiration cannot be forced (my own fact of awareness); it either is or isn't. It can carry one during periods of desolation and embolden one when the harvest is bountiful.

As Dr. G so often said, there are many paths into the forest. Some of us simply need more time to see the forest despite the trees. §

Etre disponible :
Un art de vivre façon Caleb Gattegno

Martine Widmer

"On ne peut pas intervenir avec des projections, des attentes ; c'est exclu. On est disponible. C'est une étrange place que celle d'être disponible."

- C. Gattegno, séminaire A la recherche de ma place

« Installez-vous là, en demi-cercle devant le tableau. Non, non, ne prenez pas vos feuilles ni vos crayons, laissez tout, venez vous asseoir, simplement ! ». Sans un mot, Roslyn a pointé des couleurs sur un rectangle, des couleurs qui se transformaient en sons. Et c'est ainsi, au milieu des rires et de toutes sortes de bruits que nous produisions avec notre bouche, notre gorge, nos cordes vocales, du vent soufflé entre nos dents, c'est ainsi que nous avons commencé à parler … chinois ! Quel plaisir ce contact libre avec soi-même ! Je venais de découvrir le Silent Way.

Cela se passait à Besançon, durant l'été 1989. J'étais là parce que j'allais avoir, à la rentrée de septembre, la responsabilité d'une classe d'accueil (classe recevant des jeunes migrants originaires de différents pays non-francophones), à Genève. Je n'avais encore jamais enseigné le français en tant que langue seconde et j'étais tenue de me former en FLE. Français Langue Etrangère. Rien que ne je connaisse déjà. De la linguistique, de la grammaire, de l'analyse du discours, bref des exposés de spécialistes, mais pas grand-chose que je puisse utiliser dans ma classe à la rentrée. Par bonheur, dans ce programme aride, une rubrique alléchante : «Présentation d' approches non conventionnelles ». C'est dans ce cadre que Roslyn Young faisait une présentation du Silent Way. A cette époque, j'enseignais le français depuis une dizaine d'années dans des classes « ordinaires » - par opposition aux classes d'accueil-, des classes pour adolescents francophones de 12 à 15 ans. J'en étais arrivée à un point de saturation. L'effort consacré à la préparation des leçons et l'énergie dépensée pendant les cours étaient disproportionnés par rapport à l'investissement et aux résultats de mes élèves. J'étais à deux doigts de quitter l'enseignement. Aussi, lorsque Roslyn m'apprend qu'une formation à la pédagogie de Gattegno démarre à la fin de l'été, sans hésiter je m'inscris.

Et c'est là que tout a commencé à changer ! Tout ? Je n'arrive pas bien à mesurer l'étendue de l'influence de Gattegno dans mon existence. D'autant qu'il y en a d'autres, d'influences, en tout cas une autre, celle du bouddhisme tibétain et de l'un de ses maîtres, à peu près en même temps. Cependant, cela deviendra de plus en plus évident au fil du temps, entre Gattegno et moi, il y a rencontre. Alors que nous ne sous sommes jamais vus ! Par rencontre, je veux parler de ces quelques êtres qui auront jalonné mon existence et mise au contact de moi-même dans un dialogue intérieur dynamique. Je me sentais solitaire, avec des questions qui ne trouvaient d'écho nulle part. Soudain, voilà quelqu'un qui dit des choses passionnantes, qui me comprend, nous parlons la même langue, même si, pour ma part, je ne comprends pas tout ce qu'il dit !

Gattegno, depuis que je le fréquente, est devenu un maître et un ami. C'est un précurseur, il est plus loin que moi sur le chemin, mais c'est le même chemin, je ne me sens pas différente de lui. C'est un complice. Et bien sûr, c'est un maître, il m'ouvre la voie, cette piste de la connaissance dans l'expérimentation de soi-même, dans l'exploration de l'humain.

J'utilise sans cesse les outils qu'il a mis en circulation, ses propositions pédagogiques, le matériel qu'il a créé. Ma vie professionnelle en a été transformée. J'ai été amenée à travailler dans toutes sortes de structures. Plus de fatigue, mais un immense enthousiasme. Une image me revenait sans cesse pour caractériser mon nouveau rapport à mon travail, celle du paysan qui travaille sa terre. Il a semé et ça pousse, le résultat est visible ! Mais pas seulement du côté des élèves… Pratiquer la subordination de l'enseignement à l'apprentissage, utiliser le matériel inventé par Gattegno, cela produit plus d'effet que le « simple » fait de devenir un bon professeur avec des élèves qui sont en réussite et qui apprennent avec plaisir. On n'utilise pas impunément la pédagodie de Gattegno ! Ce que je demandais à mes élèves –« Pourquoi fais-tu cela ? » ; « N'y a-t-il pas une autre façon d'y arriver ? » ; « Tu es sûr de toi ? » ; « Et toi, qu'en penses-tu ? », cette interrogation permanente sur les critères mis en place, les démarches entreprises, je l'ai faite mienne. A tout bout de champ, dans tous les domaines de la vie, des phrases-clés me reviennent, qui me recentrent. Des phrases qui me placent toute droite, disponible face à l'inconnu que j'explore là en ce moment. Une phrase du style : « Je suis un système apprenant », par exemple, me met aussitôt, à la fois dans la confiance de mes possibilités en tant qu'être humain, et dans la mobilisation de l'énergie nécessaire pour creuser – j'ai envie de dire, au sens propre ! – creuser dans la matière, tant l'activité d'exploration parfois me semble concrètement palpitante.

Maintenant, je m'interroge sur la possibilité d'aller à la racine des minuscules mouvements énergétiques à la base d'enchaînements de pensées générateurs, par exemple, d'angoisse, plus généralement de chaînes d'automatismes destructeurs et de les transformer, de les effacer en les remplaçant par un autre mouvement… Pourquoi ? Mais pour aller vers toujours plus de liberté !

> " Instead of attempting to develop teacher-proof methods of teaching, we are proposing to enhance the role of the teacher and to make all teachers into associates in the elaboration of a Science of Education. "
>
> - Dr. Caleb Gattegno

The Science of Education – Part 1: Theoretical Considerations Second Edition (2010), p149.

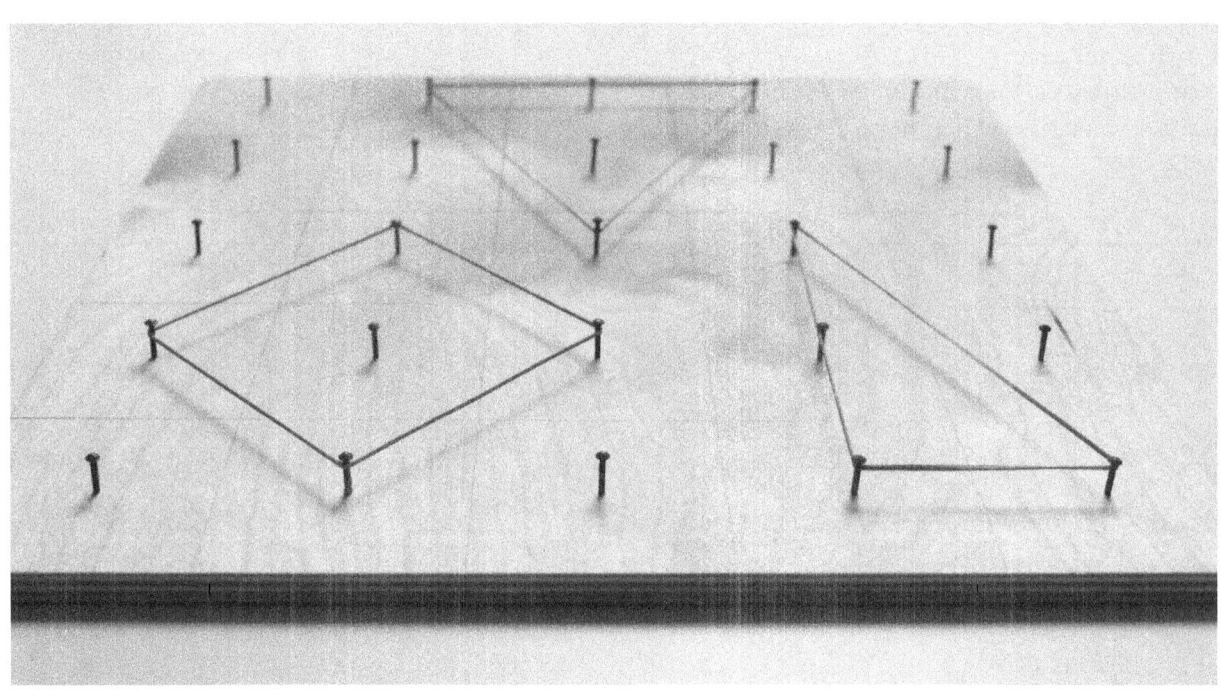

The Geoboard is one of Dr. Caleb Gattegno's many contributions to the teaching of mathematics. While in the hospital and lying on his back, Dr. Gattegno used the ceiling tiles as a way to model geometric shapes. Out of this he created the Geoboard, used in mathematics classrooms throughout the world, though few people are aware of their inventor.

An Original Thinker

Dr. Diane Larsen-Freeman

When I was first introduced to the ideas of Caleb Gattegno in the late 1970s, I must confess that their wisdom was not immediately obvious to me. In fact, if truth be told, I was rather resistant to them initially. It was only because colleagues in the MAT program at the School for International Training (SIT), whom I respected a great deal, were so positive about his teachings that I eventually opened myself to them. I am very grateful for the example set by my colleagues because much of what Gattegno said and wrote has become the foundation of my own teaching practice.

I teach a linguistics course every fall to University of Michigan undergraduate students, entitled "Perspectives on Second Language Learning and Second Language Instruction." There is a Gattegno-inspired reason that the two major foci of this course are sequenced this way. I begin the course by telling my students that teaching begins with learning. During the first module of the course, we examine what it takes to learn and to know another language. An assignment for this module is for students to write personal, reflective, language learning autobiographies. The autobiographies are quite remarkable, if for no other reason than that the students often remark that they have never before been in touch with their own learning, nor met one of their teachers who showed interest in it.

We go on in the course to look at second language instruction in light of the awareness that they have come to about learning. I take them through a series of experiential exercises, which I have designed to "educate their awareness." I set before them challenges, which I believe they can face, and I stand back to watch the students grapple with them. I try not to do for them what they can do for themselves. My only guidance is to question them — I have come to believe in the power of a good question. Perhaps it is poetic justice that not all my students take so kindly to my approach initially. They want me to tell them the answers to the questions I pose, and not have to work to discover for themselves. Often, though, they come around, and just as I witnessed at SIT when Gattegno would visit, frequently it is the students who are the most vociferous in their initial response to the teaching who become most ardent in their support later.

Gattegno's ideas have influenced me in many ways beyond those that I consciously draw on in this course. In fact, I find it disconcerting, but nonetheless true, that there are times when I think I have come up with an original thought, one that I speak and write about, only to later realize that its seed was sown by Gattegno a long time ago.

To give one example, I have been preoccupied for some time with what Alfred North Whitehead called "the inert knowledge problem" — the failure of students to use what they have learned in the classroom once they are outside of the classroom. I pondered the problem for some time, and I did a fairly extensive search of the psychological literature dealing with the failure of "transfer." What I came up with from the literature review was the need for the teacher to create "psychologically authentic" learning opportunities, where the conditions of learning and the conditions of use are aligned. Only then will transfer take place, the psychologists say. Psychologically authentic learning opportunities are ones where students take initiative to use language in meaningful ways in keeping with the stage that they have reached. Although I never heard Gattegno use the term "psychologically authentic learning opportunities," it seems to me that that was precisely what he was creating with his Silent Way approach.

In addition, I note that researchers are only now discovering what Gattegno taught so many years ago about the contribution of sleep to learning. Further, "my" notions of learning not being caused by teaching, of the usefulness of organic syllabi, and of the fractal structure of language are all ideas that I thought of as original at first, and only later came to realize my indebtedness to Gattegno for them. His original and provocative thinking, his brilliant insights, and his perseverance in following a question where it took him will all continue to influence me and bear fruit in my own professional and personal development.

Silence Amplifies: The Loud Silent Way

Adrian Underhill

Dr. G once told a story from his time in Ethiopia of seeing many villagers gather for a meeting, and wondering how such a large and vociferous group were going to hear each other in the important matters to be discussed. But once it started, everyone was so quiet and listened with such attention that each person could hear and be heard easily. His conclusion? That silence amplifies.

A discovery for me has been how a certain quality of 'silence' can render learning audible, visible, tangible and palpable. As a teacher, I can see what I am working with, and what to do next, and not have to guess what is going on in the students, since I am learning them just as they are learning the language.

I cannot really separate myself as a teacher from myself as a learner. I am all the time called a teacher, a teacher of people learning English, a teacher of other teachers, and a teacher of myself, but all this teaching is dependent on my learning. To assist my students' learning I need to be learning alongside them, and in the same moment. I gradually came to see how my learning and my teaching are not two separate activities but two sides of the same coin.

A principle that Dr. G stated when I first met him in London in July 1976 was summed up in his phrase, "to put on spectacles that enable us to see learning," which comes to mind whenever I find myself witnessing the inner moves of learning taking place in me, or a student, or both at the same time. Being sometimes able to see learning as it happens is partly due to my realizing that there is something to see, and partly due to the instruments I use that allow learning to become visible. These instruments do several things at the same time: they allow focus on specific learnings that are the right size for the learner, they enable the inner moves of that learning to be visible, and they enable me also to engage in 'learning the student,' so we are both on the 'same side of the learning fence,' as Dr. G put it.

At this first meeting, I experienced Dr. G's uncompromising stance in front of the traditional

> "If I am watchful I can see how learning finds its way into the nooks and crannies of a challenge"

teaching orthodoxy – a stance I came to admire deeply. Though it was never easy, even for him, it came with the territory he had mapped out. At the end of that meeting I went up to him and said, "You are doing something and I want more of it. How can I start?" "You have already started," was his typically succinct and probably kind reply. In 1977, I invited Cecilia Bartoli to give two weekend seminars in the Queens Hotel in Hastings, and myself and many others never looked back.

The instruments I use to teach the Silent Way may be objects like Cuisenaire Rods, or charts, or the use of the pointer. They may be attributes such as patience, curiosity, intuition, or timeliness. And they may be procedures like rephrasing sentences, making a lot of language from few words, letting some small observation hang in silence for a moment longer, enabling students to invent what they can from what they've got, or simply reducing interferences in the natural processes of learning. Dr. G would say that the problem with learning is never in the learning, but interference in the learning, and one of the qualities of silence is the reduction of such.

Some of the interfering behaviors I find in myself as a teacher include over-eagerness to help, the need to be liked, impatience, wishing that the student would somehow be different from the way they are, seeing mistakes as merely a nuisance, equating student correctness with student learning, and the subtle encouragement of them to please me, and so on. When I first met the phrase "The Subordination of Teaching to Learning," I heard it as saying something like "teaching exists solely to support learning, so get your priorities the right way around, and let your teaching be guided by the students' learning." As I accumulated experiences of 'seeing learning,' this phrase revealed further subtle insights. For example, if I am watchful I can see how learning finds its way into the nooks and crannies of a challenge, rather like a fine penetrating oil, and how the activity of teaching can shape itself according to the flowing contours of this learning. Therefore the attention of the teacher has to be with the learner, to see what these shapes might be and to shape any intervention accordingly. Thus the teacher teaches by learning the student, yet at the end of it the student can say, "In fact, I did it myself, but I could not have done it without you (and your learning of me)."

I began to see this after a small episode at a seminar in the early '80s when Dr. G proposed we take it in turns to facilitate some activity for the group. In the middle of my turn there was suddenly a roar from the back, "Stop teaching!" he bellowed. It was shocking and hilarious, and in that moment a penny dropped. I had been immersed in my "teacher's agenda" quite oblivious of the students' learning or how it could guide me.

If I ask myself what draws me to this way of teaching then I might answer that I have found in the Subordination of Teaching to Learning an experience of becoming more myself, and also a source of a great joy. My sense is that at these times I am connected to evolution itself, and to whatever it is that moves it. I experience this also when I am engaged in my learning along with others who are similarly engaged. Then I experience a kind of community of engagement, a collective shift of learning, and something moves within and between us. As Dr. G said, learning is contagious, and perhaps also bigger than us.

I have added to my first understanding of the Subordination of Teaching to Learning by seeing that I cannot separate my teaching from my learning or from the students learning, they are all part of the same equation. And as I get closer to my learning I can not only see it, but feel it as uplifting and joyful, and ordinary. And just as the village meeting was amplified by the quality of silence, so the small moves of learning become louder due to qualities of silence that arise quite naturally when I allow learning to teach me.

***

We had been through a long and challenging day, that seemed to end in a near riot. I was sitting beside Dr. G at dinner, and he said to me:

"You know, this is a very good way of working."

"What way of working?" I inquired naively, still quaking from the potential civil disturbance whose flames he appeared to have been heartily fanning, while also marveling at his relaxed nonchalance.

"Finding the baby in us," he said, "that is always the place to start."

So this is the Silent Way!
原点へ近づく喜び

Etsuko Nagasawa

Ever since encountering the Silent Way in 1991, I have been studying French and English the Silent Way, participating in Silent Way workshops, and teaching Japanese the Silent Way. Some 20 years have passed in the meantime.

The opportunities given to me for being in touch with Dr. Gattegno have been limited to watching his Silent Way videos, listening to the audio recordings, and reading his books and newsletters. The only experience of meeting Dr. Gattegno for me, therefore, was through the 70 hour ESL the Silent Way video program. When I saw it, I was probably already in my third year of teaching the Silent Way.

Driven by a strong conviction that I was not going to miss a moment of what goes on in the classes, I viewed the video with tremendous curiosity and concentration. Because of the energy the Silent Way embraces, which can make me aware of the enormous power I store in myself, I'm still filled with an electric thrill when I recall that experience.

My eyes were opened with a new awareness when I observed that there, the teacher was not teaching, not to speak of his silence. I thought I was aiming at teaching my classes like that every day, but I was filled with my own endless questions such as, "What is the teacher doing? What are the learners doing?" and I realized that one question gave birth to a new one, and they kept on growing in my consciousness. Overwhelmed again and again by the energy that was involved, and overcome by the feeling of awe, I thought, "So, this is the Silent Way!" I finally found the trigger which helped me to return to a brisk-minded novice. What hit me then and there has become my motivation to advance, and I cherish it even now.

At the same time, as I did not have the opportunity to meet Dr. Gattegno in person, the anecdotes I occasionally heard from Fusako Allard reverberate in my heart, making me feel his personality vividly, and make me able to get in contact with his firm conviction. The messages that Fusako would unfold with, "At such a time, Dr. Gattegno would say . . ." gave me the frame of reference to capture the Silent Way from its original point.

I feel that it would be difficult for me, even if given 100 or 200 years, to become a person who can truly practice the Silent Way and the theory behind the Gattegno Approach. For some reason, however, Gattegno's words hit my mind with a thud whenever I reach for his writings. It is meaningful for me, as who I am now, to be able to see that clues are hidden in those words for me to come a step nearer to something substantial.

Meeting the Silent Way, the meaning of 'to learn' for me has become 'to meet the unknown' and 'to admit my ignorance.' I have learned both the joy of meeting new awarenesses, and the humbleness of accepting my ignorant self with docility. I can declare I love 'teaching' and 'learning.' My present objective is to conduct such classes where "each student can feel for himself his own progress."

I would like to take this opportunity to express my heart-felt gratitude for the support I get for my daily classes, and the power I get to continue my journey from Dr. Gattegno's Silent Way.

原点へ近づく喜び

1991年、サイレント・ウェイに出会って以来、フランス語や英語を学び、ワークショップに出たり、日本語を教えたりする中で、約20年…。

Dr.ガテーニョに触れる機会は、過去のワークショップの記録テープやインタビューのビデオ、著書、ニューズレターなどだけだが、唯一Dr.ガテーニョに出会えたのが『70 hour ESL the Silent Way Course』のビデオだ。まだ、サイレント・ウェイで教えることを始めて3年目ぐらいの時だった。そこで起こっていることを一瞬たりとも見逃すまいという思いにかられ、ものすごい好奇心とものすごい集中力でビデオを見た。やはりサイレント・ウェイには、自分の中にある、すごい力を実感させてくれるエネルギーがあるのだろう。その時のことは、今思い起こしてもワクワクする体験だ。

そこでは、教師の「沈黙」は言うまでもなく、教師が言語を「教えていない」ことを目の当たりにし、あらためて目を見開いた。日々、そんな授業を目指していたはずなのに、「教師は何をしているのか、学習者は何をしているのか…」と、次々と湧いてくる疑問。そして、一つの疑問は新たな疑問となり内面で成長し続けることを実感した。そこに存在するエネルギーに圧倒され、「これがサイレント・ウェイなのか？！」と打ちのめされるような気持ちを何度も味わいながらも、「ああ、これがサイレント・ウェイなんだなあ…」と清々しい気持ちで初心に戻るきっかけを得た。その時のこの気持ちが、今でも私自身が前に進むチャレンジの原動力になっている。

また、Dr.ガテーニョに直接出会う機会のなかった私にとって、アラード房子氏から折りにふれ聞くエピソードは、どれも心に余韻を残すもので、その人柄を生き生きと感じること、その揺るぎない信念に触れることができる。「…そんな時、ガテーニョ先生はよくこう言っていたよ…」というメッセージが、サイレント・ウェイを原点からとらえる視点を与えてくれる。

サイレント・ウェイ、ひいてはガテーニョアプローチの理念の忠実な実践者となるには、あと100年、200年あっても無理だろうと思えることだが、著書などに触れると、Dr.ガテーニョの言葉は、なぜかずしんと心に響いてくる。本質的なものに一歩近づくヒントが隠されているように思えるだけでも、今の私には十分意味のあることだ。

サイレント・ウェイに出会い、私にとって「『学ぶ』ことは、未知に出会い、無知を覚る」という意味になった。新しいことに出会う喜びと、何も知らない自分自身を素直に受けとめる謙虚さを知った。そして『教える』と『学ぶ』を楽しむことができるようになったと明言できる。

今は、「一人一人の生徒が自分自身の進歩を実感できる授業」をすることが目標。Dr.ガテーニョのサイレント・ウェイが、日々の授業を支え、チャレンジを続ける力を与えてくれていることに、今あらためて心からの感動と感謝を捧げたい。§

> 教師の「沈黙」は言うまでもなく、教師が言語を「教えていない」ことを目の当たりにし、あらためて目を見開いた。

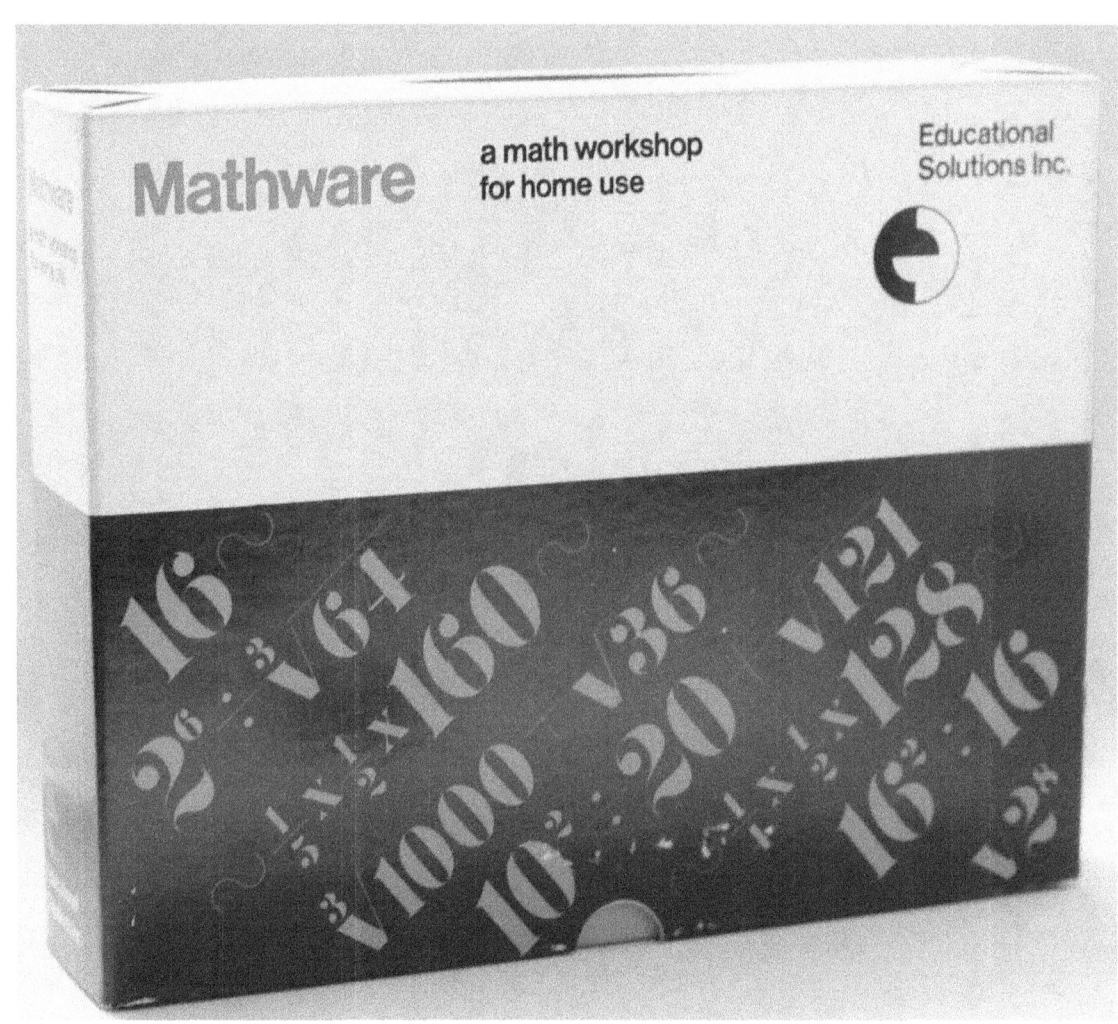

Mathware, a kit designed for the teaching of mathematics at home, created bt Dr. Gattegno in the 1980's.

"The belief that mistakes must be avoided at all cost goes against the purpose of practice, which assumes the lack of mastery and therefore the possibility of errors. If we want to be realistic, we must accept mistakes as part of learning."

– Dr. Caleb Gattegno

On Being Freer, Second Edition (2010), page 184.

Working for Caleb Gattegno

Jeremy Steele

Dr. Caleb Gattegno gave me my first employment position upon graduating from Keele University. In doing so, he ended several months of dispiriting job searching on my part, and I was immensely grateful. He took me on in his publishing company, Educational Explorers Limited, which had been described to me as "the fastest-growing educational publishing house outside London" by the professional and executive register of the labour exchange where I had in desperation finally sought help.

There were already several books in the EEL publishing list. Caleb's immediate intention at the time I was taken on in early 1963 was to produce a collection of articles he had written, in a volume to be entitled *For the Teaching of Mathematics*.

In the early '60s, the Gattegno group consisted of two Cuisenaire companies responsible for production and distribution of mathematics teaching materials, and EEL, of which I had become the sole employee. The collective staff, numbering about 15 or so, consisted of production personnel who cut, dyed, polished, boxed, and distributed Cuisenaire Rods in Reading, Berkshire, as well as about half a dozen others whose primary role was to advance Caleb's educational ideas to the public, mainly teachers. Most of this young group were recent graduates or family members, and included Caleb's daughter Lola, her husband Michael Hollyfield, Judith Wardman, Tim Crosfield and myself. We youngsters daringly referred to the maestro as 'Caleb,' though to his face I think it might have been 'Dr. G.'

Caleb showed me a pile of dusty typescripts, and explained what he had in mind. Although my title was 'assistant editor' I had neither done any editing nor been told what it entailed. So I just began reading the articles, and using a pencil. This was nearly 50 years ago, but in retrospect think I found Caleb's literary style dense and not fully idiomatic. I fancy I may have tried to simplify it, to make it more readily understandable to myself, and hence to any reader as simple as I believed myself to be. Slowly I worked through all the articles, even one I found in French among them, which I had a go at translating.

Caleb accepted my work and the volume was published. A little later he gave me more articles, and this time many of them were in French: and the outcome duly became *Volume Two*. When it was published I was astonished to find at the end of Caleb's preface: "Once again I should like to thank my young colleague Jeremy Steele for his help in making my texts more readable and for his good translations of some of my most difficult articles."

I was to work for Caleb for five years until I left to return to Australia. During this period I edited over a dozen books and as many booklets, and saw to their production through the printers, Lamport Gilbert of Gun Street. It was during this time that Words in Color, the reading program, was getting established. I went with Caleb to the printers several times to check on the production of the color charts, until he left me to supervise on my own. It was there that I learned about screens and blocks and the four-color letterpress printing process as I watched the charts coming off the presses, one by one, and talked to the machine-minders. I remember in these early days that I had seen the charts many times with their 50 or so colors, which "phoneticised written English without altering the spelling," and also how one lunchtime in London Street I resolved to learn which color stood for which sound, and had done so by the end of the day. And have never since forgotten. I was also to help Caleb with his development of the 'Lettres en Couleurs' French version of Words in Color.

I hope I may have been a slight help at least to Caleb, but it was nothing more than that. Caleb was the one with the vision and the energy and the huge agenda for getting things done. It was he who had recognized the significance of the educational tool the Belgian local primary school teacher Georges Cuisenaire had devised, and made it into a world-wide phenomenon. I recall one occasion the by-then elderly Cuisenaire, on a rare visit, staring in mystification at the Gattegno headquarters and saying in wonderment at what he had triggered off — as much to himself as to me: "C'est la compagnie que porte mon nom." Caleb had paid him a royalty on every box of Cuisenaire Rods the companies sold, and he was probably quite well off in his retirement.

film company. He hired a school room in Reading — and what better-named place might he have selected for this literacy endeavor? — along with a film crew, and had obtained a dozen or so illiterate would-be readers. This was putting money where his mouth was, for all this would have been expensive. By the close of proceedings it might be said that he succeeded, and the film was shown promotionally thereafter.

Caleb was masterfully competent, and confident, about whatever he set out to do, and could dominate

> "Caleb insisted that the learner should and would get satisfaction and motivation exclusively from his or her own knowledge of personal achievement."

Caleb had a number of aphorisms, one of which was "The Subordination of Teaching to Learning." He always avoided bestowing praise upon a learner for a progressive step made, in contrast to a common practice of heaping adulation on students for even trivial accomplishments. Caleb insisted that the learner should and would get satisfaction and motivation exclusively from his or her own knowledge of personal achievement. Many found this approach hard to accept. Another of Caleb's favorite statements, in his own inimitable idiom, was: "I can't eat and you grow fat." By this he meant that each learner has to do his or her own learning. And another, in the field of mathematics, was "algebra before arithmetic," this being the key to the use of the Cuisenaire Rods.

Caleb had, around this time, been claiming to be able to teach people to read, adult functional illiterates after a failed school career and a subsequent life experience, within a matter of hours, indeed within the course of one day, using Words in Color. This concept was taken up by *Time Magazine* in a major story on June 12, 1964. Perhaps it was this notoriety that led Caleb to the idea of his making a film to show how. There had been a previous film done by the National Film Board of Canada about him and the rods. On this later occasion, at which I was present, he would go it alone without a professional

any group. Psychology, mathematics, reading, and language teaching were some of the areas that I was aware of. In 1957, long before I had known him, he had been engaged in a literacy investigation in Ethopia, and in particular on Amharic, the official language. He had arranged like sounds in columns, however rendered in the local script. He had called the resultant sound table a "Fidel" after the Amharic word for "syallabary," or "alphabet." Subsequently he was to develop a "Fidel" for English, and another for French. I even helped a little in this venture, too, by devising sample sentences to show how the same spelling might have different sounds, as for example 'ea': "Great mean overbearing earls fear heaven heartily." But for all his language ability both as a speaker of several languages and as an analyst, Caleb always retained a heavy accent in English, just as his written English never seemed quite right to a native speaker. One word he used frequently was 'associated,' which he stressed ASSociATEd, emphasizing the first and last syllables. It always jarred, and I often wondered if I could make a difference by pointing out that the normal pronunciation of the word was assOCiated. But the moment never arrived when it seemed opportune or when I had the courage to try. For all that, it was a privilege and a pleasure to have known and had an opportunity to work with Caleb Gattegno. §

Words in Color in the classroom at the Bronx Charter School for Better Learning, 2009.

> "Teachers of reading will mainly find that the powers which help babies crack the code of the language spoken around them can be used to crack the written code much more easily than is usually believed."

— Dr. Caleb Gattegno

The Common Sense of Teaching Reading and Writing, Second Edition (2010), page 9.

Dancing a Dialogue:
Interaction with the learner and Interaction in Learning

Janice Mattina

I was one of about 10 people invited by Dr. Caleb Gattegno to attend his week-long seminar on the Subordination of Teaching to Learning, held at his offices in New York City in the winter of 1972. I learned Words in Color from my mother, Eugenie Higgins, who was the first Grade 2 teacher to use Words in Color in a public school in the USA. I had been teaching first and second grade children in public schools in Florida and California using Words in Color since 1966.

I was very excited about this invitation and I joined the group of other educators with curiosity. Among those also attending was language arts coordinator, Harriet Bentley from Rocky River, Ohio, a principal from Marin County, California, a nun, and other school administrators. We sat comfortably around the large table but were not permitted to take notes. Dr. Gattegno explained what we learned here would be within us, not on some pieces of paper.

The seminar began with the question: what is the problem of learning to read? Or, what must a child do to learn to read? We were already fumbling with that as we looked around at each other. But it became quickly apparent that Dr. Gattegno was not going to explain this to us, so we all began thinking and working. We discovered that there were five conventions of the written page that were arbitrary and therefore of necessity must be shown to the child. They were left to right, top to bottom, signs for sounds, sounds for signs, spaces between words.

Our next question was: were there any skills a child had taught himself in the acquisition of learning to talk that might be able to be used to teach him to read? After all, the printed page was the child's language just written down. If we were to read the page to the child, she would understand it. So how could we link what the child already knew, the language spoken, to what she didn't yet know, the written words? From this work we discovered the skills all children had developed in order to be speaking their native tongue. And we began to think of ways we could teach which would cause the child to use the skills she already had within her from learning to speak to learning to read. We noticed that some skills were strong and some were weak. We reasoned that we would avoid using the weakest skill, memory, and instead work with the stronger skills of visual imagery, of generalization, of stressing and ignoring, of the child's will and so on.

As we addressed those arbitrary conventions we had discussed earlier, we found that there needed to be some tools devised to help the children understand these conventions. It was then that we appreciated the coloring of the signs a, u, i, e, o, p, t, etc. so that we could speak with the child clearly without interfering with her learning. We would not call the signs by their letter names because those are not related to reading, only to spelling out loud. When we got to multiple spellings for the same sounds, (the convention is signs for sounds) again we appreciated the "bright idea" of color as Dr. Gattegno referred to the use of color coded sounds, because we didn't have to give a rule for the child to memorize or soon forget. We could simply say, we'll use this one for that word and point to the particular green spelling for 'pass' which was colored the same as the singular green 's' for 'us.'

next at that moment to facilitate our awareness so that we could know for ourselves.

So while we figured out what the problem of reading was and that the problem was now solved in the schema of Words in Color, we witnessed within ourselves what the Subordination of Teaching to Learning really was and how powerful it was for the learner. And it wasn't easy. We were held to task, we were shown respect as learners, and we were treated as if he knew we could master the task. Dr. Gattegno used a technique he called feedback. He would look pointedly at one of us and say seriously and with interest, "feedback." One would then respond from somewhere in one's being what was happening

> "Were there any skills a child had taught himself in the acquisition of learning to talk that might be able to be used to teach him to read?"

We were faced with one really challenging difference between the spoken language and the written language that needed our attention. The spoken language was in time and the written language was in space. How could we connect the two so that the child would read with the speed of speech? Another of Dr. Gattegno's bright ideas became known and understood, the pointer. By using the pointer, quickly and precisely, one could restore speed to the written words as they became oral language.

By the end of the week, we had learned a lot and Dr. Gattegno hadn't lectured to us; he hadn't been the fount of information from which knowledge flowed as in the traditional model, where teaching and the formulation of lessons were more important than learning. His focus was on our learning. And he almost danced a dialogue with us as he responded to our feedback. By interpreting our responses, our feedback, Dr. Gattegno was able to know what to do

within. After one of us spoke our feedback, Dr. Gattegno would go to another student and say, "feedback." He wouldn't say to anyone, "Oh, good, yes, you got it right." Instead, he just listened. It took a while to get used to that, so dependent had we become upon teachers to tell us if we were right or not. But we learned that what we said in our feedback was valid because it was ours and we could stand on that securely.

Only awareness is educable in human beings and by subordinating one's lessons to the responses of the learner, the learner is able to do what she has done in all of her life before she entered formal educational institutions; she is able to teach herself, to continue to be her own best teacher. She is permitted to be herself. What a gift and what potential that presents. This is our lesson as teachers, this is the message of Dr. Caleb Gattegno.

a	u	i	e	e	e	o	ö	ü		eu
	ou	ie	er	ä	ä			y		äu

a	u	i		e	e					ei
ah	uh	ih		ä	ä	o	ö	ü		eih
aa	ou	ie		äh	äh	oh	öh	üh		ai
		ieh		eh		oo	eu	y		
				ee		ow				au
										auh

ABCDEFGHIJKLMNOPQRSTUVWXYZ

d	r	n	m	l	b	s	s	w	n		z
dd	rr	nn	mm	ll	bb	sch		v	ng		zz
						ch					tz
											c

t	s	p	f		g	ch	ch	j	k	h		x
tt	ss	pp	ff		gg	g			y	g		qu
th	ß	b	v						i	ck		r
d		z		ph						ch		er
dt										c		g
										qu		j

The German Fidel, printed in 1987. ©Educational Solutions Worldwide Inc.

Une fortune sur un plateau

Suzanne Lachaise

Ecrire au sujet de Gattegno est un défi d'importance ; comment en effet résumer en quelques lignes les bouleversement intervenus dans ma vie de par ma rencontre avec cet homme d'exception ?

Après avoir « fait du Freinet » et examiné des pédagogies (Ecole Nouvelle, Montessori…) offrant plus de solutions et des angles de vue différents de ce que proposaient tant la formation professionnelle de l'Ecole Normale d'Instituteurs que les standards éducatifs – de mise dans les années soixante – après avoir imaginé et réalisé des matériels et des manières de faire en rapport avec ceux des besoins de mes élèves que je comprenais, dans des classes réservées aux élèves en difficultés, après m'être posé beaucoup de questions sur l'apprentissage et encore plus sur l'improbable efficacité de l'enseignement, aux plans techniques et épistémologiques, j'ai eu l'occasion –et la chance – de fréquenter un groupe d'enseignants en recherche qui semblaient bien avoir des pistes correspondant à mes propres démarches.

Ces enseignants avaient fait un séminaire d'été avec un pédagogue au nom étrange pour mes oreilles francophones : Caleb Gattegno. A leur contact, je découvris que toutes mes questions avaient des réponses intelligentes, techniques, que l'examen révélaient issues d'un bon sens indéniable, et fleurant le mystère de fondements plus subtils à découvrir. En outre, j'en repartis avec des questions qui ne m'ayant jamais effleurée, me mobilisèrent.

Le plus grand étonnement me vint de la simplicité des solutions alliées à une totale complexité. Je saurais plus tard faire la part du contact de la Totalité d'un univers donné et de ses parties constituantes, clés des éclairages multiples sous lesquels considérer l'univers en question.

Nous donner à voir d'un seul regard toute l'orthographe du français (de l'anglais, du russe…), tous les repésentants des sons d'une langue, toute la numération, etc. demande de son concepteur une disposition d'esprit particulière que l'analyse du problème et la synthèse des résultats ne suffisent pas seuls à expliquer.

Engagée dans cette course au trésor, séminaire après séminaire, je découvris peu à peu certaines des pistes offertes à notre réflexion, au long des 19 dernières années de sa vie.

Quel bonheur d'avoir pu transformer ma classe en centre d'expérimentation active, en laboratoire où élèves et maîtresse furent des chercheurs enthousiastes, malgré les échecs et les tâtonnements infructueux, ragaillardis par ces moments lumineux de découvertes, d'harmonie, de complicité, de réussites, qui stimulaient chacun de nous pour continuer l'aventure, la quête des prises de conscience – conscientes – de nos potentialités, mises en œuvre dans les apprentissages pour mes élèves et dans l'apprentissage de l'enseignement pour leur maîtresse.

Je suis consciente de parler de moi et non de Gattegno. Je crois que je ne suis pas capable de parler de cet homme, cela signifierait que je le connais. Je l'ai rencontré, fréquenté, côtoyé. Je l'ai beaucoup écouté, pas toujours compris. J'ai toujours été impressionnée par sa puissance mentale, par son intransigeance, son absence totale de complaisance et ce qu'il a appelé son a-moralité « je n'ai pas de morale, j'ai une éthique ». Aucune concession mais une grande compassion. Tant de facettes parfois apparemment contradictoires me font dire que cette personne particulière était bien trop complexe – tout comme son œuvre d'ailleurs – pour que je puisse prétendre « connaître » Gattegno.

De son enseignement je pris ce que mes propres aptitudes me permirent d'en retirer, consciente de son regret : « Je vous offre une fortune sur un plateau et vous prenez un centime ! ».

Dixit sa mère, « la vérité a de petites jambes, elle met du temps à se faire connaître ». Mais elle avance, n'est-ce pas ?

§

Gattegno and the McCarthy-Towne Elementary School

J. Parker Damon

The McCarthy-Towne Elementary School opened its doors to almost 600 students in September 1971. Dr. Gattegno provided the collection of Acton parents, school officials, and teachers who created the school during the preceding two or three years with the philosophical educational foundation on which the school was based. His ideas on how to teach reading with Words in Color, how to teach arithmetic and mathematics with Algebricks, and how to approach student learning of the other core subjects, served as the basis for all the curricula used at the school for the first few years.

The last half of the 1960s through the mid 1970s was an emotionally volatile time due to social, political, and educational upheavals. In Acton, Dr. Gattegno's ideas, methods, and materials challenged the status quo that the town's four other public elementary schools represented. McCarthy-Towne was created as an alternative to those schools. News articles, editorials, and letters to the editor decried the creation of a non-traditional elementary school that would employ unusual materials and methods, encourage informality in the relationships between students, teachers, parents, and other school staff, rely on student-teacher-parent conferences rather than report cards and grades, and empower teachers and parents to be voting participants in setting school objectives and priorities, policies and procedures, and evaluation of whether or not students were learning successfully and satisfactorily.

The parents of the almost 600 students in grades one through six who chose to enroll their children were taking a big risk in sending their children to MCT. There was a of lot hostility expressed toward them and the school. It was the power of Dr. Gattegno's ideas about how children should be educated and his personal ability to explain and demonstrate why his ideas made sense that convinced these parents to take the risk.

The faculty and staff who chose to be part of the startup of McCarthy-Towne were also taking a risk. Most of them were hired the preceding spring and early summer by a group of parents and the assistant superintendent. As one was hired, she or he would become part of the hiring group. I was the last person hired. I was interviewed by all the faculty and an equal number of parents, and they each had one vote. This form of democracy was used to make all major decisions regarding the school's operation from then on. Subordinating teaching to learning – a prime component of Dr. G's work – meant to us that teachers needed a lot more autonomy, authority, and responsibility than was permitted or desired in most schools at that time. If the instructional starting point was to be a focus on student learning, then teachers needed to have control over what is taught, what materials and methods are used, and how and when they are used.

Dr. Gattegno conducted two week-long workshops for the faculty and a number of parents during the summer before the school opened. Two of his Educational Solutions staff, one a specialist in the use of Words in Color, and the other in the use of Algebricks and other Educational Solutions math material, worked with teachers that summer and continued as resident staff trainers at the school on a full time basis for the next three years. Dr. Gattegno would return to McCarthy-Towne three or four times a year for at least three years to continue the school community's exploration and implementation of his ideas, materials, and methods. The faculty wanted to introduce foreign language instruction using his Silent Way approach and worked with him throughout one of the early years to see how feasible doing so might be. Unfortunately the reality of the times did not permit this initiative to get started. But, his other ideas took hold and some are still in place today.

I wondered during the latter part of the 1970s why Dr. Gattegno's ideas took hold at MCT and how MCT survived those turbulent times while other equally innovative schools did not. I now think MCT's durability came from the lucky combination of factors that came together at that time in Acton: the parents and school committee members who wanted to create educational learning experiences different from what was then available; the heady expansionism of public education during the 1960s; the hiring of an enthusiastic, smart, risk-taking young staff; and the ideas, methods, and materials presented by Dr. Gattegno in person and in his writings. The particularly helpful books at the time were *Towards a Visual Culture - Educating Through Television* and *What We Owe Children - The Subordination of Teaching to Learning*. Ronald Gross of the *New York Times* wrote about the latter book, "If Gattegno is right, then much of what goes for teaching in our schools to-day is wrong." [Quoted on the cover of *What We Owe Children*.]

"It was the power of Dr. Gattegno's ideas about how children should be educated and his personal ability to explain and demonstrate why his ideas made sense that convinced these parents to take the risk."

This latter book provided parents and teachers with much of the vision and purpose for what they wanted MCT to be like. Gattegno's ideas, more than him as a person, provided the glue that helped keep the school together during the 1970s. Caleb himself was not necessarily the right person for everyone at the school. To some he was a cult-like guru, for others an overbearing pedagogue, but for most parents and teachers his ideas were those of an insightful and challenging educational innovator. His ideas about the power of children to learn, his focus on what was at the core of learning, his use of questions to search for many possible answers rather than only one right one, and the games he created to arrive at each answer from a child's point of view was key. Dr. Gattegno's creative intellect and drive was what held us together as we sought to make learning a better experience for each of our students. §

" Our conclusion is that this computer courseware represents a multiple breakthrough in the field of education. It displays many criteria needed to define proper uses of the computer for education. It shows in concrete terms that major educational challenges can be solved and at costs in time and money ridiculously low compared with present-day costs for instruction or/and remediation. It opens the way to enlarging the curriculum, modernizing it, individualizing it, so as to serve students with every kind of gifts or impediments. It puts education technically within the modern industrial revolution — also called electronic, since students in their brains as well as on the screen, manipulate electrons. "

From the newsletter *Two of Our Breakthroughs*, by Dr. Caleb Gattegno (Vol. XI #3-4, February/ April 1980).

One of Dr. Gattegno's early companies, Educational Explorers, published the series *My Life, My Work*, which published books by over 65 authors, discussing the attributes of their various careers. Today this type of career help book is common, but at the time the concept was unheard of.

Changing Expectations
Le trajet d'un métier

Sylvain Dufros

Unlike other people, for whom work as a teacher is a vocation, I never thought about pedagogy in general, or about language learning in particular. I became a French teacher by chance, as I could have become an electrician or a musician. I wanted to work in Japan, and teaching was the first job I found. The school, where I still work, uses the Gattegno Approach, and so in addition to having no experience in teaching, I also did not choose to work with this approach; it was thrust upon me.

correct sentence in an acceptable time! I had not thought about how I learned to speak English, a learning that had not been done at school with a traditional education, but rather outside, with regular use.

In my classes, I tried to reproduce what I imagined to be an ideal class, incorporating in some way or another the approach material. I stretched the phases of work on the Sound-Color Chart to save time, and

> "[Teaching is] a job where you can be rewarded in the moment and over time, first by the observation of the awarnesses among your own students, and then by the progress they make every day."

My start as a teacher was catastrophic, as I was not adhering to the approach, which didn't fit to the image I had made of the role of a teacher in my 20 years of schooling. I was convinced that nothing was like a good book to learn. I was convinced that listening to the professor, who knows everything, would make one know as much as him.

My first real disappointment was not being able to speak Japanese upon arriving in Japan, even though I had read all the grammar books that I considered necessary to achieve this. I could not produce a

I tried to delay as much as possible the moment I would be confronted with the real problems of the class. I also found myself repeatedly trying to explain a word in French, and drowning my students and myself with dozens of new words, just to explain a single one. It also seemed impossible for me to manage classes with more than two students with this approach. I was aware that my students were not progressing, but I thought it was the daily lot of all teachers, and that I was not the cause. For me, it was the students who did not show good will, or were not made to learn languages.

But gradually, through these experiences in class, from my readings, and meetings and seminars about Gattegno's work, my prejudices have fallen one after another, and let me see a wide field to explore. I realized that mathematics is in all languages and at all levels. Isn't a sentence a sequence of sounds and words that can be reversed, added onto, or repeated, to provide a result? And like a math problem, doesn't it give its full meaning when we substitute all abstract words with more concrete ones? There are no math people or literacy people. It's just something traditional education makes us believe to justify the failure of some students in some subjects at school.

So I changed my way of thinking, and instead of interpreting the approach to make it match my expectations, I did the opposite by expressing myself as a teacher through the approach.

A fundamental principle that was difficult to grasp and put into practice was the Subordination of Teaching to Learning. It was something that didn't seem natural to me at first, but achieving it opens up endless possibilities. Each individual is different and reacts differently to what happens in the classroom. You can't work the same way with all students. The routine does not exist in a class using Gattegno approaches. This is what now makes me think that teaching is the most interesting work, and also the most difficult. It's also a job where you can be rewarded in the moment and over time, first by the observation of the awarnesses among your own students, and then by the progress they make every day.

For me, Gattegno and his work now go beyond my teaching time, and extend to my everyday life. It's a new way of looking at the world and yourself, and in everything I learn now, I'm in this state of mind. My two children are also a privileged field of investigation, especially for language learning. They teach me daily about their ways of thinking and working, and every day I use this to take care of their education, and as much as I can, to provide them what traditional education is unable to give them.

I have a special thought for all teachers who, although they put their heart and all their knowledge into their work, don't see their students progress, simply because they do not know that the work can be done differently.

Le trajet d'un métier

Contrairement à d'autres personnes, pour qui le travail d'enseignant est une vocation, je ne m'étais jamais interrogé sur la pédagogie en général, ni sur l'apprentissage des langues en particulier. Je suis devenu professeur de français par hasard, comme j'aurais pu devenir électricien ou musicien. Je voulais travailler au Japon, et professeur a été le premier poste que j'ai trouvé. L'école dans laquelle je travaille utilise l'approche Gattegno, et donc en plus de n'avoir aucune expérience dans l'enseignement, je n'ai pas non plus choisi de travailler avec cette approche par affinité, elle m'a été imposée.

Mes débuts en tant qu'enseignant ont donc été catastrophiques, n'adhérant pas moi-même à cette approche, qui remettait en cause l'image que je m'étais faite du rôle d'un enseignant, par mes vingt années de scolarité. J'étais sûr de la réalité du clivage scientifique / littéraire. J'étais persuadé que rien ne valait un bon livre pour apprendre. J'étais convaincu qu'écouter le professeur, celui qui savait, me permettrait d'en savoir autant que lui.

Ma première vraie désillusion a été de ne pas pouvoir parler japonais en arrivant au Japon, alors que j'avais lu auparavant tous les livres de grammaire que je jugeais nécessaires pour y parvenir. Je ne pouvais pas produire une phrase correcte dans un délai acceptable ! Je n'avais pas encore réfléchi à la façon dont j'avais appris à parler anglais, apprentissage qui ne s'était pas fait à l'école par un enseignement traditionnel, mais bien au contraire à l'extérieur, par une utilisation régulière.

Dans mes classes, j'essayais donc de reproduire ce que j'imaginais être une classe idéale, en y intégrant tant bien que mal le matériel de l'approche. J'allongeais ainsi les phases de travail sur le tableau de sons pour gagner du temps, et je cherchais à retarder le plus possible le moment où je serais confronté aux vrais problèmes de la classe. Je me suis aussi retrouvé à maintes reprises à tenter d'expliquer un mot en français, et à noyer mes étudiants, et moi-même, sous

(Dufros Cont.)
des dizaines de mots nouveaux, pour en expliquer un seul à l'origine. Il me semblait aussi impossible de gérer par cette approche des classes de plus de deux étudiants. J'étais conscient que mes étudiants ne progressaient pas, mais je pensais que c'était le lot quotidien de tous les professeurs, et que je n'en étais pas la cause. Pour moi, c'étaient les étudiants qui ne faisaient pas preuve de bonne volonté, ou qui n'étaient pas faits pour apprendre les langues.

subordination de l'enseignement à l'apprentissage. Travailler sur l'élève était quelque chose qui ne me semblait pas au premier abord naturel, mais y parvenir ouvre des possibilités infinies. Chaque individu est différent et réagit différemment à ce qui se passe en classe. On ne peut travailler de la même façon avec tous les étudiants, et la routine n'existe donc pas dans une classe Gattegno. Ce qui en fait maintenant pour moi le travail le plus intéressant, et

> " [Enseigner c'est] un métier où l'on peut être récompensé dans l'instant et sur la durée, d'abord par l'observation des prises de conscience chez ses étudiants, et ensuite par leurs progrès jour après jour. "

Mais petit à petit, de par ces expériences en classe, de mes lectures, et des réunions et séminaires sur le travail de Gattegno auxquels j'ai participé, mes préjugés sont tombés l'un après l'autre, et m'ont laissé face à un vaste champ à explorer. J'ai pris conscience que les mathématiques sont dans toutes les langues, et à tous les niveaux. Une phrase n'est-elle pas une suite de sons puis de mots qui peuvent s'intervertir, s'additionner, se répéter, et tout ça pour fournir un résultat ? Et tout problème de mathématiques ne prend-il pas tout son sens quand on substitue toutes les abstractions par des mots plus concrets ? Il n'y a pas de mathématiciens et de littéraires. C'est simplement ce que veut nous faire croire l'éducation traditionnelle, pour justifier les échecs de certains élèves dans certaines matières.

J'ai donc changé ma façon de faire, et au lieu d'interpréter l'approche pour qu'elle corresponde à mes attentes, j'ai fait le chemin inverse en m'exprimant à travers elle (s'exprimer ayant ici le sens de conduire une classe).

Un des principes fondamentaux qu'il m'a été difficile à appréhender et à mettre en pratique, c'est la

aussi le plus difficile. C'est aussi un métier où l'on peut être récompensé dans l'instant et sur la durée, d'abord par l'observation des prises de conscience chez ses étudiants, et ensuite par leurs progrès jour après jour.

Pour moi, Gattegno et son travail ne se limitent maintenant plus seulement à mon travail, mais s'est étendu à la vie quotidienne. C'est une nouvelle façon d'appréhender les choses, de voir le monde et de se voir soi-même, et tous les apprentissages que je fais actuellement, je les fais dans cet état d'esprit. Mes deux enfants sont aussi un terrain d'investigation privilégié, notamment pour l'apprentissage des langues. Ils m'en apprennent tous les jours sur leur fonctionnement, et tous les jours je m'en sers pour m'occuper de leur éducation, et dans la mesure du possible, leur fournir ce que l'éducation traditionnelle n'est pas capable de leur donner.

J'ai une pensée particulière pour tous les professeurs qui, bien qu'ils mettent tout leur cœur et tout leur savoir à l'ouvrage, ne voient pas venir les résultats escomptés, comme c'était le cas pour moi, tout simplement parce qu'ils n'ont pas conscience que le travail peut être fait différemment.

A Letter to Dr. G.

Dr. Barbara Villez

My daughter who, from the day of her birth, was brought up in two languages, went to a bilingual Montessori school in Paris. The school preferred that she learn to read in English first and for months I played along, without the slightest twinge, as she sounded out words passing through alphabet names (beh- ah- te, bat). This lasted for weeks and I felt she was not getting anywhere and was starting to lose interest.

I finally brought out the first English reading chart and we spent a couple of hours playing on it, so she could become familiar with the color code. When she got the idea and knew to say what she saw being pointed to, I put another chart up on a kitchen cabinet and we started to play a little while whenever we were in the kitchen. Preparing dinner, for example, I would ask her to touch a word and I would then pronounce it. After several days of that, we would do the opposite: I would say a word and she had to find it. Then I asked her to read a word that I would show on the first chart. Later I put up more charts on more cabinets and we had a lot more ground to cover. Then we alternated these activities and combined them. Soon we started putting words together and made short, sometimes silly sentences. We laughed and enjoyed the time. When she got distracted, we let it go until the next time, but often I was the first to want to stop and go into another room.

After a few weeks of this, not many, three, four, maybe five at most, I put all the charts up on the wall beside her bed in the bedroom.

One day, while dressing for school, she turned around and asked me what "anxious" meant. My eyes scanned the charts and I found that word way down the wall to the right and realized she was reading nearly any word now, on her own, silently, and that she was at the stage of acquiring vocabulary through reading.

We had done so little; just a few fun moments and she had learned to read. The following year as the school agreed for her to 'start learning how to read' in French, I quietly put the French charts up in the kitchen (the English charts were still in her room) and in one week, she had worked that code out and there was never any problem with reading after that.

My daughter must have been five when this started, but when she was seven in 1988, she suddenly said to me that she wanted to write a letter to Dr. Gattegno. Very surprised, I asked why and she answered, "Because thanks to him I can read." I said we would write the letter the next day. The next morning I found the letter announcing Dr. G's death in my mailbox.

> There is no reason, no content, no situation that can ever justify a joyless class.

Dr. G marked the lives of my children, as he did those of my students without their ever knowing him. It is incredible how the materials he created have been able to help people he never met overcome potential difficulties in learning how to read, do maths or speak a foreign language. As a teacher, I learned what to look at and how to find ways to help in particular situations, as well as how to stay out of the way.

He touched my life in many ways, making me see the consequence of what goes on in schools when we forget that we are teaching people who already start out smart. I also learned that there is no reason, no content, no situation that can ever justify a joyless class. I am now at the age Gattegno was when I first met him, and I think of him when I do things to economize my energy in class since I now get more easily tired than I did when I began teaching 40 years ago, a profession I probably would have left long ago had I not met and worked with him for those short 17 years.

§

The "Only" Statements

Dr. John Mason

I first met Caleb at an intensive weekend at Charney Manor in Oxfordshire. I had just spent a year with teacher J. G. Bennett, so I was already imbued with a cosmology and weltanschauung. This made me on the one hand sensitive to what I thought Caleb was trying to achieve, but on the other hand resistant to fully getting on board with his rather different, though not incompatible, perspective. I had several opportunities to attend Caleb's seminars, and to work through some of his writing at different times.

Of the many stimulating and attention-shifting things that I learned from Caleb (for example, "I made my brain"), the one that has perhaps played the most significant role is the notion of awareness. Having worked rather hard for some time on the notion of awareness as a form of consciousness, I felt that I had some direct experience with what might be meant by "awareness of awareness," which helped me make sense of the origins of various disciplines, particularly mathematics. With the notion of awareness being the origin, the affordance of action beautifully extends and unifies somatic and conscious actions.

During my time with Bennett I encountered the ancient Upanishadic metaphor for the human psyche as a chariot:

The chariot consists of a carriage or chariot (associated with the body or with behavior), horses (associated with the emotions and-or the senses) and a driver (associated with the intellect). The owner of the chariot is associated with will or intention, or perhaps even attention.

This image gave me a metaphoric structure for integrating the human psyche of cognition, affect and behavior. When I encountered Caleb's memorable assertion "Only awareness is educable," it made immediate sense to me, and without further thought it naturally extended itself to two further "only" statements: Only behavior is trainable, only emotion is harnessable.

I find it much more attractive to think in terms of awareness, behavior and emotion than the rather dry terms cognition, enaction and affect. The force of the "only" in each assertion helps make sense of the endemic tension between relational and instrumental understanding, between process and concept. Furthermore, it acts as a reminder that all three components are essential to deep learning.

There is much more to the chariot: the chariot itself needs looking after, by the driver, and the whole needs to be functioning otherwise the driver will simply not use the chariot. In other words, to function effectively it is necessary to have all the components of the psyche functioning, and in the case of learning (and hence teaching) mathematics, this means drawing upon all aspects of the learners' psyche. Early on I found it helpful to see the reins as mental imagery, the core power possessed by human beings that enables them to plan, indeed to direct and control the flow of energies that are released by the emotional parts of our various selves. I pondered for some time on the shafts, deciding that that these are the habits that lock us into certain characteristic behavior associated with the different selves that can take charge temporarily in place of the owner. (Here I am drawing also on a parallel image used by Plato to describe the human psyche in terms of a mansion with wayward servants and an owner who has gone away for a period).

I found this structure spoke to my experience, with the three "only's" forming three axes which make up the structure of the present moment, in Bennett's terms. I used this as the underlying structure for some publications for teachers, without being explicit about the axes or their origins, and then latterly as the Structure of a Mathematical Topic. This structure has informed all my publications for teachers and has been taken up by many others, unaware of its origins.

I also found it useful to apply the notion of awareness-of-awareness recursively, to shed light on the difference between doing mathematics, teaching mathematics, and teaching people to teach mathematics. In order to avoid complex compounds of awareness, I coined the terms awareness-in-discipline (awareness of awareness) and awareness-in-counsel (awareness of awareness-in-discipline), and this too has been taken up by various authors since.

§

Dr. Gattegno demonstrating Words in Color and the subordination of teaching to learning at a teacher training workshop. (Educational Solutions file photo.)

Ein Tor zu einer neuen Welt

Rosaria Dell'Eva

Als Cecilia Bartoli uns die S:W.-Tabelle mit den Englischlauten zeigte und sie beim Zeigen verband, um uns zuerst Englischwörter und dann kurze Sätze aussprechen zu lassen, öffnete sich mir ein Tor auf eine neue Welt, d.h. auf eine neue Weise, eine Fremdsprache zu erlernen. Die Idee die Lauten mit den Farben zu verbinden und sie durch Rechtecke auf einer Tabelle festzulegen, fand ich einfach großartig. Das Seminar fand an der Akademie für Handel und Tourismus, einem Sonderbetrieb der Handelskammer von Trient (Italien) statt. Es war Dezember 1984 und es fiel mir schwer, auf ein Wochenende in den Bergen zu verzichten, um Cecilias Seminar an der Akademie teilzunehmen. Unsere Ausbildung hätte hauptsächlich an den Wochenenden stattgefunden, da wir alle unter der Woche sehr beschäftigt waren; aber schon in den ersten Arbeitsstunden wurde mir klar, dass ich dabei war, etwas ganz Wichtiges und Besonderes für mich, für mein Leben und für meinen Beruf zu tun. Neue Energien ließen sich in mir spüren und ich ahnte, dass sich vieles an meiner Arbeit hätte verändern müssen, wenn ich diesem neuen innerlichen Impuls nachgegangen wäre. Die Akademie hatte nämlich ein Projekt mit der Forschungsinstitut CENSIS von Rom entworfen, um Fremdsprachenlehrer nach innovativen Unterrichtsmethoden auszubilden. Der Direktor des Instituts hatte Cecilia Bartoli in New York kennen gelernt und vor allem sie an der Arbeit gesehen, was ihn sofort beeindruckte. Sie wurde von ihm als "Silent Way Expertin" nach Italien eingeladen und ihr wurde die didaktische Leitung des Projektes und die Ausbildung der Lehrer zugeschrieben. Mein Glück war, dass sie eine Koordinatorin der verschiedenen Tätigkeiten brauchte und dass sie kein Deutsch konnte und deshalb kam ich unter anderen in Frage. Von da an dauerte unsere Zusammenarbeit mehrere Jahre und durch sie wurde mir möglich,

Doktor Gattegno kennen zu lernen und professionell erheblich zu wachsen.

Wegen meiner ständigen Fragerei schon in den ersten Stunden der Lehrerausbildung bezweifelte Cecilia, dass ich Interesse an dem neuen Approach hätte haben können aber ganz im Gegenteil war ich total ausgeflippt und von ihrer Arbeit besessen. Einige Vertretungserfahrungen an den Schulen hatte ich schon während der Studienzeit gemacht aber ab 1977 habe ich angefangen, definitiv Deutsch, zuerst an den Mittelschulen und dann an den Gymnasien, zu unterrichten. Seit langer Zeit war ich auf der Suche nach etwas Neuem und Sinnvollerem, das den Schülern ermöglichte, die deutsche Sprache auf eine kreativere und involvierende Art zu erlernen und da hatte ich sofort den Eindruck, das gefunden zu haben, wonach ich lange gesucht hatte.

Nach tiefem und langem Überlegen und Nachdenken über die Fähigkeiten, auf die man rechnen kann, wenn man unterrichtet, wurde uns nämlich von Cecilia eine für uns total neue und seltsame Weise gezeigt, eine Fremdsprache zu erlernen. Von Anfang an war es uns deutlich, dass die Lehrerin "nur" die Regisseurin war und sich an unsere Lernweise anpasste und dass sie ihre Arbeit unseren Reaktionen entsprechend immer wieder neu organisierte. Jeder war an den Situationen, die Cecilia uns präsentierte, geistig und physisch beteiligt. Die Zeit verlief schnell und jeder konnte auf dem eigenen Niveau arbeiten, da die Lerngruppe aus Lehrern bestand, die unterschiedliche Englischkenntnisse besaßen. Die Lehrer englischer Muttersprache konnten sich auf das Approach konzentrieren, während die anderen Lehrer die eigene Aussprache oder die eigenen Englischkenntnisse verbessern konnten.

Ganz am Anfang, statt der Arbeit, die uns Cecilia bot, zu folgen, verlor ich mich in meinen Gedanken und versuchte gleichzeitig neue Wege für das Erlernen der deutschen Sprache zu entdecken. Ich träumte schon davon, Deutsch nach diesem Approach unterrichten zu können. Dabei ist mir natürlich Vieles entgangen, was ich aber dann reichlich nachgeholt habe. Unserem Akademiedirektor machte ich nämlich sofort deutlich, dass ich den Ausbildungskurs weiter mitgemacht hätte, nur wenn er mir garantiert hätte, dass wir nach dem Englischen auch das Deutsche in Anspruch genommen und daran gearbeitet hätten. Das S.W pädagogische Material für die deutsche Sprache existierte nämlich als Prototyp und als wir Doktor Gattegno vorschlugen, das Material zu benutzen, daran zu arbeiten, es auf den neusten Stand zu bringen und es in Italien neu zu drucken, freute er sich natürlich vor allem, weil er Cecilia Bartoli vertraute, die jahrelang eine wichtige Mitarbeiterin von ihm in New York gewesen war. Ohne Bescheidenheit, muss ich aber sagen, dass ich mir inzwischen auch sein Vertrauen verdient hatte, da ich ihn Ende August 1985 bei dem Seminar "La géneration des richesses", in Maubissant in Frankreich, kennen gelernt hatte und im November desselben Jahres ein Seminar in Trient mit 100 Teilnehmern orgsanisiert hatte, was ihn sehr beeindruckte, vor allem weil ich ihn erst seit 2 Monaten kannte.

Trotz der ersten Antwort, die ich von ihm bei dem obengenannten Seminar bekam, war ich sehr angetan von ihm und von seiner Vorgehensweise, ein Problem wissenschaftlich anzunähern.

"Meine Dame, Ihnen fehlen viele Seiten über dieses Thema" war eben die Antwort, die ich von Doktor Gattegno bekam, als ich wagte, ihn zu fragen, in welchem Sinne das Wort "immanent" verwendet wurde.

Die Wichtigkeit des Zuhörens der unterschiedlichen Lauten, die Aufmerksamkeit auf die Intonation der jeweiligen Sprachen waren mir schon immer klar aber wie man damit umgehen kann und wie man jeden Schüler zum guten Gebrauch von sich selber im Sinne von gutem Gebrauch der eigenen Fähigkeiten führen kann, das machte mir den großen Unterschied. Als Lehrerin ist es für mich ganz wichtig gewesen, neue Techniken und Strategien zu entdecken und zu erlernen, um die Routine zu vermeiden und um den Schülern immer neue Herausforderungen zu bieten, damit sie ihres Potenzials bewusst werden und es mehr und besser ausnützen können. Das alles verdanke ich Doktor Gattegno sowie der große Spaß ,den ich heute immer noch am Unterrichten habe.

Neue didaktische Mittel überprüfe ich immer mit großem Interesse aber ich habe bis heute noch nichts gefunden, das besser funktioniert als das von Doktor Gattegno geschaffene Lernmaterial.

Respect for the Child's Ability To Do First Class Thinking

John Holt

What follows is an extract from the teaching diary that John Holt published as *How Children Fail*. This is the entry for October 1, 1959, quoted at length. Reproduced with permission from Perseus Books Group.

October 1, 1959

Not long ago, Dr. Gattegno taught a demonstration class at Lesley-Ellis School. I don't believe I will ever forget it. It was one of the most extraordinary and moving spectacles I have seen in all my life.

The subjects chosen for this particular demonstration were a group of severely disabled children. There were about five or six 14- or 15-year-olds. Some of them, except for unusually expressionless faces, looked quite well; the one who caught my eye was a boy at the end of the table. He was tall, pale, with black hair. I have rarely seen on a human face such anxiety and tension as showed on his. He kept darting looks around the room like a bird, as if enemies might come from any quarter left unguarded for more than a second. His tongue worked continuously in his mouth, bulging out first one cheek and then the other. Under the table, he scratched — or rather clawed — at his leg with one hand.

With no formalities or preliminaries, no icebreaking or jollying up, Gattegno went to work. It will help you see more vividly what was going on if, providing you have rods at hand, you actually do the operations I will describe. First he took two blue (9 cm) rods, and between them put a dark green (6 cm), so that between the two blue rods and above the dark green there was an empty space 3 cm long. He said to the group, "Make one like this." They did. Then he said, "Now find the rod that will just fill up that space." I don't know how the other children worked on the problem; I was watching the dark-haired boy. His movements were spasmodic, feverish. When he had picked a rod out of the pile in the center of the table, he could hardly stuff it in between his blue rods. After several trials, he and the others found that a light green (3 cm) rod would fill the space.

Then Gattegno, holding his blue rods at the upper end, shook them, so that after a bit the dark green rod fell out. Then he turned the rods over, so that now there was a 6 cm space where the dark green rod had formerly been. He asked the class to do the same. They did. Then he asked them to find the rod that would fill that space. Did they pick out of the pile the dark green rod that had just come out of that space? Not one did. Instead, more trial and error. Eventually, they all found that the dark green rod was needed.

Then Gattegno shook his rods so that the light green fell out, leaving the original empty 3 cm space, and turned them again so that the empty space was uppermost. Again he asked the children to fill the space, and again, by trial and error, they found the needed light green rod. As before, it took the dark-haired boy several trials to find the right rod. These trials seemed to be completely haphazard.

Hard as it may be to believe, Gattegno went through this cycle at least four or five times before anyone was able to pick the needed rod without hesitation and without trial and error. As I watched, I thought, "What must it be like to have so little idea of the way the world works, so little feeling for the regularity, the orderliness, the sensibleness of things?" It takes a great effort of the imagination to push oneself back, back, back to the place where we knew as little as these children. It is not just a matter of not knowing this fact or that fact; it is a matter of living in a universe like the one lived in by very young children, a universe which is utterly whimsical and unpredictable, where nothing has anything to do with anything else—with this difference, that these children had come to feel, as most very young children do not, that this universe is an enemy.

Then, as I watched, the dark-haired boy saw! Something went "click" inside his head, and for the first time, his hand visibly shaking with excitement, he reached without trial and error for the right rod.

He could hardly stuff it into the empty space. It worked! The tongue going round in the mouth, and the hand clawing away at the leg under the table doubled their pace. When the time came to turn the rods over and fill the other empty space, he was almost too excited to pick up the rod he wanted; but he got it in. "It fits! It fits!" he said, and held up the rods for all of us to see. Many of us were moved to tears, by his excitement and joy, and by our realization of the great leap of the mind he had just taken.

After a while, Gattegno did the same problem, this time using a crimson (4 cm) and yellow (5 cm) rod between the blue rods. This time the black-haired boy needed only one cycle to convince himself that these were the rods he needed. This time he was calmer, surer; he knew.

Again using the rods, Gattegno showed them what we mean when we say that one thing is half of another. He used the white (1) and red (2), and the red and the crimson (4) to demonstrate the meaning of "half." Then he asked them to find half of some of the other rods, which the dark-haired boy was able to do. Just before the end of the demonstration Gattegno showed them a brown (8) rod and asked them to find half of half of it, and this too the dark-haired boy was able to do.

I could not but feel then, as I do now, that whatever his IQ may be considered to have been, and however he may have reacted to life as he usually experienced it, this boy, during that class, had played the part of a person of high intelligence and had done intellectual work of very high quality. When we think of where he started, and where he finished, of the immense amount of mathematical territory that he covered in 40 minutes or less, it is hard not to feel that there is an extraordinary capacity locked up inside that boy.

> " It is the tragedy of his life that he will probably never again find himself with a man like Gattegno, who knows, as few teachers do, that it is his business to put himself into contact with the intelligence of his students, wherever and whatever that may be... "

It is the tragedy of his life that he will probably never again find himself with a man like Gattegno, who knows, as few teachers do, that it is his business to put himself into contact with the intelligence of his students, wherever and whatever that may be, and who has enough intuition and imagination to do it. He has not done much work with disabled children, but he saw in a moment what I might have taken days or weeks to find out, or might never have found out: that to get in touch with the intelligence of these children, to give them solid ground to stand and move on, he had to go way, way back, to the very beginning of learning and understanding. Nor was this all he brought to the session. Equally important was a kind of respect for these children, a conviction that under the right circumstances they could and would do first-class thinking. There was no condescension or pity in his manner, nor even any noticeable sympathy. For the duration of the class he and these children were no less than colleagues, trying to work out a tough problem – and working it out.

§

> "Life is an attempt of energy to do what was not possible in the molecular realm: to produce an endless evolution."
>
> - Dr. Caleb Gattegno

Evolution and Memory, Second Edition (2010), page 25.

Gattegno's Words in Color on display at the International Reading Association trade show in Chicago, 2010.

Une approche pour l'Afrique

Zouré Moumouni

Mon nom est Zouré Moumouni, né en 1971 au Burkina Faso. J'ai eu la chance de pouvoir fréquenter l'école jusqu'en première grâce à mes parents. Mais malheureusement, je n'ai pas pu aller plus loin par manque de moyens financiers, ce qui est la majorité des cas ici au Burkina.

J'ai alors décidé de devenir instituteur parce que j'aime les enfants et j'ai toujours voulu m'investir dans le social. Après deux ans de formation (alors qu'aujourd'hui, il n'y a plus que 7 mois de formation des maîtres), j'ai débuté dans des villages de brousse comme tous les jeunes instituteurs de ce pays. Puis j'ai été nommé à Bobo Dioulasso, ma ville natale, où je pratique depuis sept ans.

Travaillant dans l'école de l'association SOS Village d'Enfants, j'ai assisté à une présentation de La Lecture en Couleurs en novembre 2007 par Geneviève Godard de l'association Dounia Don Kalan, savoir lire pour s'ouvrir à la vie (DDK). Ce jour-là, je ne m'attendais pas du tout à ce que j'ai entendu et vu. J'ai découvert un outil pédagogique qui m'a paru sensationnel. J'avais l'impression que, si je l'utilisais, je pourrais enfin avoir entre les mains un matériel et une approche pédagogique qui règleraient de nombreuses difficultés dans l'apprentissage de la lecture et du français de nos élèves.

J'ai donc sauté sur l'occasion en janvier 2008 lorsque DDK a proposé une formation de formateurs. Depuis, je n'ai jamais lâché La Lecture en Couleurs et je la pratique dans ma classe. Ici, nous avons la chance de prendre une classe de CP1 et de monter chaque année avec les élèves jusqu'en CM2. Actuellement, ma classe est en CE1 et, depuis trois ans, mes élèves pratiquent très bien les sons du français sur le tableau de rectangles en couleurs. Grâce à cela, ils lisent et parlent très bien le français ce qui est un exploit dans nos conditions de travail. Une classe de même niveau dans un autre établissement est loin d'en arriver à ce résultat. Ceci, ce n'est pas dû à moi, mais à La Lecture en Couleurs. Merci Monsieur Gattegno !

Et pourtant, j'ai 104 enfants dans ma classe. Nos conditions de travail sont très précaires, nous ne disposons que de tables-bancs cassés, d'un tableau très endommagé, d'une salle très exiguë avec des enfants d'un milieu très défavorisé. En CP1, aucun ne parlait le français. J'ai la chance de parler leur langue, ce qui m'a aidé tout au début. Par contre, nombre de mes collègues n'ont pas cette chance. Leurs élèves ne parlent pas le français et eux ne parlent pas leur langue. Apprendre à lire en français dans ces conditions relève de l'extraordinaire.

Aujourd'hui, je dispose de La Lecture en Couleurs et toutes ces difficultés se sont aplanies. Le nombre d'enfants n'est même plus un problème pour moi. Ce qui importe, c'est le dynamisme et la joie d'apprendre qui sont suscités par une pédagogie attractive et ludique.

Mes élèves de CE1 lisent et comprennent ce qu'ils lisent. En plus, ils écrivent très bien. Grâce au fidel que je construis pas à pas avec eux et les textes que nous travaillons, ils ne font qu'un minimum de fautes d'orthographe.

En 14 ans de pratique, je n'aurais jamais pensé en

arriver là. L'outil Gattegno est pour moi une corde de plus à mon arc, surtout une corde en OR.

J'ai encore envie d'ajouter à mon enthousiasme de l'apprentissage de la lecture et du français, l'apport immense de cette pédagogie dans l'interdisciplinarité. J'utilise fréquemment les couleurs et le fidel pour amener des mots nouveaux en mathématiques, en géographie ou histoire... Les enfants rompus à cette pédagogie prennent parfois eux-mêmes la liberté de pointer sur les couleurs et d'essayer d'écrire des mots encore inconnus.

Ce qui me plaît beaucoup dans cette approche pédagogique, c'est que l'enfant est au centre. C'est lui qui fait son apprentissage à tous les niveaux et avec cela, ses prises de conscience. Je suis sûr que dans quelques années, ces enfants seront mieux armés pour affronter la vie parfois si dure chez nous. Ils sauront mieux qui ils sont et pourront avoir confiance en eux en toute situation.

Pour moi personnellement, pratiquer cette approche m'a ouvert beaucoup et m'a forcé à remettre en cause ma façon de faire. Elle me pousse même à aller au-delà en créant des jeux ou des procédés visant à simplifier davantage l'apprentissage.

Monsieur Gattegno m'a permis de découvrir l'algèbre de la langue et j'aime jouer avec les sons et les mots pour rendre plus plaisante encore la classe.

J'irais encore plus loin. Je pense profondément que cette approche pédagogique est tout à fait adaptée à nos pays africains et pourrait être un immense appui au développement après lequel nous courrons tant. Je suis prêt à participer à toute initiative dans ce sens. Mais pour en arriver là, il faudrait la faire connaître davantage et multiplier les formations à tous les niveaux.

TRADUCTION EN DIOULA

Nne tɔgɔ ye Zure Mumuni, nne wolola 1971, Burukina Faso. Nne ye lakɔli kɛ ka se kolɛzi ka saan wɔrɔ nan na n bangebagaw sababu ra. Nga n ma se ka tɛmɛ a kan see tanyan kama, a bi ten mɔgɔ caaman fɛ an ka jamana. O ra, nne y'a latigɛ ka kɛ lakɔlimɛliri ye, kama sɔrɔ denmisɛnw ka di n ye, a ni fana adamadenya ka di n ye.

Saan fila kalan kɔfɛ, ne ye baara daminɛ dugudeniw na, i na fɔ n tɔnyɔgɔw caaman. O kɔfɛ o ye bila Bobo dugu kɔnɔ min yen n wolo yɔrɔ ye, a saan wolonfilanan ye. Ka n to baara la 'SOS Villages d'enfants' ka tɔn lakɔliso la, n ye nin yɔrɔ ta Geneviève Godard ka Dounia Don Kalan ka tɔn na saan 2007 ka sumanladonkalo la ka kalankogwera min ye 'Lecture en Couleurs' (nyɛkalankogwɛ) ye.

N ka yeta ni n ka mɛta kɛra barinan ye n ma ni lon na. N ye kalandi cogo dɔye min ye nne kabako ya. Y'a miiri ko n y'a bila baara la, a bina nafa caaman di n ka kalandenw ma kalankogwɛ a ni tubabukan degi ta fan fɛ.

O kama, n ye nin yɔrɔ ta o kalan na o min ye kalanfaw ka kalan sanyɛlɛmakalo 2008 nan na. Kabini o tuma na, n toora k'o kalan bila baara la n ka kalanbo na. An fɛ, i bi kalandenw taa saan cɔcɔ la fo ka se n'o ye kilasi wɔrɔ nan na. Sisan n ka kalan denw bi kilasi saba nan na. A saan sabana ye, n kalandenw bi kannyɛw kalan ka nyɛ katimu kɔnɔ. O bi tubabukan kalan, ka fɔ fana ka nyɛ. N'an y'an ka kalandenw sanga ni kalanden wɛrɛw ye, a b'a ye k'o an taaw bi nyɛfɛ. O ye kalankogwekura ni sababu ye. Gattegno i ni ce.

Kasɔrɔ kalanden 104 lo bi n ka kilasi kɔnɔ. Baara kɛ minanw nyeneman te yen. Saan fɔlola, o si tun te tubabukanmɛ. Komi, nne bi julakan mɛ, o ye baara nɔgɔya. N lɔnyɔgɔn dɔw ma kɛ ni o kunadiya ye. Bii, nin kalangwekura kɛra sababu ye ka gwɛlɛya caaman kɛlɛ, bari a ka di denmisɛnw ye.

N ka kalandenw bi minw kalan, ob o famu, o bi sɛbɛri kɛ ka nyɛ, a ni filiw man ca o ka masalabolosɛbɛli la. Gattegno ka baarakɛminan le yo bɛɛ sababu ye. A ka di nne ye ka daga nyɛ o kalan na. A ni ka danyɛ kuraw sɔrɔ jatikalan, jamanakalan walima tariku ra. Danmisɛn dɔ yɛrɛ dɔ bi danyɛ dɔw sɛbɛ, an ma min kalan ban.

Nin kalankokura ra, kalandenw le bi baara fanba bɛɛ kɛ. Ne ya lɔnci ko nin kalan ni fɛ, denmisɛnw na, la o yɛrɛ la, ka se ka se sɔrɔ gwɛlɛya caaman kan.

Nin kalan ni ye nne, hakili yɛlɛ, n bi se ka tulon caaman bila senkan, a ni ka koo wɛrɛ caaman kɛ na ye. Nin kalan ni bi se ka kɛ sababu ye ka an ka farafinjamanaw giidi. Ola, nne b'a lanyini, nin kalan ka se ka waliya lakɔliso caaman na, mɛtiri yɛrɛ ka kalan sɔrɔ nin 'fɛ.

Why I Love Joining Silent Way Workshops

Kyoko Nishio

Since May 2009, I have joined about five Silent Way English workshops instructed by Donald Cherry in Tokyo. I started attending because I was studying linguistics, and was interested in how human beings acquire their first language. For me, learning English was really difficult. I started studying English when I was a junior high school student, but I could not understand grammatical rules or memorize easily, so I could not get good grades in English class. I had always wished that I could understand English, and that I could speak it as fluently as I speak my first language. I decided to study linguistics in university, where I met many foreign students from all over the world. I noticed that they were having a hard time acquiring Japanese, whereas I did not, because it is my first language. From then on I have been trying to learn more about first language acquisition.

When I joined a Silent Way workshop for the first time in May 2009, I just enjoyed spending time with the other participants and Don. I liked talking with many people who I otherwise wouldn't interact with in my daily life at the university. I thought they were thinking quite deeply about their lives, and that they were studying hard not only in their professional fields, but also in other new areas for them. I also liked learning together with different generations. I was not focusing on learning or building up my English ability at that time. Like a child, I just enjoyed the time. That's the reason I joined the workshops a couple of more times.

I started to find out what I failed to understand about English before, and I started to try to organize English structure inside my brain. It was an individual and independent process for me, although I was enjoying the time with other participants. I was really surprised when I noticed that I was reflecting inside myself during the workshops. In the Silent Way workshops, there is freedom to spend time as participants wish. Although there are many learners with various levels of English, I assume that all participants can learn something during the workshops.

Now I am an English teacher at a public junior high school. I'm teaching English to 140 second-grade students. Every day, I understand the possibility of the Gattegno Approach. I know that I'm not a good teacher yet. I cannot control my students well. I cannot explain well what they don't understand. Also, my own English still needs improvement. However, I have the confidence to become a good teacher, and I have the inspiration to become a teacher like Donald Cherry in the future. I don't want to make my students remember grammatical rules or vocabulary. I want to give my students chances to think freely and become aware of English by themselves. Of course, in junior high school, the most important job as a teacher is working on students. Teaching English is secondary, so Caleb Gattegno said, "The teacher works on the student and the student works on the language." As a language teacher, I will try hard to work on the students, and to work more with the Gattegno Approach.

§

The introduction of consonants and partnering vowels in Words in Color. (Educational Solutions file photo)

The Faster Way

Steven Quinn

I have been an English as a second language teacher for two years. I found the Silent Way about a year ago, by accident, while searching online for information about teaching pronunciation. In this past year, my world has changed forever. What I once called "teaching," I now call "fumbling around in the dark."

I became interested in language early in high school, eventually studying German at university. I never really thought much about my teachers, although I knew that some were better than others. In 10 years of study, I accumulated a large number of memorized German structures and vocabulary. But even today, speaking German triggers feelings of fear and panic, my palms become sweaty as I stammer away. At university I could not help but feel somehow dissatisfied. I spent thousands of hours studying, without ever achieving a sense of confidence and fluency.

As a trainee teacher, I thought I could change things, even if I didn't know how. I knew there must be a better way. But no one at university showed me anything different. I left Sydney University thinking that good language teaching was an eclectic soup, seasoned with this or that method according to the teacher's disposition.

When I eventually landed a job as an ESL teacher, I was thrown into a class of complete beginners, consisting mostly of illiterate refugees. Suddenly, all the elegant theories were completely useless. I couldn't translate the theory into practice. Five years of training had not prepared me at all. Almost everything I tried led to failure. All of a sudden, the eclectic soup began to look quite thin.

At university we all recited the mantra: "I take a constructivist approach; knowledge is not a list of facts." But this was always a purely verbal statement. Having no real understanding of how to do better, I did what most teachers do; I began to teach as I was taught, through drills, repetition, and grammatical explanations. I employed eclecticism with a heavy dose of the communicative approach. I was the ideal product of any respectable education faculty, but I felt like a fraud. I calmed myself with the thought that "such is language learning."

You see, conventional pedagogy designates five to 10 years of dedicated study before a person can competently speak, listen, read and write in a new tongue. The idea that "these things take time" comforted me, although only a little. My students appeared to be "unresponsive," unable to make progress from one day to the next. Looking back, I wish someone had handed me a box of rods and said, "Take these to class and shut up!" The problem was not that my students could not learn, but that I never tried to learn from them. All my talking, repetition and dancing about had no effect, and so I drank another coffee and taught harder, talking louder, repeating more, explaining again and again. I hammered away in a way that must have frustrated and paralyzed them.

Each new term brought new students and some bright idea discovered during the break. Each term I jumped from one to another; from song-like drilling, to phonics, to copy books, to grammar exercises. But looking back, I can see that my frustration with the students should have been directed at my materials and techniques. It was just a little too difficult to admit total ignorance. But there must have been a problem, else I wouldn't keep changing my approach. I was never satisfied with my teaching, and I felt the weight of my students' situation pressing down on me.

From my first day, I knew that my students were some of the most needy in Australia and that I could only help them for six months. They needed so much, in so little time. How could they learn all those words? How could they remember all the names of all the things around them? I needed to find the fastest way to teach them English.

While they cannot speak, read, or write, my students can not move freely in the community. Can I really ask my students to wait five whole years before they enter society?

I think my teaching was based primarily on fear; the fear of failure, the fear of forgetting, and the fear of publicly being shown to be inadequate. And all this classroom fear stood atop my students' greatest fear of all – "What am I to do with my life?" Their old one is gone, and here they are, at the age of 18, learning to speak like a baby, surviving on welfare payments, with almost no prospects for work.

I'm so glad to have found the Silent Way. Things are very different now. Teaching in this way, I can give the students a rapid entry into speaking, listening, reading, and writing, and therefore, an entry into social life. I can bring the students' self to the helm, and open up a new future for them, perhaps enabling them to build a new relationship with their past, and overcome their trauma.

I never thought that perhaps I didn't need to teach them loads of vocabulary, and that the more important job was to sensitize their mouths, ears, and minds to the spirit of the English language. This way, when my time with them is over, they can analyze new language and absorb it.

All my crippling anxiety was unnecessary. Now that I've begun to understand the students as they are, rather than as I would prefer them to be, my anxiety has disappeared. The students speak and I guide them. I now know that language is not a thing to be memorized, but a functioning to be acquired. And so I trigger that functioning with the rods and then guide it with feedback.

I'm still only a novice. I've never done any training, nor even seen a Silent Way class in person. I still find myself interfering when I don't really understand a problem, or seeing an error, but not really knowing how to correct it. I still have a long way to go, and my regular failures testify to this. But among the failure, some fantastic successes stand out and spur me onwards. How far I have come in these past 12 months. I feel that I've made huge strides forward, leaving "drill and kill" well behind me.

I am very lucky to have found Dr. Roslyn Young, again by accident, while trying to purchase the then-non-existant British English Charts. I learned so much while helping to edit her introductory guide to the Silent Way. If I hadn't got my hands on the book, and had the benefit of Roslyn's experience, then I would still be "fumbling around in the dark."

> "I now know that language is not a thing to be memorized, but a functioning to be acquired."

It's so exciting to come into contact with other Silent Way teachers. I can't help but feel that a renaissance in languages education is at hand. Teachers now have an independent entry to the theory and practice of Gattegno's approach to teaching languages. Of course, the road ahead is not smooth; teachers are understandably wary of new ideas, they are assailed by "innovations" and "world's best practice" dropping down on them from the education bureaucracies. Individuals must be convinced. Every teacher to whom I've demonstrated the approach can see its power, but whether they have the desire to submit themselves to years of difficult change is another question. For me, the results certainly justify the occasional hardship.

Even as a beginner, I have in 10 weeks brought students to the point where they can speak, listen, read and write in English, albeit in the small universe of a few Word Charts and some additional survival vocabulary. With these words they have listened and understood, spoken and been understood. Indeed, they have spoken independently, written independently, spelled independently, used grammar independently, and most importantly, corrected themselves in all these fields, thus proving that they have functioning criteria for the English language. By subordinating my teaching to their learning, I can give my students a good start in their new life. I thank Caleb Gattegno for showing me that in these "unresponsive" students lurks an enormous intellectual power waiting to be unleashed.

> "Language teaching becomes a scientific endeavor because the teacher is engaged in what makes things move in the proper direction knowingly and carefully through access to a continuous feedback of what students are doing here and now."
>
> — Dr. Caleb Gattegno

The Common Sense of Teaching Foreign Languages, Second Edition (2010), page 20.

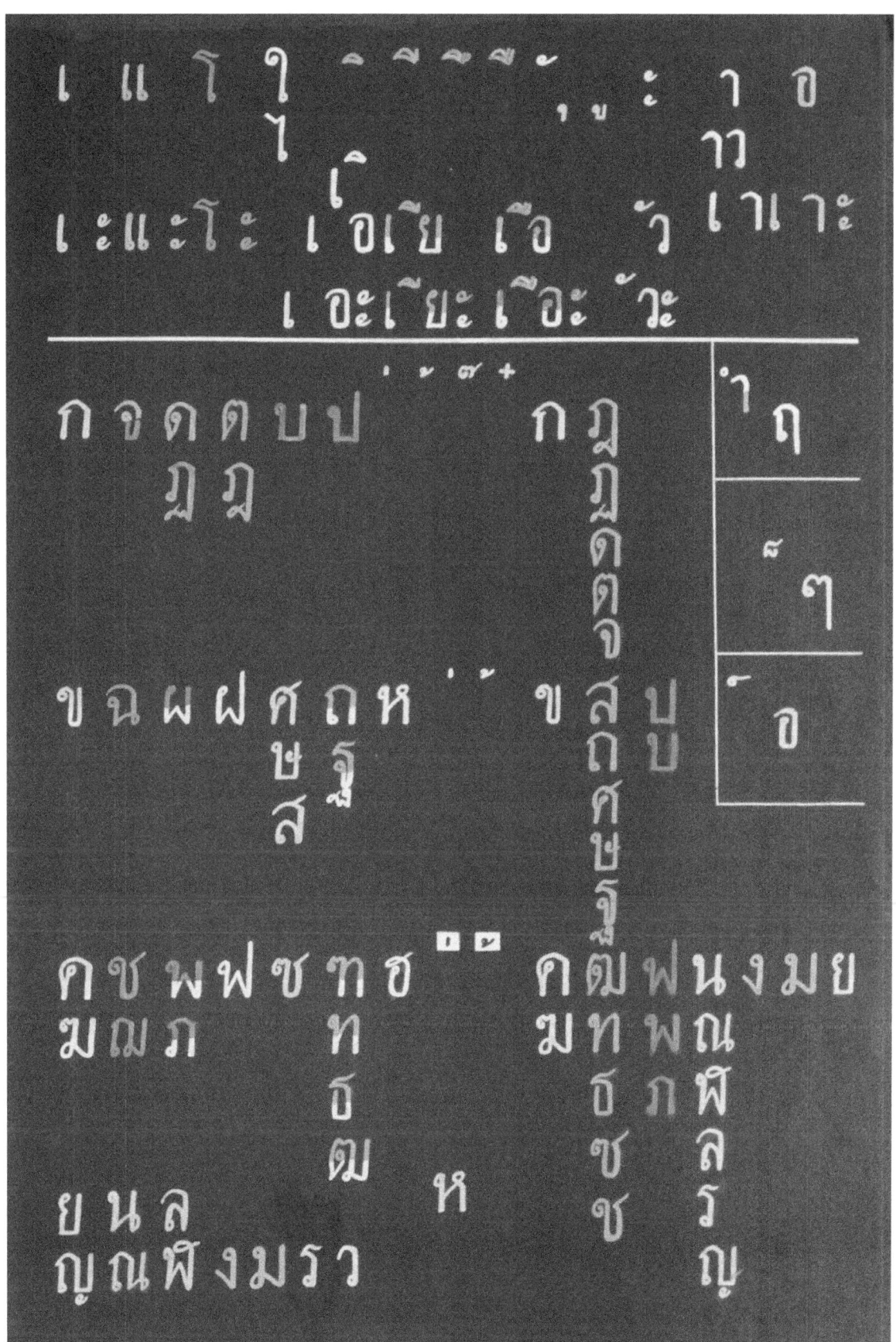

The Thai Fidel in its prototype stage. Made in 1972 with hand-painted lettering on cardboard. ©Educational Solutions Worldwide Inc.

Caleb Gattegno: A Profound and Continuing Personal Influence

Henry Liebling

"We shall only be able to serve as educators when we reach deeper and deeper into the mystery of the mind at work on itself." (Gattegno, 1963.)

I stumbled upon Gattegno's work when after teaching science and agricultural science in Zambia, I returned to England and took up a post in a Lancashire primary school where I discovered some Cuisenaire Rods deep in a cupboard. I embarked, helped by an older and much more experienced teacher and a copy of *Mathematics with Numbers in Colour* by Caleb Gattegno, found hiding on a staffroom bookshelf. I had always valued visual learning as a child and felt no different as an adult.

Watching children work with the colored rods gave me insights into their mental processes and quickly taught me things I didn't know. Patterns appeared and reappeared very readily; the algebra of some rules of arithmetic became visible. Many children found using the rods rewarding, as relationships and equivalences could be visualized, pointed out and spoken about – something I never remembered from my own childhood. I had clearly seen the benefit of using materials such as the rods to help children learn. I got an old trolley and started loading it up with maths resources, games and materials so that other teachers could share these treasures. How might I encourage my colleagues "to subordinate teaching to learning"? Later I realized how many of the resources and how much of the pedagogy I had used owed their origins or introduction to Gattegno and his colleagues in the ATAM (later to become the ATM).

Many of Caleb's questions, directed to members of his seminar audiences have stayed with me as triggers to self-investigation and to working on ways to subordinate teaching to learning. They also had the power to stimulate the production of new phrases, which I would often use with my students. They are still in my head and I think all owe their origin to G.

"What has your sleep brought you?"

"Only awareness is educable."

"Where is your awareness now?" and "Where was your awareness at the point of your conception?"

"Tell your own story, not someone else's. Tell me what you think. Speak from your own experience. Try things out for yourself."

"The person who knows the most says the least."

"A lot from a little," and, "Give them gruel." (i.e. Give students only what they cannot reasonably find by themselves and let them do the rest.)

"Say what you see."

"What patterns can you see?"

"Think to me." "You speak and I'll write."

There are also some well-worn mental scripts relating to errors, mistakes and misconceptions – especially the waste from mathematical activity, which is so valuable and such a rich and underused source of food for learning. We used the idea of the "Mantle of the Expert" or the "Expert's Chair" to encourage students to talk about the problems they were having, and how common misconceptions might be unpicked and reconstructed as a group activity.

How can you develop your awareness, especially as a young student or newly qualified teacher? Often the training forces a superficial awareness of self – through being watched by lots of pairs of eyes and assessed by tutors. How can you let this go and instead watch the learners? To Caleb's reminder that only awareness is educable, can be added (and I recall these as John Mason's words) only behavior is trainable and only emotions are harnessable. These reminders prompt teachers to become learners of their craft through a science of education.

I first thought about this whilst observing an experienced Dutch teacher in Zambia. He had a glove puppet on his left hand looking over his right shoulder at the class as he was facing the blackboard and writing on it as he explained long multiplication. The children were not looking at him; they were in dialogue with the puppet who was finding the whole experience confusing. They responded to the puppet who whispered into the teacher's ear in the hope that he might explain things a little better, a little more clearly. The children were happy to tell their doubts and fears to the puppet and the teacher could respond via the blackboard and the puppet: a very hard act to accomplish, a bit like a good ventriloquist. It started me thinking about transitional objects. A sock with an elastic band and a couple of re-enforcing rings makes a passable snake.

the learners.

If you make the effort to train yourself, you will find your attention is directed at the children's responses and you will be thinking about where to point next. It is a bit like teaching when you have lost your voice. Strangely the children feel in control. You will hear their confident voices probing the unknown while watching for signs of your approval. You and they are setting up a very powerful feedback loop. You are subordinating teaching to learning.

I could write about G's fascination with the ease with which children have learnt to talk and use their first language, about "The set of one's fingers," about the use of film and animation, about his excitement with the potential of new technology, about the concept of an "ogden" – a unit of mental energy required to

> "You and they are setting up a very powerful feedback loop. You are subordinating teaching to learning."

I have a memory of team teaching some 60 first-year undergraduate student teachers with Tony Brown. We had all made or brought a glove puppet. We were sitting on the floor. My puppet and I were talking to the students. Tony's puppet was peering behind my back and silently trying to engage/distract my puppet. The dynamics were wonderful and the students' smirks became giggles and eventually an uproar of laughter. The power of puppets as transitional objects within classrooms between staff and students had been accepted. The search for more powerful transitional devices led me to the Gattegno Place Value Chart elegantly presented by Geoff Faux.

Gattegno's Silent Way approach to using charts also works by forcing the teacher to remain virtually silent while paying very close attention to the movements and position of the pointer and the learners' responses. The teacher is a conductor developing his own repertoire of movements of the pointer on the chart while also using gestures, facial expressions and other non-verbal communication to encourage, elicit, modify and develop responses from

learn a new fact – as a means of bringing the 'cost' of learning to the attention of teachers, and encouraging them to seek opportunities for an economy of learning that directly benefits the learner.

Building on the ideas of Gattegno, Faux, and ATM "Developing Number" software, allowed Tony and me to develop our pedagogic writing, including for example, "Saying and Making Numbers" described fully in *The Really Useful Maths Book*. More recently we used developing awareness as the central concept and starting point for a website on sustainability in teacher education. How gladdened Gattegno would have been by the work of people such as Sugata Mitra.

"Because technology, at the electronic level of today, has made it possible to reach millions instead of scores, in the future all valid educational ideas will end up available on television, reaching people through computers and satellites, rather than through textbooks and teachers at schools. This era is with us already and calling us to do the new job the best we can." (Gattegno 1974)

A Teacher's Perspective On The Power of Observation

Dr. Kathleen Graves

I first encountered Dr. Gattegno in 1976 in the MAT program at the School for International Training (SIT) in Brattleboro, where I was studying to be a language teacher. Little did I know that his work would have such a profound and lasting influence on who I am and what I do as an educator. I continued to attend his seminars in Brattleboro and in New York over the years, first as a language teacher and then as a teacher educator. In Brattleboro, the seminars started on Friday evening with a kind of Socratic session. His pointed questions and comments always provoked thought, self-examination, and doubt – in one of the early seminars he told us, "You are all bad teachers," which made quite an impression on me. We would then go home to sleep and learn. The next day, we were immersed in learning language through the Silent Way, either as participants or observers. At the end of each seminar, I came away energized and eager to put into practice this exciting approach to education.

For me, the foundation of Dr. G's work is the principle of subordinating teaching to learning; I had to first understand how people learn in order to understand how to teach. This is captured in the tenet of the MAT program at SIT, "Learning tells us how to teach." Dr. G made me see that in order to understand learning, I needed to look at how people learn in the literal, empirical sense. I needed to watch what learners did, what they tried to do, and what they didn't or couldn't do. By careful observation I could perceive what they needed, provide it, and then let them get on with learning. More often than not, what they needed was for me to get out of the way. I had to give them things to do, both mental and physical — the more they did, the more they learned. I had to refrain from giving them, or doing for them, what they could do for themselves. In my first attempt at teaching language using the Silent Way, I was amazed at how easily my two colleague-students grasped and started to use Chinese. They had something to attach it to — the rods — and something to do with them that language mediated — taking and giving the rods to each other. With time to practice as I attentively (and silently) observed, they quickly made the language their own. I was hooked. I had an exhilarating sense of power, not because of what I had done, but because of what they had been able to do. I wanted to know more about how to make this happen in my future classrooms.

For five years as a language teacher, I grappled with how to be present to my learners, to grant them what they knew, but to not take anything for granted. I learned from my mistakes. It seemed alluringly efficient to give students answers or to make corrections. The result? I was doing their work for them, and they didn't learn. Or conversely, I would try to elicit what wasn't there, causing great frustration. I tried to follow Dr. G's admonition: "The students' job is to work on the language; your job is to work on the student." I experimented with the Sound-Color Chart, the Fidels and the Word Charts. When I first taught Chinese, I made my own charts; each character was color-coded by hand with felt tip pens. I used a pointer to focus the learners' attention on the language, not on me. My box of Cuisenaire Rods was always with me (a large box of the real wooden ones that I still have), ready to be counted, compared, and formed into towers so students could make predictions about their likelihood of toppling. I also used them to represent places, people, and things in ways that make meaning perceptible. The rods allowed me to observe my learners and to provide the language they needed as they needed it.

When I returned to SIT to become an educator of teachers, I found I had to work on two levels – subordinating my teaching to the learning of my teachers-in-training, while also guiding them to understand and practice it themselves. I observed countless teachers in myriad classrooms and was struck anew at how challenging it is to teach in the service of learners. In fact, the opposite was more often the case: learning was subordinated to teaching. Teaching took the form of teachers telling or displaying what they knew and, as a result, the potential for learning was untapped and often wasted. I realized that I faced the same challenge as my teachers: it was tempting to tell them what to do,

> "I tried to observe the teachers closely so that I could use their experience as the starting point for triggering an awareness of the vast potential for learning in their classrooms."

to give them the answers, to display my knowledge. I re-learned what it meant to subordinate teaching to learning. I tried to observe the teachers closely so that I could use their experience as the starting point for triggering an awareness of the vast potential for learning in their classrooms, just as Dr. G had once so closely observed and listened to us as we struggled to learn. When a teacher had one of those 'aha' moments, I felt the same exhilaration I had experienced when my two fellow graduate students told each other to "take two rods" in Chinese. It is still hard work to be ever present to the learner, but for 35 years it is exactly that work that has kept me alive to learning and to growing as a teacher.

The Influence of Gattegno – Direct and Indirect

Rosie McAndrew

I first came across the Silent Way when I was teaching at International House, Hastings. Adrian Underhill, an instrumental and inspirational figure there, had already come under the influence of Gattegno, and was to extend this influence in turn to many more of the staff with whom he worked in both training and development.

Its most immediate impact on me, in 1980, was via one of the tutors on my initial CTEFLA training course – Allan Brammall – although at the time I had no name to attach to the mysterious withholding of simplistic answers and the cryptic silences that characterized his teaching style. A little later, the management of IH made the momentous decision to run two full-blown Silent Way classes in parallel – one led by Adrian, and the other by Joe Santos. They gave Janet Carver and I a month when we shared a class, so that we could spend the rest of our timetable observing these two practitioners at work with the learners, the rods, the Fidels, and the pictures. We observed the thinking process involved in encouraging students to experiment with language, increase their awareness and their curiosity, and discover the rules without overt explanation or prescription. And as the month went by, we began to work with their students' learning ourselves.

Later on, small groups of us were enabled to attend some of Gattegno's workshops in Bristol; I went to one, where if I remember rightly, the gnomic question was "Where is the baby in you?" This provoked endless discussion and argument, with Gattegno at no point providing answers or arbitration, although I believe some people had a strong sensation that their ideas had been summarily dismissed.

He also included a demonstration lesson in elementary Arabic. The only stipulation for participating volunteers was that no one could be part of the learning group who already knew any Arabic at all. I was lucky enough to be one of the demonstration class, and relished applying myself to the discovery process, but I must admit to a sense of helplessness and frustration when someone at the other end of the group seemed to be able to apply the colors for the sounds of the words on the chart so much more quickly than I (and most of the other learners) could. It emerged that this participant did in fact already know one very particular aspect of Arabic – either the numbers from one to 10 or the days of the week – but it turned out that this was precisely what we were being taught!

When, in the post-lesson feedback, this became clear, I couldn't understand why the false beginner hadn't withdrawn from the group as soon as he realized that by answering so immediately each time, he was giving a misleading impression of how much the class had absorbed, and subverting the learning process for the rest – or why Gattegno himself didn't gently encourage him to take a back seat. But it gave me a vivid and valuable experience of the tensions that can come into play for a learner when others are getting it so much faster than you are.

My next experience as a Silent Way learner was at another workshop in Bristol set up by Piers Messum, where we learnt some basic Italian with Cecilia Bartoli. This time I think the participants were on a more even footing, or perhaps were more respectful of each others' cognitive and affective needs. At any rate, I don't remember a parallel degree of frustration interfering with the learning process, and already being a pronunciation and intonation addict, I loved the early and consistent emphasis on phonology.

Another very significant milestone in my

apprenticeship was being able to observe and participate in one of Adrian's weeklong Sound Foundations Phonology courses, so that he could hand them over to me on occasion. While not strictly a Silent Way course per se, it embodied many of the underlying principles involved, and reinforced the direction of my development as a teacher; I subsequently ran many such courses myself, both at IH and at Pilgrims, Canterbury.

There were other brief opportunities to experience language learning the Silent Way at guest seminars at IH, but by whatever route, the seeds had been sown. I never actually became a fully-fledged Silent Way practitioner; the rods are always with me, but I never quite internalized all the colors. But the spirit of subordinating teaching to learning, of working with the students' questions, at their pace – of allowing them to explore and discover rules and relationships for themselves, with phonology and the bare bones of language structure at the core – has become central to my way of working.

Now I am based in an FE college where the curriculum is paramount: lesson plans are mandatory, schemes of work have to be devised for months ahead, and progress must be measurable and measured. Needless to say, I have usually diverged from my lesson plan within the first 15 minutes, and my scheme of work has no more relevance in retrospect than it had in prospect! Naturally, my precepts do not find favor with the senior management team, but fortunately they seem to go down well with the learners.

Long live Gattegno! §

Dr. Gattegno in the 1980's. (Educational Solutions file photo.)

Appendix

About the Authors

Carole Adams and Rachel Adams Goertel
A Mother and Daughter Story 107

CAROLE ADAMS earned her master's degree from the School for International Training in Brattleboro, Vermont and has taught ESL in the Rochester City School District in New York for 23 years. She has been an online instructor with Columbia University's Business English for Employees of Companies Abroad program. Her most recent publication is a chapter in *Language Games: Innovative Activities for Teaching English* in the TESOL Classroom Practice Series. She has also been a presenter at every TESOL conference since l995.

RACHEL ADAMS GOERTEL has taught public school K-12 ESL for 15 years. She has also taught for Columbia University and the University of California, Berkeley. Currently, she is an instructor of composition and ESL at Penn State University, the Behrend College. Rachel has just completed her course work towards a Ph.D. in composition and TESOL at Indiana University of Pennsylvania. She is writing her dissertation on the use of discourse markers in the casual conversation of linguistically and culturally diverse speakers.

Fusako Allard アラード　房子
Silence: The Most Powerful Tool of All
沈黙：最も強力な教具 14

Fusako Allard was born in Osaka, Japan in 1933 and received a M.A.T. from the School for International Training in Vermont, USA. She directed the Center for Learning in Osaka for about 25 years, since 1979. Presently, she works with a few students on their Japanese, English, and French (sound only) while working with junior high school 'dropouts'; reinforcing their English and Japanese school education.

昭和８年、大阪に生まれる。School for International Training（米国バーモント州在）よりMATを獲得。1979年より２５年余り、語学文化協会（大阪在）を運営。現在、日本語、英語及びフランス語（発音のみ）のクラスを少々と中高生の学校英語の補習の手伝いを楽しんでいる。

Dr. Roann Altman
Gattegno's Body of Work:
Providing Lessons For Life 154

Roann Altman majored in Spanish in high school, studied French and Italian at Syracuse University, received a master's in English sociolinguistics at SUNY Cortland, and received a Ph.D. in applied linguistics at the University of Southern California (USC). She taught courses at USC using the Silent Way, and in 1984 became assistant director of the ESL Service Courses at UCLA. She received a Fulbright in 1989-90 to Tel Aviv University in Israel to conduct research into the process of learning Hebrew as a foreign language. She then chaired the English as a Foreign Language unit at Ben-Gurion University in Beer-Sheva for five years. Roann has been a lecturer at the English Language Institute of the University of Michigan since the late '90s.

Dr. Marti Anderson
The Silent Way: A Pedagogy of Life 77

Marti Anderson is an educator currently based in Bangkok, Thailand where she works in both face-to-face and online formats to train and support teachers in their work. She was on the faculty of the Master of Arts in Teaching program at the School for

(About the Authors Cont'd.)

International Training in Brattleboro, Vermont for 20 years where she regularly taught the Approaches to Teaching course that included a unit on the Silent Way. Marti has provided professional development opportunities to teachers on six continents, in addition to her work at SIT. She believes that educating awareness is a worthy goal that continues to be as relevant today as it was when first articulated by Gattegno.

Alma Arnould

Education From My Father 212

Alma Arnould studied French and German at University College London, Spanish at the University of Madrid, and attended the School of Interpreters in Geneva. She earned a diploma in education from Monash University in 1973, and later received a postgraduate diploma course for TESOL. From 1974 to 1996, she taught French, German, Spanish, and ESL in secondary schools around Melbourne, and taught Spanish and French to adults in several 20-hour Silent Way courses. She also organized courses with her husband before their retirement.

AURAMA

Voices from Aurama 192

ANNE BREGANI has a M.A. in political science, a B.A. in education and has been a specialized French teacher for immigrant children and teenagers for 20 years. She is a poet and has been granted literary awards for her work, most recently in 2010.

DANIELA CERRETTI has an education degree in Italian, and a B.A. in occupational therapy, in French. She taught French to children and adults. She now runs a boutique where she creates imaginative objects made of textiles.

MARIE-CLAUDE CHALLANDES spent 20 years in Haiti as a teacher trainer in literacy and mathematics for deprived populations. Back in Switzerland, she taught young immigrant children for 15 years. In 1998, she released a collection of nursery rhymes, published by Aurama.

CATHERINE DELÉTRA has a master's in specialized education and is a sign language interpreter.

BRIGITTE MESOT has a master's in psychopathology. She has been teaching French to immigrants for some years. She is also a painter and is setting up a project to combine aspects of linguistic and visual expressions.

CAROLINE DE SYBOURG has a B.A. in Romance languages. She taught Italian and has been teaching French literacy for many years. She directed theater plays in French with immigrant students from Silent Way classes. She is also an actress herself.

MAYA WEINMANN has a German degree, speaks Schwitzertütsch, German, Italian, English, and French. She has been teaching French to immigrants for 17 years and German to Swiss students. She is a musician and plays the saxophone.

Dr. Bruce Ballard

Where do Good Results Come From? 256

Bruce Ballard first met the Silent Way in 1975 when the Peace Corps taught him to speak Korean during his pre-service training in South Korea. He studied the Silent Way while serving in the Peace Corps, then took courses at Educational Solutions in New York City. Eventually he worked at Educational Solutions, assisting Patricia Perez in the Bilingual Education Department. Since then, he has taught in universities in New York, Korea, and Japan, and trained teachers in the Silent Way in half a dozen countries. In 1999, he joined Charlotte (Shasha) Balfour's company, the Skilled Writer International, which applied Gattegno's pedagogy to business writing courses. Bruce is now a staff trainer at the Bronx Charter School for Better Learning, which was set up to train new teachers in the Subordination of Teaching to Learning. He has a doctorate in applied linguistics from Teachers College, Columbia University.

Dr. Cecilia Bartoli

A Responsibility to Learn 26

Cecilia Bartoli worked at Educational Solutions in New York City from 1973 to 1979 and conducted a number of teacher training seminars around the world (United States, Canada, Great Britain, Italy, France, Greece, Japan) both on the Silent Way and on the Subordination of Teaching to Learning. She taught Italian and English using the Silent Way at a university level both in the United States and in Italy. She also headed a three-year project in Trento, Italy, for the Accademia del Turismo for the improvement of teaching English, French, and German as foreign languages. Cecilia is the author of several articles on the Subordination of Teaching to Learning, particularly related to the theory, techniques, and evaluation of the Silent Way.

Manuela Bartoli

Life Through a Silent Way Lens 78

Manuela Bartoli is a freelance consultant for private agencies and different institutions in the province of Trento, Italy. She has been working as project manager in the educational and vocational training fields, and teaching both English and Italian as second languages. She managed her own company based in Trento for 10 years, coordinating young teachers and trainers. Throughout her career Manuela has taught students from kindergarten to higher and further education. She has also been involved in language teaching for specific purposes in local SME. She holds a business diploma, and has attended a variety of postgraduate courses related to teaching, communication, language teaching, ICT, tutoring and HR management.

Dr. Joyce F. Baynes

Sharing the Gift of Math, Learning and A Better Way to Teach 202

Joyce Baynes is a graduate of Swarthmore College where she majored in mathematics. She receievd an M.A.T. degree from the Harvard University Graduate School of Education as a National Science Foundation Fellow. She also has a master's in administration and a doctorate in mathematics education from Columbia University Teachers College in New York City. Joyce taught mathematics for 18 years before moving into administration. Prior to her retirement, she was Superintendent of the Dunellen Public Schools, the Englewood Public Schools and Assistant Superintendent of the Teaneck Public Schools, all in New Jersey. She has a great love for mathematics and worked tirelessly to break down barriers that prevent students from excelling in mathematics.

Dr. Patricia Benstein

How Could I Prevent Turning Into A Teaching Zombie? 55

Patricia Benstein has experienced many different cultures as part of living and traveling in various countries. She considers Australia her home, but is currently living and teaching in Europe. She has always been attracted to philosophies and teachings that get to the essence of what is required for success. Gattegno's Silent Way holds an ongoing attraction for Patricia as a teacher because it focuses on the submission of teaching to learning.

Malik Berkane

Silent Way au Japon 95

Malik Berkane est né en 1959 à Orléans. Il habite au Japon depuis 1981, où il est Professeur de FLE à Tokyo depuis 1982 et dirige Classes de Français depuis 1989.

Bill Bernhardt

Gattegno's Aphorisms 3

Bill Bernhardt is associate professor of English at the College of Staten Island, City University of New York (CUNY) and a member of the Consortial Faculty of the CUNY Online Baccalaureate. He is a founding trustee of the Bronx Charter School for Better Learning and President of the Association for the Science of Education and the Gattegno Foundation for Education, both located in New York. He attended many workshops and seminars with Dr. Gattegno during the 1970s and '80s, and assisted in editing books authored by Gattegno. His own book, *Just Writing* (Teachers and Writers, New York, 1977) was an attempt to apply Gattegno's work to the teaching of writing in schools. *Becoming A Writer* (St. Martins Press, New York, 1986) co-authored with Peter Miller, applied the Gattegno Approach to writing for American university students. Since 1990, he has conducted workshops in teaching writing in native and foreign languages in Brazil, China, France, Japan and Vietnam.

(About the Authors Cont'd.)

Hugh Birdsall

Revolutionizing My Teaching By Doing the Opposite 48

Hugh Birdsall teaches English to Speakers of Other Languages (ESOL) at the Regional Multicultural Magnet School (RMMS), in New London, Connecticut. He has also been on the faculty of the Summer Master of Arts in Teaching Program, at the SIT Graduate Institute, in Brattleboro, Vermont for 12 years. He graduated from Yale College with a B.A. in French literature in 1975, was a member of the first class of the Alternate Route to Certification Program at Wesleyan University in 1988, and received a Master of Arts in Teaching from SIT in 1993. He has taught both English and French in various schools, and has also presented numerous teacher development workshops.

Dr. Caroline Brandt

'A Cat that Walked by Himself' 20

Caroline Brandt joined the British Council in the United Arab Emirates in 1986, where she stayed for seven years; she returned to the UAE again in 2006. During the intervening years, she lived and worked in Hong Kong, New Zealand, the UK, Bahrain, and Brunei. Currently, she teaches academic communication skills to female engineering students taking bachelor of science degrees at the Petroleum Institute in Abu Dhabi, UAE. Researching, writing, and publishing are also important parts of Caroline's life.

Chris Breen

Working on the Edge of Discomfort: Threads of a Complex Journey into Awareness 254

Chris Breen is an independent consultant in the corporate world, teaching topics linked to personal leadership and complexity and diversity. He also teaches mathematics courses for adults called Second Chance Maths; a book based on this course was published in 2003. He is an emeritus associate professor of the School of Education at the University of Cape Town (UCT) and a visiting faculty member at the UCT Graduate School of Business (GSB). He was president of the International Group for the Psychology of Mathematics Education (PME) for three years, has lectured as a visiting professor at the universities of Lisbon, Auckland, Monash and Dakar, and has given plenary conference papers internationally. In 1984, he founded the Mathematics Education Project (MEP), an NGO based at the University of Cape Town, which worked exclusively in schools that were disadvantaged by apartheid, and continued as director for 12 years.

Laurinda Brown

The Heart of the Matter: Gattegno's Awareness of the Powers of Children 90

After teaching mathematics in a secondary comprehensive school in the Bristol, UK area for 14 years, Laurinda spent five years (1988-1992) co-editing *Mathematics Teaching*, a journal of the Association of Teachers of Mathematics (ATM) in the UK, with Tony Brown (Cornwall). During this time, she also worked part-time as a curriculum developer at the Resources for Learning Development Unit. This editorship followed directly that of Dick Tahta and Ray Hemmings. An earlier editor of the journal had been David Wheeler, who went on to launch the journal *For the Learning of Mathematics*. Laurinda edited this journal from 2003 to 2007. She has been working as a teacher educator at the University of Bristol, Graduate School of Education for more than 20 years and continues to subordinate the teaching of mathematics and mathematics teaching practices. Her recent work, *The Economy of Teaching Mathematics*, is largely linked to Gattegno.

Donald Cherry

A Less-Damaging Career 208

Donald Cherry is an English teacher at Hiroshima International University. He also teaches intensive Silent Way English courses a few times a year that are organized by Silent Way Tokyo. He is a graduate of the School for International Training, where he received a Master of Arts in Teaching in 1994.

Dr. Robert (Bob) Coe

Small Vocabulary as a Big Idea 204

Robert L. Coe is a retired teacher of French, Spanish, and ESL. He taught for a number of years in New Jersey at the Pingry School, the Chatham

Boro, and Basking Ridge public schools, and in Bethlehem, Pennsylvania, at Moravian Academy and Northampton Community College. He lives with his wife, Mary Ann, in Easton, Pennsylvania, where he volunteers as a teacher of ESL at the Fowler Literacy Center of Project Easton. Reflecting on using the Silent Way, Coe says, "It has been a profoundly satisfying experience on both the professional and personal levels. It's challenging, it's fun, and it works." Coe did his undergraduate studies at Middlebury College, Middlebury, Vermont, where he earned a B.A. in French in 1961. He did his graduate studies at the Middlebury College Language Schools, earning a master's in French (Paris, 1963); a master's in Spanish (Madrid, 1973); and the degree of Doctor of Modern Languages (1977).

Alf Coles

In Pursuit of a Science of Education 5

Alf Coles is a senior lecturer in education (mathematics) at the University of Bristol, Graduate School of Education. He taught mathematics in secondary schools in the UK between 1994 and 2009. Alf came across Gattegno's work initially through his teacher training at Cambridge University, and then through joining the Association of Teachers of Mathematics' (ATM) Science of Education working group in 1995. He has been involved in classroom based research since 1995, mainly through a long-term collaboration with Laurinda Brown that has led to funded research projects, publications and one co-authored book. His research interests include: the development of classroom cultures, strategies for opening a space for inquiry in classrooms, issues of listening and hearing in the classroom, metacognition, and teacher development (including the use of video).

Dr. Clifton de Cordoba

He Said Nothing, But I Understood Everything 86

Clif de Cordoba is currently a principal of a community adult school with 13,000 students in the Los Angeles Unified School District. He is also an adjunct instructor in the adult education credential program at University of California, Los Angeles Extension. He holds a master's in applied linguistics and a Ph.D. in language teacher education. Clif is currently interested in English and Spanish literacy, school-site teacher inservicing and evaluation, and in exploring ways of computerizing Dr. Gattegno's work with language and literacy learning.

J. Parker Damon

Gattegno and the McCarthy-Towne Elementary School 284

J. Parker Damon was principal at McCarthy-Towne School, in Acton, MA from 1971 to 2000.

Dr. Ubiratan D'Ambrosio

The Talk of the Town 180

Ubiratan D'Ambrosio retired in 1994 and is emeritus professor of mathematics at the State University of Campinas in São Paulo, Brazil. He received a doctorate in mathematics from Escola de Engenharia de São Carlos, of the University of São Paulo, in 1963. In 1983, he became a Fellow of the AAAS (American Association for the Advancement of Science). He is also the recipient of the 2001 Kenneth O. May Medal of History of Mathematics, granted by the International Commission of History of Mathematics, and the recipient of the 2005 Felix Klein Medal of Mathematics Education, granted by the International Commission of Mathematics Instruction.

Ubiratan is currently a graduate advisor in several universities and professor of mathematics education at UNIBAN, Universidade Bandeirantes de São Paulo.

His past roles have included: Visiting Research Fellow at Istituto Matemático dell'Università, Genoa, Italy (1961-62); Post-doctoral Fellow (Research Associate), Brown University (1964-65); Associate Professor of Mathematics and Graduate Mathematics Chairman, SUNY at Buffalo (1966-72); Professor of Mathematics and Director of the Institute of Mathematics, Statistics and Computer Science of UNICAMP, Brazil (1972-80); Chief of the Unit of Curriculum of the Organization of American States, Washington DC (1980-82); Pro-Rector (Vice-President) for University Development, of UNICAMP, Brazil (1982-90); Visiting Professor of Mathematics, University of Illinois at Chicago (1987); and Member of the Council of the Pugwash Conferencers on Science and World Affairs (1987-1995).

(About the Authors Cont'd.)

David Davies
An Educational Awakening 76

David B. Davies was born in 1940. He received a B.A. in classics in 1962, and a certificate in education in 1964. From 1964 to 1972 he was in the UK and Paris teaching Latin, Greek, and English as a foreign language. He started his own ESL school in 1973 in the UK, and came into contact with the Silent Way in 1978. From that time on, David worked in language-school administration and teaching, until 1997. Throughout his career, he arranged seminars in the UK, led by Dr. Gattegno and others, and attended seminars in France, Switzerland, and Spain. He also arranged short summer courses (ESL, Silent Way) in the gap between the end of exam courses and early July start of 'conventional' summer courses at his school.

Dr. A.J. Sandy Dawson
Fractions Are Not Parts of Wholes 124

Sandy Dawson taught at Simon Fraser University (SFU), Vancouver, Canada from 1970 to 2000. He was director of teacher education at SFU from 1985 to 1992. It was during this time that he became aware of Gattegno's work and eventually incorporated it into all of his own teaching and administrative activities. He moved to Honolulu in 2000 to take up work with teachers of mathematics across Micronesia as the Principal Investigator (PI) for the National Science Foundation (NSF) grant administered by Pacific Resources for Education and Learning (PREL). In 2003, he joined the College of Education, University of Hawaii (UH) though still maintaining his work with PREL. Currently, he is the PI of another NSF grant cooperatively administered by PREL and UH, which is educating Micronesian mathematics educators to the doctoral and master's degree level. Sandy teaches courses for these students under the label, "Educating Mathematical Awareness," thus carrying on the Gattegno-based work begun during the '70s at SFU.

Stephen DeGiulio
Caleb Gattegno, Scientist: A Learner Remembers 252

Stephen DeGiulio is a professor of English, TESOL, linguistics, and adult education. He teaches at the Dona Ana Community College of New Mexico State University and directs a non-profit adult literacy program in the "borderlands," a multicultural micro cosmos in the U.S. southwest and Mexican north. His interests include indigenous and non-Western knowledge systems, especially pedagogy and critical social theory. His current research is in the arts as a medium for sustainable education and cultural healing with special attention to the work of Caleb Gattegno, Jiddu Krishnamurti, and Rabindranath Tagore that integrates pedagogies developed from world indigenous traditions with the Science of Education.

Rosaria Dell'Eva
Ein Tor zu einer neuen Welt 294

Seit 1977 ist Deutsch als Fremdsprache mein Fach und seit 1998 unterrichte ich an dem Neusprachlichen Gymnasium „A. Rosmini" in Trient – Italien.

Doktor Gattegno habe ich Ende August 1985 in Maubissant, in Frankreich kennen gelernt. Das verdanke ich Cecilia Bartoli, von der ich nach dem Approach Silent Way ausgebildet wurde. Sie leitete nämlich ein dreijähriges Lehrerausbildungsprojekt, das ich koordinierte und das bei der Akademie für Handel und Tourismus in Trient stattfand. Von 1985 bis 1988 besuchte ich im Sommer die Seminare, die Doktor Gattegno in Frankreich leitete und organisierte die Seminare, die er im Herbst in Trient abhielt. Nach seinem ersten erfolgreichen Seminar in Trient, beauftragte Doktor Gattegno das Fremdsprachenteam, der obengenannten Akademie, das von ihm entworfene Material zum Erlernen der deutschen und der italienischen Sprache zu ergänzen und zu veröffentlichen. Seit 1987 beschäftige ich mich auch mit Lehrerausbildung mit besonderer Aufmerksamkeit auf das S.W. Approach und auf das entsprechende Material.

Eaton Donald
Caleb Gattegno and the Well-Crafted Pedagogical Challenge 120

Eaton Donald is a phil-entrepreneur. He was first exposed to Dr. Gattegno's work in 1994 in Japan. His interest in the principles of the Science of Education led him to apply these principles to business. After being a student of Dr. Gattegno's work for 15 years, Eaton became president of Educational Solutions. Today he continues the work of the worldwide elimination of illiteracy and innumeracy. In 2009, Eaton founded the Skylar Project, which aims to replace the slums of developing countries with sustainable, low-cost, and secure housing. Eaton has a young family and shares his time between Canada, USA, and Japan.

Sylvain Dufros

Changing Expectations
Le trajet d'un métier 288

Sylvain Dufros was born in Deauville, France in 1977 and is married with two young children. After a receiving a B.A. in science, he trained as a computer programmer. Sylvain then worked four years in France as a programmer, then went to Japan to experience another culture. He has been living in Japan for nine years now, and works as director assistant and professor of French as a foreign language in a private school called Classes de Francais, in Tokyo.

Français, né à Deauville le en 1977, marié, deux enfants de quatre ans et un an. Après un Bac scientifique, j'ai suivi une formation de programmeur informatique. J'ai ensuite travaillé quatre ans en France en tant que programmeur, puis je suis parti au Japon pour découvrir une autre culture. J'y habite depuis maintenant neuf ans, et je travaille depuis le début en tant que directeur-adjoint et professeur de Français Langue Étrangère, à l'école Classes de Français, à Tokyo.

Christian Duquesne

My Personal Journey Towards Letting
Go of "No" 196

Christian Duquesne was born December 13, 1941 in Albertville, France. He studied French, Latin, and Greek at Sorbonne University in Grenoble and Paris. From 1959 to 1971 he was a middle-school and high-school French teacher, and from 1971 to 1982 he was the national manager of in-service education for adults in textile care and temporary work. In 1983, he became a founding director of a communication company (Sylicone Tele Video) in Paris. In the summer of 1985, he met Dr. Caleb Gattegno. Christian decided to change career direction in 1990 by founding an individual company (which would become "Langues du Monde") devoted to spreading, experimenting, and exploring new teaching aids for adults according to Caleb Gattegno's propositions. He has so far explored Africa, China, and France for the potentialities given by Caleb Gattegno's research in the Science of Education, in the fields of corporate culture, tools for adult literacy, language teaching and literacy.

Jean-Jacques Dutrait

Witnessing the Truth
En témoin de la vérité 246

Jean-Jacques Dutrait worked for 15 years in his orginal vocation of architect before being introduced to the Gattegno pedagogy by Claudie Gattegno. He then began running workshops for French as a second language and mathematics in corporate environments (Hervé BTP, Peugeot, Rambol). Since 1997, Jean-Jacques has been leading workshops for low income individuals on the topics of literacy and French as a second language.

Avec une formation initiale d'architecte Jean-Jacques Dutrait a exercé pendant quinze ans dans ce domaine d'activité. Il a été formé à la pédagogie Gattegno par Claudie Gattegno. Il a animé des stages de mise à niveau en français, de français langue étrangère et de mathématiques en entreprise (Hervé BTP, Peugeot, Rambol) Depuis 1997, il anime des stages en direction de publics bénéficiaires du RMI (alphabétisation, français langue étrangère, illettrisme) à raison de deux par an, en alternance.

Robert Echter

Life is a Grand Experiment 52

Robert P. Echter was born in New Haven, CT in 1947. He attended public schools, and majored in psychology at Clark University. He also has a master's in early childhood education and a sixth year degree in school administration. Robert produced not-for-profit concerts with famous rock and jazz artists for a few years in a small venue, wrote poetry, and was

(About the Authors Cont'd.)

an avid student of numismatics for 10 years. He also conducted a drop-in center for teenagers to instill a sense of community in Southern California. During the '70s, Robert taught autistic and brain damaged students at Benhaven for six years. He was interested in studying the early stages of growth, and worked with friend Louis Lerea at Benhaven, until his death. Robert went on to teach at Goddard College, to conduct teacher education projects with U.S. Office of Education funding at High School in the Community, and to teach in the New Haven, CT public schools mostly as a special education teacher with Kindergarten to Grade 8 students. He has had an abiding interest in the field of Caleb Gattegno's work since 1972.

Dr. Marietta Elliott-Kleerkoper
The Silent Way Down Under
De Silent Way Downunder 215

In a career spanning over 40 years, Marietta Elliott-Kleerkoper has taught French, German, English and ESL. Her Ph.D. featured case studies of students learning to write in English as a second language. In the late '70s and early '80s, she teamed up with Dr. Jane Orton in Australia to present seminars to teachers about the Gattegno approaches. She is now retired from teaching, but still runs writing workshops for fellow poets.

Ann Crary Evans
An Experiment in Humanizing Education 112

After leaving Educational Solutions, Ann Crary Evans attended law school and became an attorney for the Administration for Children's Services in Manhattan Family Court. She is married to Ron Evans, who was principal of I.S.201 during the struggle for community control. They are both retired.

Philippe Fagot
Caleb Gattegno, une expérience de maïeutique 88

Philippe Fagot développe auprès d'entreprises et d'institutions des programmes de culture focalisés sur la place de la couleur et du visuel dans des démarches de conception de produits nouveaux, de design, d'architecture ou d'aménagement. Orchestrés autour d'un axe théorique permettant d'associer le sensible au conceptuel, ces programmes investissent les domaines scientifiques, technologiques, anthropologiques, et artistiques. Par l'approche des neurosciences cognitives, cette transdisciplinarité implique autant le sujet (la personne) que l'objet (la matière). Cette activité de conseil est complétée par une forte implication d'enseignement, autant dans des écoles d'ingénieurs, que de design ou d'arts appliqués.

Dr. Alvino Fantini
A "Maverick" Among Thinkers 223

Alvino E. Fantini holds degrees in anthropology and applied linguistics. As senior faculty since 1964, Fantini helped turn the Sandanona Estate into the present SIT Graduate Institute. He has worked in language education (ESOL and foreign languages) and intercultural communication for over 40 years in the U.S. and abroad, in intensive and extensive programs, in education and training, in field situations and in academia, and with numerous languages and cultures. He has conducted significant field research and is published widely, including *Language Acquisition of a Bilingual Child* and *New Ways in Teaching Culture*. Fantini served as an advisory panel member to develop the National Foreign Language Standards for U.S. education, as a president of SIETAR International (Society for Intercultural Education, Training, and Research), and as recipient of its highest award. Fantini is professor emeritus at World Learning's School for International Training in Brattleboro, Vermont, and currently serves as an international consultant.

Annie Fayolle Dietl, Anna-Laura Ferro-Luzzi et Renée Wisler
Trois Enseignantes De Genève 144

Dès 1980, Anna-Laura Ferro-Luzzi, Renée Wisler et Annie Fayolle Dietl ont enseigné à des élèves faibles, puis à des élèves non- francophones de 12 à 15 ans avec la pédagogie Gattegno appliquée aux maths, au français langue seconde, voire tertiaire, et à l'allemand, avec l'accord de la direction du Collège de la Golette et de la Direction Générale du Cycle d'Orientation.

Donald Freeman
"Have You Ever Thought You Might Be Boring?" 235

Donald Freeman is on the faculty at the School of Education, University of Michigan, where he works with undergraduate and post-graduate teacher preparation in all subjects K-12. For 25 years, he was on the graduate faculty at the School of International Training, where he chaired the Department of Language Teacher Education and founded and directed the Center for Teacher Education, Training, and Research, a research and development unit that designed and implemented teacher education projects around the world. His research and design interests focus on creating new, atypical professional environments to support individual learning and institutional transformation.

Maria Gagliardo
How Staying With a Question Pays Off 102

Maria Gagliardo, B.A., M.A. is emeritus professor of language and culture at Purchase College, SUNY. She is a graduate from Hunter College, CUNY. A native of Buenos Aires, Argentina, she was a public school teacher in her country before joining the staff of Dr. Gattegno's Educational Solutions in New York City, first as a trainee and later as a bilingual consultant, in the early '70s. She worked with Dr. Gattegno in the Twin Parks Public Schools project and, in 1974, joined the faculty of the Division of Humanities of Purchase College. She was originally hired by the college to teach Spanish the Silent Way and later on, literature and Latin American civilization. She was the director of two National Endowments for the Humanities grants and of the Foreign Language Institute for secondary school teachers of foreign languages at Purchase College. Since her retirement, Maria has lived in Mar del Plata, Argentina, where she does freelance work as a teacher and consultant.

Claudie Gattegno
Ordinary Miracles 158

Claudie Gattegno began volunteer work with non-reading children in 1985 and then became involved with Professor Berges' department at the Sainte-Anne hospital in Paris. She worked with the Gattegno pedagogy for many years in the field of adult education, mainly with foreign, unschooled or illiterate people. From 1990, Claudie held one or two teacher-training sessions a year, in France, Reunion, and Mayotte. From 1992 to 1996, she ran courses for businesses and public works to help their foreign workers or French workers with little or no education. In 1996, she and her husband, Jean-Jacques Dutrait, created a successful education center in Montreuil, which has since disbanded.

Geneviève Godard
Une enseignante française à Bobo Dioulasso 72

Geneviève Godard est née en 1950 à Montpellier, ville située au sud de la France au bord de la mer Méditerranée. Elle a grandi à Paris où elle a passée un bac littéraire avant de faire des études d'allemand en France, à Münster en Allemagne de l'Ouest et à Berlin-Est. Elle y est restée trois ans, travaillant comme traductrice. A son retour en France en 1972, elle a enseignée l'allemand pendant treize ans.

Après avoir quitté le système scolaire en 1990, elle s'est mise à la recherche de solutions pour aider les enfants en difficultés scolaires, travaillant avec des orthophonistes et des spécialistes de l'audition pour élucider les questions relatives aux difficultés d'émission des sons, et suivant des formations de pédagogie, de gestion mentale, etc. C'est au cours de ces recherches qu'elle a découvert la pédagogie Gattegno.

Ghislaine Graf
Leading Ways 70

Ghislaine Graf was born in a small Swiss village not far from the Lake of Geneva. She discovered Caleb Gattegno's materials and met the "master himself" in 1968. This meeting occurred just before going to be headmistress of a kindergarten in one of the poorest districts of Dakar, where she taught La Lecture en Couleurs and mathematics and marveled at the results. In 1971 Ghislaine joined Educational Solutions. That year, she became the French teacher at St. Thomas Choir School in New York, for two years. In 1973, she was hired by the Red Cross in

(About the Authors Cont'd.)

Switzerland to teach French the Silent Way to the area's first Chilean refugees. The door to an important part of her commitment in teaching languages to immigrants had opened, and remains open to this day. She worked for two years as a specialized educator for addicted women, created the first Subtitling for the Deaf for the Swiss French-speaking Television from 1984 to 1989, and taught English to executives of international companies in France, England, and Germany for several years. She has also been leading seminars in many settings, and for Aurama for many years.

Dr. Kathleen Graves

A Teacher's Perspective on the Power of Observation 310

Kathleen Graves is associate professor of education practice at the School of Education, University of Michigan. She started her career as an English teacher in Taiwan and later taught in the US, Japan, and Brazil. She became a full-time teacher educator in 1982 at the School for International Training in Brattleboro, Vermont where she taught methodology, linguistics, and curriculum design for 26 years. She has worked on curriculum renewal and language teacher education in the US, Algeria, Bahrain, Brazil, Japan, and Korea. Her research focuses on teaching and learning as the heart of a curriculum, and supporting teachers' professional development as the key to successful educational and curricular reform. She is interested in helping teachers to 'think curricularly' and to develop a reflective practice both individually and collaboratively. She is the editor/author of two books on course design, *Teachers as Course Developers* and *Designing Language Courses*. She is the series editor of TESOL's Language Curriculum Development series. She has also co-authored two textbook series for English language learners. She has a master's in teaching languages from the School for International Training and a Ph.D. in applied linguistics from Lancaster University, UK.

Dr. Jim Green

Reflections on Gattegno, Learning Lakota, and More 152

Jim Green received his doctorate at the University of Minnesota. His dissertation, Paradigm Adherence and the Great Debate on Reading, used the Gattegno color charts (Lakota) to conduct the following experiment: Will teacher education faculty on either side of the reading debate adapt their preferred paradigm after a positive learning experience with Words in Color? Jim has taught at the Sisseton Wahpeton Tribal College, South Dakota State University, and the University of Alaska Anchorage. He currently works with the federal Equity Assistance Center (University of Colorado Boulder) and the Monarch Center for Tribal Colleges (University of Illinois Chicago). He resides in South Dakota with his wife Bernice and granddaughter Ciara. Several of his informal lessons for Lakota the Silent Way can be found on YouTube.

Laura Guajardo

A Man Ahead of His Time Recuerdos Agradecidos 133

Laura Guajardo's professional life has so far been very rich and fulfilling, both for her students and for herself. She is still in communication with many past students, some that she taught more than 20 years ago, and continues to get positive feedback from current students. She says Dr. Gattegno impacted her personal life just as much. Through his summer seminars in Europe, she met many wonderful people, some whom became lifelong friends, and was able to learn something from everyone. She also credits Gattegno's essay *On Death* for the great serenity she experienced after the passing of her husband. Laura is very happy to see that there are so many new groups of people in the world spreading Dr. Gattegno's pedagogical approaches.

Nací en la ciudad de México en 1949. Pasé la mayor parte de mi infancia en México. A los 12 años me fui un año a Nueva York y un año a Toronto. Cuando cumplí 19 años me fui a París en donde me case con un Suizo. Fui interprete durante algunos años. Conocí a Cecilia Bartoli quien me presentó al Doctor Gattegno. Trabajé durante muchos años en una escuela de idiomas que trabajaba con muchas compañías multinacionales. He enseñado en Francia, Italia, Suiza y México. Actualmente paso el invierno en México y el resto del tiempo entre París y mi granja en Suiza, desde donde se ve la casa en la que vivió el Doctor Gattegno cuando vivía allá.

Soré Hadara
Le rôle que Caleb Gattegno peut jouer au Burkina Faso 237

Soré Hadara, appelé le plus souvent Adéré, est né au Burkina Faso à Bobo Dioulasso en 1969. Il travaille comme animateur de langues.

Dr. Paula Hajar
The Foundation of My Teaching: A Belief in the Genius of Human Beings 98

Paula Hajar is the professional development specialist in mathematics at the Bronx Charter School for Better Learning, founded in 2003 in New York. Over the years, she has taught grades 1-8, with a specialty in mathematics. In addition to teaching for two years at Horace Mann, she spent 11 years in various capacities at The Day School (now the Trevor Day School) in New York. She earned her doctorate in 1993 at the Harvard Graduate School of Education, and from 1994 to1997 was a professor of education at Teachers College, Columbia University. In 1998, she began a series of administrative positions in public school systems in northern New Jersey and Westchester, and in 2003 left all that to help found Bronx Better Learning with Ted Swartz and Daniel Tamulonis.

Steve Hirschhorn
Seeing 'I' to 'I' 221

Steve Hirschhorn was launched into his career by the inspirational training of International House, Hastings, which sadly no longer exists. He then spent 15 years teaching and learning in Italy, and building up his own businesses, one of which taught Silent Way downstairs and Suggestopedia upstairs. In the late '90s, Steve returned from Italy, completed a master's in Applied Linguistics, received a Postgraduate Certificate in Higher Education (PGCHE), won two awards for excellence in teaching, and became a Fellow of the Higher Education Academy. He also taught various master's modules, delivered hundreds of teacher training courses, and wrote numerous articles for professional journals. He continues to train teachers and always includes modules on the Cuisenaire Rods and the Silent Way. Steve is currently principal of Eckersley Oxford, a well-established and highly respected language school in Oxford.

Michael Hollyfield
My Time with Dr. G and His Overwhelming Flow of Creativity 238

Michael Hollyfield started his career as a navigation officer in the British Merchant Navy. When through illness he could no longer continue in this job, he moved to London and found work as a salesman. At this time he met his future wife, Lola Gattegno, and in 1961 met her father, Dr. Caleb Gattegno, who invited him to attend a weeklong teacher-training course in the use of Cuisenaire Rods. This experience made a great impression. He switched careers again and joined Gattegno's Reading-based operation, eventually becoming director of the Cuisenaire Company of the UK. He is still with the company which has now moved from Reading to West Wales.

John Holt
Respect for the Child's Ability to do First Class Thinking 296

John Caldwell Holt was born in 1923 in New York City and died in 1985. Upon graduating from university, he served a three-year tour of duty with the United States Navy, then worked his way up to the executive director position of United World Federalists, an organization of anti-war and anti-nuclear advocates. John later became a fifth-grade teacher and a supporter of school reform and home-schooling. In 1964, he authored *How Children Fail*, excerpted in this book, in which he criticized traditional education methods. He followed up this work with *How Children Learn* (1967), and *Instead of Education: Way to Help People Do Things Better* (1976).

Maritée Juge
Je n'imagine pas enseigner le français autrement 104

Maritée Juge est née en 1954 à Antibes. Elle y passe son enfance et son adolescence. Après un détour par Aix-

(About the Authors Cont'd.)

en-Provence, elle obtient une licence de philosophie à Paris où elle travaille au montage de longs métrages et de documentaires pendant une dizaine d'années. En 1987, elle obtient une maîtrise de géographie (spécialité aménagement du territoire). En 2009, un concours de circonstances l'amène à donner des cours d'alphabétisation à Vallauris. Se sentant démunie au point de vue méthodologique, elle cherche à se former et participe à un stage animé par Roslyn Young et ensuite la « formation de formateurs » dispensée par Claudie Gattegno et Jean Jacques Dutrait. Depuis le printemps 2010, elle intervient, comme formatrice en français langue étrangère et alphabétisation, auprès des jeunes mineurs étrangers du Foyer de l'Enfance des Alpes-Maritimes et auprès d'un groupe d'adultes étrangers, à Saint-André de la Roche, dans le cadre de la Politique de la Ville.

Suzanne Lachaise

Une fortune sur un plateau 283

Suzanne Lachaise a suivi, de 1970 à 1988, quasiment tous les stages animés par Caleb Gattegno en France et en Suisse. Elle est l'un des membres fondateurs d'Une Ecole Pour Demain où elle a animé de nombreux stages. Enseignante maintenant retraitée de l'Education Nationale, sa carrière a été principalement axée sur l'enseignement en milieu spécialisé, dont 27 années auprès d'enfants sourds et malentendants, après un court passage en classes primaires à plusieurs cours, en maternelle et en classes de perfectionnement. Entre 1996 et 2000 elle a enseigné le français langue étrangère au Japon et contribué dans ce cadre à la formation d'enseignants à Silent Way. Elle fait partie du conseil d'administration de l'association depuis sa création en 1978, et en occupe la fonction de présidente depuis 2008.

Dr. Diane Larsen-Freeman

An Original Thinker 269

Diane Larsen-Freeman (Ph.D. in linguistics, University of Michigan, 1975) is professor of education, professor of linguistics, research scientist at the English Language Institute, and faculty associate at the Center for the Study of Complex Systems at the University of Michigan, Ann Arbor. She is also a distinguished senior faculty fellow at the Graduate SIT Institute in Brattleboro, Vermont. Diane Larsen-Freeman has been a conference speaker in over 65 countries and has published over 100 articles, and several books, in her areas of interest: second language acquisition, language teacher education, applied linguistics, language teaching methodology, and complexity theory. Her book *Complex Systems and Applied Linguistics* (co-authored with Lynne Cameron, Oxford University Press, 2008) was awarded the 2009 Kenneth W. Mildenberger prize from the Modern Language Association. From 1980 to 1985, Diane was editor of the journal *Language Learning*, and she currently serves on its board of directors. In 1997, Diane was inducted into the Vermont Academy of Arts and Sciences. In 2000, she received the lifetime achievement award from Heinle/Cengage Publishers. In 2009 to 2010, she was awarded a Fulbright Distinguished Chair at the University of Innsbruck, Austria. Also, in 2009 she received an honorary doctorate from the Hellenic American University in Athens, Greece. In 2011, she was awarded the Distinguished Scholarship and Service Award by the American Association for Applied Linguists.

Maurice Laurent

Caleb Gattegno aujourd'hui : quelques réflexions 110

D'abord enseignant en France, Maurice Laurent rejoint l'École Internationale de Genève en 1970. Il y enseigne jusqu'en 2000 le Français et les Mathématiques dans les premières classes du secondaire, et y assume aussi des responsabilités administratives et pédagogiques. M. Laurent a rencontré C. Gattegno en 1969. Inspiré par ses recherches et ses propositions, il participe à de nombreux séminaires que dirige le chercheur en Suisse, en France, aux États-Unis et en Grande Bretagne. Depuis trente ans, il conduit lui-même des sessions de réflexion et de formation pédagogiques centrées sur l'approche définie par C.G. : La Subordination de l'Enseignement à l'apprentissage. Avec Christiane Laurent, il a mis au point 2 didacticiels : Dictées en couleurs et S'éduquer à orthographier. Ils ont aussi mis au point des supports pour enseigner la langue française : expression orale et écrite, grammaire, orthographe, conjugaison… M. Laurent est aussi l'auteur de 2 livres : Les jeunes, la langue, la grammaire. Au sein de l'association Une Éducation Pour Demain, il est chargé avec deux ou trois autres personnes de la formation de groupes d'enseignants désirant s'approprier les outils de l'approche Gattegno.

Alain L'Hôte

Un plaisir pour la vie 225

Instituteur de 1972 à 2004, Alain L'Hôte a commencé sa carrière en faisant des remplacements de maîtres absents dans des classes très diverses avec des populations d'enfants de 8 à 16 ans, souvent en difficultés. Puis il a travaillé dans des classes primaires ordinaires pour finir sa carrière avec des classes de C.P. (première année du primaire en France)Il a commencé à utiliser les outils proposés par Caleb Gattegno au début des années 80, date à laquelle il a rencontré l'association Une École Pour Demain (aujourd'hui Une Éducation pour Demain). Très vite il a rejoint le Conseil d'Administration de l'association dont il fait toujours partie. Il a été de longues années au Bureau de l'association et a occupé la responsabilité de Président durant trois années. Il anime des stages de formation en Lecture en Couleurs depuis de nombreuses années.

Henry Liebling

Caleb Gattegno: A Profound and Continuing Personal Influence 308

Henry Liebling currently develops a website with ESCalate for Education for Sustainability and Global Learning in teacher education, launched in June 2008. He helped introduce agricultural science into the Zambian secondary curriculum in 1970, leading science and the school farm at Mwinilunga Secondary School. Returning to Lancashire in 1973 with a growing interest in self-help, community, and sustainability, he helped set up an Oxfam group and shop, chaired a parish council, and taught for 10 years in an urban primary school, introducing science, technology, and early IT. He co-authored Sand Harvest (a computer role-play simulation of life in the Sahel) for CWDE in 1986. He led primary maths education at Marjon for 16 years, writing *Getting Started* a guide for newly qualified teachers (1999) and co-authoring *The Really Useful Maths Book* with Tony Brown in 2005.

Wojciech Łukaszewicz

Taking the Learner into Account: An Effective Remedy for Becoming a Better Teacher 174

Wojciech Łukaszewicz studied Polish and theatre, but it was English that shaped his professional life. He started teaching in 1990, and in 1997 opened Global Village Language School in Białystok, northeast Poland, where he still works. He only recently took interest in the Silent Way in his quest for more effective learning and teaching.

Isabelle Luter Doussain

Approaching the Approach
L'évolution d'une approche 230

Isabelle Luter Doussain discovered Caleb Gattegno's pedagogical approach six years ago at Une Education Pour Demain (An Education for the Future) in Besançon, France, where she participated in initiation and training sessions. Motivated by the techniques she was learning, she began seeking other associations that practice the approach. She currently works as an FSL (French as a Second Language) teacher in the Paris area.

Luigi Magnano

No Tricks, But There is
Magic in the Technique 39

Luigi (Louis) Magnano worked as a teacher, bilingual coordinator, and administrator for the Hartford Board of Education in Hartford, Connecticut from 1974 to 1983. He is presently self-employed, living in Italy, Marina di Massa (MS) Tuscany. He enjoys giving lessons whenever possible to those wishing to open their minds through use of the Silent Way.

Brendan Marcus

Living, Learning, Teaching
En vivant, en apprenant, en enseignant 58

Brendan Marcus is a teacher of French and English

(About the Authors Cont'd.)

as foreign languages. He was introduced to the Gattegno Approach while working in Japan, and has been a practitioner of the Silent Way for the past eight years. Back in France since 2007, he has broadened his study of awareness through exploring the fields of reading and writing, mathematics, computers, and recently, parenthood.

Brendan Marcus est enseignant de français et d'anglais langues étrangères. Il a été initié à l'approche Gattegno via son travail au Japon, et est un praticien du Silent Way depuis huit ans. De retour en France en 2007, il a élargi son étude des prises de consciences vers les domaines de la lecture et de l'écriture, des mathématiques, de l'informatique, et plus récemment, à celui d'être parent.

Dr. John Mason

The "Only" Statements 292

John Mason started teaching when he was 15, tutoring younger students in mathematics, and has kept it up for over 50 years. As an undergraduate, he studied mathematics, physics, and chemistry, and then received a M.Sc. and Ph.D. in mathematics. John joined the Open University in the UK in 1970, learning how to make radio and television programs, and writing distance-teaching materials. He designed the university's first summer-schools, which lasted for 25 years, and involved as many as 5,000 students over a span of 11 weeks on three sites simultaneously. He went on to spend one year in the company of 130 companions under the guidance of J. G. Bennett, mathematician and mystic. John was a founder member of the Open University Centre for Mathematics Education and defacto leader for some 15 years. He met Dr. Caleb Gattegno in 1981 over a week at Charney Manor and participated in several subsequent workshops. He retired from the Open University in 2009, but continues to be a senior research fellow at the department of education at Oxford University where he sometimes teaches. He initiated the mathemapedia component of the NCETM website, and continues to work on mathematical problems by himself and with anyone willing to participate. John also leads workshops and seminars in mathematics education around the world when invited.

Janice Mattina

Dancing a Dialogue: Interaction with the Learner and Interaction in Learning 280

Janice Mattina has been an educator for more than 40 years. Trained in the Gattegno approach to teaching reading and math, and a certified Montessori instructor for over 30 years, she started Center Montessori School for her own children in 1976 to provide an alternative education in an environment respectful of the whole child. As a graduate of the University of South Florida in Tampa, a public school teacher both in California and Florida, a Words in Color reading and Algebricks math consultant, a parent and teacher instructor in redirecting children's behavior, and expert on instructing children on conflict resolution, Janice has devoted her life to children and helping give them the tools to live happier, more fulfilling lives. Janice is a proud parent of four and grandparent to six children (all of whom attend the school she founded). In her spare time, she writes poetry about nature and wildlife.

Dr. Marilyn Maye

Exceeding Expectations 36

Marilyn Maye is assistant professor in the Department of Educational Leadership at New Jersey City University, and a mathematics education consultant for state and national organizations. She has been a middle school mathematics teacher and coach in the New York City public schools, lecturer in mathematics in the City University of New York, and assistant superintendent in an urban New Jersey school district. A graduate of Swarthmore College, Harvard Graduate School of Education, and Columbia University Graduate School of Arts and Sciences, she earned her doctorate in education from Columbia University, Teachers College. She is a founding trustee of the Bronx Charter School for Better Learning in New York City, and a member of the Board of the African Christian Teachers Association. She and her husband, Warren L. Maye have co-authored *Orita: Rites of Passage for Youth of African Descent in America*.

Rosie McAndrew
The Influence of Gattegno – Direct and Indirect 312

Rosie McAndrew is a grammar and pronunciation specialist who has been teaching English as a Foreign Language (EFL) for over 30 years. She now has her own company teaching and accommodating students one on one in her home in Hastings, United Kingdom.

Dr. Piers Messum
Insights from Gattegno 166

Piers Messum studied mathematics and law as an undergraduate in university. He then worked for two spells in the computer software business (as a programmer and then a salesman), but between these he taught English in Japan and came across the work of Caleb Gattegno there. In 1991, he started to teach English by an approximation to the Silent Way. He spent nearly 11 years on a Ph.D. thesis entitled "On the Role of Imitation in Learning to Pronounce" which describes non-imitative mechanisms by which children might learn to pronounce English. Piers lives in London and teaches English and some math.

Klara Miller-Fuehren
Meine Begegnungen mit dem Genie Dr. Gattegno 34

Klara Miller-Fuehren wohnt in Rimsting am Chiemsee, Deutschland. Sie ist gebürtige Deutsche und lebte 30 Jahre im Ausland, davon 10 Jahre in Paris. Dort studierte sie Schauspielerei und arbeitete jahrelang als Schauspielerin. Um ihr Studium zu finanzieren, arbeitete sie von 1979 -1983 „Pour l'Education de Demain" in Paris und weil sie so begeistert war vom Silent Way, machte sie die Ausbildung bei Cecilia Bartoli und Barbara Villez.

Sie unterrichtete Deutsch mit dem „Silent Way" in großen Firmen wie SNECMA, Englisch für Angestellte des Fernsehsenders TV 1 an der Sorbonne. An vielen Wochenenden lehrte sie Englisch oder Deutsch in Paris, Bordeaux, Besançon und Genf. Auch stellte sie den Silent Way den Lehrern der Universität Bielefeld und an anderen deutschen Schulen vor, wie auch auf Messen in Paris. 1983 verließ sie Frankreich. Inzwischen ist sie verheiratet und hat zwei erwachsene Kinder.

Obwohl sie jetzt nicht mehr unterrichtet, weiß sie das Genie Dr. Gattegno immer noch sehr zu schätzen, denn diese Zeit in Paris war für sie prägend für das ganze Leben. Seit 1998 arbeitet sie als Erzählerin und Regisseurin in Oberbayern.

Dr. Katherine Mitchell
Caleb Gattegno: As I Remember Him 182

Katherine A. Mitchell received her Ph.D. in reading from New York University. She worked on the staff of Educational Solutions for 10 years, teaching and conducting workshops on Words in Color and Gattegno Mathematics for teachers across the United States and in England, Switzerland, and Northern Africa. For 28 years, she worked with the Alabama Department of Education. In her last position as assistant state superintendent of education for reading, Katherine created and directed the Alabama Reading Initiative, which saw Alabama's Grade 4 reading scores on the National Assessment of Educational Progress (NAEP) increase more than scores in any other state in the history of NAEP assessment. Katherine has served on several national boards and technical advisory groups, and received multiple awards for her work in literacy.

Dr. Patrick Moran
"Why Am I Doing This?"..............127

Patrick Moran has been a member of the SIT Graduate Institute faculty of the M.A.T. Program since 1977. Pat has taught a variety of courses there, including language teaching methods. He has a special interest in the interface of intercultural communication and second language education. He is also an illustrator of language learning and teaching materials.

Zouré Moumouni
Une approche pour l'Afrique 300

Zouré Moumouni est né en 1971 à Bobo Dioulasso au Burkina Faso. Il a fréquenté l'école jusqu'en première, mais il n'a pas pu aller plus loin par manque

(About the Authors Cont'd.)

de moyens financiers. Il a alors décidé de devenir instituteur pour s'investir dans le social. Après deux ans de formation, il a débuté dans des villages de brousse. Puis il a retourné à sa ville natale, Bobo Dioulasso, où il pratique depuis sept ans.

Etsuko Nagasawa 長澤 悦子
So this is the Silent Way! 原点へ近づく喜び 272

Etsuko Nagasawa was born in 1960 in Kyoto Prefecture, and now resides in Osaka City. She graduated from the Kansai University of Foreign Studies (Spanish Language Section of Foreign Language Department) in Osaka in 1983 with a B.A. degree in Spanish. She started her career as a Japanese language instructor in 1993, working for a Japanese language school in Kobe, where she has taught ever since. She has also been working for the Center for Learning in Osaka since 1997 with Fusako Allard. She established the Silent Way Language Center in Osaka in 2005 with the aim to make it a place where both learners and teachers of languages can function practicing the spirit of the Silent Way. To this end, she makes continuous endeavors by offering language courses, and organizing and leading research activities.

1960年、京都生まれ。大阪在住。1983年、関西外国語大学外国語学部スペイン語学科卒業。 1993年〜日本語学校(神戸)日本語教師。1995年〜『語学文化協会(大阪)』アラード房子氏のもとで、サイレントウェイを学ぶ。1997年〜『語学文化協会(大阪)』日本語教師。 2005年、『SW Language Center(大阪)』設立。SWで言語を学ぶ人、SWで言語を教える人の実践の場として機能することを目指して、言語コースの提供、研究会活動等を続けている。

Kyoko Nishio
Why I Love Joining Silent Way Workshops 302

Kyoko Nishio teaches English to junior high school students in Japan. She recently completed her first year teaching English. She studied linguistics in university, focusing on psycholinguistics. She has taken several Silent Way English workshops instructed by Donald Cherry in Tokyo, and hopes to find her own way of teaching by studying the Silent Way more in the future.

Noriko Ogino
The Real Learning:Educating My Self 229

Noriko Ogino worked as a flight attendant for Scandinavian Air Lines for 30 years after graduating from the economics department of Keio University in Tokyo, Japan. She took a year's absence to attend the School for International Training (SIT), receiving a M.A.T. in 1991. She first participated in a Silent Way workshop offered by the Center in Osaka, Japan, studying Italian the Silent Way. Since then, she has been involved in studying the Gattegno Approach and the Silent Way, and since 2002, she has been one of the staff members of the Gattegno Approach Study Group and Silent Way Tokyo.

Dr. Masayuki Onishi
In the Midst of a Whirlwind 260

Masayuki Onishi is a linguist specialising in the documentation of minority languages spoken in Bougainville (Papua New Guinea), Northeast India, and Okinawa, Japan. He has also been working on the modern literature and folk culture of Bengal (India and Bangladesh) since the 1970s. He has translated many works of modern Bengali writers into Japanese. In addition, he has been developing an audio database of traditional Bengali folk and religious songs in collaboration with local researchers and performers. He is currently employed as a senior researcher at RIHN (Research Institute for Humanity and Nature), Kyoto, Japan, working for a project entitled "Environmental Change and the Indus Civilization." He has worked as a foreign language teacher and an organizer of foreign language programs in different institutions for 35 years. He regularly teaches Japanese, Bengali, and English, and occasionally conducts Silent Way workshops. He has experimentally developed a full set of Bengali language charts with the assistance of Piers Messum and Roslyn Young, and a Sound-Color Chart of Japanese with the assistance of Fusako Allard.

Dr. Jane Orton
Two Simple Drawings That Changed My Teaching Forever 138

Jane Orton, Ph.D., is director of the Chinese Teacher Training Centre in the Melbourne Graduate School of Education, The University of Melbourne, Australia, where she coordinated modern languages education for 20 years. A speaker of English, French, and Chinese, her research interests are intercultural communication and nonverbal communication, and she has published particularly on kinesic expression and identity. Jane first encountered Gattegno's work through Silent Way classes in ESL, being taught in Melbourne schools. After some time living in France, she spent three years working with Caleb Gattegno, first at Schools for the Future and then at Educational Solutions, Inc. During her two years in New York, she taught Silent Way French daily to three classes of boy sopranos at the Choir School of St. Thomas' Church Fifth Avenue, developed Silent Way materials for a number of languages, and gave regular seminars and intensive French language courses for ESI. In her third year in the US, she opened a branch office of ESI in New Haven, Connecticut.

Lindsay Pearson
Transcending Barriers to Become a Better Learner 23

Lindsay Pearson is an ESL instructor at the Riverside Language Program, where she has been on staff since 1981. She has taught at various other institutions and has been a mentor to master's degree candidates in TESL from the School for International Training, the New School, and New York University. She also coordinates ESL evening classes in several branches of the New York Public Library. In 1992, she founded English for Clear Expression in Medicine and the Sciences, a business that specializes in on-site communication improvement for physicians and scientific researchers. From 1979 to 1981, she worked at Educational Solutions in New York City as an education consultant, then as west coast regional manager. She graduated with a B.A. Magna Cum Laude, and a M.A. in TESL, both from Hunter College of the City University of NY. Lindsay is also a member of Pi Delta Phi (Société d'Honneur Française), and the New York Academy of Science.

Esaie Pierre
Ignoring the Threat of Violence for the Hope of Becoming a Better Teacher 244

Esaie Pierre is a senior research scientist for an international pharmaceutical company. He received his B.A. in biology and M.A. in in neuroendocrinology from Rutgers University. Esaie immigrated from Haiti to the United States in 1981 at the age of 12. Believing that education is the key to Haiti's future, he co-founded ELAT, a professional development project for teachers of elementary schools, focused on the materials and pedagogy developed and popularized by Caleb Gattegno. Esaie is also on the board of directors of Beyond Borders, an organization that focuses on the division created by growing economic disparity in the world.

John Pint
Standing on the Shoulders of Dr. G 8

Upon receiving a master's degree in TESL in 1971, John Pint was employed by Educational Solutions, Inc. and was sent to California by Dr. Caleb Gattegno to introduce West-Coast teachers to the Silent Way. He subsequently lived and worked with teachers and students in Korea, Spain, France, Saudi Arabia, and Mexico, where he presently continues to teach while writing a column for The Guadalajara Reporter. John is author of *Outdoors in Western Mexico*, *The Desert Caves of Saudi Arabia*, and several books for teachers and students of EFL, such as *Telephone Talk*, *Encounter English—The Britannica Method* and *The Adventures of Lucky Luke—Stories and Exercises to Develop Comprehension and Vocabulary*. John and his wife Susy have also co-authored *Discovering the Silent Way—With an Introduction by Caleb Gattegno*, a manuscript edited by Dr. Gattegno and awaiting publication.

Dr. Arthur Powell
Transformation: From Ideology to Science ...92

(About the Authors Cont'd.)

Arthur B. Powell is associate professor of mathematics education and chair of the department of urban education at the Newark campus of Rutgers University, New Jersey, and faculty research scientist and associate director of the Robert B. Davis Institute for Learning of the Graduate School of Education in New Brunswick. He received his B.A. in mathematics and statistics from Hampshire College, Amherst, MA; his M.A. in mathematics from the University of Michigan, Ann Arbor, MI; and his Ph.D. in mathematics education from Rutgers University, New Brunswick, NJ. He is the co-author and co-editor of several books, and co-developer of ELAT, a professional development project for teachers of elementary schools, focused on the materials and pedagogy developed and popularized by Caleb Gattegno. In 2003, he also co-founded the Bronx Charter School for Better Learning, where Gattegno's approach to the teaching of reading, world languages, social studies, science, and mathematics are practiced.

Steven Quinn

The Faster Way 304

Steven Quinn was born in Sydney, Australia, and is 25 years old. He gained a Bachelor of Arts and Bachelor of Education at Sydney University in 2008. He has been teaching at an intensive English language center in Melbourne for two years, working with illiterate refugees from all over the world, but mainly from Afghanistan and Sudan. Steven has been teaching the Silent Way for about a year. During this time, he has been working with Dr. Roslyn Young on her book, *An Introduction to the Silent Way*. He helped her to edit the book and shaped the content a little with what he calls "novice questions." He has also established a website for beginning Silent Way teachers.

Jim Reed

The Summer with Dr. G 109

Jim Reed studied modern languages and literatures and spent his working life teaching at Oxford University, first as fellow and tutor in German at St John's College (1963-1988) and later as the University's taylor professor of the German language and literature and fellow of the Queen's College (1989-2004). In retirement he continues to study modern languages and literatures.

Riverside Language Program

Dr. Gattegno and the Riverside Language Program 82

PHYLLIS BERMAN, co-founder and co-director of the Riverside Language Program in New York City since 1979, has been an ESOL teacher and teacher trainer in high school, college, and adult education settings. A student of Caleb Gattegno at Educational Solutions in the 1970s, she continued her study of the Silent Way with Shakti Gattegno, who offered special workshops for the staff of RLP in recent years. She also studied Counseling-Learning/Community Language Learning with Father Charles Curran, now deceased, and Dr. Jenny Rardin during that same period, and integrated the two approaches in her classroom work with ESOL students and teachers.

LANE SEROTA has been with the Riverside Language Program in New York City since 1980, as an ESL instructor in its daytime classes, as a coordinator and supervisor for the evening ESL classes provided by Riverside in conjunction with the New York Public Library in numerous library branches throughout the city, and as a mentor to student interns from the School for International Training in Brattleboro, Vermont. She first began studying at Educational Solutions in New York City in 1976, taking various workshops with Dr. Gattegno, many of his brilliant staff, and Shakti Gattegno, eventually enrolling in Dr. Gattegno's Program for Advanced Study in the Silent Way. After completing the coursework requirements for this program, she was observed by Dr. Gattegno and approved by him as a Silent Way teacher.

NORMA ELLIOTT is currently the associate director at Riverside Language Program in New York City. She was introduced to the Silent Way at York House in Barcelona, Spain, in the 1980s. Later, Norma moved back to the United States, specifically New York, and began to work at the Riverside Language Program, which has also been a home for Silent Way practitioners. Norma thanks Shelly Liu for introducing her to the Chinese language via the

Silent Way in 1980. Shelly Liu, in some magical way, awoke a passion for Mandarin that has lasted for over 20 years.

LIA PESCE is currently the workshop coordinator at the Riverside Language Program, where she has previously been an ESOL teacher. She is also a teacher of ESOL for adult learners in classes held in collaboration with the Riverside Language Program and the New York Public Library. Following the completion of her graduate language teaching education at New York University, she enrolled in an internship at the Riverside Language Program to further enhance her experience and confidence in the classroom. It was during this internship that Dr. Gattegno's Silent Way became a fundamental part of her teaching and learning philosophy, and has continued to be ever since.

Bill Robbins
Transferable Skills 44

Bill Robbins was born in 1944 and lived in the former Belgian colony of the Congo until just short of his sixteenth birthday. He attended four different high schools before going to university in a small Midwestern institute in the U.S., majoring in history and political science with training to become a teacher. In 1966, he went to Vietnam as an English teacher with International Voluntary Services, followed by a stint with the U.S. Peace Corps in Thailand. He spent over a decade in Japan where he developed his understanding of, and skills in using the Silent Way. He now resides in Australia.

Raymonde Rocourt
Gattegno en Haïti 128

Raymonde Rocourt est née en Haïti en 1949 de la famille Héraux. Elle a fait ses études classiques et supérieures dans son pays d'origine. Dès son plus jeune âge, elle s'est intéressée à l'enseignement. Sa formation de base fut empreinte de la méthode Freinet qu'elle a appliquée pendant quatre ans au Nouveau Collège Bird, un Collège suisse établi en Haïti à l'époque. Au bout de quelques années, elle s'est tournée vers l'administration dans une compagnie aérienne américaine pendant vingt-trois ans. Là encore, une de ses tâches était celle d'entrainer le personnel affecté au service à la clientèle. Pour le faire, elle mettait à profit ses connaissances en pédagogie. Mais lorsqu'elle a découvert Caleb Gattegno, elle a eu l'envie de revenir dans l'éducation avec le défi d'apporter un sang neuf, un enseignement diversifié, dynamique, puissant, nouveau et efficace à son pays. C'est ainsi que depuis 1997, Mme Raymonde Rocourt, à travers son école fondamentale Aux Alizés, fait la promotion des techniques Gattegno pour un apprentissage conscient, valable et durable pour les jeunes Haïtiens.

Daniel Roder
Une rencontre avec Gattegno ou plus précisément avec sa pédagogie 210

Daniel Roder est présentement le gérant du cabinet Virgule, un conseil en ressources humaines créé in 2003 en Lorraine.

Véronique Rodoz
Une nouvelle vision grâce à la Lecture en couleurs 33

Véronique Rodoz est née en 1962. Elle habite un petit village dans la région de Montbéliard, en Franche-Comté, dans l'Est de la France, très proche de la Suisse Romande et de l'Allemagne. Elle est enseignante depuis 1981, et a enseignée longtemps en petite section de maternelle, puis elle s'est spécialisée dans l'aide aux enfants en difficultés. A la fin de son année de formation spécialisée, elle a rencontré la pédagogie Gattegno sous la forme d'une intervention sur la Lecture en couleurs faite par une de ses collègues en formation. Depuis ce moment, elle n'a pas cessé de faire des stages, un, puis deux, puis trois par an, pour s'engager enfin dans une formation générale proposée par Une Éducation Pour Demain (pendant 5 ans voire plus). Elle a commencée à utiliser cette pédagogie avec des enfants en difficultés scolaires, puis, depuis 2006, avec des enfants handicapés ayant des Troubles Envahissants du Développement. Parallèlement, l'approche Gattegno a transformé peu à peu sa vision du monde.

Carol Finch Cone Rose

(About the Authors Cont'd.)

To the Best of Our Abilities 135

Carol Rose was born in 1933 in Champaign, Illinois, and was educated at University of Illinois Laboratory High School, where Dr. Gattegno worked with Max Biebermann to initiate new math in the early 1950s. She later attended Middlebury College, University of Illinois, Yale University, and University of Paris – specialties in Russian, French literature and linguistics, and clinical psychology at Paris VII. She was a teacher of English as a second language (Achimota School, Ghana, Paris II), and had a professional practice as a psychotherapist and reading specialist at Hospital St. Anne, Paris, using Dr. Gatttegno's pedagogy. She also worked in private practice in reading difficulties, and has published regarding remediation in reading and mathematics.

Allen Rozelle

Some Facts of Awareness 264

Allen Rozelle has been in touch with The Subordination of Teaching to Learning since 1971 and working directly with it and its associated materials since 1974. He taught English in Paris from 1968 to 1979. He then moved to Geneva where he taught English, History and Geography in the bilingual section of the middle school at the International School of Geneva. During that time, he also attended Educational Solutions sponsored workshops, did teacher training, taught adult ESL classes, and worked with students in Hebrew, using the video series Hebrew, the Silent Way. He now lives in Santa Cruz, California, where he teaches ESL as a volunteer with the Santa Cruz Literacy Project.

Christiane Rozet

This Work Transformed Me
Ce travaille m'a transformé 162

Christiane Rozet spent her career as a kindergarten teacher, first in the countryside, then in the city of Besançon, France. She met Dr. Gattegno in 1982 and worked with him until he died. She has transcribed most of the seminars Gattegno gave in France, about 20 in all. She retired from National Education in 1992. She continues to work as secretary of the association Une Education Pour Demain, a job she has held since 1990.

Christiane Rozet a passé toute sa carrière comme institutrice en école maternelle, d'abord à la campagne, puis à Besançon. Elle a rencontré Gattegno en 1982 et a travaillé avec lui jusqu'à sa mort. Elle a transcrit la plupart des séminaires que Gattegno a animé en France, une vingtaine en tout. Elle a pris sa retraite de l'Education Nationale en 1992 mais a continué de travailler en tant que secrétaire de l'association Une Education Pour Demain, poste qu'elle occupe depuis 1990.

Dr. Michel Sagaz

Silence, apprentissage et
méta-apprentissage 187

Michel Sagaz est Docteur de l'Université de Toulouse-Le Mirail (France), en Sciences du Langage. Il est actuellement Maître de Conférences à l'Université de Kumamoto (Japon). Ses domaines d'intérêts incluent notamment les sciences cognitives, la conception des modèles didactiques d'enseignement-apprentissage des langues étrangères et leur cohérence théorico-pratique. Il a été sensibilisé à l'Approche Silencieuse à partir de 2001. Vivement intéressé par cette approche, il a entrepris de faire des recherches dans ce domaine. Dans sa thèse de Doctorat (2007), l'auteur propose une étude du rôle constructif des apprenants dans l'Approche Silencieuse dans laquelle il examine la pertinence de la notion de « subordination de l'enseignement à l'apprentissage » en s'intéressant spécifiquement aux interrelations entre les paramètres cognitifs et méthodologiques qu'implique le modèle didactique relatif à cette approche.

Edna Shaw

Facing Change the Gattegno Way 30

Edna Shaw was born in 1924 in Townsville, a far north-eastern port in Queensland, Australia. Her hopes to pursue teacher training in the south suddenly faded with the outbreak of World War II. She gained a Public Service appointment to the Great Northern Railways, which played a vital role in troop deployment in the Pacific War, and was also a part-time VAD (Voluntary Aid Detachment), giving nursing aid to sick and wounded troops at the military hospital. With peace in the Pacific declared, she went to Royal Melbourne Hospital for four years of general training and staff nursing. Edna then took midwifery training at Crown Street Women's Hospital, Sydney, followed by a third Certificate in Infant Welfare. Years of charge work followed in nursery, pediatrics, post-natal care, and work with those with cerebral palsy. She then earned a degree in fine arts and philosophy at Melbourne University, which opened the path to teaching.

Kazuko Shimizu 清水和子
It Takes the Time it Takes
何かをするのに　かかるだけの時間がかかる …………168

Kazuko Shimizu began teaching Japanese as a second language in 1974, at first by a conventional method, and later with the Silent Way, having met Fusako Allard in 1979. She was enchanted by the Silent Way and participated in the center's activities, such as hand-painting Silent Way Japanese charts, trying to improve them. She introduced the Silent Way to the Japan Association of Language Teachers with Fusako, and participated in various seminars and workshops learning such things as Vietnamese and Korean. After Dr. G's death, Kazuko continually had opportunities to learn from various people invited from the U.S., Italy, and France, as well as from local colleagues who studied and used the Silent Way. Due to the drastic change of lifestyle after the Hanshin- Awaji earthquake in 1995, among other problems, she stopped teaching. Kazuko now runs a space to offer yoga, chi-gon, etc. with her family in Kobe.

1974年に第二言語としての日本語を教え始める。最初は従来のやり方で教えていたが、1979年にアラード房子さんに出会い、サイレント・ウェイを知ってからはSWに魅せられ、SWで教えはじめた。房子さんたちと一緒に日本語のサウンド・カラー・チャート、フィデル、語彙のチャートなどの改良に従事。よりよい授業を目指して、房子さんからいろいろ示唆を受ける。また、日本語学教師の会（JALT）で、房子さんとSWを紹介。と同時に一緒にいろいろなセミナーやワークショップにも参加。Dr. Gのセミナー仲間などからベトナム語や韓国語をならったりもした。Dr.Gの没後もUS、イタリア、韓国、フランスなどから招かれたSW、さらにはガテーニョ・アプローチを研究、実践する人々によるセミナーなど学ぶ機会をたくさんもらった。1995年の阪神大震災のあとの急激な生活の変化と個人的な問題から教えることをやめ、神戸でヨガや気功などのスペースを家族で経営している。

Junko Shinada 品田潤子
A Fascination with Pronunciation
発音の魅力 …………198

Junko Shinada was born in 1957 and currently lives in Tokyo, Japan. She has been working as a Japanese language teacher since 1984. She met the Silent Way in 1988 during Spanish and English workshops led by Dr. Gattegno offered by the Center, in Japan. Since then, she has been studying the Gattegno Approaches and the Silent Way. Since 2002, she has been one of the staff members of the Gattegno Approach Study Group and Silent Way Tokyo, which is engaged in holding workshops.

1957年生まれ。東京在住。1984年より日本語教師。1988年5月、語学文化協会が大阪と東京で開催したガテーニョ博士によるスペイン語と英語のワークショップに参加し、サイレント・ウエイと出会う。以後現在に至るまで、ガテーニョ・アプローチの勉強を続けている。2002年より、ガテーニョ・アプローチ研究会に参加し、「サイレントウエイ東京」のスタッフとして、サイレントウエイとガテーニョ・アプローチのワークショップの企画、運営に従事している。

Jeremy Steele
Working for Caleb Gattegno …………276

Jeremy Steele was born in Adelaide, grew up in Perth, and in 1954, at the age of 15 joined his family in Italy. At the end of 1955, with some competency in Italian but no life plan, he traveled to London. A hostel roommate encouraged him to complete his school education by correspondence, in Italian and French, which duly led to university admission to Keele in 1958. Upon graduating in Arts four years later, he worked for Caleb Gattegno's Educational Explorers educational publishing company as assistant editor. Five years later, he joined the Hodder publishing group with a view to representing its educational interests in Australia. After a further five years with Hodders, he embarked on a 25-year career in administration with the University of Sydney, in publications and public

(About the Authors Cont'd.)

relations. His interest in languages led to enquiries into the Sydney Aboriginal language, and following retirement in 1999, Jeremy completed a master's degree by research on this subject in 2005, thereafter allowing the thesis to be placed on the internet. He has continued to develop and refine his databases of Australian indigenous languages, mostly in New South Wales, and makes occasional additions to his language blog.

Dr. Earl Stevick
Humanism in Language Teaching 115

Earl Stevick was born in Sioux City, Iowa, midway between the Great War and the Great Depression. Except for one year in Africa, he has always lived in the United States. He is widowed, with three adult children, seven grandchildren, and five great-grandchildren. Since the death of his wife in 2003, he has been a resident in an assisted living facility in Lexington, Virginia.

Dr. Theodore Swartz
Three Lessons Learned From
An Uncompromising Man 219

Theodore Swartz first saw Caleb Gattegno teach in the early 1970s, when Gattegno conducted a demonstration lesson at his school. He worked for Gattegno from 1972 to 1979 and has continued to study and teach about the Subordination of Teaching to Learning since then. Theodore was a first grade teacher during Bronx Better Learning's first two years of operation. He later served as the school's executive director, and now is a professional development specialist, training teachers in all aspects of the subordination of teaching to learning. With a Ph.D. in Educational Psychology, Special Education, from New York University, Dr. Swartz has served in a wide variety of school positions, including: an elementary and intermediate school teacher in the Bushwick and Ocean Hill-Brownsville sections in Brooklyn; a special education teacher in an elementary school on Staten Island; an adjunct assistant and associate professor of English, including remedial reading and writing, with the City University of New York; and the principal of an elementary school in Putnam County, New York.

Daniel Tamulonis
From the Congo to the Bronx 66

Daniel Fergus Tamulonis was born in Pottsville, Pennsylvania, U.S.A. After graduating with a B.A. in theatre from Pennsylvania State University in 1975, he joined the U.S. Peace Corps and spent the next five years in Zaïre (now the Democratic Republic of the Congo). He then studied puppetry at the University of Connecticut and toured nationally with the Center for Puppetry Arts. He continued his graduate studies in TESOL at Teachers College, Columbia University, and spent years teaching around New York State. He returned to New York City to become the director of the Peace Corps Fellows Program at Teachers College for 10 years. In 2002, he began working on teacher training in elementary schools using Words in Color. This led to his work with the Bronx Charter School for Better Learning, where Daniel currently teaches kindergarten.

Te Ataarangi
The Māori Revival 40

Te Ataarangi was developed in the late 1970s by Dr. Kāterina Te Heikōkō Mataira and Ngoingoi Pewhairangi. It was designed as a community-based program for adult Māori language learning. The program is modeled on the Silent Way approach developed by Dr. Caleb Gattegno, utilizing Cuisenaire Rods (rākau) and spoken language. This is in direct contrast to traditional grammar-based, academic approaches. Gattegno's methodology was further developed to incorporate Māori values and customs, and Te Ataarangi was born. Originally these programs were delivered by native speakers of the Māori language who were trained to become tutors. In over 30 years since its inception, Te Ataarangi has taught thousands of adults to speak Māori. Thank you to Maureen Muller and her colleagues for providing this article.

Dr. Leslie Turpin
"I Didn't Do it, You Did":
A Great Lesson Learned 25

Leslie Turpin has been a language teacher since 1980 and a teacher educator in the M.A.T. Program at SIT since 1989. She has a M.A.T. from SIT and a Ph.D.

from the California Institute for Integral Studies. She currently works as managing director of Sandglass Theater in Putney, Vermont.

Adrian Underhill

Silence Amplifies: The Loud Silent Way 270

Adrian Underhill is an international Enhanced Language Training (ELT) consultant and trainer. As a consultant, he provides training and consultancy to leadership and management of ELT organizations, and as a trainer, runs courses. In addition, Adrian writes for teachers and speaks at conferences. He was director of the International Teacher Training Institute at International House in Hastings, Australia until 1999, and is a past president of the International Association of Teachers of English as a Foreign Language (IATEFL). Adrian started the first IATEFL interest group dedicated to teacher development. Of the many influences on his work the most profound and all-encompassing has been the work of Dr. Caleb Gattegno, who Adrian first met in 1976. He feels huge gratitude to him for his piercing insight and vision, and for being constantly ahead of his time. Adrian Underhill's other interests include working in his organic garden and improvising music with his jazz band.

Dr. Barbara Villez

A Letter to Dr. G 291

Barbara Villez is a professor at the University of Paris 8 (Vincennes-St Denis), where she teaches in the departments of Didactics, Law, and Media Studies. She discovered the Silent Way at the very beginning of her teaching career and was able to study with Dr. Gattegno and Cecilia Bartoli in New York and Paris. She worked for the Paris association (Pour l'éducation de Demain), which organized Silent Way language weekends, courses in companies, and seminars with Dr. G to enable European teachers to work with him during these trips. Her collaboration with Dr. G lasted 17 years and he continues to have a strong influence on her ideas about teaching and learning. Barbara has taught language to students of all ages from three to 77 years old. Now at the University, she does a teaching ethics class which is largely based on Dr. Gattegno's pedagogical approach.

Michiko Watabe

The Audacious Learner and Teacher in Me 63

Michiko Watabe teaches English and Japanese in Japan. She first met the Silent Way in the early 1980s through workshops for language teachers. Later, she took Dr. Gattegno's workshop as part of the M.A. program at the School for International Training in Vermont, USA. Her thoughts on learning and teaching began to change drastically after that. Michiko continued learning the Silent Way from Ms. Fusako Allard through teacher training, and from Dr. Roslyn Young in various workshops.

Andrew Weiler

The Road to Inspired Teaching 130

Andrew Weiler has been teaching the Silent Way since 1978. In that time, he has trained hundreds of adult students in ESL, as well as taught Hungarian and Indonesian. He has trained language teachers in the Silent Way across all sectors of education throughout Australia, as well as having organized Silent Way language classes in a number of languages. He was instrumental in bringing Gattegno and other Silent Way practitioners to Australia to expose and train teachers in the Silent Way. Andrew is currently working on a book which combines applications of the Science of Education with what learners can do for themselves.

Martine Widmer

Être disponible: Un art de vivre façon Caleb Gattegno 266

Martine Widmer est née en 1954. Après des études de Lettres à l'Université de Genève, où elle vit, elle suit l'obligatoire mais inutile formation pédagogique pour devenir professeur de français dans l'enseignement secondaire. En 1989, elle découvre la pédagogie de Gattegno qu'elle n'aura donc jamais eu l'occasion de rencontrer personnellement. Elle participe à une formation intensive au Silent Way organisée par Une Education Pour Demain, à Besançon, et ensuite à de nombreux stages animés par des « anciens » chevronnés pour approfondir sa découverte du

(About the Authors Cont'd.)

travail de Gattegno. Sa vie professionnelle en est complètement renouvelée. De nouveaux champs d'activités s'ouvrent alors à elle. Depuis, elle enseigne le français sous toutes ses formes, dans toutes sortes de structures, à des élèves de tous âges et de toutes origines sociales. Elle s'occupe également de l'animation de différents groupes de travail constitués d'enseignants désireux de s'initier à la pédagogie de Gattegno.

Yoko Yasuda

I Went Looking for a Match
And Found a Volcano 242

Yoko Yasuda was born in 1967 in Tokyo. She is one of the members of Silent Way Tokyo and president of the Rainbow Laboratory. Yoko met the Silent Way learning to teach Japanese as a foreign language, studying under Fusako Allard. She now runs Silent Way Tokyo, organizing workshops for learning the Silent Way, and using the Gattegno Approach, with Noriko Ogino and Junko Shinada. She is a Japanese teacher with the Silent Way and also teaches the Alexander technique for use of the self, maintaining the Subordination of Teaching to Learning in all of her classes.

Dr. Roslyn Young

How Caleb Gattegno Influenced My Life 12

Roslyn Young worked as an English teacher in a secondary school in Australia for several years before leaving for France. She started working at the Centre de Linguistique Appliquée (CLA) of the University of Franche-Comté in Besançon in 1968 and spent her career there teaching English in intensive courses. She earned a doctorate in 1990, and her thesis made Gattegno's work more accessible to many people when it was published by Une Education Pour Demain (UEPD). Roslyn began giving workshops for UEPD in 1983 and has given workshops in France, Japan, Switzerland, Reunion Island, and other countries as well. She has also presented Gattegno's work in congresses in various countries, has published articles on different aspects of Gattegno's work, and has translated many of his works into French. She was president of UEPD for several years in the '80s and '90s, then vice-president and treasurer of the Association.

Michel et Nathanaël Zobel

A Father's Reading Laboratory 176
I Have Experienced the Gattegno Approach
Mon expérience avec l'approche Gattegno 177

After following various seminars with Caleb Gattegno between 1980 and 1988, in France and in Switzerland, Michel had the opportunity to join the "Formation Générale à l'approche pédagogique proposée par Caleb Gattegno" in Besançon, France, just when his son Nathanaël started his first year at primary school in 2004. For five years, Nathanaël and Michel experienced daily what the Subordination of Teaching to Learning means in the first learning experiences at school. After those five years, they both reached the end of a cycle. Nathanaël successfully finished his cycle at primary school and went to secondary school. Michel finished his "Formation Générale à l'approche pédagogique proposée par Caleb Gattegno" and was much more conscious of what is involved from a pedagogical point of view.

Après avoir suivi de nombreux séminaires avec Caleb Gattegno entre 1980 et 1988, en France et en Suisse, Michel Zobel, le père de Nathanaël, eu l'opportunité, au moment même où son fils, entrait en première année d'école primaire, en 2004, de rejoindre à Besançon, en France, la « Formation Générale à l'approche pédagogique proposée par Caleb Gattegno ». Pendant cinq années, ils ont pu partager au quotidien, chacun à partir de ses propres découvertes, ce que peut être une expérience de subordination de l'enseignement à l'apprentissage, dans le cadre des premiers apprentissages scolaires. Au bout de ces cinq années, ils ont arrivés chacun au bout d'un cycle. Nathanaël a terminé avec succès son cycle à l'école primaire et est entré au collège. Pour sa part, Michel est arrivé au bout de sa « Formation Générale à l'approche pédagogique proposée par Caleb Gattegno », en étant beaucoup plus conscient des enjeux sur le plan pédagogique.

Chronology of Dr. Caleb Gattegno

1911

Born in Alexandria, Egypt as the eighth of nine children.

1932-1936

High-school mathematics teacher at the Lycée Français in Alexandria (Mission Laïque Française).

1937

Doctorate of Mathematics at the University of Basel, Switzerland.

1938-1945

Founder and director of the Centre d'Études Supérieures Scientifiques et Techniques in Cairo.

1944-1988

Wrote more than 120 books and 500 articles in scientific and other journals in a dozen countries. (See the bibliography of his works.)

1945-1946

Visiting mathematics professor at the University of Liverpool.

1946-1957

Mathematics teacher and teacher trainer for grammar schools in the London area and at the University of Liverpool.

1948

Master of Arts in Education at the University of London, with a thesis entitled "The Mathematical Definition of Education."

1951

Doctorate of Philosophy at the University of Lille, France.

1952

- Founder of the Association for Teaching Aids in Mathematics, in Britain. This organization continues to exist as the Association of Teachers of Mathematics (ATM).
- Founder of *Mathematics Teaching*, a journal for the Association for Teaching Aids in Mathematics.
- Translator of Jean Piaget, from French to English.
- Docteur ès Lettres (Philosophy) at the University of Lille: Recherches sur une pédagogie de l'affectivité.

(Chronology Cont'd.)

1953

First introduction to Belgian schoolmaster Georges Cuisenaire, and the Cuisenaire Rods. Gattegno immediately began work on the development of a mathematics curriculum based on the rods.

1954

Founder of the Cuisenaire Company in England; served as its director until 1986. The Cuisenaire Company published over 70 authors, including Gattegno between 1960 and 1982. The company had branches in seven countries during this time.

1957

Member of the United Nations mission to Ethiopia, with the objective of finding a solution to the high illiteracy rates there.

1961

Ground-breaking work in the field of math with the film, *Mathematics at Your Fingertips*.

1962

Release of the first edition of Words in Color.

1968

Founder of Educational Solutions Inc, in New York, NY, USA.

1970

Pop Up first airs on NBC in the United States as an educational alternative to commercials.

1971-1987

Wrote the *Educational Solutions Newsletter* five times annually.

1972

Published an article in *Mathematics Teaching* called "A Prelude to the Science of Education."

1977

- Release of the second edition of Words in Color – includes diphthongs shown as two colors, and more words per chart.

- Release of the Silent Way in American English.

1979

Release of English the Silent Way video program, consisting of 140 recorded half-hour lessons.

1986

Release of Infused Reading English – a literacy software program developed for the Apple Macintosh computer.

1987-1988

Published *The Science of Education* treatise as a series of books.

1988

Died in Paris, France.

Bibliography of Dr. Caleb Gattegno

1937

"Les cas essentiellement géodésiques des équations de Hamilton-Jacobi intégrables par séparation des variables."
Unpublished D. Phil. thesis. Basle University.

1941

"Contribution à l'étude psychologique du Trac."
Bulletin de l'Institut d'Egypte.

1943

"Les problèmes de l'éducation de l'après guerre."
Le Progrès Egyptien.

1944

Les enfants et nous - Causerie pédagogique.
Les Lettres françaises, (Cairo).

Six contes pour enfants.
Les Lettres françaises, (Cairo).

1945

"Analyze générale et topologie de l'espace des connaissances."
Bulletin de l'Institut d'Egypte, N° 28.

"Etude sur le Jeu."
Bulletin de l'Institut d'Egypte, N° 27.

1946

"Studies in the Structure of the Mind."
Mind, Vol.. LV, N° 219.

1947

"Mathematics and the Child."
The Mathematical Gazette, Vol.. 31, N° 296, (England).
Reprinted in *For the Teaching of Mathematics Vol..1,* 1963.

1948

"Psychologie du Dessin Enfantin."
Enfance, N° 5, (France).

"The Use of Mistakes in the Teaching of Mathematics."
The Mathematical Gazette, Vol.. 32, N° unknown, (England).

"The Mathematical Definition of Education."
Unpublished M.A. thesis. London University, (England).

"Substitutes and Examples."
The Mathematical Gazette, Vol..33, N° 304, (England).
Reprinted in *For the Teaching of Mathematics, Vol..1,* 1963.

(Bibliography Cont'd.)

1949

Représentation conforme à la frontière.
with A.M. Ostrowski; General Domain, 2 Vols., Gauthiers-Villars, (Paris).

"International N.E.F. Conference in Brussels."
The New Era, Vol.. 30, N° 9.

"Further Experiments in International Education."
The New Era, Vol.. 31, N° 10.

1951

"Adolescent Thought and its Bearing on Mathematics Learning."
Revue Belge de Psychologie et de Pédagogie, Vol.. 13, N° 55-56, (Belgium). Reprinted in *For the Teaching of Mathematics, Vol.. 2,* 1963.

"Remarks on Mental Structures."
Enfance, N° 3, (France). Reprinted in *For the Teaching of Mathematics, Vol.. 2,* 1963.

Play, Dreams and Imitation.
(Translation, with F. M. Hodgson) by Jean Piaget. Heinemann, (Melbourne, London, Toronto) and W W Norton, (New York).

The Child's Conception of Number.
(Translation, with F. M. Hodgson) by Jean Piaget. Routledge & Kegan Paul, (London).

"Les fondements de l'éducation."
Dialectica, N° 18. Reprinted in *For the Teaching of Mathematics, Vol.. 2,* 1963.

1952

Introduction à la psychologie de l'affectivité et à l'éducation à l'amour.
Delachaux and Niestlé, (Neuchâtel and Paris). English translation titled *The Adolescent and his Self*, Educational Explorers, (Reading, England), 1962.

"A New Theory of the Image."
Introduction à la psychologie de l'affectivité et à l'éducation à l'amour, Annexe 3. Delachaux et Niestlé, (France). Reprinted in *For the Teaching of Mathematics, Vol.. 2,* 1963.

"Note on Pythagoras' Theorem."
The Mathematics Teacher, Vol.. 45, N° 1, (United States). Reprinted in *For the Teaching of Mathematics, Vol.. 1,* 1963.

"A Note on the Teaching of Mathematics."
Journal of General Education, Vol.. VI, N° 4, (United States). Reprinted in *For the Teaching of Mathematics, Vol.. 1,* 1963.

"Investigation through Teaching."
Nederlansch Tijdschrift voor de Psychologie, Vol.. 7, N° 3, (Netherlands). Reprinted in *For the Teaching of Mathematics. Vol.. 2,* 1963.

"Three Dimensional Vision and its Psychological Application to the Teaching of Mathematics."
Gymnasium Helveticum, Vol.. 6, N° 5, (Basel, Switzerland). Reprinted in *For the Teaching of Mathematics, Vol.. 2,* 1963.

Un Nouveau Phénomène Psychosomatique.
with Alphonse Gay; Delachaux et Niestlé, (Paris).

1953

"Mathematical Thinking and the Use of the Senses."
Bulletin of the Association for Teaching Aids in Mathematics, Vol.. 1, N° 1. Reprinted in *For the Teaching of Mathematics, Vol.. 2,* 1963.

"Notes sur les nombres en couleurs."
Le Moniteur des Instituteurs, (Tamines, Belgium). Reprinted as "Notes on Monsieur Cuisenaire's Invention" in *For the Teaching of Mathematics, Vol.. 2,* 1963.

"Numbers in Colour."
Bulletin of the Association for Teaching Aids in Mathematics, Vol.. 2.

1954

Conscience de la conscience.
Le Cercle du Livre. Second edition, Delachaux et Niestlé, (Paris), 1967.

Huit contes pour enfants.
Ducolet-Roulin. Second edition *Huit Contes* (New York), 1967. Translated to English as *Eight Tales*, 1968.

"Notes in Intuition in Mathematics."
Mathematica & Paedagogia, N° 3, (Belgium). Reprinted in *For the Teaching of Mathematics, Vol.. 1,* 1963.

"Number and Colour."
New Era for Home and School, (England). Reprinted in *For the Teaching of Mathematics, Vol.. 3,* 1963.

"The Use of Mistakes in the Teaching of Mathematics."
The Mathematical Gazette, Vol.. 37, N° 323. Reprinted in *For the Teaching of Mathematics, Vol.. 1,* 1963.

"The Idea of Dynamic Patterns in Geometry."
The Mathematical Gazette, Vol.. 38, N° 325, (England). Reprinted in *For the Teaching of Mathematics, Vol.. 3,* 1963.

"Arithmetic with Colored Rods."
The Times Educational Supplement, (England). Reprinted in *For the Teaching of Mathematics, Vol.. 3,* 1963.

"Brazier's Park Weekend."
Bulletin of the Association for Teaching Aids in Mathematics, N° 3.

"The Gattegno Geoboards."
Bulletin of the Association for Teaching Aids in Mathematics, N° 3.

Numbers in Colour.
with Georges Cuisenaire; Heinemann, (England).

"Le rôle de l'intuition en mathématiques."
Math & Paedogogica, N° 3. Translation in *For the Teaching of Mathematics, Vol.. 1,* 1963.

"The Objective Study of Sensitivity."

Radio Perception.

"Georges Cuisenaire's Numbers in Colour."
Mathematica & Paedagogia, N° 4, (Belgium). Reprinted in For the Teaching of Mathematics, Vol.. 3, 1963.

1955

"Arithmetic and the Child."
Il Centro. Bulletin du Centro Didattico Nazionale di Studie Documentazione, N° 5, (Florence, Italy). Reprinted in *For the Teaching of Mathematics, Vol.. 3,* 1963.

"Arithmetic and Colour."
Il Centro. Bulletin du Centro Didattico Nazionale di Studie Documentazione, N° 5, (Florence, Italy). Reprinted in *For the Teaching of Mathematics, Vol.. 3,* 1963.

"Mathematics Teaching and ATAM."
Mathematics Teaching, N° 1.

"Pupils' Reactions to Geometrical Classifications Considerations."
Mathematica & Paedagogia, N° 9, (Belgium). Reprinted in *For the Teaching of Mathematics, Vol.. 2,* 1963.

"Theoretical Remarks on the Cuisenaire Material."
Mathematica & Paedagogia, N° 9, (Belgium). Reprinted in *For the Teaching of Mathematics, Vol.. 3,* 1963.

1956

"The Study of Arithmetic with the Help of Colour Associated with Length."
Le Courrier de la Recherche Pédagogique, N° 6, (Paris). Reprinted in *For the Teaching of Mathematics, Vol.. 3,* 1963.

"Some Problems involved in the Teaching of Mathematics."
Nastava Matematike I Fizike, Vol.. V, N° 1, (Belgrade).

(Bibliography Cont'd.)

Reprinted in *For the Teaching of Mathematics, Vol.. 1*, 1963.

"Introducing the Concept of the Set."
The Arithmetic Teacher, Vol.. III, N° 3, (United States). Reprinted in *For the Teaching of Mathematics, Vol.. 3*, 1963.

Teaching Mathematics to Deaf Children.
Educational Explorers, (Reading, England).

"Mathematics and the Deaf."
Teaching Mathematics to Deaf Children, Introduction. Reprinted in *For the Teaching of Mathematics, Vol.. 2*, 1963.

Teaching Mathematics in an Expanding Economy.
Section 1 (Primary). Educational Explorers (Reading, England).

Les nombres en couleurs.
with Georges Cuisenaire; Delachaux et Niestlé Translation of *Numbers in Colour*, 1954.

Numeros en color.
with Georges Cuisenaire; Min Ed, (Madrid). Translation of *Numbers in Colour*, 1954.

Numbers in Colour - Film Strip Notes.
The Cuisenaire Company, (UK).

"New Methods of Teaching Arithmetic."
Arithmetic Teacher, 3.3. Reprinted in *For the Teaching of Mathematics, Vol.. 2*, 1963

"Notes for Administrators."
Unpublished. Reprinted in *For the Teaching of Mathematics, Vol.. 3*, 1963

"Quelques problèmes que pose l'enseignement des mathématiques."
Nastaya Nat Fiz, 5.1. Reprinted in *For the Teaching of Mathematics, Vol.. 1*, 1963.

"L'arithmétique basée sur la couleur."
Courier Rech Ped, 4. Reprinted in *For the Teaching of Mathematics, Vol.. 3*, 1963.

1957

"Reforming Mathematics Teaching."
The Times Educational Supplement, (England). Reprinted in *For the Teaching of Mathematics, Vol.. 1*, 1963.

"A Matter of Relationships."
British Columbia Teacher, September-October, (Canada). Reprinted in *For the Teaching of Mathematics, Vol.. 3*, 1963.

"On Teaching Mathematics."
British Columbia Teacher, September-October, (Canada). Reprinted in *For the Teaching of Mathematics, Vol.. 3*, 1963.

"Can American Education Teach us Anything."
Mathematics Teaching, N° 5.

"Mathematics for All."
Restricted printing, 1960, (New York). Reprinted in *For the Teaching of Mathematics, Vol.. 3*, 1963.

"Learning Mathematics - a Practical Solution."
Impulse, N° 2, Mitchell Engineering and the Journal Press, (London). Reprinted in *For the Teaching of Mathematics, Vol.. 3*, 1963.

Arithmetic with Numbers in Colour.
Books 1-3, Heinemann, (England).

L'arithmétique avec les nombres en couleurs.
Books 1-3, Delachaux et Niestlé, (Paris). Translation of *Arithmetic with Numbers in Colour*, 1957.

Arithmetica con numeros en color.
Books 1-3, (Madrid). Translation of Arithmetic with Numbers in Colour, 1957.

1958

Arithmetic with Numbers in Colour.
Books 4-6, Cuisenaire Company, (Reading, England).

L'arithmétique avec les nombres en couleurs.

Books 4-6, Delachaux et Niestlé, (Paris). Translation of *Arithmetic with Numbers in Colour*, 1958.

Arithmetica con numeros en color.
Books 4-6, Delachaux et Niestlé, (Paris). Translation of *Arithmetic with Numbers in Colour*, 1958.

"Notes on a Radical Transformation in the Teaching of Mathematics."
Currents in Modern Thought, January, (New York). Reprinted in For the Teaching of Mathematics, Vol.. 3, 1963.

"Mathematical and Mental Structures."
Bulletin de l'Association des Professeurs de l'Enseignement Public, March, (Paris). Reprinted in *For the Teaching of Mathematics, Vol.. 2*, 1963.

Le Matériel pour l'enseignement des mathématiques
Delachaux et Niestlé, (Paris).

"La perception et l'action."
Le matériel pour l'enseignement des mathématiques, Chapitre 1, Delachaux et Niestlé, (Paris). Reprinted as "Perception and Action as Bases of Mathematical Thought" in *For the Teaching of Mathematics, Vol.. 2*, 1963.

"L'enseignement par le film mathématique."
Le matériel pour l'enseignement des mathématiques, Chapitre 7, Delachaux et Niestlé, (Paris). Reprinted as "Teaching Through Mathematical Films" in *For the Teaching of Mathematics, Vol.. 2*, 1963.

"Les matériels multivalents."
Le matériel pour l'enseignement des mathématiques, Delachaux et Niestlé, (Paris). Reprinted as "Multivalent Materials" in *For the Teaching of Mathematics, Vol.. 3*, 1963.

The Individual Geoboard.
Cuisenaire Company, (Reading, England).

"Mathematics and Mental Structures."
Bulletin APMEP, March. Reprinted in *For the Teaching of Mathematics, Vol.. 3*, 1963.

"A Message from the President."
Mathematics Teaching, N° 7.

Educão para o amor.
Editôra Fundo de Cultura S.A. Translated excerpt in *Introduction à la psychologie de l'affectivité et à l'éducation à l'amour*, Delachaux et Niestlé, 1952.

Mathematics with Numbers in Colour: Book A.
Cuisenaire Company of America.

"Observations on the Teaching of Mathematics in the United States."
The Mathematics Teacher, LI 3.

From Actions to Operations.
Cuisenaire Company, (Reading, England).

Teaching Mathematics in an Expanding Economy.
Cuisenaire Company, (Reading, England). Revised edition.

1959

"Thinking Afresh about Arithmetic."
The Arithmetic Teacher, February, (United States). Reprinted in For the Teaching of Mathematics, Vol.. 3, 1963.

Mathematics with Numbers in Colour: Books B-D.
Cuisenaire Company of America.

1960

Arithmetica con numeros en color: Books 4-5.
Cuisenaire de España. Translation of *Arithmetic with Numbers in Colour*, 1958.

"What Matters Most."
Mathematics Teaching N° 12, March, (England). Reprinted in *For the Teaching of Mathematics, Vol.. 1*, 1963.

"Mathematics and the Needs of Society."
French radio program on *CBC Radio Canada*, December 6, 1960. Text translated into English by the author for inclusion in *For the Teaching of Mathematics, Vol.. 1*, 1963.

Now Johnny can do Arithmetic.
Educational Explorers, (Reading, England). Translated into French under the title *Enfin, Freddy comprend l'arithmétique*, 1967, Delachaux et Niestlé (Neuchâtel et Paris).

Modern Mathematics with Numbers in Colour.
Educational Explorers, (Reading, England).

(Bibliography Cont'd.)

Arithmetic Arithmestics.
Educational Explorers, (Reading, England).

Initiation à la méthode: les nombres en couleurs.
with Georges Cuisenaire; Delachaux et Niestlé, (Neuchâtel, Switzerland). Second edition under the French title *Initiation aux nombres en couleurs*. Delachaux et Niestlé (Neuchâtel et Paris). Translation of *Numbers in Colour*, 1954.

"La pédagogie des mathématiques."
CIEAEM: *L'enseignement des mathématiques*, Delachaux et Niestlé, (Paris).

"Letter."
Mathematics Teaching, N° 11.

"Obituary: Puig Adam."
Mathematics Teaching, N° 13.

Arithmetica con numeros en color: Books 6-7.
Cuisenaire de España. Translation of *Arithmetic with Numbers in Colour*, 1961.

"La Pedagogia della Matematica."
L'insegnamento della Matematica, la Nuova Italia editrice, (Italy).

A Teacher's Introduction to Cuisenaire-Gattegno Methods.
Cuisenaire Company of America, US edition Educational Explorers.

1961

A Teacher's Introduction to the Cuisenaire-Gattegno Method.
Hebrew version, Cuisenaire Company of Israel, translated 1960.

"Reality and the Learning of Mathematics."
Education Vol.. 10, N° 5, (New Zealand). Reprinted in *For the Teaching of Mathematics, Vol.. 3*, 1963.

"Formalisation and Sterilisation."
The Mathematics Teacher, Vol.. LIV, N° 7, (United States). Reprinted in *For the Teaching of Mathematics, Vol.. 1*, 1963.

Arithmetic with Numbers in Colour: Books 7-9.
Educational Explorers, (Reading England).

L'arithmétique avec les nombres en couleurs: Books 7-8.
Delachaux et Niestlé. Translation of *Arithmetic with Numbers in Colour*, 1961.

Arithmetica con numeros en color: Books 7-8.
(Madrid). Translation of Arithmetic with Numbers in Colour, 1961.

"Why Study Mathematics?"
The Washington Post Sunday Magazine, September. Reprinted in *For the Teaching of Mathematics, Vol.. 1*, 1963, (United States).

"Una visión 'práctica' para España."
En relacion con el problema de enseñanza de las matematicas, (Homenaje a Dr. Pedro Puig Adam), Direccion General de Enseñanza Media, (Madrid).

Guide introductif aux nombres en couleurs.
Delachaux et Niestlé, (Paris). Translation of *A Teacher's introduction to Numbers in Colour*, 1960.

Apuntes correspondientes a las clases dictadas por el profesor Gattegno.
Institutos de investigaciones y estudios pedagogicos.

1962

L'aritmetica con I numeri in coloure - I numeri da 1 a 10.
Edizioni Calderini translation of *Arithmetic with Numbers in Colour*, 1958.

Mathematics with Numbers in Colour: Books 1-7.
Educational Explorers, (Reading, England).

Nombres en couleurs: Cahier de travail.
Delachaux et Niestlé, (Neuchâtel et Paris).

The Adolescent and his Self.
Educational Explorers, (Reading England). Translation of *Introduction à la psychologie de l'affectivité et à l'éducation à l'amour*, Delachaux et Niestlé, 1952.

Fiches de travail Nos 1 à 15 pour les nombres en couleurs.

Delachaux et Niestlé, (Paris).

Morphologico-algebric Approach to Reading and Writing.
Photocopy. Educational Explorers, (Reading, England).

Words in Colour - Teachers' Guide.
Photocopy. Educational Explorers, (Reading, England).

Words in Colour: Background and Principles.
Chicago: Xerox Corporation. Educational Explorers, (Reading, England).

Words in Colour - Book of Stories .
Educational Explorers, (Reading, England).

Words in Colour - Word Building Book.
Educational Explorers, (Reading, England).

Words in Colour - Reading Primer Books 1- 3.
Educational Explorers, (Reading, England). Reprinted in 2010 as Reading Primer R0&R1, R2, and R3.

Words in Colour - Worksheets 1 - 7.
Educational Explorers, (Reading, England).

Words in Colour - Worksheets 8 - 14.
Educational Explorers, (Reading, England).

Words in Colour - The Word Cards.
Educational Explorers, (Reading, England).

Words in Colour and The Silent Way - The Standard English Fidel.
Educational Explorers, (Reading, England).

Words in Colour - The Standard English Word Charts.
Educational Explorers, (Reading, England).

Words in Colour – Filmstrip.
Educational Explorers, (Reading, England).

The Silent Way - EFL Word Charts: Standard English edition.
Educational Explorers, (Reading, England).

Words in Color - Teacher's Guide.
Learning Materials Inc. (subsidiary of Encyclopaedia Britannica Press Inc, Chicago).

Words in Color - Background and Principles.
Learning Materials Inc. (subsidiary of Encyclopaedia Britannica Press Inc, Chicago).

Words in Color - Book of Stories.
Learning Materials Inc. (subsidiary of Encyclopaedia Britannica Press Inc, Chicago).

Words in Color - Word Building Book.
Learning Materials Inc. (subsidiary of Encyclopaedia Britannica Press Inc, Chicago).

Words in Color - Reading Primer Books 1- 3.
Learning Materials Inc. (subsidiary of Encyclopaedia Britannica Press Inc, Chicago).

Words in Color - Worksheets 1 - 7.
Learning Materials Inc. (subsidiary of Encyclopaedia Britannica Press Inc, Chicago).

Words in Color - Worksheets 8 - 14.
Learning Materials Inc. (subsidiary of Encyclopaedia Britannica Press Inc, Chicago).

Words in Color - The Word Cards.
Learning Materials Inc. (subsidiary of Encyclopaedia Britannica Press Inc, Chicago).

Words in Color - The North American English Fidel.
Educational Explorers, (Reading, England).

Words in Color - The North American English Word Charts.
Educational Explorers, (Reading, England).

Mathématiques avec les nombres en couleurs: Book B.
(Canadian Edition), Delachaux et Niestlé, (Paris).

Arithmetica con numeros en colour: Book 8.
Cuisenaire de España. Translation of *Arithmetic with Numbers in Colour*, 1961.

Introducción a la psicología de la afecti.
Espasa-Calpe, SA. Translation of *Introduction à la psychologie de l'affectivité et à l'éducation à l'amour*, Delachaux et Niestlé, 1952.

O zeca já pode aprender aritmética.
Cuisenaire de Portugal. Translation of *Now Johnny Can do Arithmetic*, 1960.

Elementos de matematica moderna.
Cuisenaire de España. Translation of *Modern*

(Bibliography Cont'd.)

Mathematics, 1960.

Gattegno Worksheets 1-15.
In three booklets. The Cuisenaire Company, (New Zealand).

1963

"Why My Books Are as They Are."
Cuisenaire News, N° 3. Reprinted in *For the Teaching of Mathematics, Vol. 3*, 1963.

"Discovering Cuisenaire."
Cuisenaire News, N° 3, January. (England) Reprinted in *For the Teaching of Mathematics Vol. 3*, 1963.

"The Place of Colour in Mathematics Learning."
Mathematics Teaching, N° 23, summer. Reprinted in *For the Teaching of Mathematics Vol. 3*, 1963.

For the Teaching of Mathematics.
Educational Explorers, (Reading, England) Vol.1, Vol. 2, Vol. 3.

Teaching Foreign Languages in Schools the Silent Way.
Educational Explorers, (Reading, England) Second edition in 1972, Educational Solutions, (New York)

Study of Energy: Forms of Energy.
Educational Explorers, (Reading, England)

The Silent Way - French Word Charts.
Educational Explorers (Reading, England)

The Silent Way - French Fidel.
Educational Explorers (Reading, England)

Notes on Words in Colour.
Educational Explorers (Reading, England)

Arithmetica con numeros en color: Book 9.
Cuisenaire de España (trans of Arithmetic with Numbers in Colour 1961)

Letras en Colour-Nuevo metodo de enseñanza de la lectura y la escritura.
Cuisenaire de España.

1964

"Teaching Reading, An Indefinitely Renewable Problem."
Spelling Progress Bulletin, Fall 1964 pp15-1

"Words in Colour System."
Forward Trends 7 4: 141-144. Chapter 6.

Mathématiques avec les nombres en couleurs: Book C.
(Canadian edition), Delachaux et Niestlé, (Paris).

For the Teaching of Elementary Mathematics.
Cuisenaire Co of America. US edition of *For the Teaching of Mathematics,* 1963.

Endlich kann Robert rechnen.
Cuisenaire Lehrmittel GMBH. Translation of *Now Johnny Can Do Arithmetic*, 1960.

Mathematik mit Zahlen in Farben: Books 1-2.
Cuisenaire Lehrmittel GMBH. Translation of *Mathemematics with Numbers in Colour*, 1962.

1965

Pour un enseignement dynamique des mathématiques.
Delachaux et Niestlé, (Neuchâtel, Switzerland). Translation of *For the Teaching of Mathematics*, 1963.

Notes on Building Geometry.
The Cuisenaire Company, (Reading, UK) (revised translation of Costruiamo ... 1964)

A Thousand Sentences.
The Cuisenaire Company, (Reading, UK)

Ocho cuentos.
Educational Explorers, (Reading, England). Translation of *Huit Contes*, 1954.

El libro de las mil frases.
Educational Explorers. Translation of *A Thousand Sentences*, 1965.

"Mathematics and Imagery."
Mathematics Teaching, Journal of the Association of

Teachers of Mathematics, N° 33, (England).

"Ten Years of Mathematics Teaching"
Mathematics Teaching, Journal of the Association of Teachers of Mathematics, N° 33 (England).

Arithmetic with Numbers in Colour
Hebrew version, Cuisenaire Company of Israel, 1957.

"A Teacher's Guide to Using Words in Colour"
Spelling Progress Bulletin, Summer 1965.

1966

Mathématiques avec les nombres en couleurs.
Delachaux et Niestlé, (Neuchâtel et Paris). 12 volumes. Translation of *Mathematics with Numbers in Colour*, 1962.

Manuel A : Les nombres de 1 à 20 et jusqu'à 100.

Manuel B : Les nombres jusqu'à 1000. Procédés de calcul.

Manuel C: Mesures canadiennes

Manuel 4 : Les nombres jusqu'à 1000 : propriétés et opérations

Manuel 5: Fractions ordinaires et décimales. Pourcentages.

Manuel 6: Les nombres et leurs propriétés.

Manuel 7: Les unités de mesure et le système métrique.

Manuel 8: Problèmes et situations quantatives.

Manuel 9: Algèbre et géométrie pour les écoles priMayres.

"Words in Colour."
J Money, The Disabled Reader. John Hopkins University Press, (United States).

Arithmetic with Numbers in Colour.
(Hebrew version), Cuisenaire Company of Israel, 1958.

La lecture en couleurs: guide du maître.
Delachaux et Niestlé, (Paris).

La lecture en couleurs - pour construire mes mots.
Delachaux et Niestlé, (Paris).

La lecture en couleurs - les premiers pas.
Delachaux et Niestlé, (Paris).

La lecture en couleurs - tout les sons du français.
Delachaux et Niestlé, (Paris).

La lecture en couleurs - tout les signes du français.
Delachaux et Niestlé, (Paris).

La lecture en couleurs - livre des 40 petits récits.
Delachaux et Niestlé, (Paris). Translated as *Book of Stories*, 1962.

La lecture en couleurs - Le jeu de cartes grammatical.
Delachaux et Niestlé, (Paris).

La lecture en couleurs - cahiers d'exercices 1 à 7.
Delachaux et Niestlé, (Paris).

La lecture en couleurs - cahiers d'exercices 8 à 14.
Delachaux et Niestlé, (Paris).

"What does 'Words in Colour' Demand of Us?"
Schools for the Future, (New York).

"Report on One Month's Experiment in PS113."
Schools for the Future, (New York).

1967

Huit Contes.
Educational Explorers, second edition, (Reading, England).

Enfin, Freddy comprend l'arithmétique.
Delachaux et Niestlé, (Paris). Translation of *Now Johnny Can Do Arithmetic*, 1960.

Obituary: Jean-Louis Nicolet.
Mathematics Teaching, Journal of the Association of Teachers of Mathematics, N° 38, (England).

"Functioning as a Mathematician."
Mathematics Teaching, Journal of the Association of Teachers of Mathematics, N° 39, (England).

Le livre des mille phrases.
Educational Solutions, (New York). Adapted from the English version *A Thousand Sentences*.

Trente-six Instantanés.

(Bibliography Cont'd.)
Educational Solutions, (New York).

Narraciones breves.
Educational Explorers, (New York). Translation of *Trente-six instantanés*, 1967.

Eléments de mathématiques modernes par les nombres en couleurs.
Delachaux et Niestlé, (Neuchâtel et Paris). Translation of *Modern Mathematics with Numbers in Colour*, 1960.

1968

Lessons with Cuisenaire Rods - Notes on the Filmstrip Numbers in Colour.
The Cuisenaire Company, (Reading, England).

The Silent Way for Teaching English as a Second Language.
Educational Explorers, (Reading, England).

Words in Colour - Further Reading.
Educational Explorers, (Reading, England).

Teaching Reading with 'Words in Colour.'
Educational Solutions, (New York).

Eight Tales.
Educational Explorers, (Reading, England). Translation of *Huit Contes*, 1954.

Short Passages.
Educational Explorers, (Reading, England). Translation of *Trente-six instantanés*, 1967.

Geoboard Geometry.
Educational Explorers (Reading, England). New and revised edition of *From Actions to Operations*, 1958.

"Rechenunterricht in neuer Sicht."
Der Mathematik - unterricht, Ernst Klett Verlag (Germany).

L'aritmetica con I numeri in coloure - I numeri da 1 a 20 e fino a 100.
Edizioni Calderini, translation of *Mathematics with Numbers in Colour*, 1962.

The White Canary Papercraft Litho Ltd, (Hayes, Middlesex)

1969

Reading with Words in Colour.
Educational Explorers, (Reading, England).

Towards a Visual Culture.
Outerbridge & Dienstfrey, (New York).

Vers une culture visuelle.
Delachaux et Niestlé, (Neuchâtel et Paris). Translation of *Towards a Visual Culture*, 1969.

"The Ideal School."
G Kinney, *The ideal school*, Kagy Press.

1970

"The Human Element in Mathematics."
Mathematical Reflections, ed. Association of Teachers of Mathematics, Cambridge University Press, (England).

"Notes on a New Epistemology: Teaching and Education."
Mathematics Teaching, Journal of the Association of Teachers of Mathematics, N° 50, (England).

"Notes on a New Epistemology: Teaching and Education."
Mathematics Teaching, Journal of the Association of Teachers of Mathematics, N° 50, (England).

What We Owe Children, The Subordination of Teaching to Learning.
Outerbridge and Diensfrey, (New York).

"The Problem of Reading is Solved."
Harvard Educational Review, 40.2.

The Morphologico-Algebraic Approach to the Teaching of Reading and Writing English.
Educational Explorers, (Reading, England).

1971

What We Owe Children, The Subordination of Teaching to Learning.
Routledge and Kegan Paul, (London).

Geoboard Geometry.
Educational Solutions, (New York). New edition *Teaching Mathematics to Deaf Children,* 1956.

Zur didaktik des mathematikunterrichts, Schroedel.
With others. Translation of *CIEAEM,* 1958/1960.

1972

"A Prelude to the Science of Education."
Mathematics Teaching, Journal of the Association of Teachers of Mathematics, N° 59, (England).

Ces enfants nos maîtres, ou la subordination de l'enseignement à l'apprentissage.
Delachaux et Niestlé, (Neuchâtel, Switzerland). Translation of *What We Owe Children,* Outerbridge and Dienstfrey, 1970, (New York).

1973

In the Beginning There Were No Words: The Universe of Babies.
Educational Solutions, (New York).

An Experimental School: A Study of a Possible Renewal of Public Education.
Educational Solutions, (New York).

Notes for Parents on Words in Colour.
Educational Solutions, (New York). Revised edition, 1979.

"Looking Ahead to an Adult Association."
Mathematics Teaching, Journal of the Association of Teachers of Mathematics, N° 62, (England).

"Teaching Reading Via the Medium of Television."
Educational Technology, 1.9.

"Some Remarks and Additions on the Silent Way."
Idiom, 4.2.

Educational Solutions Newsletter Volume 2.
Educational Solutions, (New York).

"The Silent Way (SW)."
EdSol Newsletter Vol. 3, N° 1, October 1973, Educational Solutions, (New York).

"The Improvement of Teachers."
EdSol Newsletter Vol. 3, N° 2, December 1973, Educational Solutions, (New York).

"Mathematics."
EdSol Newsletter Vol. 2, N° 3, March 1973, Educational Solutions, (New York).

"Bilingualism."
EdSol Newsletter Vol. 2, N° 4, April 1973, Educational Solutions, (New York).

"Reading."
EdSol Newsletter Vol. 2, N° 5, May 1973, Educational Solutions, (New York).

1974

The Common Sense of Teaching Mathematics.
Educational Solutions, (New York).

"Our Work on Remediation."
EdSol Newsletter Vol. 4, N° 1, September 1974, Educational Solutions, (New York).

"On Evaluation."
EdSol Newsletter Vol. 4, N° 2, December 1974, Educational Solutions, (New York).

"Involving the Paraprofessionals."
EdSol Newsletter Vol. 3, N° 3, February 1974, Educational Solutions, (New York).

"Let the Public Speak."
EdSol Newsletter Vol. 3, N° 4, April 1974, Educational Solutions, (New York).

"Thoughts for the Summer."
EdSol Newsletter Vol. 3, N° 5, June 1974, Educational Solutions, (New York).

(Bibliography Cont'd.)

1975

Of Boys and Girls.
Educational Solutions, (New York). Restricted Printing.

On Being Freer.
Educational Solutions, (New York). Restricted Printing.

The Mind Teaches the Brain.
Educational Solutions, (New York). Restricted Printing. Revised edition 1988.

"Letter."
Mathematics Teaching, N° 70.

"ESL, The Silent Way."
EdSol Newsletter Vol. 4, N° 3, February 1975, Educational Solutions, (New York).

"On Early Childhood."
EdSol Newsletter Vol. 4 , N° 4, April 1975, Educational Solutions, (New York).

"Affectivity and Learning."
EdSol Newsletter Vol. 4, N° 5, June 1975, Educational Solutions, (New York).

"Intuition and Complexity."
EdSol Newsletter Vol. 5, N° 1, September 1975, Educational Solutions, (New York).

"Teachers are Made."
EdSol Newsletter Vol. 5 N° 2 - N° 3, December 1975-February 1976, Educational Solutions, (New York).

1976

The Common Sense of Teaching Foreign Languages.
Educational Solutions, (New York).

"Le cerveau."
Bulletin de liaison, Face à l'éducation N° 1 pp. 1-26; N° 2. pp. 1-45; N° 3. pp. 1-25. (Lyon).

"The Silent Way."
J. Fanselow & Crymes, R. (eds), *On TESOL 76* (Washington D.C.: TESOL).

"On Literary."
EdSol Newsletter Vol. 5, N° 4, April 1976, Educational Solutions, (New York).

"On Knowledge."
EdSol Newsletter Vol. 5, N° 5, June 1976, Educational Solutions ,(New York).

"Back to Basics."
EdSol Newsletter Vol. 6, N° 1, September 1976, Educational Solutions, (New York).

"On Mistakes."
EdSol Newsletter Vol. 6, N° 2- N° 3, December 1976-February 1977, Educational Solutions, (New York).

1977

"L'intuition."
Bulletin de liaison, Face à l'éducation N° 1. pp.15-29; N° 2. pp. 3-34; N° 3. pp. 4-25; N° 4. pp. 1-31; N° 5. pp. 1-21. (Lyon).

"La nourriture."
Bulletin de liaison, Face à l'éducation N° 3. pp. 1-3. (Lyon).

Evolution and Memory.
Educational Solutions, (New York). Restricted Printing.

On Love.
Educational Solutions, (New York). Restricted Printing.

"Awareness of the Awareness."
Chapter 2 of *The Science of Education*, published in 1987, Educational Solutions, (New York).

"The Facts of Awareness."
Chapter 3 of *The Science of Education*, published in 1987, Educational Solutions, (New York).

"Affectivity and Learning."
Chapter 4 of *The Science of Education*, published in

1987, Educational Solutions, (New York).

"The Birth of the Language Video Project."
EdSol Newsletter Vol. 6, N° 4- N°5, April-June 1977, Educational Solutions, (New York).

"Aspects of Language Learning."
EdSol Newsletter Vol. 7, N° 1, September 1977, Educational Solutions, (New York).

"Further Insights in Leaning Languages."
EdSol Newsletter Vol. 7, N° 2, December 1977, Educational Solutions, (New York).

1978

De l'Intuition.
Une Ecole Pour Demain, (Lyon).

Deux Conférences: Besançon 1976, Lyon 1977.
Une Ecole Pour Demain, (Lyon).

On Death: An Essay.
Educational Solutions, (New York). Restricted printing.

"On Spelling."
Chapter 6 of *The Common Sense of Teaching Reading and Writing*, published in 1985, Educational Solutions, (New York). Restricted Printing.

De l'Affectivité.
Une Ecole Pour Demain, (Lyon).

"Subordinating Teaching to Learning."
The Real World, 11 5-9.

"Evaluating Students' Progress."
C H Blatchford & J Schachter (eds), *On TESOL '78*, TESOL.

"The United States and the World: On Education."
EdSol Newsletter Vol. 7, N° 3, February 1978, Educational Solutions, (New York).

"On Feedback."
EdSol Newsletter Vol. 7, N° 4, April 1978, Educational Solutions, (New York).

"In Favor of Bilingualism."
EdSol Newsletter Vol. 7, N° 5, June 1978, Educational Solutions, (New York).

"Storytelling and Storytellers."
EdSol Newsletter Vol. 8, N° 1, September 1978, Educational Solutions, (New York).

"Problems and Solutions."
EdSol Newsletter Vol. 8 N° 2, December 1978, Educational Solutions, (New York).

1979

English the Silent Way: A Video Program.
With others. Educational Solutions, (New York).

Du Temps, Quatre volumes.
Une Ecole Pour Demain, (Lyon). Restricted printing.

Who Cares about Health?
Educational Solutions, (New York). Restricted Printing.

Notes for Teachers on Animated Geometry.
Educational Solutions, (New York).

El Dominio De La Ortografia Español.
Educational Solutions, (New York).

"Where to Look for New Light."
Lecture reprint, Assoc Child Learning Disabilities, (Quebec, Canada).

"The Year of the Child: Entering the World/Early Childhood."
EdSol Newsletter Vol. 8, N° 3, February 1979, Educational Solutions, (New York).

"The Year of the Child: The Elementary School Years."
EdSol Newsletter Vol. 8, N° 4, April 1979, Educational Solutions, (New York).

"The Year of the Child: Adolescence."
EdSol Newsletter Vol. 8, N° 5, June 1979, Educational Solutions, (New York).

"The Year of the Child: The Child in Everyone of Us."

(Bibliography Cont'd.)
Educational Solutions, (New York).

"The Year of the Child- Knowing: Epistemology and Psyschology."
EdSol Newsletter Vol. 9, N° 2, December 1979, Educational Solutions, (New York).

1980

Math Mini Tests.
Educational Solutions, New York.

"Ces enfants nos maîtres."
dans la série "La conscience éducatrice" in *De l'Éducation, N° 1*, Une École pour Demain, (Lyon). Interview with Caleb Gattegno for France-Culture by Jeanne Gruson. pp. 1-5.

"Vers une culture visuelle."
dans la série "La conscience éducatrice" in *De l'éducation, N° 2*, Une Ecole pour Demain, (Lyon). Interview with Caleb Gattegno for France-Culture by Jeanne Gruson. pp. 1-4.

"Seule la conscience est éducable en l'homme."
dans la série "La conscience éducatrice" in *De l'éducation, N° 2*, Une Ecole pour Demain, (Lyon). Interview with Caleb Gattegno for France-Culture by Jeanne Gruson. pp. 5-8.

"Affectivité et apprentissage" dans la série "La conscience éducatrice."
dans la série "La conscience éducatrice" in *De l'éducation, N° 3*, Une Ecole pour Demain, (Lyon). Interview with Caleb Gattegno for France-Culture by Jeanne Gruson. pp. 1-5.

"La Subordination de l'Enseignement à l'Apprentissage."
dans la série "La conscience éducatrice" in *De l'éducation, N° 3*, Une Ecole pour Demain, (Lyon). Interview by Caleb Gattegno for France-Culture by Jeanne Gruson. pp. 5-9.

"The Foundation of Geometry."
For the Learning of Mathematics, 1.1.

"A Seminar on Problem Solving."
For the Learning of Mathematics, 2.1.

"Children and Mathematics: A New Appraisal."
Mathematics Teaching, N° 94.

"The Effectiveness of the Silent Way Method in the Teaching of Maori as a Second Language."
with Katarina Mataira, Dissertation: Thesis (M.Ed.) - University of Waikato, (New Zealand).

"Reflections on 40 years work."
Proc Canadian Maths Ed Study Group. Republished 1989.

"Mathematics: Visible and Tangible."
EdSol Newsletter Vol. 9, N° 3, February 1980, Educational Solutions, (New York).

"Our Impact Here and There."
EdSol Newsletter Vol. 9, N° 4, April 1980, Educational Solutions, (New York).

"Computers in Education."
EdSol Newsletter Vol. 9, N° 5, June 1980, Educational Solutions, (New York).

"A New Braille and Other Topics."
EdSol Newsletter Vol. 10, N° 1, September 1980, Educational Solutions, (New York).

"Clinic Cases."
EdSol Newsletter Vol. 10, N° 2, December 1980, Educational Solutions, (New York).

1981

Animated Geometry - Notes for Teachers.
Monograph, Educational Solutions, (New York).

"Learning Disabilities."
EdSol Newsletter Vol. 10, N° 3, February 1981, Educational Solutions, (New York).

"Teaching the Deaf."
EdSol Newsletter Vol. 10, N° 4, April 1981, Educational Solutions, (New York).

"Are We All Not Handicapped."
EdSol Newsletter Vol. 10, N° 5, June 1981, Educational Solutions, (New York).

"The Computer and the Mind."
EdSol Newsletter Vol. 11, N° 1, September 1981, Educational Solutions, (New York).

"Solving Problems."
EdSol Newsletter Vol. 11, N° 2, December 1981, Educational Solutions, (New York).

1982

L'Énergie et les énergies.
Une Ecole Pour Demain, (Lyon). Restricted printing. Three volumes.

"Much Language and Little Vocabulary."
Blair, R. (ed.) *Innovative Approaches to Language Teaching*, Newbury House p 197-200 (Rowley, MA).

"Perception."
Blair, R. (ed.) *Innovative Approaches to Language Teaching*, Newbury House p 201-203 (Rowley, MA)

"Two of Our Breakthroughs."
EdSol Newsletter Vol. 11, N° 3- N° 4, February-April 1982, Educational Solutions, (New York).

"Energy, Time, Evolutionary Impasses and Man."
EdSol Newsletter Vol. 11, N° 5, June 1982, Educational Solutions, (New York).

"The Origins and Evolutions of Language."
EdSol Newsletter Vol. 12, N° 1, September 1982, Educational Solutions, (New York).

"Transfer of Learning."
EdSol Newsletter Vol. 12, N° 2, December 1982, Educational Solutions, (New York).

"On Algebra."
Mathematics Teaching, Journal of the Association of Teachers of Mathematics, N° 105, (England).

1983

"The Economics of Education."
EdSol Newsletter Vol. 12, N° 3, February 1983, Educational Solutions, (New York).

"Time: Public and Private."
EdSol Newsletter Vol. 12, N° 4, April 1983, Educational Solutions, (New York).

"Looking Back and Then, Forward."
EdSol Newsletter Vol. 12, N° 5, June 1983, Educational Solutions, (New York).

"Making Silent Way Materials."
EdSol Newsletter Vol. 13, N° 1, September 1983, Educational Solutions, (New York).

"The Need to Know."
EdSol Newsletter Vol. 13, N° 2, December 1983, Educational Solutions, (New York).

1984

"Curriculum and Epistemology I."
For the Learning of Mathematics. Vol. 4, N° 2.

"Curriculum and Epistemology II."
For the Learning of Mathematics. Vol. 4, N°.3.

"On Sleep."
Mathematics Teaching, Journal of the Association of Teachers of Mathematics, N° 106, (England).

"Infinity."
Mathematics Teaching, Journal of the Association of Teachers of Mathematics, N° 107, (England).

"Notes on Adolescence."
Mathematics Teaching, Journal of the Association of Teachers of Mathematics, N° 108, (England).

Infused Reading in French: Notes for Teachers.
Educational Solutions, (New York).

Infused Reading in Inupiaq: Notes for Teachers.
Educational Solutions, (New York).

Ma mort.
Une Ecole Pour Demain, (Lyon).

"Homo Economus."
EdSol Newsletter Vol. 13, N° 3, February 1984, Educational Solutions, (New York).

(Bibliography Cont'd.)

"Man Must Experiment."
EdSol Newsletter Vol.. 13, N° 4, April 1984, Educational Solutions, (New York).

"Whence Mortality."
EdSol Newsletter Vol.. 13, N° 5, June 1984, Educational Solutions, (New York).

"Understanding Disagreements."
EdSol Newsletter Vol.. 14, N° 1, September 1984, Educational Solutions, (New York).

"The Powers of Self Education Maintained."
EdSol Newsletter Vol.. 14, N° 2, December 1984, Educational Solutions, (New York).

1985

The Common Sense of Teaching Reading and Writing.
Educational Solutions, (New York). Restricted Printing.

The Science of Education Chapter 13: The Learning and Teaching of Foreign Languages.
Published in 1987, Educational Solutions, (New York). Restricted Printing.

Infused reading in Ojibwe: Notes for Teachers.
Educational Solutions, (New York).

"Knowledge and Experience."
Mathematics Teaching, Journal of the Association of Teachers of Mathematics, N° 110, (England).

De L1 à L2 - la relation entre l'apprentissage de la langue maternelle et celui d'autres langues.
Pour l'éducation de la conscience, (Besançon).

Les forces psychiques qui nous aident.
Une Ecole Pour Demain, (Besançon).

"What's a Good Question."
EdSol Newsletter Vol.. 14, N° 3, February 1985, Educational Solutions, (New York).

"A Reconsideration of the Sciences."
EdSol Newsletter Vol.. 14, N° 4, April 1985, Educational Solutions, (New York).

"The Silent Way and Zen."
EdSol Newsletter Vol.. 14, N° 5, June 1985, Educational Solutions, (New York).

"What is Man?"
EdSol Newsletter Vol.. 15, N° 1- N° 2, September – December 1985, Educational Solutions, (New York).

1986

L'Univers des Bébés.
Une Ecole Pour Demain, (Besançon). Translation of *In the Beginning There Were No Words: The Universe of Babies.*

La génération des richesses.
Deux Volumes, Une Ecole Pour Demain, (Besançon).

The Generation of Wealth.
Educational Solutions, (New York). Restricted Printing.

"Memory and Retention."
Chapitre 5 of *The Science of Education*, published in 1987, Educational Solutions, (New York). Restricted Printing.

"Operations on Integers."
Mathematics Teaching, Journal of the Association of Teachers of Mathematics, N° 114, (England).

"On Being Amazed."
Mathematics Teaching, Journal of the Association of Teachers of Mathematics, N° 116, (England).

"Origins."
Mathematics Teaching, Journal of the Association of Teachers of Mathematics, N° 1 Theoretical Considerations 17, (England).

Infused Reading in English: Notes for Teachers.
Educational Solutions, (New York).

Infused Reading in German: Notes for Teachers.
Educational Solutions, (New York).

Infused Reading in Italian: Notes for Teachers.
Educational Solutions, (New York).

"Sleep Revisited."
EdSol Newsletter Vol.. 15, N° 3- N° 4, February-April 1986, Educational Solutions, (New York).

"Can Language Teachers Be Open Minded?"
EdSol Newsletter Vol.. 15, N° 5, June 1986, Educational Solutions, (New York).

"Collective Experiments: One & Two."
EdSol Newsletter Vol.. 16, N° 1, September 1986, Educational Solutions, (New York).

"A Workable Model for Health."
EdSol Newsletter Vol.. 16, N° 2- N° 4, February-April 1986, Educational Solutions, (New York).

1987

Vers une théorie générale de la relativité humaine.
Une Ecole Pour Demain, (Besançon).

L'Amour.
Une Ecole Pour Demain. (Besançon).

Etre Libre.
Une Ecole Pour Demain, (Besançon).

De la Santé.
Une Ecole Pour Demain, (Besançon).

"Caleb Gattegno's Achievements."
EdSol Newsletter Vol.. 16, N° 5, June 1987, Educational Solutions, (New York).

"From Pre-Humanity to Humanity."
EdSol Newsletter Vol.. 17, N° 1, September 1987, Educational Solutions, (New York).

"Education and the Present World Crisis."
EdSol Newsletter Vol.. 17, N° 2, December 1987, Educational Solutions, (New York).

Peut-on penser en termes positifs à l'avenir de nos enfants?
Une Ecole Pour Demain, (Besançon).

Les disciplines spirituelles qui nous aident à vivre et à être heureux.
Une Ecole Pour Demain, (Besançon).

La Lecture en Couleurs.
Une Ecole Pour Demain, (Besançon) New edition, 1997.

1988

"Reflections on Forty Years of Work on Mathematics Teaching."
For the Learning of Mathematics Kingston, FLM Publishing Association, November.

"Of Music and Language."
EdSol Newsletter Vol.. 17, N° 3, February 1988, Educational Solutions, (New York).

"Collective Experiment Series: The Hebrew Jewish Experiment."
EdSol Newsletter Vol.. 17, N° 4- N° 5, April-June 1988, Educational Solutions, (New York).

2010

Know Your Children As They Are: A Book For Parents.
Educational Solutions, (New York).

The Mind Teaches the Brain.
(1975, Reprinted 2010) Educational Solutions, (New York).

Evolution and Memory.
(1977, Reprinted 2010) Educational Solutions, (New York).

On Being Freer.
(1975, Reprinted 2010) Educational Solutions, (New York).

The Adolescent and His Will.
Educational Solutions, (New York).

Of Boys and Girls.
(1975, Reprinted 2010) Educational Solutions, (New York).

What We Owe Children.
(1970, Reprinted 2010) Educational Solutions, (New York).

(Bibliography Cont'd.)

Towards a Visual Culture.
(1969, Reprinted 2010) Educational Solutions, (New York).

The Universe of Babies, In the Beginning There Were No Words.
(1973, Reprinted 2010) Educational Solutions, (New York).

The Common Sense of Teaching Mathematics.
(1974, Reprinted 2010) Educational Solutions, (New York).

The Common Sense of Teaching Foreign Languages.
(1976, Reprinted 2010) Educational Solutions, (New York).

The Common Sense of Teaching Reading and Writing.
(1985, Reprinted 2010) Educational Solutions, (New York).

The Science of Education Part 1: Theoretical Considerations.
Educational Solutions, (New York).

The Science of Education Part 2B: The Awareness of Mathematization.
Educational Solutions, (New York).

The Science of Education Chapter 13: The Learning and Teaching of Foreign Languages.
(1985, Reprinted 2010) Educational Solutions, (New York).

Now Johnny Can Do Arithmetic.
(1960, Reprinted 2010) Educational Solutions, (New York).

Teaching Foreign Languages in Schools the Silent Way.
(1963, Reprinted 2010) Educational Solutions, (New York).

A Thousand Sentences.
(1965, Revised and reprinted 2010) Educational Solutions, (New York).

Teaching Reading With Words in Color: A Scientific Study of the Problems of Reading.
(1968, Reprinted 2010) Educational Solutions, (New York).

Eight Tales.
(1968, Reprinted 2010) Educational Solutions, (New York).

Short Passages.
(1968, Reprinted 2010) Educational Solutions (New York)

Book of Stories.
(1962, Reprinted 2010) Educational Solutions, (New York).

Reading Primer R0 & R1.
(Originally published in 1963 as Words in Colour - Primer book 1- 3) Educational Solutions, (New York).

Reading Primer R2.
(Originally published in 1963 as Words in Colour - Primer book 1- 3) Educational Solutions, (New York).

Reading Primer R3.
(Originally published in 1963 as Words in Colour - Primer book 1- 3) Educational Solutions, (New York).

Student Workbook 1.
Educational Solutions, (New York).

Student Workbook 2.
Educational Solutions, (New York).

Gattegno Mathematics Textbook 1: Qualitative Arithmetic- The Study of Numbers From 1-20.
(1970, Reprinted 2010) Educational Solutions, (New York).

2011

Gattegno Mathematics Textbook 2: Study of Numbers up to 1,000. The Four Operations.
(1970, Reprinted 2011) Educational Solutions, (New York).

Gattegno Mathematics Textbook 4: Fractions – Decimals – Percentages.
(1970, Reprinted 2011) Educational Solutions, (New York).

Gattegno Mathematics Textbook 5: Study of Numbers.
(1970, Reprinted 2011) Educational Solutions, (New York).

Mathematics with Numbers in Color: Book VI.
(1961, Reprinted 2011) Educational Solutions, (New York).

Mathematics with Numbers in Color: Book VII.
(1966, Reprinted 2011) Educational Solutions, (New York).

On Love.
(1977, Reprinted 2011) Educational Solutions, (New York).

On Death.
(1978, Reprinted 2011) Educational Solutions, (New York).

For the Teaching of Mathematics Volume 1.
(1963, Reprinted 2011) Educational Solutions, (New York).

For the Teaching of Mathematics Volume 2: Psychological Studies on Films.
(1963, Reprinted 2011) Educational Solutions, (New York).

For the Teaching of Mathematics Volume 3: Elementary Mathematics.
(1963, Reprinted 2011) Educational Solutions, (New York).

A Teacher's Introduction to Arithmetic.
(1954, Reprinted 2011) Educational Solutions, (New York).

Modern Mathematics.
(1960, Reprinted 2011) Educational Solutions, (New York).

La science de l'éducation Partie 1: Considérations théoriques (1988, traduction 2011).
Educational Solutions, (New York).

La science de l'éducation : Partie 2B: Conscience de la mathématisation (1985, traduction 2011).
Educational Solutions, (New York).

La science de l'éducation : Chapitre 13 : L'apprentisage et l'enseignement des langues étrangère (1985, traduction 2011).
Educational Solutions, (New York).

Ocho Cuentos.
(1965, Reprinted 2011) Educational Solutions, (New York).

Narraciones Breves.
(1967, Reprinted 2011) Educational Solutions, (New York).

El Libro de las Mil Frases.
(1965, Reprinted 2011) Educational Solutions, (New York).

Hojas de Trabajo 1 a 6.
Educational Solutions, (New York).

Leocolor Libro 1.
Educational Solutions, (New York).

Leocolor Libro 2.
Educational Solutions, (New York).

www.ingramcontent.com/pod-product-compliance
Lightning Source LLC
Chambersburg PA
CBHW060257240426
43661CB00060B/2814